AF607818

LAW AND THE VISUAL

Representations, Technologies, and Critique

Law and the Visual

Representations, Technologies, and Critique

EDITED BY DESMOND MANDERSON

UNIVERSITY OF TORONTO PRESS
Toronto Buffalo London

Toronto Buffalo London
utorontopress.com

ISBN 978-1-4426-3031-4

Library and Archives Canada Cataloguing in Publication

Law and the visual : representations, technologies, and critique / edited by Desmond Manderson.

Includes bibliographical references and index.
ISBN 978-1-4426-3031-4 (cloth)

1. Law and art – History. I. Manderson, Desmond, editor

K3778.L39 2018 344'.097 C2017-903466-9

Every effort has been made to contact copyright holders; in the event of an error or omission, please notify the publisher.

University of Toronto Press acknowledges the financial assistance to its publishing program of the Canada Council for the Arts and the Ontario Arts Council, an agency of the Government of Ontario.

Canada Council for the Arts Conseil des Arts du Canada

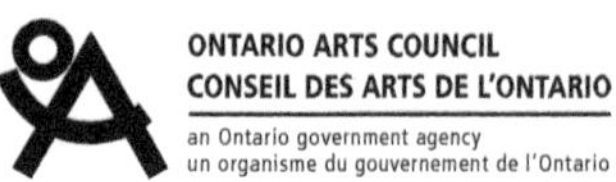

Funded by the Government of Canada | Financé par le gouvernement du Canada | Canada

Contents

LAW AND THE VISUAL

Representations, Technologies, and Critique

Introduction: Imaginal Law

DESMOND MANDERSON

Background

As Carlo Ginzburg pointed out, the problem with using visual material to explain other spheres of human activity, and the other way around – Panofsky and then W.J.T. Mitchell called it "iconology," while for Mieke Bal it is "cultural analysis"[1] – is what *kind* of evidence they provide for the nature of social interactions and social change, now or in the past.[2] For Erwin Panofsky, the question lay at the heart of his project. It led him to overreach – or so Ginzburg thought – in claiming that the highest (or deepest) level of interpretation of an image or art practice aims to reconstruct the "underlying principles which reveal the basic attitude of a nation, a period, a class, a religious or philosophical persuasion – unconsciously qualified by one personality and condensed into one work."[3] E.H. Gombrich also remained unconvinced. He famously cautioned against the tendency to slip from real connections to mere *geistgeschichtliche Paralleln*.[4] But even the great defender of formalist art history ultimately had recourse to a kind of social understanding of art from which he had initially thought to mark his distance.[5] Gombrich was no doubt right when he said that paintings reference other paintings more than they reference "the real world"; but it can't be turtles all the way down.[6] In the end, "history ... put out quietly at the door, re-enters through the window."[7] This ambiguous interdependence arises not because there is something distinctive about visual representations – but because there is not. Any text forms a tapestry along with the many texts and forces that surround it. Each thread both participates in and constitutes a web that began long before and continues long after. It makes no more sense to speak of a particular image or set of images as "evidence" of an independent legal idea or event, than to speak of the stars as evidence of the night. They are objects that partake of the same reality.

Forget thinking in terms of visual evidence for some external fact that could be conceived as being separate from it. Think instead of visual *discourse*, a network of the symbolic expression of values, ideas, and feelings, in which we are always already enmeshed. This is what Chiara Bottici calls "the imaginal." She means neither the individual faculty of the imagination, nor the social context of the imaginary, but something between the two.[8] The use of the word imaginal acknowledges the enormous power of images to communicate ideas and norms, to frame experiences, to constitute relations, to generate the emotions that construct the world we live in. Political discourse, as she pointedly argues, is not particularly imaginative nowadays, and it's certainly not imaginary. But it is fought out increasingly in the realm of and through the medium of images.[9] The same could be said of legal discourse. But the term imaginal also demands that we take into account not just the *conceptual* power of images, a bias towards immateriality and abstraction shared by both the imagination and the imaginary. Rather, images here have a physical presence – as artworks, photographs, representations, and the like. This emphasis on visual media as vital components of the discursive operations that organize and interpret normative, aesthetic, and legal structures around us, and in accounting for the effects of their material manifestations, their living presence, invites the kind of engaged and specific "case studies" around the relationship between legal and visual discourses that sit at the heart of this book.

If we accept that visual studies concerns the relationship between images and the discourses they realize, legitimate, or set in motion, then this book's claim for their importance in law is very far from new. It is as old, if not as the hills, then at least as Hammurabi's Code (c. 1750 BC).[10] That great basalt plinth marked, in the detail and specificity of the written laws it set down, an important development in law's textual presence. But equally important is the image of legality that crowns the stele and materializes out of its black-headed stone. Here we see the shining Babylonian sun god, the god of justice Shamash, flames sprouting from his shoulders, giving Hammurabi a ring and a staff as signs of his authority.[11] The connection is made explicit in the Prologue: "Then Anu and Bel delighted the flesh of mankind by calling me, the renowned prince, the god-fearing Hammurabi, to establish justice in the earth, to destroy the base and the wicked, and to hold back the strong from oppressing the feeble: to shine like the sun-god upon the black-headed men and to illuminate the land."[12]

Clearly, then, law is making a claim not just through the use of images but *about* images; about the legal system's relationship to light and vision, the coming together of its power to illuminate and the illumination of its power. The language of light is not just a metaphor for the law; it is its origin and its justification.

Now in fact this imaginal law, a law of and in the image, is a great deal more venerable than Hammurabi. In the Louvre where it now resides, on the wall next to it, we find an almost identical image dated hundreds, up to a thousand years *earlier*.[13] The temporal distance is staggering. What we might naively describe as an image of Hammurabi is not a picture of the king at all. By his time it was already an ancient, conventional, even ritual evocation of a familiar trope. The iconography of the image was an enduring stamp of legitimation and authority; Hammurabi's revolution was to appropriate it in order to justify specific legal obligations.

Many of those who have studied how images and visual media both illuminate and influence questions of legitimation, authority, and obligation have arrived at these interests from scholarly fields other than law. Perhaps the example of Michel Foucault is too obvious, a profoundly influential philosopher of history who was interested in questions of law and social relations, on the one hand, and in the evidence to be gleaned from a rich variety of visual sources, on the other. His theory of power and his eclectic source materials were two sides of the same coin. *Discipline and Punish* is a classic example. Foucault treats the striking image of Jeremy Bentham's Panopticon as the telling symptom that reveals a seminal shift in modalities of legal power and consciousness. Ever since then, legal philosophers, criminologists, and social theorists have been inspired by his insight.[14] In the first pages of *The Order of Things*, Foucault again uses a painting, this time by Velasquez, as symptomatic of a world view.[15] His analysis of *Las Meninas* unlocks the whole conceptual ordering of a society, "the representation of the space of representation."[16] Foucault's oeuvre clearly demonstrates the importance of visual material and media to our understanding of law and society, but equally to its actual material and psychological operations.

Other writers have been equally influential. Ernst Kantorowicz's *The King's Two Bodies: A Study in Medieval Political Theology*, for example, is premised precisely on the central role played by images and visual metaphors in the development of constitutional theory in the West.[17]

Eric Santner's recent book, *Royal Remains: The People's Two Bodies and the Endgames of Sovereignty*, transplants these ideas to a different historical context, but equally treats the imaginal as central elements in contemporary structures of legality and belonging.[18] Louis Marin's *Portrait of the King* offers a sustained argument on the vital function of the image – both as a symbolic concept and as a material form – in valorizing and in realizing the authority of the king.[19] "What then is a king? He is a king's portrait and that alone makes him king, and besides that he is also a man … No one knows that, on the contrary, the king is only his image, and that behind or beyond the portrait there is no king, but a man."[20] *Only* as the embodiment of a tradition, and *only* through the material, visible forms that that embodiment must take, can the king transform his will into other people's actions. In this way Marin's work very clearly manifests the dual aspects that Bottici's use of the term imaginal bridges.

These examples might serve as foundational reading for the study of law and visual studies. It has been matched by recent developments in the field of aesthetics and politics, art criticism and society, and visual studies itself. Christian Metz famously introduced the notion of a "scopic regime" to characterize the visual order of a culture or a genre capable of determining on a pre-reflective level how we see and interpret the world around us.[21] For, Martin Jay to the contrary,[22] it is hard to discern any "denigration of vision" in contemporary critical thinking – in the work, for example, of Louis Althusser, Jacques Rancière, Georges Didi-Huberman, Giorgio Agamben, Bruno Latour, or Judith Butler.[23] The term "visual studies" itself is a relatively recent adoption that reflects just this turn towards visual genres and modes of communication as these have become deeply embedded in contemporary life, including contemporary politics, regulation, and ideology. Writers like Marin, W.J.T. Mitchell, Ariella Azoulay, and Mieke Bal[24] have not hesitated to apply these approaches to radically new issues in politics and society.

Thus, the trajectory around scholarship of the image, on the one hand, and in history and social theory, on the other, has led inevitably to a new convergence. It is hardly possible to imagine any study of popular culture, social history, politics, or ideology which does *not* pay serious attention to its visual aspects and manifestations.[25] What has been particularly important for the genesis of this book has been the coupling of these trends and interests with a far more specific attention to law itself. Commencing with *Law and the Image: The Authority of*

Art and the Aesthetics of Law, a pioneering collection curated by Costas Douzinas, a legal theorist, and Lynda Nead, an art historian, legal writers have generated a new agenda and a multitude of new questions.[26] In just the last few years, the work of Alison Young, Richard Sherwin, Peter Goodrich, Judith Resnik, and Dennis Curtis has exemplified this transition.[27] In the process, new dialogues have opened with scholars in visual studies, too, demanding from them a more rigorous understanding of the effects of legal concepts on social and individual experience. Thus, the meeting of minds has not simply "applied" visual studies "to" the problem of law, as one applies an old method to a new object, but has compelled a deeper understanding of each area of human life by the other. This discursive oscillation between images as concepts and as material forms, so neatly captured in Bottici's term, might be described (with apologies to John Rawls) as a kind of "reflexive disequilibrium."[28] Imaginal law requires a constant recalibration of the dialogue between law and society, history, visual studies, and theory.

Yet pitfalls remain. A delicate balance must be struck – between past and present, universal and particular, concepts and materials. One risk is that of dilettantism, which is perhaps inherent (but not of course inevitable) in any such interdisciplinary enterprise. Another is the danger of an insufficient specificity in the use of both legal and visual sources, relying instead on too airy abstraction or assertions. The use of the word imaginal here demands precisely that we pay attention to the granular connections, influences, and mutual imbrication of the discourses of law and the visual, in particular works and in specific historical or cultural contexts. The very best work in this exciting new field has shown an impressive willingness to deploy highly detailed analyses of images, works of art, and visual media. Their material sensitivity has illuminated in new and imaginative ways the experience and nature of law at moments of important transition. Their analytical sophistication has contributed to crucial debates on the role of aesthetics and images in the character of law in the modern world.

Law and the Visual

Law and the Visual: Representations, Technologies, and Critique presents readers, students, and scholars across many disciplines with state-of-the-art research on the many different ways in which legal and visual discourses both illuminate and constitute one another. This accounts for the diversity of the collection but equally for its unifying features.

The authors include both legal theorists and critics, and art historians and critics, as well as several writers who have straddled these disciplines for many years now. The seriousness with which each discipline addresses the questions and orientation of the other is immediately apparent, whether in the legal sophistication displayed in the work of art historians, including Cristina Martinez or Stefan Huygenbaert, for example, or the aesthetic sophistication in the work of legal scholars including Sherally Munshi, Honni van Rijswijk, and Alison Young.[29]

I have emphasized the specificity of aesthetic analysis as an important feature of imaginal law. Each chapter addresses the specific details of the works or bodies of works of art, and the law or bodies of law that are its equal focus. Our contributors are not content to talk about "law" in some amorphous sense but "laws" as unique objects of study: the Engravers' Act of 1735; the French, Belgian, and Liberian Constitutions, the case of *United States v. Thind*, Australia's Immigration Acts, the Khmer Rouge Tribunal, the Netherlands Secret Service, Freedom of Information Acts, the County Court of Melbourne, and more. These are brought into relation not with "the image" in some generic sense, but with "images" – material visual presences. The source material studied here includes single works of art, emblems and frontispieces, heraldic devices, family photo albums, newspaper images, documentary archives, commercial reproductions, architectural decorations, stamps, statues, graffiti, and films. This astonishing diversity allows this book to exemplify the breadth of claims now being made for the relevance of visual studies to legal thought. But the chapters assembled here also exemplify a methodological commitment shared by each and every author – to take the particularities of law and the visual equally seriously.

Such a diverse range of papers poses a particular organizational challenge. They cover a wide range of legal contexts, over a historical range from the Renaissance to the contemporary world. Again in the interests of presenting readers with diverse interpretative options, the chapters employ a variety of theoretical positions. No doubt this eclecticism comes at a cost. Many of the themes and histories touched on here are worthy of a more detailed examination than has been possible within the constraints of a single chapter. But this limitation is more than made up for, at least it seems to me, by the panorama it presents readers of the dynamic intercourse between law and the visual as it has worked to shape legal ideology, technology, consciousness, and critique, over hundreds of years. Both the urgency and the changing contours of this dynamic are heightened by observing its mobile manifestations and its striking resonances.

Nevertheless, *Law and the Visual* contains within it a clear organizing principle and a clear argument. The book is structured chronologically, tracking the dialogue between law and visual media over time, and traces its effects on our shifting aesthetic and legal subjectivity. Part I deals with the origins of legal modernity from the sixteenth through the nineteenth centuries. Part II deals with the apotheosis of legal modernity in the twentieth century. Part III deals with our current predicament, which for want of a better word we might call global legal modernity. This move from history to the present day sets up resonances between what we can learn about the past and the nature of law, and our relation to it, now. Yet the essays in each of these three sections have as their distinctive focus one of three constellations of research interest that now occupy scholars in law and visual studies. These research clusters concern visual representations *about* the law, visual technologies *in* the law, and aesthetic critiques *of* the law. Each section may be taken to exemplify different ways of drawing out the dynamic interplay between legal and visual materials. Each exemplifies in different ways the dynamic interplay between legal and visual materials, and draws out, in turn, images' inherent yet problematic resources of ambivalence, of excess, and of irony. And, as we will see, the shift in emphasis over time is far from coincidental.

1. Representations: The Origins of Legal Modernity from the Sixteenth to the Nineteenth Centuries

Foucault has already shown us that in the Renaissance, classical, and colonial periods, social and legal order was essentially thought through variations on the theme of representation.[30] The power of artworks of various kinds to represent legal systems, concepts, and ideologies is a particularly productive avenue for scholarly historical inquiry. This is the approach taken by the essays in Part I, *Representations,* all of which excavate the intersection of legal and art history to illuminate changes in legal thought through legal images captured at seminal moments in its history. Like a cross-section of the fossil record, each chapter offers a case study that helps trace the emergence of a distinctive modern Western legality in the mirror of art. Visual media provide us with critical representations that distil and illuminate with remarkable clarity transitions that took place very slowly over many years or centuries: the emergence of modernity, positivism, and formalism, to name but a few, along with changing rhetorics of governance and changing notions of justice. This vocabulary, this imaginal discourse, is of more than historical significance, offering important insights into the structure of the relationship between visual discourse and legal consciousness in the contemporary world.

Chapters 1 and 2 highlight the emergence, in the course of the sixteenth century, of critical images in the visual discourse of modern law. What is particularly striking is the ambivalence and complexity of the visual resources used to evoke legal tropes that in later times came to be rendered more abstractly and, it must be said, more tritely. My own chapter in this volume explores an intriguing image by Pieter Bruegel the Elder. Placing the figure of a blindfolded Justicia at the heart of his depiction of the brutality of a legal system which was already recognizably modern, Bruegel challenges the orthodox interpretation of this trope. The visual image here both allows us to identify an important moment in legal transition and to sharpen its critique. In chapter 2, Peter Goodrich makes an even bolder claim. He argues that images were central to the articulation, synthesis, and compression of legal concepts in the medieval and early modern period. Drawing on the genre of legal emblems inaugurated by the jurist Andrea Alciato in 1531, Goodrich argues that they functioned as the unconscious of law.[31] Freud saw the ancient myths as clues to our unspoken drives, whose relevance was not historical but emblematic.[32] Goodrich likewise implies that an uncanny thread connects the liturgical, symbolic, and affective authority of the old legal emblems to the same functions performed by their modern-day descendants – "virtual, manipulable and borderless in its variable on-screen environments … on the mobile optimized web."[33]

In the chapters that follow, imaginal law is deployed to pick out key moments along the road to legal modernity. Chapters 3 and 4 concern the pivotal Enlightenment or neo-classical moment in which the relationship between law and justice, human and divine, was radically transformed. In chapter 3 we are in England. Cristina Martinez uses the legal imagery of William Hogarth to explore the implications and feelings of that transformation, and the entirely unprecedented place that written law and judicial decisions were beginning to occupy in people's lives. Not only does she demonstrate how well Hogarth understood the constitutional settlement following the Revolution of 1688. As she persuasively argues, even before Sir William Blackstone, Hogarth captures the English constitution in a precise visual form. The central proposition of this book concerns the necessary imbrication of legal and aesthetic forms. The story of Hogarth is an apt demonstration – "Whether law promoted the image or the image promoted law, the relationship could not have been more beneficial to both." In chapter 4 we are in France, but there too, although in a different way, the foundations of a modern legal system were being built on the supremacy of positivist legislation and at the same time the primacy of natural rights. Law can bridge the paradox through the mythological operation of images. Morgan Thomas explores the themes of abstraction and void in the art of Jacques-Louis David (including, lest we forget, the French flag). His art's very emptiness, its pure potential, allows both the indeterminacy of positive law and the indeterminacy of human rights to be reimagined from generation to generation. "A certain nothingness," Thomas concludes, "attesting to an encounter between art and ethics, acts to revolutionize law and thought."[34] Modern art and modern law share a secret revealed at the moment of their origin: the power of that blank slate, that immanent place of possibility, in both.

The last two chapters in this section describe the role of art and images in nation-building enterprises during the nineteenth century. Although many different studies could have been chosen, it is the thickness of their description and the diversity of their visual materials that rewards the reader. In chapter 5 Stefan Huygebaert discusses the decorations for Brussels's Cour de Cassation. Following on from the argument made in the previous chapter, he argues that the committee faced a choice between symbolism and historical realism in art that echoed and served as a placeholder for a conflict between two countervailing visions of law – one opaque, conceptual, and affective, and the other historical, positivist, authoritarian, and nationalist. Indeed, the distinction between "common-sense" and "open-ended" understandings of the nature of representation, in art and law alike, only highlights a fundamental interpretative disagreement, which art made clearer, more dramatic, and more emotionally compelling. In choosing the path of aesthetic conservatism, the legal authorities made their jurisprudential prejudices equally plain. Shane Chalmers's argument in chapter 6 is set in Liberia, a profoundly different social and legal context. Yet this brings part I full circle. In our first chapter, Bruegel's drawing exploits the ambivalence inherent in the representation of Lady Justice. In chapter 6 the very same indeterminacy within the figure of Lady Justice (in the mythical person of Matilda Newport) allows her to be filled with a variety of ideological meanings to suit shifting national needs. As every chapter in this part demonstrates, the ambiguity, the void, and the indeterminacy of the image is not a problem besetting imaginal law – it is precisely the opportunity that *empowers* it. The law of representation enables the representation of law. And again, like each of the chapters here, Chalmers refuses to reduce images to mere ciphers or emblems of battles decided elsewhere. The image of Justice exerts a power not just to illustrate but to influence the trajectory of legal transition, to shape the world as much as it shapes her.

2. Technologies: Excesses of Legal Modernity in the Twentieth Century

In the twentieth century, visual images do not lay down this burden of representation.[35] But something else is at play. One could refer again to Foucault, who emphasizes the extent to which the disciplinary and regulatory reach of the modern world exploits all the devices and desires at its disposal. As others have argued, this did not simply render juridical law obsolete. Rather, law itself increasingly deploys all manner of technological developments to further the zeal for governance.[36] In the past century, law's reach has manifestly not lessened but dispersed its effects. This corresponds to a functional dynamic that Walter Benjamin identified as the changing role of the work of art in the age of its mechanical reproduction.[37] No doubt, as Heidegger and Arendt foresaw, the triumph of technology and the instrumentalization of law went hand in hand.[38] Mechanical, not to mention digital, visual media gave new outlets to the representation of law's ideology but also offered law a new and unquestionably powerful set of legal technologies. Photography – whose early adoption by the law should not be forgotten[39] – film, the archive, the closed-circuit camera, the Internet, mobile phones, social media, and the drone are technological developments which have shaped our experience of law in the twentieth century and have in turn been woven into it. In part II, our contributors address this dangerous liaison, this complicity, and this appropriation.

Above all, these chapters argue that images and visual technologies are not just *used* by the law. Images are unruly, revealing our legal culture's shocking affective supplement, its excessive and subconscious meaning. In chapter 7 Sherally Munshi focuses on the photograph as a visual transmitter of regulatory judgment about race in immigration cases. The use of photographs in evidence demonstrates how powerfully they oscillated between facts and judgment, reading the former to confirm the latter, and using the latter as the common sense that legitimates the former. The power of the photograph comes from the self-justifying logic of this argument. But Munshi also sees the photographic archive as the repository of an excess – the suffering and the struggle that the process of assimilation demanded. The space that opens up between the photo as a token of personal suffering and as a type of legal judgment lies at the heart of law's visual technologies in the twentieth century. In chapter 8, Honni van Rijswijk studies the state's use of visual media to justify the force-feeding of suffragettes at the turn of the century, and then the internment and detention of refugees under Australian law a century later. But in this case, the excess is not of suffering but of pleasure. She reads the government as explicitly indulging and encouraging a sado-masochistic pleasure in the exertion of state power over the suffering bodies of its victims. Visuality, while it is exploited by the state, says more than it means. The *jouissance* of the legal system, assiduously denied in its legal texts, is revealed through visual materials.

In chapter 9 Maria Elander discusses the visual archive of the Cambodian genocide. She demonstrates how the process of taking and archiving the photos of thousands of victims by officials of the Pol Pot regime performed a chilling instrumental logic. It was an act of destructive power, a final statement of control, on the one hand, and a final annihilation of dignity and individuality, on the other. But the plasticity and ambivalence of the image – a snapshot of a face, seconds from extinction – demonstrates again a powerful and irreducible excess. The same photos have now been reclaimed and redeployed in the Cambodian Genocide Museum. But now they testify to the criminality of the state that took the photos, not the individuals whose photos were taken; now they are intended to demonstrate not the subjugation of individual identity but their ultimate triumph. Yet there is an uncanny similarity between these two opposite interpretations. The museum also treats these images as an archive – a collective entity, an artefact. The individual stories behind the uniform line of photos remain secret and untold. In a strange way, the legal obsession with the treatment and management of masses connects the regime that created these images with the regime that now governs them.

Chapter 10 brings the story of law's pleasures, disavowed textually but revealed visually, up to date. Connal Parsley offers a Foucauldian reading of images of torture after 9/11. In common with Van Rijswijk, he demonstrates that Foucault's relegation of the visual spectacle to an earlier, so-called juridical, legal regime must be reassessed. One of the problems facing the contemporary legal order is the increasingly traumatic division between empowered neoliberal citizens and abject others, within or without the state. It is worth recalling Carl Schmitt's notion of the enemy as law's necessary other.[40] For many people, Schmitt's arguments are tainted and shameful.[41] But the visual violence inflicted by law (and equally by social media) on those who cross some line or other intensifies daily, encouraging us to operate in this world with our "eyes wide shut" – Kubrick's phrase suggesting this wilful oscillation between seeing and not seeing, feeling and not feeling.[42] A modicum of shame would be no bad thing.

3. Critique: Irony and Legal Modernity in the Twenty-first Century

It is almost trite to note that the twenty-first century is characterized by a hyper- and even hysterical visuality that touches every aspect of our lives. In reflecting on the current status of law and the visual it is not enough to acknowledge the ideological representations and institutional technologies that envelop it. Yes, aesthetic modes are prime agents in the transmission of legal subjectivity. Yes, the power of the visual to mediate and survey our lives, to create images that assault us, control us, and constitute us, is surely in evidence. Terrorism communicates via the visceral immediacy of the image; governments are increasingly image-savvy, crafting scenes to valorize and modalize their power but equally to make us anxious and distrustful. Yet images are also prominent among our attempts to expose, critique, and unsettle the law. A little boy lies dead on a beach. A refugee from Syria cries and holds tight his child when they safely arrive off Greece. A woman vainly attempts to shield her baby from a soldier's bullet, while a photographer captures her despair. An Australian aboriginal boy in juvenile detention is hooded, handcuffed, and strapped to a chair. Visual media offer modes of breaking through our assumptions about law and justice. If part I of this collection treats the imaginal as a kind of witness to the law, and part II as its instrument or agent, part III suggests a more complicated responsibility, as if it were law's double agent.

From this perspective, the two key features we identified in previous parts of this collection – the ambivalence and excess of images – are again points of critical departure. One way of understanding their usefulness as a way of subverting the law is as irony. Irony is essentially an aesthetics of ambivalent and of excessive meaning; it operates by staging the unintended effects of juxtaposition and contrast. As Shoshana Felman says, it undoes the illusory mastery of intention. As a critical approach, irony seizes on imaginal law's indeterminacy or remainder to challenge, to undermine, and even to transform the legal system. There is nothing fundamentally new in such an approach. There is a long history of artists as sly masters of indirection. Francisco Goya would be an obvious example, as would the satirical images of law by Bruegel and Hogarth, discussed in part I.[43] Yet if it is in relation to contemporary law that art and critique are most insistently connected, this is no coincidence. On the one hand, the tension between the artist as a symbol of autonomy, and law as a symbol of power, has never been more keenly felt. On the other hand, we have never stood in greater need of art's particular gift – its capacity to radically unsettle conventional wisdom about the world around us – than now. Bygone art was, in all probability, no less critical in its response to law and power. But perhaps being so close to the problems, we can see that critique more clearly in artists' work and feel the weight of their irony.

An ironic reading of an iconic image is precisely the mode of interpretation adopted by Luis Gómez Romero in chapter 11. Analysing the history and afterlife of a famous photograph of Che Guevara, Romero demonstrates the mysterious plasticity of the visual – its ability to mean radically different things in different ideological frames. The point has already been made in this collection by Huygebaert, Thomas, and Chalmers, for example. But Romero, attending to the *contemporary* life of an image rather than its historical existence, emphasizes the stubborn resilience of the visual object.[44] "T-Shirt Guevara" has proved a bestseller for capitalism, but the irony of this exploitation continues to reproach the system that simultaneously endeavours to domesticate it. Che's face, while it has become a commodity, exceeds all objectification. Art's transformative potential thus does not recede with time; it banks up like storm clouds; it deepens like a coastal shelf.[45]

So too in chapter 12 Katherine Biber turns her attention to the explicit irony of artists appropriating secret and redacted legal documents to serve other aesthetic or political meanings. Their jarring juxtapositions, in which the indeterminate blank spaces of legal documents are made to bear meanings beyond their intention and to invade contexts they could hardly have anticipated, allow us to glimpse those brief moments in which the subterranean machinery of government reluctantly exposes itself to public view. The move, again, is one part art and one part law. Marcel Duchamp sought to undermine the authority of art by placing a urinal in a gallery; these artists seek to undermine the authority of law by placing in a gallery a comparable legal object. If it is a piss-take, we should take it seriously. Once again, in chapter 13, it is through a practice of ironic juxtaposition that art elevates to visibility the everyday legal order that passes unnoticed. Public art queers public space. The pedestrian is encouraged to shop but not to sing. We accept as natural the billboards that shout out their wares, but condemn as a crime and an affront the graffiti that resist their visual hegemony. Biber suggests that art can reveal the law that tries to stage its own disappearance; Alison Young implies that it can reveal the law that so artfully stage-manages its own appearance.

The final chapter pursues these themes in a different register. Richard Sherwin undertakes an extended discussion of two immensely moving films that attempt to come to grips with a campaign of anti-communist violence that took place in Indonesia in the 1960s, whose scale and horror have been insidiously shrouded in denial for fifty years. Octavio Paz wrote that we must confront law's visual power "*not* with another image – all images have a fatal tendency to become petrified – but with *criticism*, the acid that dissolves images."[46] Sherwin demonstrates that this is a false dichotomy. Adi, the undoubted hero of these films, can only engage in one through the other; the ironic juxtaposition he stages with such miraculous intensity is not between images but between people and the events they perpetrated.

In a truth much too strange for fiction, Adi is an optometrist. The science of seeing – and particularly of seeing more clearly – is his job and his calling. He offers a kind of visual prescription, corrective glasses to heal a moral blindness. We have need of such glasses. To understand law's representations and technologies requires a visual perspicacity that *Law and the Visual* hopes to cultivate. To adequately critique the law requires visually sophisticated resources capable of responding to visually sophisticated challenges. That was the case in the sixteenth century and it is still the case now. Over the past few years, as this book amply demonstrates, visual studies has transformed thinking and writing about the law. The question for the future is not *whether* but *how* visual media will continue to shape and transform the law itself.

NOTES

1 Erwin Panofsky, *Studies in Iconology* (Oxford: Oxford University Press, 1939); W.J.T. Mitchell, *Iconology* (Chicago: University of Chicago Press, 2013); Mieke Bal, *The Practice of Cultural Analysis* (Stanford: Stanford University Press, 1999).
2 Carlo Ginzburg, "From Aby Warburg to E.H. Gombrich," in *Myths, Emblems, Clues*, trans. John and Anne Tedeschi (London: Hutchinson Radius, 1990), 17–59.
3 Panofksy, *Studies in Iconology*, quoted in Ginzburg, "From Aby Warburg to E.H. Gombrich," 41, and see generally 41–3. See also Erwin Panofsky and Christopher Wood, *Perspective as Symbolic Form* (New York: Zone Books, 1991).
4 Quoted in Ginzburg, "From Aby Warburg to E.H. Gombrich," 43.
5 Ernst Hans Gombrich, *Art and Illusion: A Study in the Psychology of Pictorial Representation* (London: Phaidon, 1977).
6 Ginzburg, "From Aby Warburg to E.H. Gombrich," 42–59.
7 Ibid., 59.
8 Chiara Bottici, *Imaginal Politics* (New York: Columbia University Press, 2014), chap. 1.
9 Ibid., Introduction.
10 Code of Hammurabi, 225 × 55 cm, basalt stele. Louvre, c. 1792–1750 BC.
11 Jacques De Ville, "Mythology and the Image of Justice," *Law and Literature* 23 (2011): 324–64.
12 Quoted in William Seagle, *Men of Law: From Hammurabi to Holmes* (New York: Macmillan Co., 1947), 21. See also Robert Harper, *The Code of Hammurabi* (Union, NJ: Law Book Exchange, 1999).
13 Babylonian Stele. Louvre, Third Millennium BC.
14 Michel Foucault, *Discipline and Punish*, trans. Alan Sheridan (New York: Vintage Books, 1977), 195–228.
15 Michel Foucault, *The Order of Things* (New York: Vintage Books, 1973), 3–16.
16 Ibid., 16.
17 Ernst Kantorowicz, *The King's Two Bodies* (Princeton: Princeton University Press, 1997).
18 Eric Santner, *The Royal Remains: The People's Two Bodies and the Endgames of Sovereignty* (Chicago: University of Chicago Press, 2012).
19 Louis Marin, *Portrait of the King*, trans. Martha House and foreword by Tom Conley (Minneapolis: University of Minnesota Press, 1988).
20 Ibid., 218.

21 See Christian Metz, *The Imaginary Signifier* (Bloomington and Indianapolis: Indiana University Press, 1982), e.g., 61–5.

22 Martin Jay, *Downcast Eyes: The Denigration of Vision in Twentieth-Century French Thought* (Berkeley: University of California Press, 1993).

23 Louis Althusser, *Essays on Ideology* (London: Verso, 1976); Jacques Rancière, *Aesthetics and Its Discontents* (New York: Polity, 2009); Jacques Rancière, *Aisthesis – Scenes from the Aesthetic Regime of Art*, trans. Zakir Paul (London: Verso, 2013); Jacques Rancière, *The Future of the Image* (London: Verso, 2009); Georges Didi-Huberman, *Confronting Images* (Reading: Pennsylvania State University, 2005); Georges Didi-Huberman, *L'image survivante: Histoire de l'art et temps des fantômes selon Aby Warburg* (Paris: Minuit, 2002); Giorgio Agamben, *The Man Without Content* (Stanford: Stanford University Press, 1999); Bruno Latour and Peter Weibel, eds, *Iconoclash: Beyond the image Wars in Science, Religion and Art* (Cambridge, MA: MIT Press, 2002); Bruno Latour, *Picturing Science, Producing* Art (London: Routledge, 1998); Judith Butler, *Frames of War* (London: Verso, 2009).

24 Mieke Bal, "Semiotics and Art History," *The Art Bulletin* 73 (1991): 174–208; Mieke Bal, *Quoting Caravaggio* (Chicago: University of Chicago Press, 1999); Mieke Bal, *Reading "Rembrandt"* (New York: Cambridge University Press, 1991); W.J.T. Mitchell, ed., *Art and the Public Sphere* (Chicago: University of Chicago Press, 1992); W.J.T. Mitchell, *Iconology: Image, Text, Ideology* (Chicago: University of Chicago Press, 2013); W.J.T. Mitchell, *What Do Pictures Want?: The Lives and Loves of Images* (Chicago and London: University of Chicago Press, 2005; Louis Marin, *Portrait of the King*; Louis Marin, *On Representation* (Stanford: Stanford University Press, 2001); Louis Marin, *To Destroy Painting* (Chicago: University of Chicago Press, 1995); Ariella Azoulay, *The Civil Contract of Photography* (New York: Zone Books, 2008).

25 See, for example, works such as John Tagg, *The Burden of Representation* (Minneapolis: University of Minnesota Press, 1988), Nicholas Mirzoeff, *An Introduction to Visual Culture*, 2nd ed. (London: Routledge, 2009); and Nicholas Mirzoeff, *The Visual Culture Reader* (London: Routledge, 2002).

26 Costas Douzinas and Lynda Nead, eds, *Law and the Image: The Authority of Art and the Aesthetics of Law* (Chicago: University of Chicago Press, 1999).

27 Peter Goodrich, *Legal Emblems and the Art of Law* (New York: Cambridge University Press, 2014); Douzinas and Nead, eds; Judith Resnik and Dennis Curtis, *Representing Justice* (New Haven: Yale University Press, 2011); Alison Young, *Judging the Image: Art, Value, Law* (London: Routledge, 2005); Alison Young, *Street Art, Public City* (London: Routledge, 2014); Richard Sherwin, *Visualizing Law in the Age of the Digital Neo-Baroque*

(London: Routledge, 2011); Peter Goodrich and Valerie Hayaert, eds, *Genealogies of Legal Vision* (London: Routledge, 2015).

28 See John Rawls, *A Theory of Justice*, rev. ed. (Cambridge, MA: Belknap Press, 1999), 43–4.

29 See chapters 3, 5, 7, 8, and 13.

30 Michel Foucault, *The Order of Things* (London: Pantheon Books, 1970). See also the treatment of the importance of questions of representation in Walter Benjamin, *The Origin of German Tragic Drama* (London: Verso, 2009).

31 See the expanded discussion in Goodrich, *Legal Emblems and the Art of Law.*

32 Of course the literature is both voluminous and contentious. See, for example, Nadia Sels, "On the Relation of Psychology and Psychoanalysis," *Journal of the Jan Van Eyck Circle* 4 (2011): 56–70; Jean-Paul Valabrega, *Les mythes, conteurs de l'inconscient* (Paris: Payot & Rivages, 2001); Lionel Trilling, "Freud and Literature," in Lionel Trilling ed., *The Liberal Imagination* (London, Heinemann, 1964), 34–57; Graziella Nicolaïdis and Nicolas Nicolaïdis, *Mythologie grecque et psychanalyse* (Paris: Delachaux & Niestlé, 1994).

33 Peter Goodrich, this volume.

34 Morgan Thomas, this volume.

35 John Tagg, *The Burden of Representation* (Minneapolis: University of Minnesota Press, 1988).

36 Michel Foucault, *Discipline and Punish*, trans. Alan Sheridan (London: Vintage, 1975); Alan Hunt and Gary Wickham, *Foucault and Law* (London: Pluto Press, 1994).

37 Walter Benjamin, "The Work of Art in the Age of Its Mechanical Reproducibility," *Zeitschfirt fur Sozialfoschung*, May 1936, in Walter Benjamin, *Selected Writings, Vol. 3 – 1935–38*, ed. Howard Eiland and Michael Jennings (Cambridge, MA: Belknap Press, 2006), 101–33.

38 See Martin Heidegger, *The Question concerning Technology and Other Essays* (New York: HarperCollins, 1982); Hannah Arendt, *Between Past and Future* (Harmondsworth: Penguin, 1961).

39 Peter Hutchings, *The Criminal Spectre in Law, Literature and Aesthetics* (London: Routledge, 2001), 127–65.

40 Carl Schmitt, *Concept of the Political*, trans. George Schwab (Chicago: University of Chicago Press, 1996).

41 See discussions in David Dyzenhaus, ed., *Law as Politics – Carl Schmitt's Critique of Liberalism* (Durham, NC: Duke University Press, 1998).

42 Stanley Kubrick, dir., *Eyes Wide Shut* (London, 1999).

43 Francisco Goya, *El Dos de Mayo*, oil on canvas, 266 × 345 cm, Prado, 1814; *El Tres de Mayo*, oil on canvas, 266 x 345 cm, Prado, 1814; *Disasters of War*,

lithographs, 1810–1820 – see Philip Hofer, ed., *The Disasters of War* (New York: Dover Publications, 2006). For discussion of Bruegel and Hogarth, see chapters 1 and 3.

44 Jacques Derrida, "Force of Law: The 'Mystical Foundation of Authority,'" trans. Mary Quaintance, *Cardozo Law Review* 11 (1989–90): 943.

45 Philip Larkin, "This Be the Verse," in *High Windows* (London: Faber & Faber, 1974), #15.

46 Quoted in Mary Coffey, *How a Revolutionary Art Became Official Culture: Murals, Museums, and the Mexican State* (Durham, NC: Duke University Press, 2012), 179.

PART ONE

Representations – The Origins of Legal Modernity from the Sixteenth to the Nineteenth Centuries

1 Blindness Visible: Law, Time, and Bruegel's Justice

DESMOND MANDERSON

I don't think we did go blind, I think we are blind, Blind but seeing, Blind people who can see, but do not see.

José Saramago, *Blindness*[1]

Recent work has emphasized the importance of the visual arts in illuminating legal concepts, transitions, and transformations.[2] Art's affective force – its connection to bodies and feelings – reveals elements of anxiety, desire, and loss which more conventional legal materials repress. But there is another important element here. Art is often thought to be about the representation of space. Alexander Nagel and Christopher Wood argue that it is equally about the representation of time.[3] They identify two divergent temporalities of representation, the first a mode of absence in which art recalls and echoes earlier and originary forms; the second, a mode of presence embedded in linear time. The first shows art as a figure of transcendence, framed in terms of continuity. The second shows art as a figure of immanence, framed in terms of change. In Panofksy's evolutionary narrative, the art of the Renaissance exceeded that of the Middle Ages in situating its subjects within the consciousness of on-rushing time, an ascent towards the phenomenal. In Didi-Huberman's revisionist narrative, this marked a corresponding loss of the experience of time's eternity, a decline away from the noumenal. But Nagel and Wood argue that these different temporalities are not mutually exclusive. They can and do exist in the same work of art, in dialogue, sometimes even in downright opposition, to one another.[4] "The work is late, first because it succeeds some reality that it re-presents, and then late again when that re-presentation is repeated for successive recipients ... The work of art when it is late, when it repeats, when it hesitates, when it remembers, but also when it projects a future or an ideal is 'anachronic.'"[5] The "anachronic" structure of Renaissance art juxtaposes, within one visual frame, past and present, different values or ideals. This encounter between different modes of temporal experience was and still is one of fine art's great themes.

It's about time we took a good look at Bruegel's *Justicia.* Printed in 1559, it appears at first glance to be a spatial representation of law – a snapshot, a mis en scène. But it is essentially about *time.* Bruegel's image overlays three different perspectives on the hitherto unexplored relationship between time, responsibility, and legal authority, revealing the hidden anachronism of law. At the same time, law is shown not merely to be a concept or a symbolic form, but a physical practice engraved in

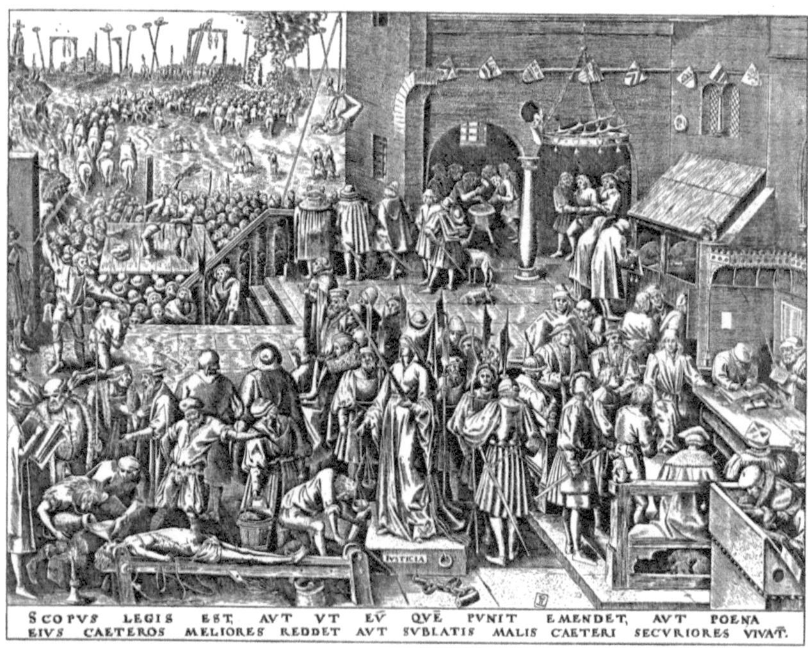

Figure 1.1 Pieter Bruegel the Elder and Philips Galle, *Justice* (*Justicia*) from *The Vices and the Virtues* (Hieronymous Cocke, 1560). Image courtesy Harris Brisbane Dick Fund, 1928, and Metropolitan Museum of Art Open Access for Scholarly Content (www.metmuseum.org).

the flesh of those who carry it out and suffer it. Bruegel was not a jurist but an artist. *Justicia* takes as its method art's anachronic discourse and power of embodiment; and presents as its thesis the role of anachronic discourse and corporeal experience to the law. These insights were pertinent to the situation of law in the sixteenth century, but they are of far broader significance than that.

The Three Temporalities of Law

Pieter Bruegel (the Elder) was one of the great artists of the Northern Renaissance.[6] Towards the beginning of his career he composed two sets of sketches for the publisher Hieronymous Cock. These were engraved by Philip Galle and published as *The Seven Deadly Sins* (1558) and *The Virtues* (1559).[7] In each case, an allegorical figure is set against an archive of illustrative incidents drawn from daily life. Neither series is comparable to the masterworks of the next ten years of Bruegel's life, before his untimely death at the age of 44. But a case can be made for the importance of *Justicia*, in particular, and for its interpretation in relation to those paintings.[8] Indeed, the level of detail in the picture alone provides importance evidence about legal practice in the sixteenth century. But more than this, Bruegel's highly original treatment of the relationship between law and justice emphasizes law as socially, corporeally, and temporally grounded.

Three axes organize Bruegel's image: an x-axis, mainly horizontal, a y-axis, vertical, and a z-axis, diagonal. These organize the pictorial space in different ways, but more to the point they trace three different ways of thinking about law's relationship to time: the present law, the future law, and the law of the past.[9] Bruegel lived during a period of radical change in the concepts of law, on the very cusp of its transformation from medieval to modern legality. He turns this transformation from a mere *fact* about legal change to a set of potential normative responses to it. The anachronic and embodied sensibility central to his art was fundamental to these insights. In the following discussion, I take as my point of departure the original pen and ink drawing – reproduced below – rather than the better-known engraving of it by Philip Galle (reproduced at the start of this essay), which was the published version.[10] Galle's work heightens the monumentality of the series and enhances its sense of three-dimensional space. But the engraving process did not exactly replicate Bruegel's drawing: it produced a mirror image of it. Turning back to the original drawing

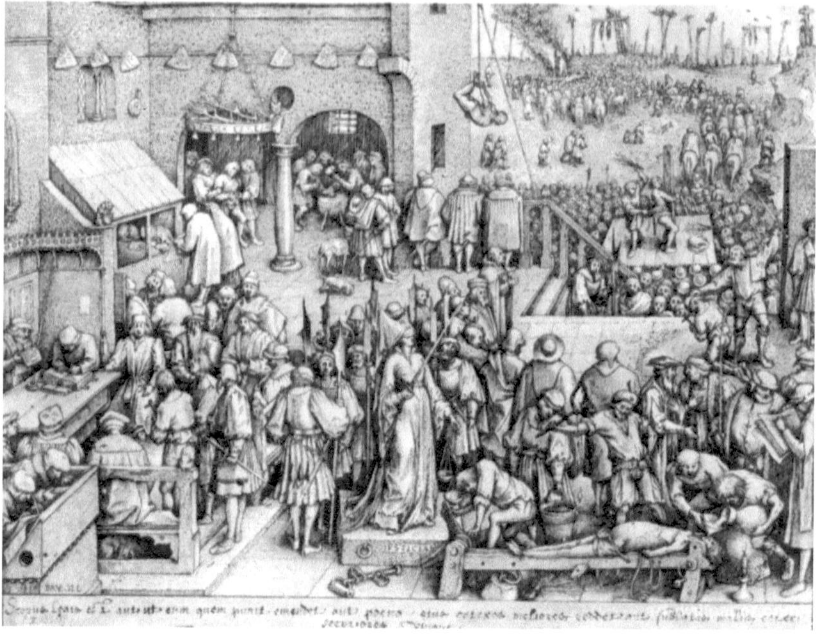

Figure 1.2 Pieter Bruegel, *Justicia* (original version, 1558–9). Image courtesy of Bibliothèque Royale de Belgique, Brussels, Belgium/Bridgeman Images.

helps to clarify its narrative intentions, particularly if we read the picture from left to right.[11]

The *x*-axis traces a legal geography. His attention to detail in the realization of the space and the distinctive features of the many people in it generate a powerful sense of realism. Starting from the left-hand side and then running horizontally along the foreground, Bruegel depicts various aspects of routine legal and administrative work. Lawyers are depicted almost without exception as traffickers in texts – reading, writing, exchanging, and notarizing. The most dramatic element is the scene of torture at the far right. This shows the forcible ingestion of large amounts of water, a practice known as "the water cure." It was commonly used in France and the Low Countries until the seventeenth century. Bruegel's depiction was probably based on a woodcut in Joost Damhoudère's book *Praxis rerum criminalium*, with which Bruegel was certainly familiar. It had been published only five years earlier, in Antwerp, where Bruegel lived,[12] and the publisher included a quotation from it as a caption to the printed version of *Justicia*.[13] Indeed, it seems likely that Bruegel's image is set in Antwerp: symbols of imperial sovereignty are conspicuously absent, replaced by shields over the town hall reflecting the corporate governance of the city, and other signs of oligarchic privileges.[14]

The *Praxis rerum criminalium* describes the water cure in some detail:

> You must undress the patient, tie both hands ... with back down and the stomach up (only shameful parts should be covered with a handkerchief or linen trousers) ... so that the body can be stretched with instruments similar to a pinion, a wheel or a rod; place a small bridle in the mouth [here, a funnel] and pour cold water on the face and body until the body is swollen, and this with the frequency and duration that the judge and jury believe the body can withstand without great danger.[15]

Bruegel's scene scrupulously follows this procedure. Damhoudère's text was far from original; he probably plagiarized most of it from an earlier textbook by Philip Wielant. What made Damhoudère's version famous were the fifty-odd woodcuts which accompanied it. In that form, it became a classic of early modern law, staying in print for well over 100 years and translated into several languages. In Damhoudère's illustration (figure 1.3), a judge is on hand to observe, record, and validate the exercise of legal violence – to authorize it and to modalize it, as Marin says.[16]

Comparing the two images, we can see that the lawyers buried in their books on the far right of Bruegel's picture likewise authorize the scene. A judge, holding a hazel rod as a sign of his authority, consults with a clerk as to what questions should be put to the accused, while beside him two jurors or assessors argue about the validity or efficacy of the procedure.[17] The same tiled floor orders both images – possibly an allusion to the *parquet* or *parket*, a level wooden floor that was already the term used to denote both the courtroom and the office of the prosecutor.[18]

More interesting than the parallels between the two images are the differences. Bruegel has brought the scene to life in quite a different way. He draws our attention to the inexorable logic of legal action, beginning as signatures in documents and ending as suffering bodies. As opposed to Damhoudère, he shows us not just the preparations for torture but their physical effects – the distended belly of the victim – and positions a candle to remind us that torture takes place in secret

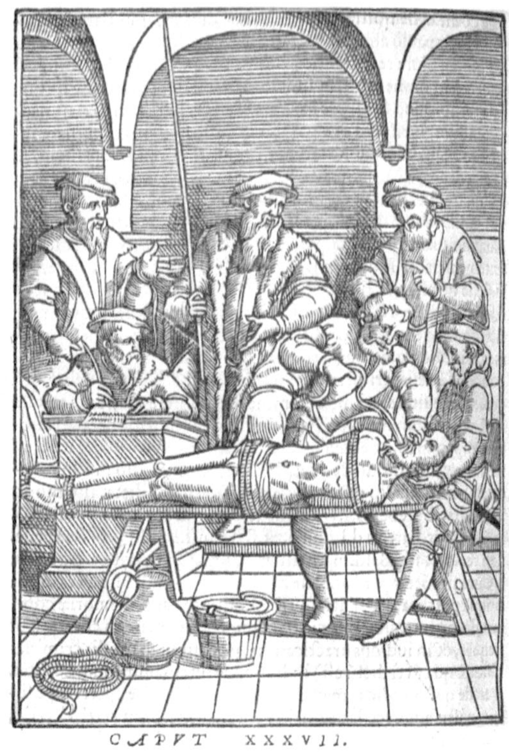

Figure 1.3 Joost Damhoudere (1507–81), *ENCHIRIDION RERUM CRIMINALIUM* (Louvain: Ex officina typographica Stephani Gualtheri & Ioannis Bathenii, 1554; 1st ed. Antwerp, 1534), 103. Permission to reproduce courtesy Yale Law Library.

and the dead of night.[19] And while Damhoudère insists on connecting lawyers' actions to these consequences, Bruegel severs them. Damhoudère's woodcut emphasizes the process of judicial authorization and supervision. The magistrate is poised to write, but his attention, and that of all the legal officials around him, remains focused on the man being tortured. Damhoudère calls this man not a victim or a prisoner or the accused, but "the patient." The word implies the extent to which he is seen to be under the care of the legal system. The process is conceived to be therapeutic, and lawyers are its doctors. *Praxis rerum criminalium* is thus a strange hymn to

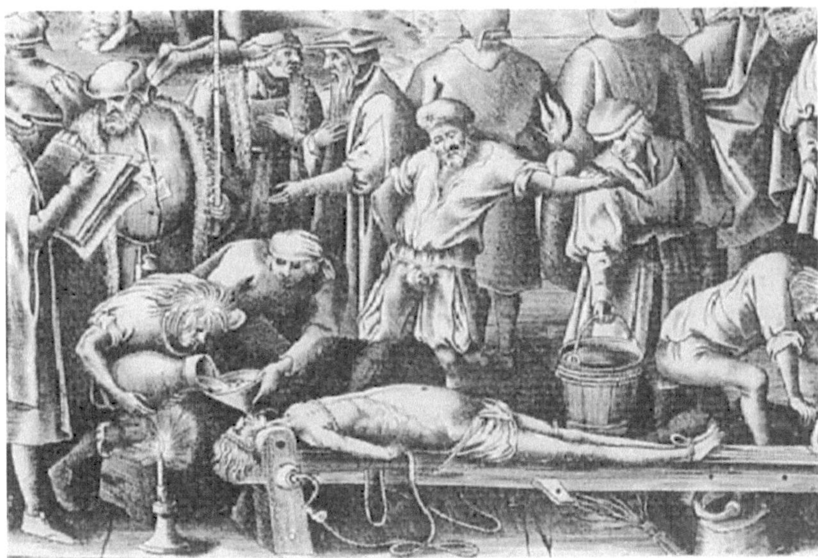

Figure 1.4 Pieter Bruegel, *Justicia* (detail, 1558–9).

judicial responsibility for the bodies that suffer under their supervision and before their eyes. By contrast, Bruegel presents the water cure as a bureaucratic enterprise divorced from any legal teleology. He draws out its routine and wholly administrative nature – one man is ready to deliver the next bucket of water right on cue, held back only by another officer swaggering like a bored security guard, while the two who actually carry out the torture do their job not so much with zeal as with due diligence. Law operates as a kind of machinery that, once set in motion, continues by itself. The lawyers that populate *Justicia* never look at what is going on around them. They have eyes only for their papers, for their "written, imperial law." When it comes to the bodily consequences of those laws, they sedulously avert their gaze.

But Bruegel's vignettes are equally anchored in a very clear temporal logic. This is law in the present tense – as it is practised here and now, in this square, in this town. The scene is both resolutely contemporary and as committed as a comic book or a film to the steady unfolding of "real time." Down the left-hand side, across the bottom of the picture, and up the right-hand edge Bruegel traces a *praxis rerum criminalium* of his own – from affidavits and a preliminary legal hearing, through interrogation under torture, before arriving at a scene of execution. The same figures are repeated throughout these scenes, in particular that of a fair-haired young man. He is bare-headed, a sign of abjection that sets him apart from the officials that surround him. In Damhoudère, too, the accused is shown bare-headed while lawyers, jurors, and judges wear hats befitting their rank.[20] The complex courtroom scene at the bottom left has been unpacked by Karl-Heinz Burmeister. Six noble jurors sit on benches around the judicial table. The judge, recognizable by his hazel staff, reads out his judgment while a clerk notes it down. Facing him, the accused is bound and downcast, holding a crucifix (a symbol of the death sentence); next to him a character witness, perhaps, entreats the judge. Behind the jurors, five members of the public look on, listening, arguing, scanning the court lists.[21] At the lower right, the scene of torture determines the guilt of the accused, and as we have seen, not only the accused but the jurors and the judge with his hazel staff reappear. Finally, we travel from crime to punishment. The accused, once more identifiable by the crucifix he still holds, is about to be executed, while a priest, a surgeon, and possibly the judge, look on. Thus, Bruegel depicts an individual criminal's journey along the assembly line of modern criminal procedure.

The modernity of this process was both a reality in Bruegel's day and a novelty. If "assembly line" seems too industrial a term, we should remember Harold Berman's claim that legal science was the first science of the West.[22] Ironically, it was the papacy that set it in motion. In 1075 Pope Gregory VII unilaterally declared the independence of the church from all secular authority. But at the same time, he announced a strikingly positivist set of reforms and arrogated to a structurally independent and hierarchical legal structure the authority to create new laws – *jus novum*.[23] This was a momentous departure from the idea of law as divine, eternal, customary, or traditional. The great Norman kings of the twelfth century, Roger of Sicily, Frederick Barbarossa, and, in England, Henry II, likewise understood monarchical power as essentially *legislative* and centralizing, advanced through a structure of legal regulation conceived as autonomous, posited, and written.[24] Thus was introduced the concept of "rule by law," if not the rule *of* law. Increasingly, a professional legal and judicial class was needed to realize it.[25]

From the thirteenth through the fifteenth centuries, the reception of Roman law, first in the universities and then across the Holy Roman

Empire, set in train a further process of centralization, textualization, bureaucratization, and regulation that touched every corner of the realm.[26] These changes were called "reformations." They enlarged administrative and regulatory control, and profoundly altered the relationship between monarchical authority and justice. As Gerald Strauss put it, princes began to think of themselves not as *guardians* of legal principles of justice, but as their *authors*.[27] Many people were troubled by the rise and rise of the legal profession. The fifteenth century saw increasing resistance, particularly in Germany, to the adoption of the imperial written law at the expense of local customary law.[28] A diatribe, such as that of Sebastian Brant in *Das Narrenschiff* (1494), was only one of a host of tracts and complaints in circulation. They displayed a deep anxiety concerning the growing power of "written" or "learned" lawyers, whose essentially technical facility made them biddable allies of the centralizing forces of the state; "a guild of sovereignty-mongers," as Jacob Moser called them.[29] By 1553, the German jurist Justin Göbler could note that "when we say 'law' without adding any other word we always mean the common, written, imperial law."[30]

Bruegel's x-axis places justice squarely within this wholly institutional, textual, human, and procedural vision of law. The contrast with earlier representations of justice is stark. Ironically, torture was not, in this context, a relic of pre-modern superstition. On the contrary, as Bruegel shows, torture was central to the modern logic of criminal procedure. In 1215, the Fourth Lateran Council abolished trial by ordeal in canon law and replaced it with the *ordo iudiciarius*.[31] From that moment on, the legal system was no longer interested in trying to summon up a manifestation of divine will. Instead, the critical problem for legal systems became how best to gather human evidence. Damhoudère treats torture not as an aspect of penal law but as part of the law of evidence, "putting the question," as the "cure" was called, to the "patient," a form of words implying both its benign purpose and its claims to scientific legitimacy.[32] Within a secularizing and institutionalizing approach to law, torture was a means not of exacting divine punishment, but of extracting human proof. It was a kind of interrogation by surgery.

In contrast, the y-axis of Bruegel's composition draws us from foreground to background, extending its temporal dimension far beyond the narrative of a single trial. What the image loses in specificity as it recedes, it gains in intensity. Across the middle of the picture Bruegel depicts several instances of corporal punishment. In a darkened cell, a man is being dragged to a block where he suffers the amputation of his hand with a butcher's knife and club; then a local variant of *strappado;* finally, a flogging. Far into the background, the crowds of onlookers lose their individuality, and become merely faces and finally faceless, controlled by a tide of soldiers, and engulfed by the gruesome apparatus of execution – gallows, pyres, and wheels. The single drama that unfolds in the foreground is being endlessly repeated through time and space. One could read that scene of violence as a history, leading from the past up to the present day. Perhaps such a reading would suggest we have come less far than one might think. But the arc of the original drawing carries us forward in time as our eyes move across the canvas and then into the background. The soldiers and citizens are shown with their backs to us. They too are moving *into* the background, not out of it. As we look into the distance, then, we look into the future, where hecatombs of the dead conjure up the image of law as an ever-growing charnel house. The foreground describes a formal, textual, and highly organized process. The distant view reveals a wasteland – dead bodies and circling crows. There is a sensory and corporeal reality to Bruegel's treatment. Bruegel's future stinks – one can almost smell the burning flesh signified by the smoke and the rotting flesh signified by the birds.

Justicia has more than a little in common with *The Triumph of Death* (1562),[33] also, in its way, a grim reminder of the future that awaits us all. The endless ranks of the dead press against the futile barricades of the dying. What makes Bruegel's image of death so powerful is his refusal to justify or glorify or remediate it. It is all hell and no paradise, which has a distinctly Protestant, indeed Lutheran, feel to it. So too, the *y*-axis of *Justicia* suggests a vision of the future in terms of doom and futility. In Ambrogio Lorenzetti's visual constitution for the city of Siena, in the Palazzo Pubblico (1338–9), law and security promise to deliver us "the effects of good government."[34] Lorenzetti paints a scene of peace and harmony and dancing in the streets. His future is utopian.

Bruegel's future, by contrast, is distinctly dystopian. We are busily building a machine of unremitting violence, he implies, driven by its own unstoppable momentum, like a tanker at sea. Klein calls the image a "festival of sadism,"[35] but as Burmeister observes, it lacks the artist's usual witty touch; no one appears to be taking pleasure from the pain.[36] The image does not have a satirical mood. Bruegel puts the question to the legal system he depicts, sounding a warning note about the cure of modern law and its side-effects.

The third or *z*-axis slices across the picture, starting from the figure of Justicia and following the line of her sword to the uppermost corner.

This diagonal line unites two figures that transcend the legal business being transacted around them; at one end, Justicia, at the other, Jesus crucified, with two mourning women at the foot of the cross. The figure of Christ had always been torn between Christ the source of justice and Christ the victim of injustice; between figures of redemption and suffering.[37] Barnouw, among others, asserts that Justice's sword, pointing to the Cross, shows how God authorizes the legal practices described by Bruegel.[38] This is not convincing. Bruegel frames early modern legality, represented through motifs of legal violence and military order, against the story of the Cross, a world-shattering act of violent *injustice*. The Cross is situated on a high promontory. Christ gazes out – not over the scene of modern law in the foreground, but over the scene of multiple executions and endless deaths in the background. As opposed to the realism of the rest of Bruegel's image, the wheels in the background (on which would have been placed the broken bodies of the executed) are planted on the end of exaggerated poles, heightening their sense of brutal desolation and establishing a visual rhythm that connects them with the Cross. Christ's gaze and position establish an affinity not with the executioners but with the executed.[39] He serves as an example of what law does, not its remedy.

While the *y*-axis introduces images of violence that steer us towards a future full of foreboding, the *z*-axis is backward-looking. Its anachronic cut interrupts the temporal march of the picture. It connects a historic moment that took place over a millennium earlier with an earlier, more personal, and less formal notion of the relationship between justice and Christian ideals. At the moment of transition, Justicia triggers the memory of a legal framework that is being broken or cast aside. She hearkens back to an earlier notion of law more deeply connected to Christian principles and to the transcendent authority of divine justice. In the words of Alciato, "It is neither the words written on parchment nor those engraved on bronze that constitute the law, but rather it is that which justice dictates, and which equity directs that bears the true name of law."[40] All this was rapidly being swept away by the forces of legal modernity. Significantly, then, the plinth on which Justicia stands has a large iron ring at its base. Links of the chain to which this ring would once have been joined lie on the ground in front of it, but the connections have been broken and only a small fragment of the whole remains.[41] The metaphor of the chain of the law, joining together the present with the past, and law with justice, suggests itself, and the symbol of this broken chain implies not just a break with the past but a destruction of memory, connection, and justification.

Justicia's costume is telling. Reznik and Curtis describe it as "an odd two-pointed cap evoking fools, courtesans, or dunces."[42] This misses the point. Justice wears a heart-shaped or horned head-dress of a type often worn by genteel women – one hundred years previously.[43] In 1559, her clothing would have seemed quaintly or ridiculously old-fashioned, just when the idea of fashion, with its connotations of the transience of time, was starting to permeate European consciousness. Erasmus, in 1528, proves the point:

> *Nosoponus:* Just look at pictures that aren't all that old, painted, say, sixty years ago, and see what was being worn by those of the fair sex belonging to prominent families or living at court. If a woman went out in public dressed like that now, the village idiots and street-urchins would pelt her with rotten fruit.
>
> *Hypologus:* Only too true. Who would put up now with a decent married woman wearing those huge horns and pyramids and cones sticking out from the top of the head ...?[44]

Justicia signals an antique ideology of law surrounded by trappings of the modern law that was superseding it – a statement both about fashion and opposed to it.

Bruegel's *Justice* is an anachronic site. The representations of the Cross and the outmoded figure of justice, both isolated from the world around them, contest the temporality and trajectory of modern legal ideas. The background, meanwhile, creates a premonition of ghoulish horror that contrasts with the descriptive neutrality of the foreground. Bruegel sees law as the site of a tension and dialogue between these three distinct temporal modes: the present in terms of institutional logic, the future in terms of the consequences of our practices, and the past in terms of the ideals and principles that might ground them. He presents law at the crossroads of these active but incommensurable discourses. The insight is that different ways of seeing our relationship to the passage of time provide different ways of engaging with social and legal change. As Goodrich discusses, the representation of law as Janus-faced, looking both back into the past and forwards into the future, was a powerful theme in the iconology of legal emblems.[45] In many of these images, law comes across as self-satisfied. But Bruegel does not see law's temporal ambivalence as merely an anodyne way of securing law's power and legitimacy. Instead, he sees these elements of legal justification and reflection as a site of discursive struggle, as problematic and contested.

Because we don't just live in the present.[46] Certainly, we live from day to day. But we plan for the future. And equally, a picture or a fragment of melody can transport us back in time, recalling for us a particular person, a promise made or broken, a hope or a regret. We suddenly remember who we were, or who we wanted to become. And we continually negotiate between these different temporal perspectives as we strive on a daily basis to justify, adjust to, or redeem our existence. Bruegel shows that law is no less dependent on all three grammars in order to sustain arguments capable of explaining its legitimacy, its efficacy, and its very existence. Arguments about law are arguments about a society's relationship to time in these multiple senses: about who we are, what we are becoming, and where we came from.

Bruegel's Blindfold

The work of Damhoudère betrays some of this anachronistic quality. The text itself is, of course, highly technical, derived from the *Constitutio criminalis Carolina Germanica* of 1532. But the woodcuts speak a different language. By and large they are lurid depictions of substantive crimes – fornication, incest, gambling, and the like. Damhoudère's images hearken back to the illustrated manuscripts of the *Sachsenspiegel*, two or three hundred years earlier.[47] Damhoudère, like Bruegel, finds himself caught between two worlds. His legal material is thoroughly modern but his images reference a much earlier folkloric legal vernacular in which the legitimation of law took preliterate and populist forms. Damhoudère transmits modern ideas but clothes them in an older and more familiar aesthetic rhetoric. New wine, one might say, in old bottles.

Is that what Bruegel's image does too? To answer this question, we need to consider in greater detail the puzzle of the blindfold worn by Justicia. There is nothing antique or old-fashioned about it. On the contrary, the blindfold is the most *modern* aspect of her clothing – an anachronism within a figure that is already anachronistic. The blindfold had only very recently entered the iconography of Western law. In 1494, the noted jurist Sebastian Brant[48] published a collection of satirical poems called *Das Narrenschiff* or *The Ship of Fools*, and commissioned several artists to illustrate it with a series of woodcuts.[49] Verse 71 is a crude satire, excoriating the corruption and cynicism of the legal profession. It concludes:

> He'll get much raillery uncouth,
> Who fights like children tooth for tooth
> And thinks that he can blind the truth.[50]

But the illustration, sometimes attributed to Albrecht Dürer, shows not truth but justice being blindfolded by a fool in a tricorn hat. The artist emphasizes the bad faith of lawyers, actively constraining justice the better to achieve their own ends. Through the window an urban vista recalls perhaps Ambrogio Lorenzetti's happy depictions of urban life.[51] On this occasion, however, the city is empty of humanity, and removed from the machinations of the law. The fool prepares Justice for her new role in a private room, like a dresser on opening night.

The appearance of this trope is not surprising. What is astounding is the speed with which it cast off its satirical edge. During the sixteenth century, official statues of blind justice – played straight, as it were – start to pop up, although in other contexts blindness continues to operate as a critique.[52] The first edition of Cesare Ripa's *Iconologia* (1593) notes that "in the opinion of Plato, nothing escapes the eyes of Justice … and by the force of her gaze she penetrates to the base of all things."[53] Ten years later, the earliest illustrated editions represent several aspects of justice, but only one of them – called "worldly" or "strict" justice – was depicted blindfolded.[54] But within a very short time, the *madonna bandita* had become a ubiquitous symbol of abstraction and neutrality, and a generic statement of the judiciary's commitment to maintain a formal ignorance of personal circumstances. As the inscription on Tübingen town hall explains, "My eyes are bound so that rich and poor appear the same."[55] In little more than a century, something cataclysmic seems to have happened to the legal imaginary.[56] The history of the image draws our attention to a complete *inversion* of established ideas, and pinpoints it in time. But this only highlights the problem of interpreting Bruegel's blindfold. Fifty years earlier and it would undoubtedly have been a critique. Fifty years later and it would undoubtedly have been a virtue. In 1559, Bruegel's image hovers right on the cusp of this revolution.

To fully interpret the meaning of Bruegel's blindfold, we need to consider two overarching features of his work. The first is his treatment of crowds. His paintings reflect the steadily urbanizing life of northern

Europe, lived increasingly in close proximity to many strangers. He captures the noise, density, and diversity of social life, not one story but one hundred jostling for recognition on the canvas.[57] Several of his works form a kind of illustrated encyclopedia of contemporary social life. *Children's Games* (1560) is so precise that historians have identified no less than eighty specific games in it; for many of them, Bruegel is our only evidence. In *Proverbs*, and in some of the peasant pictures, the canvas teems with catalogues of folk practices. *Justicia*, too, provides a scrupulous compilation of contemporary aspects of legal violence.

For this unprecedented accumulation of social details, particularly about the lives of the poor, the best analogue to Bruegel's work is that of his close contemporary, François Rabelais (1494–1553). Rabelais was also a devotee of the list, piling up instance upon instance, particular upon particular. Like Bruegel, he revelled in compiling catalogues – children's games, anatomical metaphors, cooks, fools, bodily insults, and so on. As Mikhail Bakhtin argues, this observational extravagance demystifies the socially hegemonic sentimentality of earlier literary genres.[58] Rabelais constantly contrasts myth and real life, both by paying attention to the lives of common people and in the accumulation of overwhelming empirical detail. To the romantic ideal of love, Rabelais juxtaposes copulation and farting. To the romantic ideal of religion, Rabelais juxtaposes corrupt and gluttonous friars. To the romantic ideal of war, Rabelais juxtaposes detailed descriptions of death, pain, and mutilation. At each point, Rabelais's scatological humour and forensic irony unmasks false idealizations and discloses the real experiences hidden by them.[59] Many an epic might say, "And I deliver thee, said the monk, to all the devils in hell; then at one stroke he cut off his head." But Rabelais, doctor of medical science, must tell us what happens next:

> Cutting his cranium above the petrous bone, removing both the bones of the sinciput as well as the sagittal suture, together with the greater part of the coronal bone; by doing so he sliced through both meninges and opened up deeply the two posterior ventricle-cavities of the brain: and so his cranium remained hanging down over his shoulders at the back from the membranes of the pericranium in the form of a doctoral bonnet, black above, red within.[60]

Rabelais presents an early instance of the "disenchantment of the world."[61] By observation and juxtaposition he opens up a gap between our beliefs about the world and what actually happens in it. At this point, Bakhtin insists, Rabelais's own empiricism takes on an ethical significance.[62] With a virile repertoire of humour, irony, and scenes from low life, Rabelais's readers see the life around them more honestly and judge their own illusions more critically. Thus was born the modern novel.

Bruegel's paintings appear at the same time, and with the same combination of social realism, humour, and irony. Both moral/conservative and political/radical readings of his work are too reductionist. They underestimate the carnivalesque sweep[63] of his diverse social observations. His physical realism was no doubt facilitated by the development of linear perspective,[64] which replaced romantic or ideological relationships with spatial ones. *The Beggars* is a good example.[65] On the one hand, it has been read as a coded message to the Northern resistance; on the other hand, it has been read as a conventional homily on human deceit.[66] The image certainly refuses to indulge our taste for pity. But the physical reality of the beggars ultimately *resists* the moral assumptions we attempt to project on them,[67] forcing us to confront the fraud, complacency, or bad faith of our own preconceptions, whether they run in the direction of pity or of righteousness.[68] By refusing to romanticize or moralize them, Bruegel demands we take them seriously.

In true Rabelaisian fashion, Bruegel's depiction of legal violence similarly undercuts our romantic ideals. He juxtaposes "justice" against what people actually do in its name, and how, and where. One of the most profound shocks delivered by Bruegel's image is his insistence that justice is not produced by a single transcendent authority – an ideal, a king, or a God – nor conceived in terms of a personal relationship between man and God, nor realized in a single, climactic moment of judgment. Instead, Bruegel embeds justice in a social context and in multiple, everyday social practices and institutions. He implicates all of us in daily gestures of complicity and involvement. Bruegel seems to have captured here, for the very first time, a key feature of modern law. He shows how legal regulation expanded exponentially by being diffused across multiple actors and institutions.[69] Perhaps his own artistic experience might have informed this perspective. Bruegel's *Virtues*, for example, were not the product of a single moment of artistry. It took the engraving skills of Galle and the publishing skills of Cock, not to mention the invention of the printing press, for Bruegel's images to make their way into the public domain. Bruegel was no doubt an artistic realist. He was also the first "legal realist," a good 350 years ahead of the schools of Pound, Llewellyn, or Olivecrona.[70] He reveals justice to be mundane in every sense of the world. Yet as one's eyes move back into the distance, collective action gives way to undifferentiated crowds. The legal system becomes an ornately choreographed performance intended for mass consumption. Bruegel therefore portends another key feature in the development of modern law – the rhetorical power of the spectacle of legal violence.

The second over-arching feature lies in Bruegel's approach to history. *Landscape with the Fall of Icarus, Procession to Calvary*, or *The Conversion of Paul* depart radically from conventional representations of such scenes.[71] In each case, the central event is lost amidst the riot of everyday activity that dominates the canvas. Indeed, the viewer has to look hard to locate the stories they depict. The fall of Icarus makes only the tiniest splash in a vast and indifferent sea. Christ carries his cross, largely unnoticed by the hundreds of people milling around him. Bruegel is not so much interested in the meaning of these events as in their reception. He depicts social ignorance and indifference. He encourages us to hunt out the important moment that those who were there manifestly *failed* to notice – and paints, above all, that failure.

So it could be that the real subject of *Justicia* is in fact the Crucifixion, another world-historical event which at the time seemed of only marginal importance. Jesus was one execution among many, one incident in a long campaign of occupation and subjugation. Meanwhile, men and women went about their business, wholly absorbed in the here and now. The difference between what matters to us now and what will be seen to have mattered in retrospect – in the temporality of the *futur antérieur*, as Derrida puts it[72] – is one of Bruegel's obsessions. The crucifixion is of course the *locus classicus* of this temporal ambivalence. It *destabilizes* our relationship to linear time since its meaning so radically changes, from desecration to purification, from tragedy to salvation, when it is viewed from the position of a future time regarding itself.

Bruegel is the painter par excellence of the crowd in history. He highlights our temporal blindness, our obliviousness to the wider significance of what is going on around us. The blindness of Justicia is therefore not a metaphor, but a metonym.[73] The figures in the picture pay no attention to the Virtue in their midst.[74] They are blind equally to the future and the past. This automatism or mundane self-absorption is again typical of many of Bruegel's paintings. We see it here in the disinterested diligence of the torturers and guards, occupied by the minutiae of their own activities. The lawyers and judges – with the exception of the magistrate making eye contact with the witness – are likewise absorbed only in their writing. Bruegel's technique of piling up details effectively conveys this myopic world. It is a commonplace in the discussion of linear perspective to observe that it draws viewers into the action.[75] But here Bruegel's three-dimensional space creates confusion rather than order, immersing us in multiple elements that compete for our attention. Like *Icarus* or *Saul*, *Justicia* invites viewers to share the short-sighted perspective of the characters in it. Bruegel's claustrophobic scene deprives one of a sense of belonging or an opportunity for judgment.[76]

The figure of Justicia is removed from this social hyper-activity. Rather like the original woodcut in *Das Narrenschiff*, she is depicted as passively acquiescent. The blindfold further emphasizes this divorce between symbol and action. Indeed, on closer inspection, Justicia does not appear to be alive at all. She is a statue. Her pose is static; her feet do not touch the ground, but rest on a plinth with her name on it. In all but one of the other virtues, the title floats above or on top of Bruegel's scene. But here, the word "Justicia," carved in stone, is part of the scene not a label for it. The word belongs to the statue, and a statue is part of the realm of the signifier, not the realm of the signified. All in all, the figure of Justice is more connected to "signs for the text" than to "signs for the real."[77] She is not a representation *of* the world, like Bruegel's depiction of the men and events that surround her, but a representation *within* that world – a figure of a figure, an image of an image. So the artist's drawing is neither in praise of justice nor opposed to it. It is not about justice at all; it is about the symbol or discourse of justice, and the use that men make of it. Bruegel shows himself uncannily attuned to the perils and powers of a new discursive figure, in whose name all manner of legal actions might be, indeed would be, legitimated. He seems to foreshadow how the word justice might become a coin circulating in the currency of rhetorical justification, at the mercy of those best able to seize, dress, and position her. We see Justicia guarded by a phalanx of well-armed mercenaries. But this only serves to show how far down in the world she has come; for since when has a god needed a guard? One could rather imagine her held hostage, a pawn at the mercy of others in a game of blindman's bluff. The control being exercised in this picture, soldiers crowding around the bound figure of Justicia in the foreground, and keeping a tight rein on the people in the background, make it unclear whether Justice is being protected from the people, or prevented from speaking to them.

So there is a second aspect to Justicia's blindness. It is neither an attribute nor a criticism, but an incapacity or vulnerability. Edward Snow rightly sees close parallels between *Justicia* and *Children's Games*, painted the following year. In the latter, children re-appropriate all manner of everyday objects as instruments to be used in their play. A child dressed as a monk holds a whip above a spinning-top, in a gesture that evokes some strange private ritual. But what is done in fun in *Children's Games* is done in earnest in *Justicia*. Instead of a top, it is men who are turned into instruments to be whipped, tortured, executed, and otherwise objectified for the law's pleasure. In short, justice is depicted as a kind of game – rote, instrumental, even mindless – and human beings its toys. "It clarifies what the vision of Bruegel's *Justicia* implies – that evil springs not from an innate anarchic violence but from the human capacity to detach oneself from it and administer it in the name of order."[78] The blindness of Justicia – her ritual and static quality, her passivity and her vulnerability to the will of others – is in fact central to her ability to be used or manipulated in the discourse of others.

From Bruegel's "Justice" to Bruegel's Justice

Bruegel's image sets a trap.[79] It seems to me that several interpreters of *Justicia* fall into it: they assume that Bruegel is about a conventional identification and reification of an idea that, here as elsewhere, is represented for the purposes of critique.[80] But Bruegel also charts a way out of the trap he has drawn. By making blindness *visible* he invites us to question our practices, and to resist the reification of justice in which, albeit in different ways, the legal actors and the discourse of justice are alike implicated. Bruegel includes figures of dissent at key moments in the image, showing us that at least some citizens were engaged participants in debates about the legal practices of their time. Justicia herself succeeds, almost covertly, in reminding us of the tension between the three temporal frameworks of law. She invites us to imagine the suffering experienced by each and every one of those microscopic figures sketched in the background; and suggests that the legal purposes that drive the foreground action might be ritual and pointless as children's games, inevitable as the triumph of death.

Finally, despite its otherwise claustrophobic air, Bruegel positions the spectator well above the town square, giving us access to a wider vista of the future and contemplation of the past. He positions the viewer on the same level as Christ and invites us, like him, to survey and judge the scene, not just to lose ourselves in activity. Likewise, in a composition overcrowded with business and busy-ness, one area is left strikingly clear. Empty space governs the whole centre of the image, from the initial legal actions on the left to the execution at right. This empty space suggests a possibility of otherness, of an alternative yet to be imagined or realized. Bruegel implies the transcendence or unrepresentability of justice. He gives space for critique.[81]

As a metonym, Bruegel's blindfold directs us to the manifold elements of social behaviour that in reality constitute legal practice. As an expression of vulnerability, the blindfold directs us to the plasticity of discourse. In neither case is the figure reducible either to a satire on legal practice or simply a conventional sign. Both as metonym and as vulnerability, the blindfold points to Justicia's weakness, demanding that we redirect our critical attention to our *own* involvement in what we do in law, and what we say about it. We could simply mourn this failure and continue to wait for some deus ex machina to come along and realize justice for us. But Bruegel seems to suggest that if we want justice we should stop waiting around for it. The position of Justicia's feet are suggestive. She stands in the classic pose of *contrapposto*, neither in motion nor at rest – her body poised and tense, anticipating the immanence of action not yet realized.[82] This tension and expectation, which might even be read as unease or anxiety, suggests a mental state of urgency, anticipation; Justicia is waiting for something, coiled and ready. Invoking Levinas, we could see then her vulnerability as a cry for help, a silent appeal that truly constitutes – inaugurates and brings to life – our legal subjectivity, imposing on us a duty that we cannot evade, to bring her to the point of action.[83] The blindfold's metonymic dimension embraces all of us in its critique, while the figure's dimension as incapacity and expectancy imposes a responsibility on us all.[84]

The unusual trope of the blindfold therefore injects a critical interpellation into the broader thesis of Bruegel's work. In the Low Countries but equally across Europe, the Protestant Reformation was turning from image to text, from symbol to form, and the legal Reformation was turning from custom to structure, from individual responsibility to institutional accountability, and from an all-seeing to a blinded justice. Brughel's virtue stands on the cusp of that transition. It looks back to a different set of underlying normative principles, as well as forward to the ways in which the old rhetoric would be recast in the interests of new and potent systems. Bruegel's image of *Justicia* turns this clash of temporal perspectives from a mere fact about legal change into different modes of argument about it. What we witness is a dialogue about transition, law's relationship to it, and our responsibility for it. This dialogue is charged with the characteristically violent, crowded, and disturbing corporeality of the image. Bruegel fuses his unprecedented legal realism with the profound shock of our own physical experience of law as well as its physical impact on others.

Bruegel's messages about time as a normative discourse, law as an embodied experience, and the daily social activities that make it real, continue to be relevant. Now, no less than five hundred years ago, we tend to think of law in symbolic and abstract ways – justice even more so. We treat justice as the realm of pure ideas, and law as a force of pure fact. Either way the legal system is thought of as something which is done by "them" – those others who have the power; not us – and done to "them" – those others who are its victims; not us. But Bruegel confronts those fatuous assumptions. Juris-diction means the place from where law speaks.[85] And Bruegel, above all, shows how this place is our flesh – the flesh that is subject to it, the flesh that imposes, performs, and participates in it, and the flesh that gives rise and gives meaning to its texts and institutions.[86] As Kafka was to say, the law is engraved on our bodies[87] – a vivid materiality that links together those who do it, suffer it, and witness it.

A certain blindness also unites these groups, a blindness which Bruegel succeeds in making visible and challenging. Much more recently, José Saramago's modern fable invites us to see our blindness not so much as a disability that afflicts us and from which we could be rescued, but rather as the condition or predicament of all human life.

> The only miracle we can perform is to go on living, said the woman, to preserve the fragility of life from day to day, as if it were blind and did not know where to go, and perhaps it is like that, perhaps it really does not know, it placed itself in our hands, after giving us intelligence, and this is what we have made of it. You speak as if you too were blind said the girl with the dark glasses. In a way I am, I am blind with your blindness, perhaps I might be able to see better if there were more of us who could see ...[88]

Like Saramago, the possibility of justice that Bruegel evokes is not a matter of either keeping the blindfold on or taking it off, but of seeing more truly how blind we are. In that enterprise, Bruegel's image is exemplary. The image of justice cannot be reduced to the figure of

Justice in it, but rather inheres in the whole theatre of representation, the dynamics of discourse, time, and transition that *Justicia*, as a totality, sets in motion. Bruegel does not represent or explain justice – he *does* it.

NOTES

1 José Saramago, *Blindness*, trans. Giovanni Pontiero (New York: Viking Press, 1997), 326.
2 Perhaps most notable for their encyclopedic range have been Judith Resnik and Dennis Curtis, *Representing Justice* (New Haven: Yale University Press, 2011) and Peter Goodrich, *Legal Emblems and the Art of Law* (New York: Cambridge University Press, 2014).
3 Alexander Nagel and Christopher Wood, *Anachronic Renaissance* (New York: Zone Books, 2010), 10.
4 See Erwin Panofsky, *Renaissance and Renascences in Western Art* (New York: Harper & Row, 1972); Georges Didi-Huberman, *Confronting Images: Questioning the Ends of a Certain History of Art* (Reading, PA: University of Pennsylvania Press, 2005); see Nagel and Wood, *Anachronic Renaissance*, chap. 1.
5 Ibid., 13.
6 Pieter Bruegel (The Elder), 1525–69. The spelling varies, but from 1559, he dropped the 'h' from his name.
7 See Manfred Sellink, *Bruegel:* The *Complete Paintings, Drawings, and Prints* (Bruges: Ludion, 2007), 134–51.
8 For previous discussion, in addition to sources to be cited, see Arthur Klein, *Graphic Worlds of Pieter Brugel the Elder* (New York: Dover, 1963); Pierre Francastel, *Bruegel* (Paris: Hazan, 1995); Christine Hartmann, "Unruhe in der Stadt, De gerechtigheid von Pieter Bruegel dem Älteren," in Hans-Peter Meier-Dallach, ed., *900 Jahre Zukunft* (Lindenberg: Fink, 1999), 114–22; L. Huygenbaert, "La justice vue par Bruegel," *La Metropole*, Antwerp, 11 June 1933, p. 1.
9 See the discussion of temporality in art in Louis Marin, *On Representation* (Stanford: Stanford University Press, 2001), 290–4. See also Kristeva's description of temporal orientations: teleological time, repetitive time, and monumental or eternal time; Julia Kristeva, Alice Jardine, and Harry Blake, "Women's Time," *Signs* 7, no. 1 (1981): 13–35.
10 This was also the method of the scholarly analysis by Karl Heinz Burmeister, originally in German and regrettably not yet translated into English. I have done my best to work with a Spanish translation done for

a conference in Colombia. See "'La Justicia' de 1559 de Pieter Brueghel el Viejo," trans. Camila Bordamalo y Jesús Gualdrón (online: http://scholar.googleusercontent.com/scholar?q=cache:vSbgXzLWMkkJ:scholar.google.com/&hl=en&as_sdt=0,5), originally published in Bernd Marquardt and Alois Niederstätter, eds, *Das Recht im kulturgeschichtlichen Wandel, Festschrift für Karl Heinz Burmeister zur Emeritierung* (Constanza: UVK, 2002), 553–601.

11 It could be argued that Bruegel had already compensated for this inversion in the sketch he provided to Galle, but I don't think so. One possible piece of evidence for this is the fact that his original drawing includes the label "Iustitia" on the central figure, *not* reversed.

12 Joost Damhoudère, *Praxis rerum criminalium*, first edition titled *Enchiridion rerum criminalium* (Louvain, 1534), p. 103. Online facsimile available: http://www.flickr.com/photos/yalelawlibrary/sets/72157625330407523/.

13 The text reads: "Scopus legis est, au tut ev que punit emendet, aut poena eius caeteros meliores reddet aut sublatis malis caeteri securiores vivat" ("The aim of the law is either to correct him who is punished, or to improve the others by his example, or to provide that the population live more securely by removing wrongdoers"). It is written in a different hand and a different ink than the original drawing, and seems almost certainly to have been added by Cock.

14 Burmeister, "'La Justicia' de 1559," 8–9. Dogs and antlers both reflect patrician rights to hunting.

15 Damhoudère, quoted in Burmeister, and in Michael Stolleis, ed., *Juristen. Ein biographisches Lexikon: Von der Antike bis zum 20. Jahrhundert* (Munich: C.H. Beck, 2001), 152.

16 Louis Marin, *Le portrait du roi* (Paris: Éditions de Minuit, 1981), 3.

17 Burmeister, "'La Justicia' de 1559," 6.

18 The evolution of the term is discussed at considerable length in Robert Jacob, *Images de la Justice* (Paris: Le Léopard d'Or, 1994). For etymology, see *Le Petit Robert* (Paris, 1967), 1237, which gives 1366 for the space in a *salle de justice*, and 1549 for the office of *le ministère public*. Other sources provide similar dates: Edmond Huguet, *Dictionnaire de la langue française du seizieme siècle* (Paris, 1925–73).

19 Some, including Burmeister, have suggested that the candle was used to heat up burning fat sometimes used in the torture. I do not find the explanation convincing both because the technique is not legitimated by Damhoudère and for various reasons endogenous to the image.

20 E.g., *Appello*, in Damhoudère, *Praxis rerum criminalium*, 516.

21 Burmeister, "'La Justicia' de 1559," 5–6.

22 Harold Berman, *Law and Revolution: The Foundation of the Western Legal Tradition* (Cambridge, MA, 1983), 151–64.
23 See *Dictatus Papae* (1075), repr. in Brian Tierney, ed., *The Middle Ages*, vol. 1: *Sources of Medieval History*, 4th ed. (New York, 1983), 142–3. See Uta-Renate Blumenthal, "History and Tradition in Eleventh-Century Rome," *Catholic Historical Review* 79, no. 2 (1993): 185–96.
24 Berman, *Law and Revolution*, 19–22, 80–96, 202–3.
25 Ibid., 405–57, 440–4; see Desmond Manderson, "Statuta and Acts: Interpretation, Music, and Early English Legislation," *Yale Journal of Law and the Humanities* 7 (1995): 317–66.
26 See Kenneth Pennington, *The Prince and the Law* (Berkeley, 1993); Emanuele Conte, "Roman Law vs. Customs in a Changing Society," in P. Andersen and Mia Münster-Swendsen, eds, *Custom: The Development and Use of a Legal Concept in the Middle Ages*, Proceedings of the Fifth Carlsberg Academic Conference on Medieval Legal History (Copenhagen: DJØF Publishing, 2009), 33–49.
27 Gerald Strauss, *Law, Resistance and the State: The Opposition to Roman Law in Reformation Germany* (Princeton, NJ, 1986), 150–1.
28 See Strauss, *Law, Resistance and the State*; Paul Vinogradoff, *Roman Law in Medieval Europe* (Oxford, 1929, 1961), 139–42.
29 In Strauss, *Law, Resistance and the State*, 142.
30 Ibid., 90.
31 Pennington, *The Prince and the Law*, 47, 134–5. Laurentius, also c. 1215, is already articulating law in these terms, already emphasizing law's attributes in terms of its form not its source.
32 Damhoudère, *Praxis rerum criminalium*.
33 Pieter Bruegel, *Triumph of Death*, oil on canvas, Museo del Prado, Madrid, 1562.
34 Ambrogio Lorenzetti, *The Effects of Good Government*, fresco, Palazzo Pubblico, Siena, 1338–9.
35 Graphic Worlds of Pieter Brugel the Elder, 126.
36 Burmeister, "'La Justicia' de 1559."
37 Jacob, *Images de la Justice*, 59–62.
38 Adriaan Jacob Barnou, The Fantasy of Pieter Brueghel (New York: Lear, 1947).
39 "And Jesus said unto him, 'Verily I say unto thee, today shalt thou be with me in paradise'"; Luke 23:43.
40 Alciato, "Emblems," in Goodrich, *Legal Emblems and the Art of Law*, 77. See also Desmond Manderson, "The Metastases of Myth: Legal Images as Transitional Phenomena," forthcoming.

41 I am very grateful to Peter Goodrich for his enormously helpful explication of these elements in the image, which had stymied me for many months beforehand.
42 Reznik and Curtis, *Representing Justice*, 72.
43 For excellent examples in French and Flemish art 1400–50, see online gallery: http://en.wikipedia.org/wiki/1400%E2%80%931500_in_European_fashion#Style_gallery_.E2.80.93_Northern_Europe_1400s.E2.80.931440s.
44 Desiderius Erasmus, "The Ciceronian" (1528), in A.H.T. Levi, ed., *Collected Works of Erasmus*, vol. 6: *Literary and Educational Writings* (Toronto: University of Toronto Press, 1986), 381. See also Nagel and Wood, *Anachronic Renaissance*, 92 and 88–92 passim.
45 Goodrich, *Legal Emblems and the Art of Law*, xix–xxi.
46 See M.M. Bakhtin, "Forms of Time and Chronotypes of the Novel," in Michael Holquist, ed., *The Dialogic Imagination: Four Essays by M.M. Bakhtin*, trans. C. Emerson and M. Holquist (Austin, 1981), 84–258.
47 Illuminated manuscripts exist in Heidelberg, Oldenburg, Dresden, and Wolfenbüttel (c. 1290–1360).
48 See Sebastian Brant, *Das Narrenschiff* (Basel, 1494), in Edwin Zeydel, ed. and trans., *The Ship of Fools* (New York, 1944), 6–7.
49 See also Sebastian Brant, *The Ship of Fools*, trans. William Gillis (London, 1971).
50 #71, "Quarrelling and Going to Court," in Brant, *The Ship of Fools*, 236. An alternative translation: "Very often he feels the heckler's barbs / Who always quarrels like a child / And wants to make the truth blind" (Leo Unglaub).
51 Ambrogio Lorenzetti, *Allegory of Good Government, Allegory of Bad Government, Effects of Bad Government in the City, Effects of Good Government in the City*, and *Effects of Good Government in the Country*, Palazzo Pubblico, Siena (1338–9). See Richard Mohr, "The Christian Origins of Secularism and the Rule of Law," in Nassein Hosen and Richard Mohr, eds, *Law and Religion in Public Life* (Abingdon, 2011); Quentin Skinner, "Ambrogio Lorenzetti's Buon Governo Frescoes: Two Old Questions, Two New Answers," *Journal of the Warburg and Courtauld Institutes* 62 (1999): 1–28; Quentin Skinner, "Ambrogio Lorenzetti: The Artist as Political Philosopher," *Proceedings of the British Academy* 72 (1986): 1–56; Nicolai Rubinstein, "Political Ideas in Sienese Art: The Frescoes by Ambrogio Lorenzetti and Taddeo di Bartolo in the Palazzo Pubblico," *Journal of the Warburg and Courtauld Institutes* 21 (1958): 179–207; Cary Nederman, "The Meaning of 'Aristotelianism' in Medieval Moral and Political Thought,"

Journal of the History of Ideas 57 (1996): 563–85; Maria Luisa Meoni, *Utopia and Reality in Ambrogio Lorenzetti's Good Government* (Florence, 2005).

52 Reznik and Curtis, *Representing Justice*, 62–75.

53 Cesare Ripa, *Iconologia*, 2 vols. (New York, 1976) (Padua, 1611 and Paris, 1644; first published Rome, 1593 and first illustrated edition Rome, 1603).

54 Ibid.

55 Resnik and Curtis, *Representations of Justice*, 75.

56 Jacques De Ville, "Mythology and the Images of Justice," *Law and Literature* 23 (2011): 324.

57 Pieter Brugel, *The Procession to Calvary*, oil on canvas, Kunsthistorisches Museum, Vienna, 1564; *Conversion of Paul*, oil on canvas, Kunsthistorisches Museum, Vienna, 1567; *Suicide of Saul*, oil on canvas, Kunsthistorisches Museum, Vienna, 1562; *Battle between Carnival and Lent*, oil on canvas, Kunsthistorisches Museum, Vienna, 1559; *The Peasant Wedding*, oil on canvas, Kunsthistorisches Museum, Vienna, 1568; *The Peasant Dance*, oil on canvas, Kunsthistorisches Museum, Vienna, 1568.

58 M.M. Bakhtin, *Rabelais and His World* (Bloomington, IN, [1965] 1984).

59 M.M. Bakhtin, "Forms of Time and Chronotypes of the novel," in Holquist, ed., pp. 168–72. See also Bakhtin, *Rabelais and His World*. There is something to be said for connecting Rabelais' potty-mouth with that of Martin Luther, and in the process connecting the reformations of religion and literature; I am not sure who has made the argument.

60 François Rabelais, *Gargantua and Pantagruel*, trans. M.A. Screech (London, [1532] 2006), 340.

61 Max Weber, "Some Categories of Interpretive Sociology," *Sociological Quarterly* 22, no. 2 (1981): 151–80.

62 M.M. Bakhtin, "Epic and Novel," in Holquist, ed., *The Dialogic Imagination*, 7.

63 Bakhtin, *Rabelais*; see also Shanti Elliot, "Carnival and Dialogue in Bakhtin's Poetics of Folklore," *Folklore Forum* 30 (1999); Bruegel, *The Battle between Carnival and Lent*.

64 Samuel Edgerton, *The Mirror, the Window and the Telescope* (Ithaca, 2009), 145.

65 Pieter Bruegel, *The Beggars (The Cripples)*, oil on canvas, Louvre, Paris, 1568.

66 Gibson, *Bruegel*, 184.

67 A similar analysis informs interpretations of the depiction by Diane Arbus of "deviant and marginal people": see Diane Arbus, *Diane Arbus* (Millerton, NY, 1972).

68 Snow, *Children's Games*, 76.

69 See Scott Veitch, *Law and Irresponsibility: On the Legitimation of Human Suffering* (Abingdon, 2007); E.W. Mathes and A. Kahn, "Diffusion of

Responsibility and Extreme Behavior," *Journal of Personality and Social Psychology* 31 (1975): 881–6; M.A. Wallach, N. Kogan, and D.J. Bem, "Diffusion of Responsibility and Level of Risk Taking in Groups," *Journal of Abnormal and Social Psychology* 68 (1964): 263–74; Gustave Le Bon, *The Crowd: A Study of the Popular Mind* (London, 1995 [1897]).

70 Karl Llewellyn, *Jurisprudence: Realism in Theory and Practice* (Chicago, 1962); Karl Llewellyn, "A Realistic Jurisprudence – The Next Step," *Columbia Law Review*, April 1930: 431–65; William Twining, *Karl Llewellyn and the Realist Movement* (Cambridge, 2012); Roscoe Pound, "The Call for a Realist Jurisprudence," *Harvard Law Review* 44 (1931): 697–711; Jes Bjarup, "The Philosophy of Scandinavian Legal Realism," *Ratio Juris* 18, no. 1 (1931): 1–15; Karl Olivecrona, "Realism and Idealism: Some Reflections on the Cardinal Point in Legal Philosophy," *NYU Law Review* 26 (1951): 120; Karl Olivecrona, *Law as Fact* (Copenhagen, 1939).

71 Pieter Brugel, *The Procession to Calvary*, oil on canvas, Kunsthistorisches Museum, Vienna, 1564; *Conversion of Paul*, oil on canvas, Kunsthistorisches Museum, Vienna, 1567; *Landscape with the Fall of Icarus*, oil on canvas (possibly copy of lost original), Royal Museums of Fine Arts of Belgium, Brussels, 1554–5.

72 Jacques Derrida, "Declarations of Independence 1," *New Political Science* 7, no. 1 (1986): 7–15.

73 See also a remark on this point by I. Bennett Capers, "Blind Justice," *Yale Journal of Law & the Humanities* 24 (2012): 189.

74 Capers, "Blind Justice."

75 Erwin Panofsky, *Perspective as Symbolic Form* (New York, 1991); Hubert Damisch, *A Theory of Cloud: Toward a History of Painting* (Stanford, CA., 2002).

76 Compare the discussion of space and perspective in Damisch, *A Theory of Cloud*, 170.

77 Mieke Bal, "De-disciplining the Eye," *Critical Inquiry* 16 (1990): 506–31. The exception is *Temperance*, whose name flows on the hem of her skirt. This figure too stands at some remove from the action, as if she too were a sign of it and not a participant in it.

78 Snow, *Children's Games*, 118.

79 Henry James, "New York Preface" to *The Turn of the Screw* (Ware, 1993), xxxii–xxxiii); see Shoshana Felman, "Turning the Screw of Interpretation," *Yale French Studies* 55/56 (1977): 185ff.

80 See Mieke Bal, "His Master's Eye," in David Levin, ed., *Modernity and the Hegemony of Vision* (Berkeley, 1993), 379–404.

81 I am grateful to Oliver Watts for drawing this crucial aesthetic element of the picture to my attention and reflecting on its meaning. For further on

the role of empty space in the representation of legal and divine authority, see Peter Goodrich, "The Iconography of Nothing: Blank Spaces and the Representation of Law in Edward VI and the Pope," in Douzinas and Neald, eds, *Law and the Image*, 89–114.

82 Cf. Michelangelo's *David*, the power of which is generated precisely because the boy's body is portrayed *before* the slingshot is thrown.

83 Emmanuel Levinas, *Autrement qu'être ou au-delà de l'essence* (Paris, 1974); Emmanuel Levinas, *Difficile liberté* (Paris, 1976); *Difficult Freedom: Essays on Judaism*, trans. Sean Hand (London, 1990).

84 Levinas, *Difficult Freedom*.

85 See esp. Shaunnagh Dorsett and Shaun McVeigh, "Questions of Jurisdiction," in Shaun McVeigh, ed., *Jurisprudence of Jurisdiction* (Abingdon, 2007), 3–18; Shaunnagh Dorsett and Shaun McVeigh, *Jurisdiction* (Abingdon, 2012), 4–5.

86 Peter Rush, "An Altered Jurisdiction: Corporeal Traces of Law," *Griffith Law Review* 6 (1997): 144–68.

87 Franz Kafka, "In the Penal Colony" (1919), in Franz Kafka, *Collected Stories*, trans. Willa and Edwin Muir (New York, 1993), 129–43.

88 José Saramago, *Blindness*, trans. Giovanni Pontiero (New York: Harcourt Brace, 1997), 297.

2 Faces and Frames of Government

PETER GOODRICH

Desire, with its dimension of depth, disfigures the Law. And simultaneously, by the same token, it is illegible, hence hidden.

Jean-François Lyotard[1]

I will open with the question of openings and will thus start at a distance from my theme of law and the *mens emblematica*, the return of the emblem, of visible desire in the media of governance. I will borrow from a brilliant work by the film scholar Laurence Moinereau on film credits to unfold the essential issue, which is that of the role of the image as the mode of access to and animation of the juridical in the social.[2] How does a textual discipline, an arcane and often foreign set of books of law engage and bind the quotidian and vernacular realm of its subjects? The answer is that it has to open to the social, lawyers have to perform the law, and enact in a properly theatrical sense the roles and the places, the *personae*, the doctrinal themes and subjects, the drama and reverberations of legality. The letters have to come to life and this is where the study of film credits is of great interest.

Moinereau's book on film credits is addressed to that crucial liminal instance of letters entering the imagistic space of the film and announcing the title, the author/director and the other dramatis personae of the movie that will follow (or that is ending). The immediate issue is that of the transformation of the letters as they appear on screen. This is no ordinary text but rather the metamorphosis of the word into a figure, the unfolding of the verbal into an image within a plurality of images. The scriptural becomes pictorial. The fixed gothic letters of the juridical and other printed inscriptions, the black and white, ink on paper, suddenly blossoms, moves, opens to colour, is encompassed by music and juxtaposed with other images. The text becomes a visible part of a theatrical narrative, a frame and supplement to the enactment of a story. Start with a simple though fond example, that of the opening credits of Tornatore's *Cinema Paradiso*. The camera is focused on an open window looking out to sea. A thin curtain shimmers back and forth suggesting a theatrical opening of the stage, and of the play. A boat in the middle distance indicates a journey, a Homeric odyssey, while the urn on the window sill is a figure of mortality, of dust to dust and ashes to ashes.

The window is not only, however, an opening out, but also a lens into the interior and a frequent metaphor in art and analysis of intimacy and of the soul – *quod quidem mihi pro aperta finestra*, just to digress, meaning that it is for me an open window, an interior visible.[3] The outside mirrors the interior, the external journey is but the evidence of an internal epic. Thus, the letters announcing the name of the director of the film, Guiseppe Tornatore, are in yellow, signifying light, diffusion, and event, while the sea is blue, signifying night and eternity, the context in which illumination and transport occur. The letters themselves are italicized, slanted forward, as if in motion, ready for the journey, the epic that the film will unravel. Accompanied by Ennio Morricone's lyrically mournful nostalgic theme tune, the name of the director immediately under the urn and on the edge of the panoramic vista, suggests that this is the narrative of a life, a history, a *momento mori*. The letters evaporate into ideas, into that interior of meaning which is seen through the window, through the opening. The next shot indeed pans into the room rather than out to sea, and the interior and contemporary replaces the archetypal and atemporal. For our introductory purposes the significant feature of the credits is thus their presence on screen as figures within a visual tableau, a scene in relation to which the letters are to be viewed as much as read and into which they rapidly dissolve in imitation of the classical motto *usus libri, non lectio prudentes facit* – it is the use of the book, not reading that generates wisdom and law.

A second and stronger example can be taken from the magnificent and recent *La Grande Bellezza* of Sorentino (figure 2.1). It is a film addressed to literature, art, and criticism, in which the fate of art, of the great beauty, is emblematized in a scene where a naked female performance artist runs full tilt into a wall of rock (and collapses). Early in the film, after a lengthy dance scene, the camera pans back to a wide shot of the rooftop where the dance is taking place in the context of Rome at night. Just as the scene is ending and immediately prior to the cut

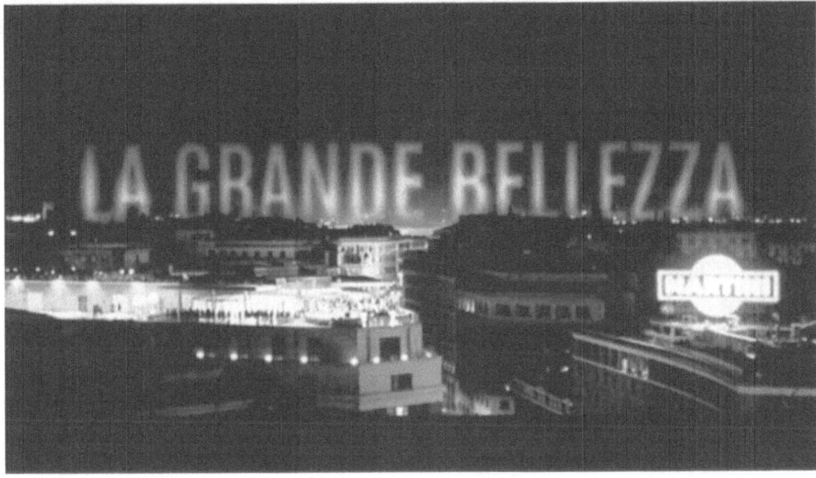

Figure 2.1 Title card, *La Grande Bellezza* (Dir. Paolo Sorrentino, 2013). Reproduced courtesy of Indigo Films.

to another protagonist leaving by car, the title of the movie appears oneirically, the letters flashing fleetingly in yellow light behind the rooftop and dancing figures. The letters come and go so rapidly that most viewers do not recall the title credits, the *litera*, that introduce the name, identity, and theme of the film. Such an evanescent and swift transition from image to letter to image, the glimpse of the literary desire among the images, perfectly condenses the themes of a film that is concerned precisely with the vanishing of literature, the pointlessness of authorship in the search for an ultimately non-existent "great beauty." The principal protagonist of the movie, Jep Gambardella, wrote a successful novella in his youth, and has not written anything more. He spends much of the movie declining to publish any more books, let alone compilations of his journalism. In one of the finest scenes in the movie, Jep excoriates the literary pretentions and absurd manoeuvres and manipulations of the *soi-disant* litterateur, the successful TV host Stefania. The movie, in sum, is about the vanishing character of the literary, the decline and disappearance of letters, and the title credits, the brief mirage of illuminations in the form of letters that immediately vanish, brilliantly capture the essential narrative and theme of the film.

The letters are intermediate elements in the visual trajectory of the movie. They are forms that appear – desire, motive, and theme made visible momentarily as apparent words, namely, figures of the story that will play out theatrically in the film. At the same time, as title credits the letters are heavy signifiers that bear a significant claim to authorship and possession. The letters are in that sense proprietary and juristic as well as nominative and authorial. It is worth thinking briefly about the status of the title credit in law. *Titulus* or title of entry, it can usefully be recalled, is in early common law "properly when a man hath lawful entry into lands whereof another is seised, for which he can have no action."[4] The root of this common law entitlement to enter a property that you do not possess resides in the fact that you own the *fee*, literally the faith upon which the land is held. It derives from a civilian gloss which notes *titulus pro tractatu accipitur*, title accedes to the work, but here of course the work is the relay of images, the motion picture that the letters notice, sign, honour, and credit.[5] We thus need to add to the titles their credit, because it is precisely the credit of titles and not title entry that is also at issue. Here the titular are those letters, those figures, the nomination to which credit, from *credo* meaning trust or belief, be given, to which something is owed. Thus, the titles are signs of honour, in the old language dignities that, ironically, given how briefly they are on screen, will not die. *Iustus titulus* means just cause, that the *causa* be real and by extension that it belong to the *ius imaginum*, the order of images, the titles of honour that constitute the order of visible being. The title credit of our particular film, L.G.B., here marks the just cause, the reality, of a great beauty that does not exist and thus figures a desire that can only ever be transitorily glimpsed, an aesthetic that resides in the event of images that will always flee into the umbrageous space of the visible rather than the verbal.

In sum, by way of opening, the title credit plays an exemplary role. It indicates a just cause for the entry of letters into the domain of images where they do not obviously belong. The letters participate only momentarily in the space of images, they are the fleeting figures that give shape to the greater visual flow of the film. In that the letters become figures, they become *exempla* of the desire that subtends and disrupts the filmic movement by their simple incursion, their apparition and evaporation. More strongly, the black letters, the inkpots of law, the *litera mortua* of rules and property, of maxims and schemes, are now, despite themselves, animate letters, ambulant figures of a desire that is expressed in but exceeds the limitations of writing.

It is in the *fingo*, the "I make" of the figure, in the shaping and moulding of form, that the illocutionary force of the sign becomes manifest.

The figure, both oratorical and visual, is the bearer of the subtextual and emotive impetus of discourse, and carries in its mutation, in its reshaping of language, the unconscious and liturgical power of the word of the law as text, as movement, and as psychic command. Where Freud returned to classical Hellenic mythology to explain the narrative structure of desire, the argument here is both similar and different in that I will use early modern representations of the classical figures of thought, as figured in predominantly legal emblem books, to evidence the continuance, the anachronic character of the images that bear the tradition into its modern subjectivity. The continuingly theatrical forms of the social depend upon the subjective attachment of the dramatis personae of our institutions and social forms to the images of our places, and the figures of our roles as plurally relayed through an inheritance of visual exemplars that constitute our visiocratic regimes of interior governance.

An Introduction to the Political Theology of the Letter

As the instance of the title credit indicates, the exemplary letter has to be animated, unfolded, and extended into life. What, as Nietzsche put it, is the use of a book that does not lead beyond all books? The sentiment is an expansive one. The letters of the title have to leave the treatment, the script, the scroll-page and appear on-screen, rise from the book, and enter the narrative and trajectory of ambulant and visible being. The film credits destabilize our conventional biblical and juristic sense of text as inscription, as imprinted, engraved, and permanently fixed in writing – *scripta manent, verba volent*. The letters on-screen demonstrate, often in the most vivid form, the imagistic context and surround, the visual and auditory environment and theatrical scene that must always, if often secretively, accompany mere letters and make them meaningful.

The early lawyers adhered to the maxim *pro lectione pictura est*, the picture takes the place of knowing how to read, and an accompanying norm that gave the image – the painting – priority over its material support, the page and the ink, or the pigment and tableau that housed it. In our example of the credits, the legal maxim can be inverted. If the picture is to be read, the words are to be viewed. The early modern ecclesiastical lawyers understood this well, arguing that the image was the text of the interior, an "inward book" no less, according to the Oxford canon lawyer and Catholic theologian Nicholas Sanders. In this argument, as also in film, the image precedes the word. The text should ideally make scripture visible so that the reader can see the words – *videbant voces* – and hence witness through these visible words, through the ritual of their incantation, through the performance of the sacrament, the inward image of which the word is but the report.[6] The image, Sanders also notes, "has no person of its own," but rather is a pattern of a prior cause, a reference to a truth that has no image, the narrative or myth of an ultimate reason, the truth as such. So Sanders, in Augustinian fashion, constantly and consistently endeavours to "change the shape of words into another form" and so make them visible and apprehensible for the instruction of the faithful and so as to elicit obedience to law. The canon lawyer who ended his days as a papal *nuncio* to Ireland had an excellent sense of the priority and importance of the image and of its essential role in the relay of the text, and it is precisely this transmission of the word via and among images, as a visible sign, that forms the principal argument that Moinereau develops in relation to the letters that appear, flower, and disappear among the images in film.[7] In the polarities that she develops, text and image, reading and viewing, narrative and figuration come to be intertwined rather than simply opposed, and it is this thesis, the attention to the imagistic context of legal texts, law's visible words, as well as the figuration that animates these texts, that makes them in their own right figures of authority, images of norms, that I will here pursue.

If we turn to the position or plight of humanist lawyers in the rapidly changing contexts of contemporary practice, the relation of legal texts to new media, to images, screens, and the generally evanescent and mobile digital modes of public manifestation of law is of huge import. The Psalmist's dictum that man walks among images (*in imagine ambulat homo*) has a very modern resonance; although in a juridical context the drive is most often to exclude the image and the theatrocracy that it connotes from the increasingly embattled and porous textual sanctuaries of law. The predominant view is that cameras should be kept away from the courtroom or at least they should be cabined, restrained, and incidental to trial. By the same token, images should remain outside the library, and external to the collections and other scriptural bodies of law. At best, the legal argument goes, the image can in some incidental manner facilitate the textual transmission of law, and the logical passage of rules. The visual should be restrained and secondary to a legal reason and judgment that is predicated, however ironic this may seem to non-lawyers, upon texts, upon print technology and the resilient black letters of law.

In the analysis that follows I will argue that the subordination of the image to the letter, the hierarchy that puts reading ahead of vision, and places the text outside and above law's visible presence is technically inaccurate and, increasingly, obviously misleading. First, historically, and I will use the example of common law, the image and specifically the *ius imaginum* frames and legitimates law. The image introduces the text and opens letters to vision, what I will term the *ambulatio* of the eye that relays the performances that make law, in the antique rhetorical formula, both seen and understood. Second, theoretically, the text needs finally, or once again, to be apprehended as a sign, as itself an image among images. This is not to argue that words are pictures, although they may also be conceived as such, but rather to acknowledge the increasingly evident sense in which the legal text has become virtual, manipulable, and borderless in its variable on-screen environments: including those of the classroom, chambers, courtroom, newscast, taxi-TV, smartphone, congress, or whatever other parliamentary scene inaugurates the creation of law.

Mos britannicus

In certain respects the advent of the digital mirrors the invention and cultural impact of print. One technology introduced linearity, the other pixellation, one ink, the other pulse codes. The early modern era that follows on from the invention of the press indeed witnessed a war of images, and for over a hundred years the use of images and the radical distinction of icon and idol, *latria* and *dulia*, proper and illicit avenues of worship, were the most pressing – life and death – issues of theological, legal, and political debate.[8] Law was never immune to the violent disputations and legal method borrowed from the theological debates in proposing a scriptural method of textual transmission that paid only marginal attention, peripheral respect to the highly controversial status of images in the propagation of belief. In the lawyer's argot, to know the law is not to know the words but the force and power (*vim ac potestatem*) that underlies all meaning. The clues as to law's relation to, valuation of, and use of images thus has to attend to what the historian Carlo Ginzburg, following Morelli and Freud, terms the marginal and incidental that provides the clue to the hidden meaning of the work.[9]

My first example is from the humanist lawyer and antiquarian John Selden's *Titles of Honor*, first published in 1610. This work is the first common law treatise to address what the Romans termed *ius imaginum*, the notes of dignities (*notitia dignitatum*), the signs of military, administrative, and ecclesiastical offices. It is a work on images in a juristic sense, but it begins with a defence of learning against "the common enemy Ignorance" and its neighbour, "some fragment of Knowledge supported only with an illiberal exercise of depraved Reason."[10] The disciplines are to be protected, and this requires a jurisdiction for knowledge and law, signs that will mark and tend the spaces and places of the juridical in the social. The disciplines, for Selden, are an archipelago, islands that need vexillological marking, signs, titles of dignity, and images of office that will announce before and beyond language, the authority of the disciplines. The point can be made succinctly with an image of Britannia taken from *Titles of Honor* (figure 2.2). Here we literally see Britannia in an architectural rather than a properly emblematic figuration. The island is a castle, *turris iustitiae*, and we see the three portals of entry to administration, the *comes Britanniae* mentioned immediately below the ensign of Britain. The image is a note of dignity, *nobilia portenta*, and Selden goes on to argue that it is the universal law, Justinian's codification in particular, that provides the sources and interpretations for the use of images as devices of communication throughout the Christian world – *nobilitas Christiana* as he puts it at one point. It is out of the books of "Civill Learning" that the Precepts and Directions that permit us to recognize the images of dignity and office, "the Faces and Frames of Government," can be found.[11] The image opens our access to and knowledge of administration, and this is in essence a knowledge of signs that is taken from a universal law shared by all the common lawyers of Europe.

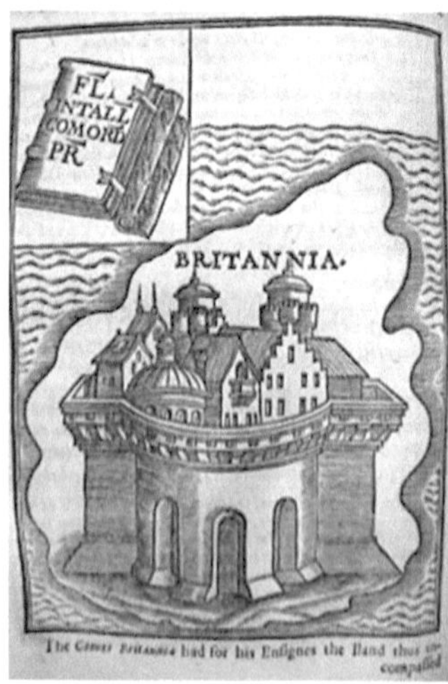

Figure 2.2 John Selden, *Titles of Honor* (London: Stansby, 1631), p. 324. Reproduced by permission of P. Goodrich.

The image itself deserves a further brief viewing. The ensign shows the island and "one faire building (to denote the chief Citie, it seems)." This is not a map but an official mark of governance and jurisdiction produced by the Clerks of the Crown. It is vexillological as much as it is representational. It shows, it demonstrates, it is the very image of authority and supports its claim by placing in the top-right corner, in the space of precedence, *dexter chief*, "a Booke," *Foelix liber*, that signals government under the dominion of the order and precedence demonstrated by these letters.[12] The president of the Clerks has issued this instrument and ordered this tabulation of governmental and administrative powers contained within the closed and clasped book, and the scroll that abuts it. Such, however, is not all. There is a further and crucial claim, the in-between of islands that the image portrays in a series of three sets of lines or inscriptions. First, those of the plough, the common land, and common food that subtends the city and passes imperceptibly from land to architecture and building. Then the lines that surround the island, the straight lines of inscription, of writing, of *nulla dies sine linea*, of law. Then third and finally the wavy lines of the sea, whose very presence in the image indicates, Selden claims, that the sea itself, as portrayed, belongs within and is subject to the jurisdiction of the island, an argument pursued much further in *Mare clausum* (The Closed Sea).[13] What is important is that the "imaginarie lines" that mark and so incorporate or territorialize the sea are drawn and entered into the book. The sea becomes like print, the image enters the text in the same manner that the text enters and endeavours to inscribe the sea, at least in imagination. The wavy lines look like writing, the script, one might say, of the illiterate, if by that we mean the force of arms that take the place of language, where discourse is impossible.

Giving an image, a "face and frame" to governance opens the legal and legitimate sites of power to view. At the same time, law is opened to images and pictures enter the juridical text. Boundaries are broken precisely in the manner of the island-hopping method of humanistic legal study. More than that, the book in our ensign is itself an image within an image. It is clasped with what appears to be a plea roll in front of it, and then this pair of writings are placed at the top right, *dexter chief*, of the image and separated from the rest of the device by means of two straight lines that box it into a rectangle whose bottom-left corner touches our island Britannia. The book, the *foelix liber* of legally etched dignities, the record of administrative offices, the collation and interpretation of the signs of governance are all recorded here, in this island book, in this clasped and closed, dominating image of an esoteric text.

The depiction of the book clearly includes an enigma, the acronym on the cover of the clasp-closed book, whose meaning even Selden is uncertain about. He cites Pancirolus and so immediately invokes sources beyond Britannia, and laws that are international rather than local. The definition of an enigma is a dark saying, meaning an opaque or condensed statement that is plural in meaning and so hard to interpret. The image can thus convey beautifully what words will likely confuse or occlude. The words in the image indeed have to be interpreted in the light and context of the image. They are part of the picture, the letters have become figures, the words symbols. It is thus no accident, but rather in anticipation of what follows that this book of images begins with an allegory which the rhetoricians define explicitly as a dissimulation, an enigmatic and coded statement that requires dis-encryption.[14]

The treatise on the law of images obviously and emblematically enough constitutes a direct expression of the relationship of text to picture, print to depiction. In one immediate sense the book *Titles of Honor* contains an image of a book, *foelix liber* in our example, out of which emerges an image first of writing, of a plea roll or scroll with wavy lines on it, with scribble, and then an image of authority, an ensign of Britannia, and all of her lines and inscriptions are portrayed visually. The book is an image, and then, of course, the image is itself a book (*liber pauperum*) for the unlearned, an internal book for theologians, as also a visible sign, a vexillological note and warning for the traveller, the stranger, the foreigner, and the enemy. Then, even though the *foelix liber* is clasped and closed, it is evident from the images adjoining or extruding from it that the boundaries of the book, the limits of the text, are fluid, porous, and in important senses visibly uncertain. The book flows into the image, the image enters the book, just as the island merges with the sea and equally enters the space of the book. This leads to a second example of the hieroglyphic and hierarchical quality of the image as a sign of law, as the complement and transport of words, as a letter signifying the *nomos* of transmission of an interior relay.

The depiction in question is common to devices and emblem books, whence my example is taken, from Rollenhagen as reproduced by the common lawyer George Wither (figure 2.3).[15] It is expressly an "Hieroglyphick" according to the explanatory verse, and shows a pelican piercing its breast with its beak and suckling its young with its blood. The image is that of the fulfilment of the law, there being no greater love than the sacrifice of oneself for one's children, flock, or fellows: "His *Heart* was pierc'd that he their *Soules* might save."[16] It is for Wither a holy emblem, a metaphor or more properly in this case a metonymy

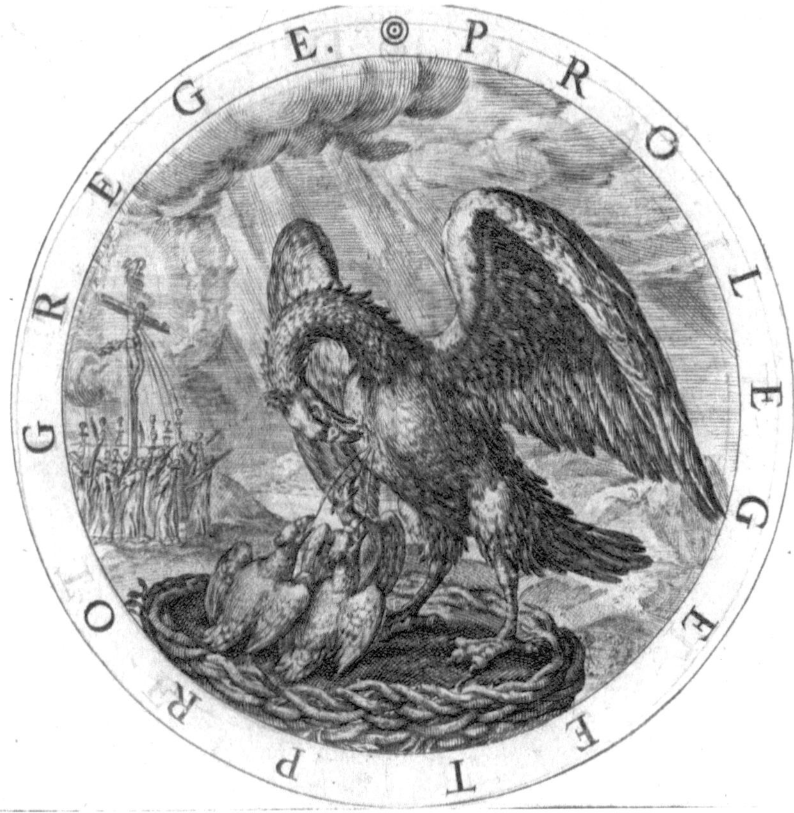

Figure 2.3 George Wither, *A Collection of Emblemes Ancient and Moderne* (London: Allot, 1635), 154. Reproduced by courtesy of P. Goodrich.

for the crucifixion of Christ for our sins, the background of the picture indeed showing the saviour on the Cross, his chest pierced and blood flowing into the raised chalices of priests below: "Lift up thy soule to him who dy'd for thee." Some details are important. In the background Christ on the Cross emits three streams of blood, a trinity of remissions of sins. The Cross itself is encircled by light and a halo of clouds, signifying that Christ is divine and already beyond or gone, impossibly unified, both above and below, spiritual and temporal. The pelican is portrayed in a more tellurian form. Heavenly rays emanate from the clouds onto the pelican, but it is firmly on the ground, a sign in Horapollo and Artemidorus that the bird is foolish and imprudent, but in Christian symbolism it is a mark of the pelican's "deare *Mercies*" and "bloudy *Passion*." The bird is foolish in the same sense that the three fledglings are foolish: all have sinned and need to atone for errors that pertain not to this world or ground but to the imaginary and other world.

The visual structure of the emblematical is viewed laterally, and at least in the armorial handbooks, from top right to bottom left, an optical axis which in this picture moves from the crucifixion, in the background and above, to the nest and self-sacrifice in the foreground. The theological message, the repetition of the sacrifice, is reasonably evident but is only part of the significance of the image. Take first the simple question of perspective. What is distant and less visible is more important and directive than what is immediate and foregrounded. The perspective law of the ego, as Nietzsche calls it, has to be reversed. What is closest to the self is the least important, and the law of self-sacrifice, the emblematic immolation of the pelican, confirms this vividly. By similar token, the depiction of sacrifice itself, of the body pierced and bleeding, also indicates the primacy of the invisible and internal over the external carapace and visible form. "For the law and for the people" (*pro lege et pro grege*) suggests a law that is unseeable and internal, a law enclosed in the dark storehouse of the chest, an *anima legis* that constitutes the pulmonary and pectoral interiority and drive of law. The chest has to be pierced for the law to come out and in this sense the emblem goes within, is inserted as a visual avenue to the transmission of an inner law. It is quite evidently the divine law, the invisible inscription of the Ten Commandments on the heart of the subject that is depicted and transmitted as *ius non scriptum*, as image. The crucial point in interpreting the picture is to realize that it is in opening the body, in releasing the interior inscription, the invisible law of nature and of God, that the subject both fulfils their civic duty and attains grace.

The earlier humanist, Hadrianus Junius, is explicit on the point. The verse subscription to the equivalent emblem, in his *Emblemata*, enjoins the subject *perscrutare animum*, search your soul and then open your breast – your chest, your heart – to release the law and knowledge, dissimulating and hiding nothing – *nihil occultum*.[17] For the humanist the law is that of letters, of *Respublica litteraria* and the sacred inspirations of the muses, including poetry, art, music, and the "sciences liberall," as the common lawyers called them. Dedicated to the chief justice of the Netherlands, the corollary themes of just judgment and the proper transmission of law is peculiarly significant if not particularly explicit in Junius's discussion of the emblem. Law and not arms, letters rather than force, art and not war were the express trajectories of justice that his *emblemata* sought. The motto *quod in te est, prone* – bring to light what is inside you, instructs in the wounding that is necessary to open the body to law, and connect speech to the unwritten tablets, the *ius non scriptum*, of the heart. There is a method of knowing, teaching, and ruling that requires an opening of the soul, and more vividly a piercing of the body, so as to allow for the exhalation or ex-sanguination of knowledge. The phrase that Junius uses is *Musarum fores semper apertae* – the doors of the Muses should always be open. In humanist juristic theory, mimicking the relevant theology, the first instrument of law is faith, the dictate of the heart, the glimmering of eternal power. The Roman faith in instruments – *de fide instrumentorum* – is here a faith in the justice of the inner books, the interior writings, the texts that are stored in the chest of the sovereign and the subject alike.

Ambulatio and Vision

The words open into the visual and symbolic, the aesthetic and imaginary, and in the manner of the theatrical draw the viewer into the narrative portrayed.[18] The contemporary theologians were indeed most vociferous as to the priority of the imagistic: *maior est imago quam oratio* – an image is greater than any speech, says the Oxford professor of theology Nicholas Sanders in response to John Jewel's *Defence of the Church of England*.[19] He argues at length that it is only through images that we can remember and adore Christ: *per imaginem Christum recordamur et adoramus*.[20] The fervour and enthusiasm of faith is only fully excited by images. Vehement affection (*compunctionem*) is stirred up by visual recollection, by the sign of the prototype, and the image binds the subject on earth as she will be bound by wit in heaven.[21]

It is neither accidental nor unimportant that the sacrament was produced through the ritual of making the word visible, bringing it to life, animating the dormant and quickening the past. This is the essential role of theatre in the enactment of social life and in the spectacular character of sovereignty in its dual forms. It would be most surprising if law did not borrow from these techniques and utilize these avenues to the binding of collectivity and the generation of reverence and legitimacy. Agamben indeed in *Opus Dei*, a recent work, has made the point that the ritual of trial is predicated upon the liturgical effect, the making present and manifest of what the mystery promises.[22] In his philological argument the liturgy is predicated upon the old legal form of the *legis actio sacramenti*, the action in law which puts what is said into effect or, in the language of the Twelve Tables, *si quis nexum faciet mancipiumque, uti lingua nuncupassit, ita ius esto* – if anyone makes a bond or conveyance, as it is said so shall it be done.

From the juristic perspective law has to be brought to life, made active, visible, and internalized as a vital precept, a living principle. The legitimacy of law depends in other words upon its sovereignty, its spectacular and, in Agamben's terms, otiose but glorious (reverential) presence.[23] Returning to our last emblem and the concept of the source of the image and of authority, of truth and law being *semper apertus*, we are witness precisely to the face and frame of a social and institutional scene. Here the law walks visibly and actively opens the breast of the pelican, the interior law that is ultimately in the Anglican tradition *ius quaesitum alteri*, a law lodged in the other, in nature, custom, use, and tradition. What is juristically important in the image is the principle of animation, of insufflation, of bringing to life, of making ambulate. Thus, Bacon in his *Maximes* begins precisely with the notion of the legal text as *litera mortua*, dead letters, a closed and dormant *foelix liber*, a sleeping book. The words mean nothing; they are closed and inaccessible until Caesar brings them to life: *Iura suum, legesque; tulit iustissimus auctor* – by which he intends that Caesar, the lion, the sovereign lifts up and presents this most just author of laws. It is the spirit of the source that suffuses the sovereign, and as intermediary and vicarious author he alone, in Bacon's hyperbolic dedicatory epistle, can render a mere text, a collection or code, into *proprium and sanctissimum templum iustitiae consecratum* – into the proper and most holy consecration of the temple of justice.[24]

What is necessary, though less evident in the text alone than in the emblem and image, is an opening of the book and the transmission of the letters into life, which is to say into the city, the institution, the subjects of law. For Bacon the Latin maxim with all its authority, authenticity, sovereignty, and majesty, its aura of great justice, its sacred and consecrated dignity, acts as the animating principle of laws, which is to say of texts. The gathering of the laws, the collections, the tomes, are termed *acta in toga*, acts in robes, the work of lawyers and compilers who generate those texts that form the books of law and constitute, according to Bacon, the honour and undying dignity of the sovereign who promulgates them. War may be necessary, and victories may be significant, but *gesta in armis*, deeds of arms, are merely great, whereas the promulgation of laws founds the claim to immortality. Arms may mark the body, but laws inscribe the soul. Letters, and in our case specifically the figure of the book, the image of the tome, opens the domain of materiality, the landscape, nature, and society to the literary and artistic representation of their invisible pattern, their natural order, their fingerpost, their source.

The sovereign conceived as *anima legis*, or as *viva vox iuris*, the active voice of law, positions the image that represents this authority as a crucial mediation of the principle of legality. It is not enough to have law on the books. It is inadequate to store the rules in the library, in collections and compilations, when what is necessary is the animation and incorporation of law into life. The rules of law have to be converted into rules of life, into a *modus vivendi* that inscribes the very structure of subject and sociality. The subject in the end has to open to law and incorporate the principle of structure and sociality, and thus also, and in imitation of the sovereign, it is the subject who must animate the law and allow it to speak through them. The subject, to borrow from Legendre, has to become a living emblem of the law and so must accept the insertion of the emblematical as the animating principle of personality, of *ius imaginum*. The subject has to open to law and the image is the means and medium of such opening, a principle of the visual that can be addressed initially by looking to the opening of the legal text, the threshold, the frontispiece. The face and frame of textual governance, to use Selden's expression again, is the opening image of the book of law, the titular depiction, the portal and emblem of the text that follows.

Moinereau argues decisively, following Lyotard's Freudian adaptations in *Discourse, Figure* that the film credits both condense, which is to say compress, a multitude of themes, and also displace, that is decentre, the manifest content of the film. The displacement is tied to the condensation but adds the key element of how we think in images, which is to say an associative thought appropriate to *signa translata*, to the figurative and transported symbols of dream: "In sum displacement designates the trajectory of figural interpretation, one which the spatial metaphor allows us to conceive in terms of the model of *ambulatio*."[25] Adopting a similar interpretative strategy for the visual in the legal, we can argue that the juristic equivalent of the film credits is the frontispiece and other imagery in books of law. I will take one common example. There is no text without images, no words without pictures – a point that can lead us to one slightly later example, this time from the 1608 title page of Guido Pancirolus, *Notitia utraque dignitatum*, the source of much of Selden's *Titles of Honor* (figure 2.4).[26]

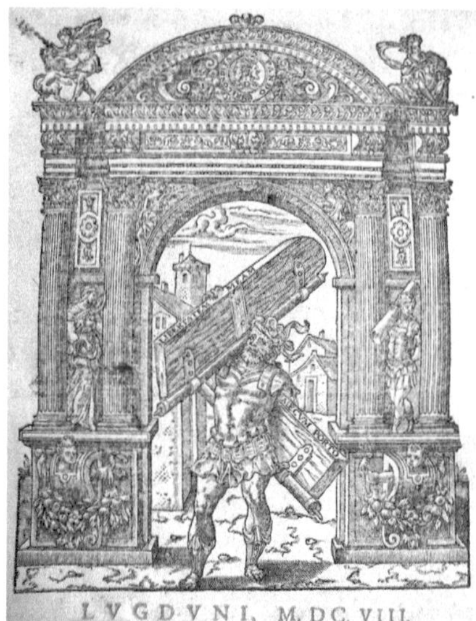

Figure 2.4 Guido Pancirolus, *Notitia utraque dignitatum* (Lugudini: Gabiano, 1608), frontispiece. Reproduced courtesy of P. Goodrich.

Atop the image is the emblematic lawgiver and god of gates, the two-faced Janus, with the standard motto *recondita pando*, I reveal the hidden. The picture that accompanies this emblem is that of a twin-columned, triumphal arch through which Samson is emerging, carrying two doors, the portals to the city. Where Janus most usually represents the necessity of looking in front and behind, to past and future, Samson's doors are inscribed with the motto *libertatem meam, mecum porto*, I am the bearer of my own liberty. Wisdom and self-knowledge are figured on the columns on the right, and labour on the left. In the centre of the picture Samson is in the process of taking away the barriers, the doors to the city, the divide between outside and inside. He thus declares peace as the achievement of subjects who are willing to take up the call of liberty that is also, in this context, the call of Christ. The doors are held aloft and as a fairly explicit cross, the sign of Christ, of course, and also of multiplication, but the message is evident: to be free means to serve God and pass under the triumphal arch, the yoke of *pax Christiana*, within which the order of the spectacular, the approved, and glorious symbols of administration and office are contained and performed.

The image is of opening, of the doors that bar the city being removed, and the interior of the depiction, the stage of civility and honour that the work will note, is now accessible and visible, free for entry and egress.

The image, in short, opens the book to the world, at the same time as it opens the law to vision and juxtaposes the lectoral to the pictorial. The image on the title page, taken from Pancirolus, and confirmed by the earlier discussion of insular drift and bleeding emblems, mediates between discourse and figure, text and subject, word and action. Moinereau's work on film credits, developed through a reading of Lyotard and Didi-Huberman, argues that reading and vision are distinct methods and different enterprises. When letters are introduced into film, we stop reading and start to view the words. By the same token, in the examples that I have used, when images are inserted into texts, pictures into discourse, then the order and hierarchy of disciplines is broken down; words and images intermingle, suffuse and escape the text. The letter becomes a figure, the text a sign, and there is a trajectory from word, to figure, to theatre, to scene, to screen. The process of animating *lex* is that of changing how we view the text of law and in particular allowing for a free interchange between interior and exterior, word and action, signature and deed.

At the level of method, and particularly of juristic technique, of hermeneutics, the strict rule introduced or at least confirmed by Bartolus in his *Tractatus de insigniis*, that the reader focus solely upon the line and move the eyes from left to right along the page, needs to be supplemented and corrected. The eye, to borrow from Moinereau's adaptation of Pierre Frankastel's work on space and figuration, moves laterally when viewing: "The fact is that the eye wanders (*se promène*) over the surface of the image which evidences a temporality of apprehension of the forms of the signifier which is different to that of scanning letters."[27] The eye traces numerous paths and connections, it circulates around the tableau and deciphers it by "a very precise act of figurative intellection," which Frankastel baptizes *ambulatio*.[28] The passage from the graphic to the figurative is facilitated by the expansion of the letter into the scene of images. The letter is set free from its envelope, it gains depth and weight, colour and sound, it becomes an image or, to borrow from the proper biblical source, John 1.14, "And the word was made flesh and dwelt among us and we saw his glory (*videmus gloriam*) … full of grace and truth."[29]

Incarnadine Jurisprudence

The example of film credits, of letters that transform into figures, is simply an *exemplum*, an emblem of the visual character and metaphoric power of letter and word, the fact of their depth. The division of discourse and figure, word and image borrows again from Freud's *The Interpretation of Dreams* and specifically his elaboration of the image as the medium of dream work to elicit the two principal axes of interpretation already discussed, those of condensation and displacement. Condensation refers to the compression of the dream and thus to the enigmatic and layered quality of the figure as the singular representation or point of intersection of several associative chains. As a nodal point, the condensation is also marked by intensity of energy and excess of meaning, which is itself the result of displacement. The latter term refers to the decentring characteristic of the dream. It draws the analyst's attention to the latent content of the dream, which exists in a lateral and otherwise focused relation to its manifest content. As Lyotard translates this, "The position of art is a refutation of the position of discourse ... Art stands in alterity as plasticity and desire, a curved expanse against invariability and reason, diacritical space."[30] To this we must also add the confluence of the two media, of the vocal and the visual, letter and image: "One only has to allow oneself to slip into the well of discourse to find the eye lodged at its core ... The figure is both without and within." To borrow from the medieval philosophers, *ubi amor, ibi oculos* – where the eye is, there is love.[31]

The latter maxim can help define the stakes of the visual in the legal, that of the covert role of desire in the promulgation and expounding of *nomos*, in the decisions of law. Turning to the discourse of jurisprudence, the first principle of method is that of *procedere ad similia*, of the refusal of difference in the paradoxical form of a profession of similitude and the power of likeness.[32] Roman and common lawyers alike determined to follow precedent – to observe the rule – and to follow the path and pattern of prior determination. Analogy, particularly in common law, is the first desideratum of decision. In the system of writs, it was necessary to show an exact similitude between the circumstances of the writ and the case in hand, while in later law a more lenient but nonetheless consistent demand is made for comparability of circumstances, for the appearance of likeness. There is already an element of the visual in the dictate of likeness and the apprehension of similitude, but before one addresses such visual dictates of the appearance of likeness there is the question of the modality of the method itself.

Procedere ad similia is at root a Roman maxim, but takes on a peculiar methodological significance in common law. It requires a degree of attention which must start with the notion of proceeding – in the medieval Latin that Bracton uses, not only to go forth, to advance, to move forward, but also to act in law, to bring proceedings. We are talking here of movement and process, of action and specifically institutional action and thus of interaction. Frankastel referred to *ambulatio* as the proper designation of the movement of the eye over the picture, and it is worth noting the biblical root of ambulation in the Psalmist's dictum *in imagine ambulat homo*, which Augustine picks up and emphasizes.[33] That images and imagination are the motors of movement, the spurs of human action, is of course one connotation of this reference, but its broader ambit of significance is rhetorical and designates that most crucial dimension of oratory, that of *actio*, of gesture, performance, and delivery. It is precisely in ambulating among images, in proceeding in the hierarchy of persons, that the scopic regime of the figurative enters the text. It is by means of images that words become acts, which is to say, expand and perform what they say.

Conclusion: Image and Wound

The classical maxim of common law method, derivative though it may be, that legal reason proceed *ad similia*, depends upon a conception of semblance that rapidly imports both desire and depth, image and figure into the elaboration of the language of law. Interpretation, which is to say reading, requires imagination, or in Plowden's law French, *imaginer* means to plot and scheme, while in its normative designation it requires the expansion and contraction, the depth and the height of equity as the amplifier of the intent, the kernel and interior of meaning. Plowden in fact introduces his discussion of the internal sense of legal words by remarking that in judgments the reader can see that the words are not the law: "*De cest iudgment, et le cause poyes veyer, (lecteur) que les parolles del ley, ne sont le ley.*" In the rhetorical art of delivery, in the *actiones* that reflect the ambulations that the advocate desires, the first and principal desideratum of argument is *procedere ad apparentiam*, to proceed according to appearances, so as to fit the words to the images. The auditor, and by extension the reader, becomes the viewer and seeks, according to the juridico-theological dogma of the day, the internal sense, the kernel, the unseen meaning, the form or figure that the word and the image both harbour and conceal.

The theological position is that the image, which is a vanishing sign, an indicator, a transient and transparent signpost to the higher and hidden cause, is by dint of such evanescence or intermediary function, closer to the source of meaning than the word. The reformers would disagree but for common lawyers, Anglicans, the visual sign, be it *verba visibilia*, icon or image, leads *ab imagine ad rem significatam* with the greater rapidity. The viewing *ad apparentiam* is here the most probative and facilitative method of apprehension and suggests the key novelty that this paper has attempted to introduce, namely, the lesson of the image as intermediary, as the go-between, the mediator of word and sense through which the text opens to vision. Lyotard talks of the desire embedded in the depths of the word as disfiguring law, but the better description is of law refigured, amplified, expanded, insufflated, and justified. For the art historian Georges Didi-Huberman, the starting point for affectively invested viewing is to recognize the role of desire – *ubi amor, ibi oculus*, where the eye is, there also is love – which is to say passion, attachment, investment, and projection. The *rend* of the image, in his terminology, makes rendering judgment, the enactment of equity and justice, possible.[34]

For the art historian the critical point is that images live, they breathe, which is to say expand and contract, rise and fall, insufflate and exhale according to the relay of the eye and the sentience of the viewer. The Roman Catholic Church had an investiture ritual in which there would be a ceremonial opening of the mouth of the newly appointed cardinal to the law of the pontiff. *Apertio oris* meant a laying of hands upon the lips of the neophyte so as to open the mouth and bring the subject to institutional speech. This is an active gesture, an embodiment as well as a transmission and what I want to suggest in conclusion is that there is an equivalent and prior ritual of apprehension which is that of opening to images (*aperire imagines*). The image is the threshold, the portal of understanding, and it is the image that both literally and metaphorically opens up viewer and viewed. No reading without looking, no significance without signification, no message without its medium.

In theological terms, the opening of the image is the opening of the body, the access to the interior, to the soul. Such access is labile, fluid, and wounded, the biblical injunction being the requirement that "they shall look upon him whom they pierced (*Videbunt in quem transfixerunt*)." As Didi-Huberman elaborates, the image is in this sense an incarnation: "The *open image* will thus designate less a privileged category of images than a privileged moment, an image event where, upon contact with the real, the aspectual organization of the similar (*semblable*) is rendered asunder and torn apart (*se déchire*)."[35] The power of the image resides in this transgression of the boundary between interior and exterior and between life and death in that the motif of the crucifixion is precisely one of opening, of release, of rebirth through death. What matters, what drives the image is what cannot be seen, an interior that in opening out, risks exposure and potentially death. In its biblical trajectory the enigma of the image is that it both brings the unseen cause near and simultaneously acts as a sign of the invisible and distant: "and then shall they see the Son of man coming in a cloud with power and great glory."[36] Only part objects, blood, exterior, are visible while the cloud, *maiestas*, and *Gloria* require figuration for their transmission to be possible. There is always, in sum, more transmitted than seen and that is the ultimate significance of the image, that it is more than it appears, that it is *imago pietatis*, a sign of the eternal and unknowable realm of the divine father, or in our case the author of law.

The earlier emblem of the law, the pelican that wounds itself to feed its young, is one such exemplary instance of opening of the image. The unbroken circle that forms the habitus of the pelican and its young is a symbol of eternity and so also connotes death, the sacrifice of the parent for the children, of Christ for humanity, and of the past for the future. The figure of Janus, an alternative depictive figure of law, also connotes a close correlation between death and opening, image and law. The deluge killed the wicked and opened the world to a new start. The key in the hand of the sovereign figure is equally an emblem of opening, of portals, thresholds, transitions, and relays. Where there are images, there is both wounding and opening, danger and possibility, transgression and law: "To open means to found: to signal the origin so as to institute a future. That is why it is not enough to see from a distance. That is why, even from a distance, one must *incorporate the opening*."[37] The Pelican's young incorporate the blood of the parent, in the manner of the Eucharist, whose function is also that of transmitting the opening of the flesh so as to render it carnally memorable: so as to incorporate it, so as to pass on the order, both spectacle and honour, that the image represents.

That the image of the divine arrives *in nube*, in a cloud, captures both the enigma and the depth of the image. What opens, opens onto and into a passage to other images as well as to images of the infinite. The reader scans the words on the page but the viewer of the text, the watcher or *speculator*, the looker and searcher of the book, follows a trajectory into and out of the text. The root is again biblical in that the opacity of the cloud signals the enigma of simultaneously viewing and being viewed. In opening to the image, the image also opens to us, we see and are seen: "No creature is invisible in his sight: but all things are naked and open to his eyes, to whom our speech is directed."[38] I have tried to expand that insight by reference to film credits and the emblematic interplay of word and image in peripheral contexts that nonetheless are significant in film and in apprehending the visual in law. Following Didi-Huberman's lead, I will conclude by arguing that *anima legis* is precisely a matter of images, of that excess or beyond of words that animates the manipulation of the text and the interlocution of legal action. The rhetorical *actio* has always been concerned with the manipulation of images, with bringing to life, making vivid, enacting and performing, and my point is simply that new media, the digital with all its current environments, networks, and screens makes the image ever more active, mobile, and present. This would not be interesting but for the boundaries that it breaks, the thresholds it crosses and the openings that it promises. As the text opens, the image is revealed, and as the image enters the text, the words come to life. The image is the site not simply of animation but of viewing and of being viewed. *Haec imago*, this face, ironically, is never just this face, and by the same token this text, this law, is never precisely how it appears, nor the *semblable* of any singular reason.

NOTES

1 Jean-François Lyotard, *Discourse, Figure* (Minneapolis: University of Minnesota Press, 2011), 237.
2 Laurence Moinereau, *Le générique de film: De la lettre à la figure* (Rennes: Presses Universitaires de Rennes, 1995).
3 On the *bifrons* window, the opening out and the looking in, see Gérard Wajcman, *Fenêtre: Chroniques du regard de l'intime* (Paris: Verdier, 2004).
4 John Cowell, *The Interpreter* [1607] (Cambridge: Legat, 1684) – *titulus est justa causa possidendi quod nostrum est.*
5 The gloss is given in Stephano Daoyz, *Iuris civilis* [*Septimus Tomus: indicem et summam rerum ac verborum omnium*] (Lugduni: J. Pillehotte, 1612) s.v. *titulus.*
6 Nicholas Sanders, *A Treatise of the Images of Christ and of His Saints: And that it is unlawfull to breake them, and lawfull to honor them* (Omers: Heigham, 1566; 1624 ed.), 162. One could endeavour a mirroring maxim: *pro visione scriptura est.*
7 Moinereau, *Le générique de film*, 215.

8 Margaret Aston, *England's Iconoclasts: Laws against Images* (Oxford: Clarendon Press, 1988) remains the most thorough study of the Anglican debates; Peter Goodrich, *Oedipus Lex: Psychoanalysis, History, Law* (Berkeley: University of California Press, 1995) addresses some of the parallel debates at common law.
9 Carlo Ginzburg, *Myths, Emblems, and Clues* (London: Radius, 1990).
10 Selden, *Titles of Honor* (London: Stansby, 1631), 2nd ed., n.p. (dedication).
11 Ibid., fol. 2r (The Preface).
12 The code on the book, FLINTALLCOMORDPR, is an acronym: *Foelix liber iniunctus Notariis Laterculi continens mandata ordine Principis*, according to Pancirolus, *De Notitia utraque dignitatum* (Lyon: Gabbiano, 1608).
13 John Selden, *Of the Dominion, Or, Ownership of the Sea* (London: Du Gard, 1652).
14 On allegory, dissimulation, and enigma, see the barrister George Puttenham, *The Art of English Poesy* (1589) (Ithaca: Cornell University Press, 2007), 270–3; and on enigma see Peter Goodrich, *Legal Emblems and the Art of Law* (Cambridge: Cambridge University Press, 2014), 55–9.
15 For diverse examples, see Hadrianus Junius, *Emblemata … Aenigmatum libellus* (Antwerp: Plantyn, 1565), 13; Gabriel Rollenhagen, *Nucleus emblematum selectissimorum centuria secunda* (Cologne: Passei, 1613), 20; George Wither, *A Collection of Emblemes, ancient and moderne* (London: Allot, 1635), 154; Henri Estienne, *The Art of Making Devises* (London: Holden, 1650), 7.
16 Wither, *A Collection of Emblemes*, 154.
17 Junius, *Emblemata*, emblem VII, p. 13 and discussed on 78–9.
18 Sanders, *A Treatise of the Images of Christ and of His Saints.*
19 Ibid., 252
20 Ibid., 57–8.
21 Ibid., 254.
22 Giorgio Agamben, Opus Dei: *An Archaeology of Duty* (Stanford: Stanford University Press, 2013), 36.
23 Giorgio Agamben, *The Kingdom and the Glory* (Stanford: Stanford University Press, 2012).
24 Francis Bacon, *The Elements of the Common Lawes of England* (London: More, 1630), epistle dedicatory.
25 Moinereau, *Le générique*, 143.
26 Guido Pancirolus, *De Notitia utraque dignitatum* (Lugudini: Gabiano, 1608).
27 Moinereau, *Le générique*, 15.
28 Ibid.
29 Specifically, in the Vulgate: *et Verbum caro factum est et habitavit in nobis et videmus gloriam … plenum gratiae et veritatis.*

30 Jean-François Lyotard, *Discourse, Figure* [1971] (Minneapolis: University of Minnesota Press, 2011), 7.

31 For discussion, see Georges Didi-Huberman, *Fra Angelico: Dissemblance and Figuration* (Chicago: University of Chicago Press, 1995), 217–21. See also Didi-Huberman, *Confronting Images* (State Park: Penn State University Press, 2005), 139ff. on figuring and becoming visible.

32 Bracton, *De legibus et consuetudinibus legum Angliae*, fol. 1 b: *Si similia evenerint, per simile judicentur, cum bona sit occasio a similibus procedere ad similia* – if like cases have occurred, they are to be judged by the like rule, since it is the proper method to proceed from like things to like.

33 Psalm 38.

34 Didi-Huberman, *Confronting Images*, 140.

35 Didi-Huberman, *L'image ouverte: Motifs de l'incarnation dans les arts visuels* (Paris: Gallimard, 2007), 35.

36 Luke 21.27: *et tunc videbunt Filium hominis in nube cum potestate magna et majestate.*

37 Didi-Huberman, *L'image ouverte*, 50.

38 Hebrews 4.13: *et non est ulla creatura invisiblis in conspectus eius: omnia autem nuda et aperta sunt oculis eius ad quem nobis sermo.*

3 An Emblematic Representation of Law: Hogarth and the Engravers' Act

CRISTINA S. MARTINEZ

It is a pleasing labour of the mind to solve the most difficult problems; allegories and riddles, trifling as they are, afford the mind amusement: and with what delight does it follow the well-connected thread of a play, or novel, which ever increases as the plot thickens, and ends most pleas'd, when that is most distinctly unravell'd.

William Hogarth, *The Analysis of Beauty*[1]

The painter and engraver William Hogarth commemorated the enactment of the Engravers' Act in 1735 with the print commonly known as *Crowns, Mitres, Maces, etc* (1754). The image represents a variety of regal, legal, and heraldic emblems united by straight lines emanating from a royal crown. It represents law as a system of signs and symbols and opens up questions about law's orderliness and disarray, visibility and textuality, possibilities and constraints. Hogarth offers a richly encoded and enigmatic picture where the viewer becomes a meaning maker, not unlike any lawyer working on the elucidation of texts. What motives lie behind the image and Hogarth's frequent use of the crown? And what exactly is law according to Hogarth's emblematic representation?

This essay addresses the dynamic relationship between the visual and the legal within the context of print production in eighteenth-century England and, more particularly, in Hogarth's little-studied illustrations of law. It takes into consideration Hogarth's earlier representation, *Royalty, Episcopacy, and Law* (1724), which inspires doubt, even terror, and shows the king, clergy, and judiciary as interlocked institutions exercising power. The later print *Crowns, Mitres, Maces, etc* raises the question of the visible manifestation of law and its impact, in both the promulgation of copyright law and the assertion of a specifically English aesthetic. The present essay explores whether the law became more visible through its existence in the image and, whether, in fact, the image was transformed by law's iconic presence.

The Crown

Crowns, Mitres, Maces, etc (figure 3.1) presents the viewer with an enigmatic code. The royal crown, like a sun, sheds rays onto cluttered symbols, shields, and signs. The coronets of baron, viscount, earl, duke, and the Prince of Wales, each illustrated with their respective ornaments and silk velvet lining, represent the power, lineage, and glory of the law. Other piled-up signs of office and trophies reinforce the print's message. The Chancellor's great seal, the Speaker's hat, the Marshal of London's fur cap, and the cap of liberty allude to the rights and duties that make up law. Also included are a few books with no title or author, alluding to law's obscure textuality. The representation of a copy of the Engravers' Act, which was the first legislation to grant copyright protection to engravings, and the presence of the laudatory text below the picture show that the image was not intended to stand alone, but to be read in conjunction with its textual support. Each symbol is only a part of the whole. All the elements are carefully placed, and framed, in three separate divisions, within the margins of an overblown column. The illustration (like the distinctive element of the capital) is at the top, followed below by the publication line and the dedicatory text (in place of the column), and the inscription or receipt for subscribing (as pedestal) at the bottom. This orderly structure enhances the monumentality of law and its prominent role as a pillar of English society.

According to Hogarth's biographer John Nichols, Hogarth published the print "immediately after"[2] the Act. But Nichols's dating is unlikely since no 1735 edition has been identified and, as pointed out by Ronald Paulson, the words "at present" in the inscription of the print seem to indicate "a sizable lapse of time between the Act and the print."[3] But why, then, did Hogarth want to convey his "grateful acknowledgement" to the legislature, in 1754, two decades after the Act? As evidenced in Thomas Jeffereys's case against Richard Baldwin and other booksellers, which came before Lord Hardwicke in Chancery on 22 March 1753, the Act only protected artists who, like Hogarth, designed and engraved their prints.[4] Printsellers like Jeffereys, who, for a price, were assigned copyright by the designer, were not protected under the

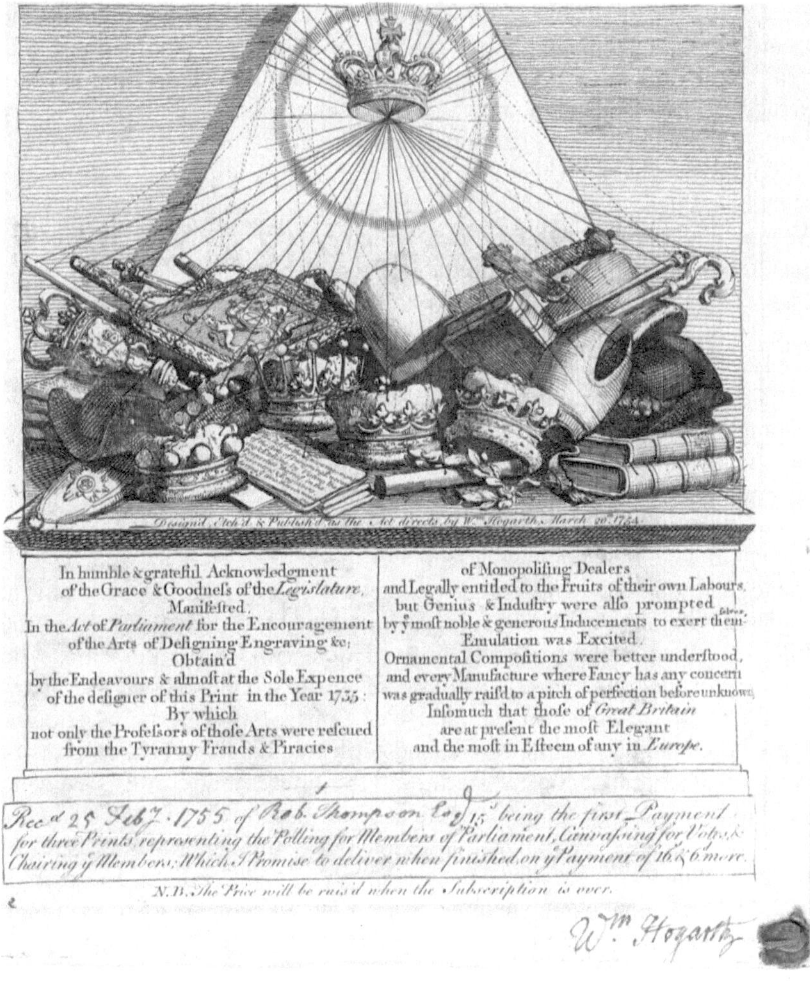

Figure 3.1 William Hogarth, *Crowns, Mitres, Maces, etc*, Fourth state, etching, 1754. Courtesy of the Lewis Walpole Library, Yale University.

Act. In his ruling, Lord Hardwicke agreed with the defendants that the print depicting the view of the Society of British Herring Fishery was not a work of ingenuity by the plaintiff: "It is not within the statute, which was made for encouragement of genius and art; if it was, any person who employs a printer or engraver would be so too."[5] Although the decision did not affect Hogarth's commercial interests, it came at a significant time, for as late as 1751 the engraver and antiquarian George Vertue severely criticized the Act, which did not satisfy the interests of petitioners like him. He emphatically stated:

> if the act of parliament made to encourage ingravers in England had been plain full and strong as I did propose it at the Committee of the parliament – it might be of true benefit to those artists that became superior in skill. and practice –
>
> That is that the license shoud be all those who Engrav'd works from paintings of any kind if they did actually do them originally from paintings – or statues or buildings – or any other artfull works[6]

Hogarth blamed his friend, the lawyer William Huggins, for drafting and wording the Bill "so loosely and vaguely."[7] However, when the bill was given its first reading in the House of Lords, John Pine, who had an interest in protecting his set of prints – copied from the Spanish Armada tapestries in the House of Lords – as well as his engraving of the Magna Carta embellished with twenty-five coats of arms of King John's barons, commented that "the Engravers would have been glad to have had the Bill more general, but that the House of Commons were not inclined to make it so extensive."[8] Indeed, the exclusion of reproductive engravers may have been a political tactic by Hogarth in order to promote English art.[9] As seen in *The Battle of the Pictures* (1745), which he used as the subscription ticket to the sale of his works at an auction, Hogarth condemned the prevailing taste of English collectors for Old Master paintings. The print represents Hogarth's contempt for imported paintings and their numerous reproductive prints, which the Act did not protect.

While the Act protected Hogarth's interests, it aimed to promote the public good by rescuing, as the print's inscription declares, those with inventive capacities "from the Tyranny Frauds & Piracies of Monopolising Dealers" and offering "noble & generous inducements" encouraging the art of engraving. Diverting attention from the Act's weaknesses, Hogarth praised its effects:

> Emulation was excited, Ornamental Compositions were better understood, and every Manufacture where Fancy has any concern was gradually rais'd to a pitch of perfection before unknown, Insomuch that those of *Great Britain* are at present the most Elegant and the most in Esteem of any in *Europe*.[10]

How could Hogarth, who was so proud, not praise his Act, particularly after it had been modelled on his own experience as an engraver? Vexed by the unauthorized copies "in all sizes and manner" of his *Harlot's Progress*, he had "applied to Parliament"[11] to protect his original designs and, in particular, *A Rake's Progress*, which he was planning to publish in 1733.[12] Two decades later, Hogarth still claimed authorship of the Act. The inscription proudly proclaims it was "Obtained by the Endeavours & almost at the Sole Expence" of Hogarth. No reference is made to the contribution of the six fellow other artists who also signed the petition.

The uneasy relationship with fellow artists and the new legal circumstances prompted Hogarth to pay tribute to the legislature with a print that alluded to law as a principle and point of transcendent order and unity and exposed the complex mechanics of lawmaking. As the print shows, law belongs to the order of divinity and of sovereignty, on the one hand, and the executive and the administrative, on the other. According to Goodrich,

> It is this double form that modern law inherits from theology in the distinction between legislative power and executive action, substance and relation, norm and decision. Sovereign power rules as a transcendent form, as a universal expression and carrier of the image of the absolute, but it is the executive and the administration that govern, that execute the details and determine right and wrong action.[13]

If the print's overall structure directs attention to law's sovereignty, its omnipotence and pervasiveness, the straight and dotted lines underline the working relations between Crown and Parliament or, to use the biographer Allan Cunningham's words, "the united wisdom of king, lords, and commons."[14] The imposing image is markedly different from Hogarth's earlier and mostly hostile representations of law. Rather than focusing on law's agents or its abuses, he conveys a deep sense of the mixed nature of the Crown.

After the so-called Glorious Revolution of 1688, the establishment of a limited monarchy was effectively secured by Parliament. As the celebrated jurist William Blackstone was to write, "The whole is prevented from separation, and artificially connected together by the mixed nature of the crown, which is a part of the legislative, and the sole executive magistrate."[15] He observes that Parliament

> hath sovereign and uncontrollable authority in making, confirming, enlarging, restraining, abrogating, repealing, reviving, and expounding of laws ... : this being the place where that absolute despotic power, which must in all governments reside somewhere, is entrusted by the constitution of these kingdoms.[16]

By the 1750s, Parliament "was being hailed as a legislative giant of unprecedented and unparalleled power."[17] England's broad economic changes stimulated the growth of new market practices and financial instruments which led to the proliferation of laws. By the time of George III, Parliament was enacting four times the number of statutes that it had in the reign of William III.[18] Public acts were printed by the king's printer and republished in newspapers, magazines, and collections of statutes. Hogarth's representation of "An Act ..." sticking out of a man's pocket in *A Country Inn at Election Time* (1747) shows how deeply they had penetrated everyday experience.

Hogarth soon came to recognize the appeal of the majestic symbols of office so pervasive in English culture. Crowns are prominently and carefully displayed in the emblematic print of *The Lottery* as early as 1724, and more lavishly in the series of paintings (1742–3) and engravings (1745) entitled *Marriage A-la-Mode* which, alluding to the vain and reckless choices of a couple whose marriage was arranged by their ambitious fathers, includes a notable display of scattered coronets on the picture frames, the footstool, the earl's crutch, the curtained alcove and the body of one of the dogs in the first scene, as well as the bed and dressing mirror on the fourth scene. The crowns point to the prominence of rank and noble lineage in marriage, as can also be seen in the five honourable ladies whose different ranks are pointed out by their coronets in Hogarth's curious display *The Five Orders of Periwigs* (1761). So fascinated was Hogarth with the visible emblems of royal authority that he used a regal coronet in the very creation of a new order of architecture in the design for a frontispiece.[19]

Crowns, Mitres, Maces, etc was issued as a subscription ticket for the *Election* series (1755–8), which ridiculed the English electoral process. The works, inspired by the 1754 election campaign in Oxfordshire, exposed the state of contemporary politics in eighteenth-century Britain. As Matthew Craske points out, they are "about party politics without revealing the party political prejudices of the artist."[20] Hogarth, however, makes a bold political move in the third state of the subscription ticket. He replaces the coronet of Frederick, Prince of Wales, positioned below the crown of laurel leaves, with that of the youngest son of George II, the Duke of Cumberland, a gesture that may be seen as a personal expression of loyalty to the victor of Culloden.[21] Frederick, who was heir to the throne and at loggerheads with his father, had died in 1751. By providing a choice of prints, Hogarth was giving the subscriber a means to make a statement of allegiance and assert his position in relation to government, while increasing his market potential among the public.[22] The fine line between law and the political realm was often indistinct, as the prints make apparent.

As a subscription ticket, the print expressed a contractual obligation and served as a mode of advertising.[23] It functioned as a receipt to subscribers for the prints of the *Election* series, which, as the caption reads, Hogarth promised "to deliver when finished."[24] But, signed by Hogarth and displaying the date and the name of the subscriber, the ticket became collectible in its own right at a time when new forms of property and commerce were emerging. As Martin A. Kayman explains:

> [...] the development, through the seventeenth and eighteenth centuries, of government debt, lottery tickets, insurance policies, bonds or shares in joint-stock companies, options for their future purchase or sale, bills of exchange, discount bills, endorsable bearer bonds, and promissory notes or bank notes, as well as the generalised increase in the importance of contracts testified to the fact that property was undergoing a profound change. Rather than the natural solidity of land, property was increasingly taking the form of signifiers of abstract value, paper bearing promises of future expectations, whose reality at the moment was only imaginary, and whose value was defined not by substance or use, but by a deferred closure, or by the rice for which it could be sold, or people could be persuaded to believe it might later fetch.[25]

In this context, prints became more and more desirable as commodities.[26] Hogarth became a brand name himself. In the 1740s, his profile picture, copied from *The Gate of Calais*, appears in a richly decorated frame in the trade card of John Smith, map and printseller of Cheapside, London. The card was drawn by Carle Vanloo and indicates the importance and high esteem in which the artist was held in the printing trade. A copy of Hogarth's self-portrait is also displayed on the trade card of Ryall and Withy, Booksellers & Printsellers at "Hogarth's Head and Dial" in Fleet Street.[27] The framed portrait of Hogarth is elegantly adorned with a clock and three crowns on top.[28]

The crown, therefore, is a frequent trope in Hogarth's allegorical engravings and paintings. It appears subtly but still noticeable in the 1746 print of Lord Lovat, the Jacobite supporter tried for high treason for his participation in the failed attempt to restore the Young Pretender to the English throne. It is possible to interpret the modest and faint carved motif of two angels holding a crown in the backrest of the chair as a symbolic reference to the transition of power from Crown to Parliament. This view is further accentuated when the image is compared to its companion, the satirical portrait of John Wilkes Esq. (1763) which Hogarth produced in response to Wilkes's trial for seditious libel in May 1763. Significantly, the attenuated form of the chair in which the defiant politician sits has no carvings on it. Indeed, Lovat marks the end of an era as he was the last man in Britain to be beheaded on Tower Hill, London. Hogarth, who had eagerly pursued royal patronage in the 1730s, was a partisan of the 1688 Revolution and a constitutional monarchist. In 1747, the regal symbol appears more prominently, and with greater solemnity, in the margin of each of the twelve prints of *Industry and Idleness*. Affixed like a stamp, it appears in the top corners, making the print appear as if it was a royal product, and thereby as precious, exclusive, and worthy of protection. The wide distribution of his prints further consolidated the message.

The royal crown is again prominently displayed in the lower left corner of the crowded image of *Strolling Actresses Dressing in a Barn*. In 1737, the Stage Licensing Act imposed tight restrictions on the British stage. The legislation, hastily passed through Parliament to suppress Henry Fielding's satirical pieces on Robert Walpole and his ministry, was a political measure intended to censor all new plays and control itinerant theatre companies.[29] In a significant manner, at the lower left, we see a printed copy of the Act. Far from inspiring awe and reverence, however, it is placed like a mat, on top of the royal crown under the baby's bowl and thus suggesting Hogarth's contempt. The crown is played down in this chaotic backstage setting where a kitten plays with the regal orb in the foreground. Such a frivolous treatment contrasts with Hogarth's full-length portrait of David Garrick as Richard III (1745). The king is portrayed awakening from a nightmare in his royal tent on the morning of the battle of Bosworth Field. Caught off guard, he reaches for his sword, placed near the crown beside a framed crucifix. Hogarth's complex and multifaceted portrait of king/actor/man appeals to the aesthetic of the stage and uses the symbolism and persuasive force of the crown to convey the mystique of monarchical authority. It draws attention to the very question of representation, which, as Louis Marin notes, "is at once the action of putting before one's eyes the quality of being a sign or person that holds the place of another."[30] Hogarth links the performative nature of kingship and the kingly nature of performance through their shared deployment of theatrical gestures, elaborate costumes, and symbolic props, just like he had done in his earlier representation of Henry VIII and Anne Boleyn (c. 1728). The engraving, which was based on Colley Cibber's production of Henry VIII, displays a royal crown held by two angels (struggling in their effort to support it) and the prominent throne of state with a crown on top in an elegant baroque setting. The picture reflects on the king's political allegiances and shifting loyalties. The empty throne, evoking the monarch's office rather than the person of the king, alludes to the succession of the Crown.

Through his incessant representations, Hogarth conveys the slippage between Crown and king that Paul D. Halliday so eloquently identifies in his analysis of Blackstone's conception of England's constitutional monarchy. "Blackstone's crown, not his king, provides the site of and impetus for mixture and thus acts as the force generating a transformed regal constitution's distinctive unification of powers."[31] Hogarth, who had been appointed sergeant painter to the king in 1757, appears to become during the Seven Years' War increasingly supportive of King George III and his minister Lord Bute.

Tellingly, in the frantic scene of a city on fire in *The Times*, plate 1 (figure 3.2), a courageous fireman constitutes the focal point of three streams of attack at the centre of the image. Hogarth distils the king's presence into the allegorical image of a fireman, represented like a statue on the pedestal-like base of the "Union Office." With the assistance of the officers operating the engine around him, he directs a stream of water into the world consumed by flames, represented by a globe. The crown and the initials G.R. on the prominent badge on his arm underline the strength, symbolic value, and unifying power of the crown.

The image can be compared to Richard Wilson's painting *The Inner Temple after the Fire of 4 January 1737*, where Frederick, Prince of Wales,

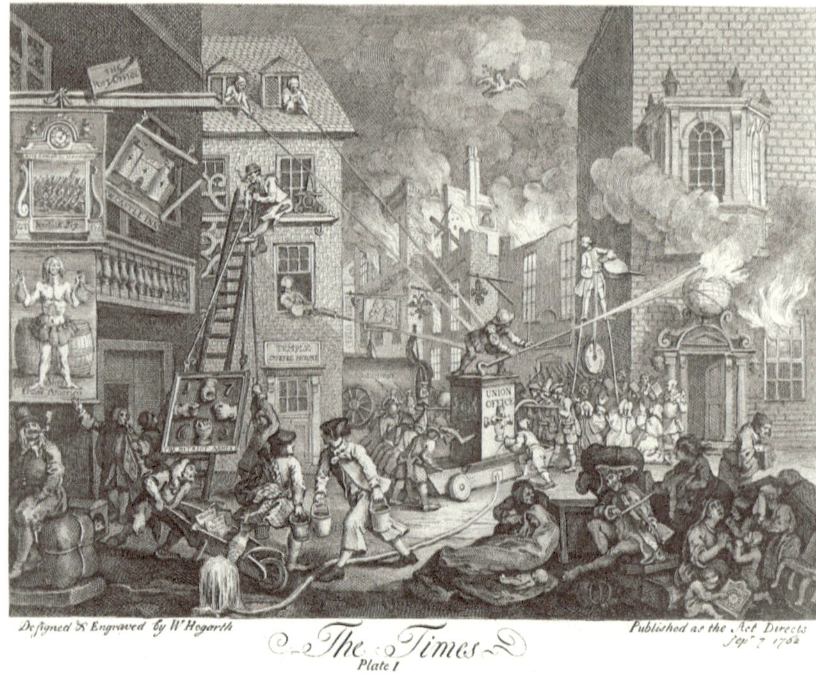

Figure 3.2 William Hogarth, *The Times*, plate 1, Third state, etching and engraving, 1762. Courtesy of the Lewis Walpole Library, Yale University.

is represented in the passive role of spectator. The prince, who was said to have helped in putting the fire out, is shown dressed in Garter robes inspecting the devastating scene while the men in the left operate the water engine.[32] In contrast, Hogarth offers a dignified and heroic image, which, in the direction of the lines and strong diagonals, seems to evoke a Union Jack or British Flag. In keeping with Blackstone's conception of a disembodied king, Hogarth invokes the crown as the actor preserving the peace of the nation. The unified support of secular forces rather than of God to identify the monarch lays emphasis on the de-sacralization of the monarchy and the legitimized and established power of the constitutional monarchy of Britain. Aligning himself with the supporters of Lord Bute against the war policies of William Pitt and his party, Hogarth explains that the print was aimed to promote "Peace and unanimity and so to put the opposers of this humane purpose in a light which gave offence to the Fomenters of destruction in the minds of the people."[33]

In 1761, Hogarth goes further and embodies Blackstone's very notion of the king as "the fountain of justice and general conservator of the peace of the kingdom."[34] In the *Frontispiece* for the *Catalogue of Pictures exhibited in Spring Gardens,* he represents the king as a sculpted bust in a shell-shaped niche surmounted by a crown at the top of a monument.[35] The allegorical figure of Britannia channels the water from the lion's head spout into three delicately intertwined saplings symbolizing the fine arts of painting, sculpture, and architecture. Once again, Hogarth's image evokes the tripartite constitution that Lord Viscount Bolingbroke had celebrated as the "tree" which produced "that delicious and wholesome fruit" of "liberty."[36] The royal monument in the rocky landscape conforms to Blackstone's definition of the king as "reservoir."[37] Hogarth, who had received little royal support and patronage from George II, creates an imposing image meant to flatter the king and celebrate the beginning of a new era.[38]

Hogarth's hope for a cultural revival under the new king did not last long. In 1764, drastically, and defiantly, a battered crown juts out of the lower edge of the picture in a deserted and ruined landscape in Hogarth's last work, *The Bathos* (1764). The crown is joined by other ruined objects: a broken bell, a tombstone ornamented by a skull, a tower in ruins, the vestiges of a capital of the Ionic order, and the painter's own cracked palette. Included in the pile of abandoned and disfigured objects is a burning copy of Hogarth's print of *The Times*. The abandoned crown in pieces attests to the fading royal mystique and presents a discouraging scene in which law and justice have left the earth.

Hogarth's illustration of the crown could not contrast more sharply with the visible splendour of *Crowns, Mitres, Maces, etc.* His commemorative image emphasizes the crown as the focal symbol of governance, set within a circle or orb, itself enclosed in a triangle, out of which radiates multiple lines of authority. Like a sun rising, the orb projects outside the frame, conferring divinity and mystery to the spatial configuration of law. Hogarth reinforces the message of an imageless space with the figure of an incomplete triangle, whose missing apex reaches out towards an invisible transcendence. The triangle is flanked by parallel lines stretching out on each side. The blank interior space interrupts and disrupts the horizontal linearity commonly associated with law's black lettered texts, suggesting a space of possibility and providing a means through which to glimpse the dynamic, unfinished, and incomplete qualities of law. As Peter Goodrich explains, "The empty space is never simply empty: it sublimates, it displaces, it transgresses and so acts as the most extravagant and most paradoxical or liminal of figures."[39] Hogarth's graphic illustration of law both marks a symbolic absence and displays a monumental presence.

The figure of the pyramid, with an eye substituting for the crown, became a widespread revolutionary symbol in engravings celebrating the Declaration of the Rights of Man and other printed Republican materials.[40] The masonic symbol also appears on the American fifty-dollar bill issued in 1778. But for Hogarth the pyramid or "triangular glass" appears on the title page of the *Analysis of Beauty*, published in 1753, one year before the print.[41] It is, he states, one of the "most expressive figures that can be thought of to signify not only beauty and grace, but the whole *order of form*."[42] It is dynamic:

> There is no object composed of straight lines, that has so much variety, with so few parts, as the pyramid: and it is its constantly varying from its base gradually upwards in every situation of the eye, (without giving the idea of sameness, as the eye moves round it) that has made it be esteem'd in all ages.[43]

Hogarth's prominent display of the word "Variety" at the base of the pyramid resonates with the vitality and variety of law in *Crowns, Mitres, Maces, etc.* The viewer's eye moves across the various focal points making connections and establishing correspondences. Far from simple accumulation, Hogarth insisted on "composed variety; for variety uncomposed, and without design, is confusion and deformity."[44] His apprehension of the world of forms is no different from his apprehension of the world of law. Hogarth aims to reconcile variety with order in both.

Furthermore, Hogarth seeks to establish a correlation with the laws of optics. His friend Joshua Kirby had published an illustrated treatise on perspective the same year as Hogarth's print dedicated to the artist, whom the author praises with "Gratitude and Affection" as "a Genius in the Art of Design."[45] Tellingly, as Douglas Fordham points out, "Illustration 30 shows lines from objects at various distances converging on the lens of a single eye and then inverts those lines onto the back of the retina. This is the only plate in the book that takes on the same hourglass shape of converging and departing lines as that in the subscription ticket."[46] The system of converging straight lines, on the one hand,

and refracted dotted lines, on the other, signal the different, sometimes intersecting, parts of government while the crown, in place of an eye, or sun, keeps watch over the ensemble.

Hogarth expressed allegiance to the Crown but placed little emphasis on the physical person of the king. Unlike Sir Joshua Reynolds and Allan Ramsay, whose royal portraits underscored the king's regal body and dignity, Hogarth's king is disembodied and metonymized through the crown. As Sir Edward Coke had explained, the king had two bodies, one "natural" and "subject to death" and the other "political" and "immortal."[47] Aware of the mysterious and representational power of the crown as metaphor, the seventeenth-century jurist described the King's crown as the "hieroglyph"[48] of law. No artist renders the concept visually better than Hogarth.

The Telescope and the Moon, Here and There

Hogarth provides a view of the law organized around a dominating, overseeing gaze, in *Crowns, Mitres, Maces, etc*. Yet he conveys a much colder representation of the nation's governing institutions in *Royalty, Episcopacy, and Law* (figure 3.3). Hogarth's 1724 print, advertised as "a very rare hieroglyphic Print, composed of emblematic attributes, and no human features or limbs,"[49] renders a space where a tightly controlled hierarchical order is felt. The social distance and strangeness of king, bishop, and judge is exacerbated by the distanced and inhospitable world in which they are placed. The rulers are seen through the lens of a telescope as if on some cold and inconstant moon. Is Hogarth, and equally importantly, the spectator (for he sees through the powerful lens of the telescope), in search of new and hidden truths about the affairs of state? Are these "inhabitants of the moon" meant to draw attention to the alien and unsympathetic character of England's rulers?

The reference to hieroglyphs is not accidental. It suggests the enigmatic logic of an ancient and mysterious cult, governed by symbolic arcana whose use the viewer can only guess.[50] Human interaction has been replaced by a semiotic system which can only be deciphered by initiates. Hogarth, in fact, may have intended to provide an explanation, as some figures have letters placed over and beneath them following the conventions of scientific illustrations.

Hogarth's figures have no faces, no expressions. The head of the king as a coin bearing a traditional profile head in simple outline, which possibly represents King James II, alludes to the traditional dominance of aristocratic wealth and privilege that continued after the 1688 Revolution. The bishop's Jew's harp may be interpreted as ancient and biblical, on the one hand, and shamanistic and mystical, on the other. The deceptively simple instrument, which required a high degree of skill to play, excited curiosity and awe-inspiring mystical qualities.[51] The judge's face has been transformed into his gavel, connoting the court's combination of force or violence with order and authority. Hogarth deploys a fantastic or theatrical world where the mask, depriving each figure of human expressiveness, is the very means of showing and revealing a face. It is through the mask that economic power (the coin), obfuscatory skill (the Jew's harp), and force (the gavel) are signified.

The three rulers, set against three distinguishable backgrounds made up of horizontal and vertical lines and a grid pattern, appear to work in a joint effort suggesting cooperation. They govern comfortably seated on their elevated stands or podiums, floating in the clouds. Although the king sits lower than the judge and bishop, his throne is half decorated with vertical lines topped by clouds that suggest his divine provenance. He holds an orb and sceptre with crescent-moons on top, a reminder of the passage of time, and that all reigns come to an end. The judge, wearing judicial robes and a long wig, holds a large sword pointing upwards which, although evoking the conventional representation of justice, seems to contradict his purpose in interpreting and pronouncing the words of law without coercion. The bishop, the only figure to have a hand, plucks the Jew's harp; but curiously that which is set vibrating through the rope is the handle fastened to a book and connected to a mincer which pumps out money. The association between clockwork logic and semiotic secrecy – a system that is both machine-like and mystical – is strongly felt. According to the mid-seventeenth-century radical Gerrard Winstanley: "Kingly power depends upon the Law, and upon buying and selling; and these three depend upon the Clergy, to bewitch the people to conform; and all of them depend upon Kingly power by his force, to compel subjection from those that will not be bewitched."[52]

Hogarth creates an image of spectacular machinery that is at once resistant to interpretation and open for inspection. The connection drawn between men in the moon and the alien powers all around us is telling of the post-Newtonian world. Jonathan Swift's *Gulliver's Travels*, first published in 1726, delved into "the mysterious meaning of words, syllables and letters" devised by conspirators –

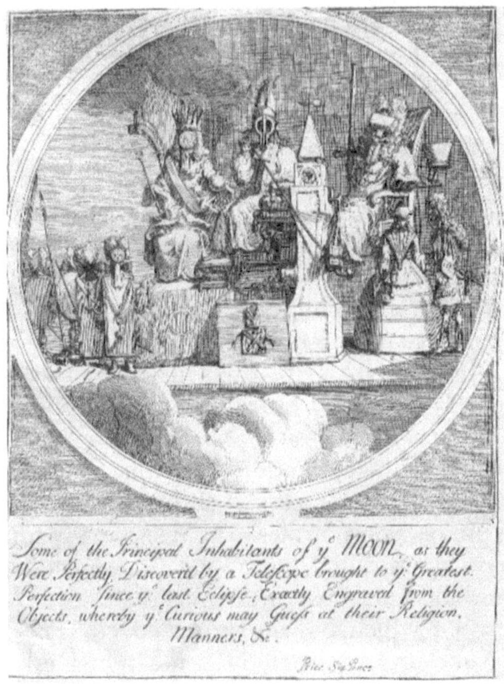

Figure 3.3 William Hogarth, *Royalty, Episcopacy, and Law (Some of the Principal Inhabitants of Ye Moon)*, etching and engraving, 1724. Courtesy of the Lewis Walpole Library, Yale University.

> for instance, they can discover a closestool to signify a privy council; a flock of geese, a senate; a lame dog, an invader; the plague, a standing army; a buzzard, a prime minister; the gout, a high-priest; a gibbet, a secretary of state; a chamber-pot, a committee of grandees; a sieve, a court-lady; a broom, a revolution; a mouse-trap, an employment; a bottomless pit, a treasury; a sink, a court; a cap and bells, a favourite; a broken reed, a court of justice; an empty tun, a general; a running sore, the administration.[53]

Hogarth's image recalls Swift's burlesqued jargon, which was in turn inspired by the trial of Bishop Attebury, a Jacobite accused of treason in 1723.[54] It is in this political context and against a background driven by scientific interest, amusement, and discovery that Hogarth uncovers and scrutinizes the truths of the state, church, and law.

From the print's caption we learn that these are *Some of the Principle inhabitants in ye Moon, as they were Perfectly Discover'd by a Telescope brought to ye Greatest Perfection since the last Eclipse*. Hogarth makes reference to a recent lunar eclipse and captures the popular excitement over the moon and its cycles as well as the new telescopic discoveries in England. In 1724 Samuel Molyneux, Member of Parliament and fellow of the Royal Society of London, had constructed one of the earliest reflecting telescopes.[55] Making distant and faint objects appear closer to the observer, the telescope altered man's view of the universe and captivated the imagination.[56] The problem with the telescope, as William Blake points out, is that it "alter[s] the ratio of the Spectators Organs, but leave[s] Objects untouch'd."[57] Hogarth's image represents a space-time in which a formally instituted order is magnified but left untouched. His interest is in the very process of focusing, which, as Roberta Kevelson notes, "is the first stage of inquiry" or "that which signals inquiry to begin."[58] It is thus in the process of observing the truths of the state that Hogarth's image concentrates. The telescope permitted Hogarth to project a space in which the "here" and "there" could be simultaneously displayed. Ultimately, what the image represents is the circular lens of the telescope, which, like the prominent circle in *Crowns, Mitres, Maces, etc*, protrudes out of the frame and can be viewed as bringing together the temporal and the celestial in one image. Hogarth wants the viewer to focus as scrupulously as possible, for as he was intensely aware, "observation is simply the beginning of heresy."[59]

Lawful Image, Visible Law

Under the 1735 Act words became an integral part of engravings. The appearance of the date of publication and the name of the proprietor were necessary to the legal protection of the image. Little is known about the origins of the formulation "Published according to Act of Parliament" – or any of its variants – but they were generally included in the so-called publication line, which appeared for the first time in Hogarth's modern series of *A Rake's Progress* (1735) and was only used in England.[60] But what, if anything, was the unique contribution of the English publication line?

In *Crowns, Mitres, Maces, etc*, the italicized words, *Design'd, Etch'd & Publish'd as the Act directs by Wm. Hogarth, March 20th 1754*, do not run near the left or right margin, as in most of Hogarth's prints, but are carefully centred. They occupy a position between the inside and the outside of the image and seem, on the one hand, to be a supplement, a superfluous addition to an already complete whole and, on the other hand, to be necessary, remedying a deficiency and so making explicit the lack in what had seemed whole.[61] The publication line stabilizes and brings forward an authoritative force that contrasts with the image's emblematic character and indeterminacy.

Medieval images used inscriptions in Latin to reinforce religious and political messages, while in the early modern period, captions and texts found at the bottom of prints often indicated the names of the engraver and inventor or cited patrons as indications of prestige, but they had "no particular legal standing."[62] In the sixteenth century, royal and papal permissions existed in the form of privileges, which were used to indicate the print's approved and protected status. A privilege was "granted on an individual basis" as a "special grace" and "favour," as opposed to being a form of property recognized and protected by law.[63] Unlike the English copyright system, which was free and did not control the content of printed material, the procedure for obtaining a privilege was costly and included obtaining a licence, which served as a censoring mechanism. It was not consistently required to include the privilege in the book or print, or to record it with a notary.[64] Authors or printers, however, preferred to include the inscription *cum privilegio*, as it had an admonitory effect and conferred prestige on the work.

Like Hogarth, the painter and engraver Albrecht Dürer was a shrewd entrepreneur. Both artists shared an overriding concern with copies and succeeded in developing new marketing techniques. According to Vasari, Dürer took legal action against the Italian engraver Marcantonio Raimondi, who copied his woodcuts from the *Life of the Virgin* series.[65] The courts permitted Raimondi to copy the prints but prohibited him from using Dürer's monogram, which the artist affixed as symbol of authority and personal guarantee of his authorship.[66] Hogarth, by contrast, does not establish his authority over the image with a personal device. He relied on the authority of law. His image is the body on which the law is inscribed.[67] It is overtly sanctioned by law and so bears two originators on its face, one legal and one aesthetic.

It is of importance to note that the publication line functions as an icon not an index. It does not refer to a legal presence; it *is* a legal presence. Like J.L. Austin's "performative utterances," which do not state facts but perform an action,[68] its effect derives not from the words of the law but from the image of the law. The line is performative in its iterability and citationality. Reprinted on every engraving, like paper currency and other common forms of legal tender, it can never be original.[69] Every "repetition is a transgression," Gilles Deleuze writes, "It puts into question, it denounces its nominal or general character in favour of a more profound and more artistic reality."[70]

Prints, which served didactic, political, and entertaining purposes, brought law into the streets and the hands of patrons and collectors. But how did the buyers of such prints respond to the intrusion of law on the image? Was the effect of the publication line to enact, to enforce, to promulgate, to warn, or to prohibit? One curious reference alluding to the line's role and value appears in a 1779 anonymous print entitled *The Family Compact*, where the kings of Spain and France are shown holding hands and standing with the devil on a map of the British colonies. The political print satirizes the alliance between Spain and France against England and displays a prominent text on the left-hand side: "Published Nov. 1, 1779 whether by Act or Order is not Material Provided it Sells." Doubting the efficacy of the Act and ridiculing the role of formalities, it ultimately stresses how economic interests are the creator's main concern.

The 1735 Act did not specify that the words "Published according to Act of Parliament" be written on each print, but engravers included them and used a variety of forms. Hogarth favoured the phrase "Published according to Act of Parliament" over "Published as the Act directs."[71] In an informative analysis of Hogarth's prints, a nineteenth-century reviewer observes that the latter form offers an advantage over the former as it indicates "at least some reliance on justice," noting that "it was possible, in fact, to resent the appearance of these words exactly as one resents the intrusive sayings of a bore."[72] The Act provided "exquisite guidelines" that "'directed' artists to do certain things which, being done, would suffice, it was hoped, to defeat the 'hunger' of knaves, and pilferers of art's reward," but "it did not enforce its directions; … the said Act had really put the claims of artists to property in their own 'inventions' into a concrete, but very ineffectual form."[73]

The reviewer is right to point out that the publication line was ineffective as a protection against unauthorized copies, but fails to recognize that it succeeded as a mode of visibility and publicity. The German traveller Friedrich Wendeborn notes that in Germany, where English prints were widely collected, "the words *published as the Act directs*, or *according to Act of Parliament*" were taken to mean "published by the express order of parliament, and therefore had an additional value."[74] This is of the utmost significance, for the international commodity value of English prints, whose political messages and complex emblematic contexts were largely incomprehensible to foreign buyers,[75] was associated with their legal status. The publication line, appearing in rather large and prominent lettering in some prints,[76] points to the legal and mercantile landscape that distinguished England from France and other countries. Indeed, the words "According to Act of Parliament" catch the eye of the viewer in the illustrated designs of the cabinet-maker Thomas Chippendale, known for the fashionable furniture creations named after him. They become a sort of trademark linked to the uniquely English designs, engraved and published in the famous pattern book *The Gentleman and Cabinet-maker's Director* (1754), highly in demand and largely copied in England and abroad.

Engravings and maps did not carry the same aura of authenticity and prestige as paintings, yet surpassed them in legal protection, at least until the 1862 Fine Art Copyright Act.[77] It was prints, at the bottom of the hierarchy and excluded from academic honours, which formed a bond with law. The significance of the relationship was greater than Hogarth realized. *Crowns, Mitres, Maces, etc* presents a hierarchical structure in which image, law, and commerce interwove legal and economic relations and enforced political liberties and economic rights. The print's true meaning, as I have tried to demonstrate, lies in the intersecting histories, codes, and infrastructures of these not so distinct spheres. The copyright inscription itself became a symbol or trademark that promoted and enhanced the reputation of a distinctly English aesthetic, not to mention the reputation of English liberties, rights, and law. Visual and legal elements built on one another. Whether law promoted the image or the image promoted law, the relationship could not have been more favourable to both.

NOTES

I am thankful to Desmond Manderson for his invitation to participate in the conference in Canberra and his helpful suggestions. I also want to thank Peter Schneck for his valuable comments.

1 William Hogarth, *The Analysis of Beauty* (1753), ed. Ronald Paulson (New Haven and London: Yale University Press, 1997), 33.

2 John Nichols, *Biographical Anecdotes of William Hogarth; with A Catalogue of His Works Chronologically Arranged; and Occasional Remarks*, 3rd ed. (London: Printed for J. Nichols, 1785), 39.

3 Ronald Paulson, *Hogarth's Graphic Works*, 3rd rev. ed. (London: Print Room, 1989), 161.

4 Nichols explains that the printseller Jeffereys "employed an artist to draw and engrave a print representing the British Herring Fishery; and, having paid him for it; took an assignment of the right to the property in it accruing to the Artist by the act of parliament. [Baldwin] ... pirated it in a smaller size, and Jeffereys brought his bill for an injunction." Nichols, *Biographical Anecdotes*, 38.

5 *Jeffereys v. Baldwin* (1753). Charles Ambler, *Reports of Cases Argued and Determined in the High Court of Chancery*, 2nd ed. (London: Joseph Butterworth, 1828), 164.

6 George Vertue, *Note Books*, ed. Lionel Cust and Arthur M. Hind, 5 vols. (London: Walpole Society, 1933–4), vol. 3, 156 (original spelling and punctuation).

7 Allan Cunningham, *The Lives of the Most Eminent British Painters, Sculptors, and Architects*, vol. 1, 2nd ed. (London: John Murray, 1830), 107.

8 As cited in Ronald Paulson, *Hogarth: His Life, Art, and Times*, vol. 1 (New Haven and London: Yale University Press, 1971), 362.

9 See Ilaria Bignami, "The Accompaniment to Patronage. A Study of the Origins, Rise and Development of an Institutional System for the Arts in Britain 1692–1768," PhD thesis (Courtauld Institute of Art, University of London, 1988), 307–9.

10 In his "Autobiographical Notes," Hogarth wrote that the Act had contributed to the great improvement of engraving in Britain, "there being more business of that kind done in this Town than in Paris or any where else and as well." William Hogarth, "Autobiographical Notes," in *The Analysis of Beauty* (1753), ed. Joseph Burke (Oxford: Clarendon Press, 1955), 216. The French observer Jean-André Rouquet stated similarly that before the act "there were only two print shops in London; but since this act, they suddenly increased to some hundreds: and if we consider the number and abilities of the engravers who are now in that metropolis, we must allow that of all arts relative to design, that of engraving has made the greatest progress in England." Jean-André Rouquet, *The Present State of the Arts in England* (London, 1755), 28. A thorough study evaluating the number of print shops and the market's size and geographical limits before and after the act remains to be completed.

11 Hogarth, "Autobiographical Notes," 216.

12 See David Kunzle, "Plagiaries-by-Memory of the Rake's Progress and the Genesis of Hogarth's Second Picture Story," *Journal of the Warburg and Courtauld Institutes* 29 (1966): 311–48.
13 Peter Goodrich, "Specters of Law: Why the History of the Legal Spectacle Has Not Been Written," *UC Irvine Law Review* 1, no. 3 (2011): 794.
14 Cunningham, *Lives*, vol. 1, 108.
15 William Blackstone, *Commentaries on the Laws of England, 1765–1769*, vol. 1, (Chicago and London: University of Chicago Press, 1979), 151.
16 Ibid., 156.
17 Paul Langford, *Public Life and the Propertied Englishman, 1689–1798* (Oxford: Clarendon Press, 1991), 43.
18 David Lieberman, *The Province of Legislation Determined: Legal Theory in Eighteenth-Century Britain* (Cambridge: Cambridge University Press, 1989), 13–17 and 28; David Lemmings, *Law and Government in England during the Long Eighteenth Century: From Consent to Command* (Basingstoke: Palgrave-Macmillan, 2011), 166–7.
19 Nichols, *Biographical Anecdotes*, 371.
20 Matthew Craske, *William Hogarth*, British Artists series (London: Tate Publishing, 2000), 10.
21 This is noted by Paulson in *Hogarth*, vol. 2, 204–6.
22 For a detailed analysis of the various states and subscribers see Mark McNally, "The Marketing Techniques of William Hogarth (1697–1764), Artist and Engraver," PhD thesis (Durham University, 2014), 123–35.
23 On the subscription method of selling prints see Sarah Lloyd, "Ticketing the British Eighteenth Century: 'A thing … never heard before,'" *Journal of Social History* 46, no. 4 (2013): 843–71; Frederick D. Leach, "William Hogarth's Subscription Tickets: A Vehicle for Eighteenth Century Satire on Contemporary Taste," PhD thesis (Iowa State University, 1937).
24 The subscriber in the image shown here is Robert Thompson, Esq.
25 Martin A. Kayman, "Lawful Writing: Common Law, Statute and Properties of Literature," *New Literary History* 27, no. 4 (1996): 767–8.
26 For an excellent discussion of caricature's cultural power and how it functioned as "an alternate currency" see Ian Haywood's chapter 2 in *Romanticism and Caricature* (Cambridge: Cambridge University Press, 2013), 33–57.
27 *Trade tokens and book plates*, Lewis Walpole Library (LWL, 66 726 T675 quarto, 7).
28 Hogarth himself produced a number of trade cards and included shop signs and signboards in his works. See Ambrose Heal, *London Tradesmen's Cards of the XVIII Century: An Account of Their Origin and Use* (New York:

Dover Publications, 1968), 63–6; Julie Anne Lambert, *Nation of Shopkeepers: Trade Ephemera from 1654 to the 1860s in the John Johnson Collection* (Oxford: Bodleian Library, 2001).

29 See P.T. Crean, "The Stage Licensing Act of 1737," in *Modern Philology* 35, no. 3 (February 1938): 239–55; L.W. Conolly, *The Censorship of English Drama 1737–1824* (San Marino: Huntington Library, 1976).

30 Louis Marin, *Portrait of the King*, trans. M.M. Houle (Basingstoke: Macmillan, 1988), 8.

31 Paul D. Halliday, "Blackstone's King," in *Re-Interpreting Blackstone's Commentaries: A Seminal Text in National and International Contexts*, ed. Wilfrid Prest (Oxford and Portland: Hart Publishing, 2014), 180–1.

32 It is reported that the prince "stayed from 12 at night till 6 in the morning directing the soldiers and encouraging the firemen to work both by his presence and money, and 'tis said he did a great service." As quoted in Kimerly Rorschach, "Frederick, Prince of Wales (1707–1751), as a Patron of the Visual Arts: Princely Patriotism and Political Propaganda," PhD thesis (Yale University, 1985), vol. 1, 110.

33 Hogarth, "Autobiographical Notes," 221.

34 1 *Commentaries*, 257.

35 The context is important for "the emblematic frontispiece was often described as the 'soul' or 'ratio' (meaning) of the book." See Alastair Fowler, "The Emblem as a Literary Genre," in *Deviceful Settings: The English Renaissance Emblem and Its Contexts*, ed. Michael Bath and Daniel Russell (New York: AMS Press, 1999), 18.

36 *The Works of the Late Right Honourable Henry St. John, Lord Viscount Bolingbroke*, 8 vols. (London, 1809), vol. 3, 201.

37 1 *Commentaries*, 257.

38 It is not known whether Hogarth was entrusted, in 1728, with the task of engraving the Great Seal of England onto a silver platter made by Paul de Lamerie for Robert Walpole. In 1733, Hogarth had made a preparatory oil sketch of the royal family in an elegantly rendered garden setting representing George II and Queen Caroline, the young prince, and the princesses.

39 Peter Goodrich, *Law and the Image: The Authority of Art and the Aesthetics of Law*, ed. Costas Douzinas and Lynda Nead (Chicago: University of Chicago Press, 1999), 92 and 94.

40 See Susan Maslan's chapter 3 in *Revolutionary Acts: Theater, Democracy, and the French Revolution* (Baltimore: Johns Hopkins University Press, 2005), 125–82.

41 The triangular prism may be an allusion to the painter Giles Hussey's scheme of triangles, which Hogarth didn't like. Hogarth's contemporary

George Vertue wrote that "Hogarth (in opposition to Hussey. scheem of Triangles.) much comments on the inimitable curve or beauty of the S undulating motion line, admired and inimitable in the ancient great Sculptors & painters." Vertue, *Note Books*, 3 (1936), 126 (original spelling and punctuation). See Sheila O'Connell, "An Explanation of Hogarth's *'Analysis of Beauty,'*" *Burlington Magazine*, 126 (1984), 32–4.

42 Hogarth, *Analysis of Beauty*, 11 (original emphasis).

43 Ibid., 30.

44 Ibid., 28.

45 Joshua Kirby, *Dr. Brook Taylor's Method of Perspective Made Easy, Both in Theory and in Practice*, Book 1 (Ipswich, 1754).

46 Douglas Fordham, "Hogarth's Act and the Professional Caricaturist," in *Hogarth's Legacy*, ed. Cynthia Ellen Roman (New Haven: The Lewis Walpole Library, Yale University, 2016), 29.

47 Edward Coke, "Postnati: Calvin's Case, 7 Reports" (1608), 10. Cited in Ernst H. Kantorowicz, *The King's Two Bodies: A Study in Medieval Theology* (Princeton: Princeton University Press, 1957), 423 n. 362.

48 Coke, "Calvin's Case," 11a–11b. Cited in Kantorowicz, *King's Two Bodies*, 16.

49 As cited in Paulson, *Hogarth's Graphic Works*, 54.

50 The Rosetta stone was not discovered until 1799 during Napoleon Bonaparte's Egyptian campaign and was deciphered in 1822. Thus, Egyptian hieroglyphs in the eighteenth century remained a mystery and undecipherable. See Liselotte Dieckmann, *Hieroglyphics: The History of a Literary Symbol* (St Louis: Washington University Press, 1970).

51 The instrument circulated widely in Europe from the sixteenth to nineteenth centuries. It was associated with merchants and pedlars, as seen in Pieter Bruegel the Elder's comic engraving *The Merchant Robbed by Monkeys* (1562). See Leonard Fox, *The Jew's Harp: A Comprehensive Anthology* (Lewisburg: Bucknell University Press, 1988); Gjermund Kolltveit, "The Jew's Harp in Western Europe: Trade, Communication and Innovation, 1150–1500," *Yearbook for Traditional Music* 41 (2009): 42–61.

52 Gerrard Winstanley, *The Law of Freedom* (1652), as cited in Ronald Paulson, *Hogarth's Harlot: Sacred Parody in Enlightenment England* (Baltimore and London: Johns Hopkins University Press, 2003), 67–8.

53 Jonathan Swift, *Travels into several remote nations of the world. By Lemuel Gulliver* (London, 1766), 182.

54 English artists were particularly known for their use of emblems, a tradition that, as Sheila O'Connell points out, "developed in response to the suppression of naturalistic imagery at the Reformation." Sheila

O'Connell, "Curious and Entertaining – Prints of London and Londoners," in *London 1753*, ed. Sheila O'Connell (Boston: David R. Godine, 2003), 40.

55 Samuel Molyneux has been identified as the "Occult Philosopher searching into the Depth of things" in Hogarth's later print *Cunicularii, or The Wise Men of Godliman in Consultation* (1726). *The Gentleman's Magazine*, April 1842, 366–8.

56 The optical instrument appeared frequently in political prints and caricatures. In 1803, for example, James Gillray's print *The King of Brobdingnag and Gulliver* shows the king peering through a compact telescope at the miniature figure of Napoleon in the palm of his hand. This may be interpreted as a playful allusion to Swift's *Gulliver's Travels* (where the traveller appears tiny in comparison with the giants of the fictional land of Brobdingnag) and the magnifying effect of the telescope, which makes an image of a distant object appear closer.

57 William Blake, *Milton*, in *The Poetical Works of William Blake*, ed. Edwin J. Ellis, vol. 1 (London: Chatto & Windus, 1906), 496.

58 Roberta Kevelson, "The New Realism and Lawlessness in Kaleidoscope," in *Law and Semiotics*, vol. 2, ed. Roberta Kevelso (New York and London: Plenum Press, 1988), 190.

59 Steven Wilf, "Law/Text/Past," *UC Irvine Law Review* 1, no. 3 (2011): 564.

60 The act did not extend to Ireland until 1836 ("An Act to extend the Protection of Copyright in Prints and Engravings to Ireland," 6 & 7 Will. IV, c. 59). It is worth noting that the term "copyright" was first used in the nineteenth century (Copyright Act, 1801, 41 Geo. III, c. 107).

61 Jacques Derrida, *The Truth in Painting*, trans. Geoff Bennington and Ian MacCleod (Chicago: University of Chicago Press, 1987), 59–71.

62 Rebecca Zorach and Elizabeth Rodini, "On Imitation and Invention: An Introduction to the Reproductive Print," in *Paper Museums: The Reproductive Print in Europe, 1500–1800* (Chicago: The David and Alfred Smart Museum of Art, University of Chicago, 2005), 12–13.

63 Christopher L.C.E. Witcombe, *Copyright in the Renaissance: Prints and the Privilegio in Sixteenth-Century Venice and Rome* (Leiden and Boston: Brill, 2004) and Jane C. Ginsburg, "Proto-Property in Literary and Artistic Works: Sixteenth-Century Papal Printing Privileges," *Columbia Journal of Law & the Arts* 36, no. 3 (2013): 345–458; also Lisa Pon, *Raphael, Dürer, and Marcantonio Raimondi: Copying and the Italian Renaissance Print* (New Haven and London: Yale University Press, 2004), 39. I am grateful to Lisa Pon for her comments.

64 I am thankful to Jane C. Ginsburg for pointing out that practices varied with different popes. See her chart published as an appendix in Ginsburg,

"Proto-Property in Literary and Artistic Works," 377–458. For a study of the printing privilege in France, see Peter Fuhring, "The Print Privilege in Eighteenth-Century France – I," *Print Quarterly* 2, no. 3 (September 1985): 175–93; Kathie Scott, "Authorship, the Académie, and the Market in Early Modern France," *Oxford Art Journal* 21, no. 1 (1998): 27–41.

65 Pon, *Raphael, Dürer, and Marcantonio Raimondi*, 39–66.

66 See Joseph Leo Koerner's enlightening discussion of images and symbols of authority in chapter 10 "The Law of Authorship" in *The Moment of Self-Portraiture in German Renaissance* (Chicago and London: University of Chicago Press, 1993) 203–23. Also, Witcombe, *Copyright in the Renaissance*, 81–6; Joanna Kostylo, "From Gunpowder to Print: The Common Origins of Copyright and Patent," in *Privilege and Property: Essays on the History of Copyright*, ed. Ronan Deazley, Martin Kretschmer, and Lionel Bentley (Cambridge: Open Book Publishers, 2010), 43.

67 As Drucilla Cornell points out in reference to Kafka's *Penal Colony*, "We will only know the meaning of a legal proposition as it is engraved on our backs." Drucilla Cornell, *The Philosophy of the Limit* (New York: Routledge, 1992) 94.

68 John L. Austin, *How to Do Things with Words*, ed. J.O. Urmson and Marina Sbisà (Cambridge: Cambridge University Press, 1962).

69 Those seeking copyright protection are fated "to imitate an ever anterior, ever original gesture." Roland Barthes, *The Rustle of Language*, trans. Richard Howard (Oxford: Basil Blackwell, 1986) 53.

70 Gilles Deleuze, *Difference and Repetition*, trans. Paul Patton (New York: Columbia University Press, 1994), 3.

71 Among other forms are "Published according to a late Act" – i.e., *Slavery* (1738) and *Orator H-y laying the independent rump ghosts* (1746) – and "Published according to Law" – *The Scotchman fox'd, or, The lawyer outwitted* (1756) and *Iphigenia's late procession from Kingston to Bristol* (1776). Keenly aware of the practice followed by English engravers, the French engraver Hubert-François Gravelot, working in England from 1732 until 1745, includes the line "Entered According to Act of Parliament" in his design for *The Itinerant Handy-Craftsman or Caleb turn'd Tinker*, published in 1740. The English formulations were the precursors of the American designation "Entered according to Act of Congress," which, in 1802, became a requirement for copyright protection. The U.S. Copyright Act 1802 (Amendment of the 1790 Act). See *Primary Sources on Copyright (1450–1900)*, ed. L. Bently and M. Kretschmer, www.copyrighthistory.org.

72 F.G. Stephens, "Hogarth and the Pirates," *The Portfolio: An Artistic Periodical* 15 (1884): 2 and 4. The author further explains that "when [the

form 'Published as the Act directs'] came into vogue Parliament had vouchsafed to take upon itself the pretence of promising protection against robbers of artists' property, genius, earnings, or what not, the ownership of which that Act indicated, although it did not secure it against spoliation." Ibid., 4.

73 Ibid.

74 Gebhard Friedrich August Wendeborn, *A View of England Towards the Close of the Eighteenth Century*, 2 vols. (London, 1791), vol. 2, 216–17.

75 As Wendeborn comments, "very few of those who pay dearly for them" knew "any thing of the characters and transactions which occasioned such caricatures." Ibid., 213–14.

76 This is the case, for example, in a *View of Ranby's House* (1781), a relatively small print published by Jane Hogarth and representing the view of a cultivated field across Hogarth's house at Chiswick.

77 See *Primary Sources on Copyright (1450–1900)*, www.copyrighthistory.org/record/uk_1862.

4 Law and the Revolutionary Motif after Jacques-Louis David

MORGAN THOMAS

The notion of the motif in art is closely associated with Paul Cézanne. With regard to his studies of Mont Sainte-Victoire in Provence, for example, which he painted again and again at the end of his life, Cézanne would write of studying *sur le motif*. In Cézanne's pictorial system, the motif – the motive or motivation for making the picture, the thing attracting the painter's interest – was typically a figure, a scene, or an object.[1] The thing that began as an external motif became, in the process of painting, a pictorial motif. Yet the motif could sometimes be "internal" rather than "external," when it took the form of some "imaginary" subject matter, like a fantasy or vision, for example.[2] Cézanne was interested in the circuit of connections between the medium, the painter, and the motif of a picture. His idiosyncratic notion of the motif served his declared aims of "ridding the mind of the formulas of our illustrious predecessors" and "forgetting how things appeared before our time."[3] The eclipsing of the distance between subject and object implied in this conception of painting was an assault on a still pervasive academicism in art.

Cézanne's idea of the motif might invite us to consider the question of the relationship between the radical plasticity of pictorial modernism and the anterior motif – legal, historical, political – of a *revolutionary* transformation that is hardly containable within an aesthetic or pictorial frame. In the late eighteenth century, revolutionary art and thought already drew upon the notion of a radical form of judgment bent on "ridding the mind of the formulas of our illustrious predecessors" and an active forgetting of "how things appeared before our time." A revolution works towards practical ends, in particular the elusive goal of realizing an emancipatory vision of justice and law. It is a movement and a vision instituting an irruptive and consequential engagement with history and politics. Revolution, Paolo Viola writes, "is a political transformation, which has the constitution as its object. It is not only the control of political power, but a durable change in the structure of authority itself."[4]

Mostly unforeseen waves of insurgency and revolutionary activity have marked the last decade, for example with the so-called Arab Spring, yet in the cultural landscape of the affluent West the idea of revolution or of a revolutionary subjectivity seems to have little actual force or currency. Today a "motivational deficit" is said to plague contemporary life and revolution is conceivable only metaphorically, as a dream or gimmick.[5] By now, the "comic dimension" of any appeal to radicality in contemporary art and culture is even taken to be a consequence of the disjunction between the revolutionary qualities we regularly ascribe to artworks (regarding their formal qualities, degree of autonomy, and so on) and the political meaning of revolution.[6]

Yet there are historical occasions where the conjunction of revolution and visual art is no longer or not yet a joke. These occasions deserve attention, even if they attest to a revolutionary demand that is scarcely graspable in our present.[7] Before and after Cézanne, revolutions have consisted in unprecedented, excessive, and typically violent acts that mark and re-mark the limits of legitimacy and illegitimacy, sovereign and subject, inside and outside, imaginary and real. In an analogous way, the revolutionary motif in art recurrently touches on what is most contingent and groundless in modern forms of legality and judgment. If we want to see where revolutionary thought remains indispensable to concepts of justice and law and where it no longer speaks in the present, it is interesting to look again at significant moments of revolutionary art and visuality with special regard to their efficacy, complexity, and allure.

Here I focus on one motif, empty space or blankness, and one artist, Jacques-Louis David, whose path as a cultural and political figure between 1784 and 1793 exemplifies the legislative ambition of the French Revolution and the ethical and aesthetic questions that came with it. I argue that it is the quasi-emblematic figuration of absence, blankness, and material inconsistency at the centre of things, and, associated with this, the repeated enactment of a breakdown of vision and representation in David's artistic production, that stays with us today as the vital remainder of his revolutionary modernity. It is also possible,

I suggest, to discern points of resonance between the indeterminate yet distinctive spaces of David's paintings and other projects in the revolutionary period and the conjunction of revolutionary ideas and (non-) motifs of abstraction and invisibility in the work of contemporary artists operating outside or at the peripheries of the West today. Perhaps equally significant is the distance that separates the marginal cultural position of the revolutionary motif in contemporary life and the decisiveness, momentum, and all-or-nothing logic of this motif in the late eighteenth century.

Emblems of Law and Revolution

On 25 and 26 January 2011, Ahmed Basiony, one of a handful of digital media artists then active in Egypt, recorded silent video footage during the first and second nights of mass demonstrations in Tahrir Square in Cairo. Basiony was shot and killed by police when he returned to Tahrir Square to continue filming on 28 January. The footage he left behind remains raw material. In one sequence Basiony's camera pans to show the scale of the protests, in which over 700,000 people are thought to have participated. For half a minute it swings back and forth between the elated movements of a man who waves the national flag of Egypt in all directions from a high platform and the crowd watching below (figure 4.1).[8] In the hands of the flag-bearer and, again, in the frame of Basiony's viewfinder, the flag announces a form of popular authority and sovereignty that refuses the prevailing order while eliding its own precarious relation to existing laws and forms of political authority. In its affirmation of a new popular sovereignty – in situ, in Basiony's video recording – the flag becomes a screen onto which the captivated onlookers in the square, and others elsewhere, imaginatively project another destiny.

The French tricolour was designed in 1794, epoch of the Law of Suspects and the Terror, at the request of the revolutionary Convention. The flag's design is widely (yet not universally) attributed in France to David, a member of the revolutionary Convention and former painter to Louis XVI.[9] A consistently recognized national flag did not exist in France until the Revolution. In 1790, an earlier version of the tricolour – yet one that we would not recognize as the French flag today – had been introduced. It featured a band of white, flanked by red and blue, considered to be the colours of Paris and worn in the form of the cap or *cocarde* during the storming of the Bastille.

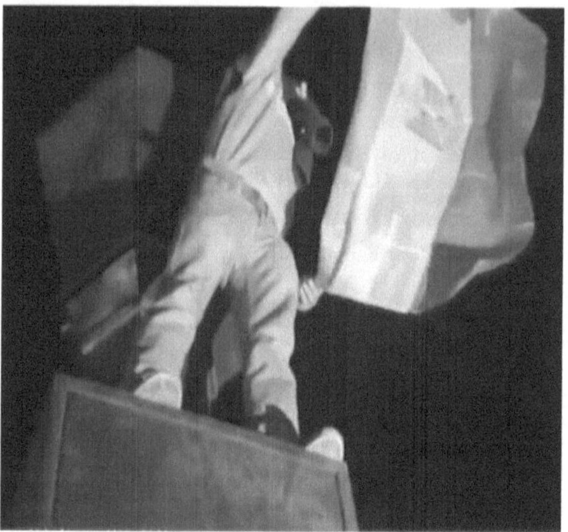

Figure 4.1 Ahmed Basiony, from a documentary video, 25–26 January 2011, Cairo. Video still. Courtesy of the Estate of Ahmed Basiony.

The 1794 modification to the 1790 flag makes a seemingly minor, yet decisive, change. David – if it was him – alters the order of the colours. Instead of running from left to right, red, to white, and then blue, the progression is now blue, white, and red. Why? Perhaps we can hypothesize that the additional resonances of the colours came into play. In the Western tradition the eye conventionally reads visual designs from left to right, as it does text. In most flag designs the wind, hypothetically, blows the same way. Blue, with yellow *fleurs-de-lys* interspersed through it, was emblematic of the Bourbon dynasty. All-red flags were far more visible than the tricolour during the Revolution. They were associated with the Jacobins' radical politics and the blood of revolutionary martyrs, which was also a running motif in David's work. From this point of view, the sequence signals a historical progression, a revolutionary movement. The blue recalled the Bourbons, and therefore the past. Paired with red, it evoked the city of Paris. A plain white flag had functioned as a symbol of France as far back as the fifteenth century. The new flag's white field in this sense anchors the design in France's history, yet perhaps also operates symbolically in other, more elusive ways. It interpellates an ellipsis into the composition, mediating the disparate intensities of the blue and red fields. The red, finally, recalls the all-red Jacobin flag and its Parisian provenance. It now signals the way the wind is blowing, a destiny. The flag of 1794 thus gives France a striking yet deeply resonant new face.[10]

The Tahrir Square footage and the revolutionary tricolour share several features. The tricolour's bold abstraction was a novelty when it was designed. Similarly, with its low-visibility, foregrounded framing, and digital format, Basiony's recording employs multiple modes of abstraction. The tricolour's colour sequence implies movement. Basiony's handheld camera moves and at the same time captures movement. Functionality is also vital. In the Cairo footage, the flag-bearer's gestures serve an almost choreographic purpose; the recording also exemplifies the role of digital media in making the protests in Cairo widely visible. Similarly, the tricolour served a ritual, legitimating function in the new Republic. On the other hand, regarding questions of authority, signature, and intentionality, both the flag and the video appear peculiarly ungrounded, like "sovereign accidents," to use Georges Didi-Huberman's formulation.[11] Neither presents itself *as* art. The most striking thing about them is their aporetic character, the potential energy they seem barely able to contain. In each case a certain blankness at the level of the signifier – a far-reaching indeterminacy, an opacity, an anonymity – is keyed to a situation in which a radical destabilization of forms of symbolic authority, including conventions of visual representation, takes place. If we think of the logic of the Kantian sublime, this type of communicative aporia – occasioned by a "negative" presentation, an iconoclasm, an "*absence* of form" – paradoxically "unbridles" the imagination, giving it "much to think." These non-presentations, if anything, run the risk of inciting *too much* emotion, *too much* enthusiasm, according to Kant.[12]

The French and Egyptian Revolutions invite reflection on questions of spectatorship and judgment because of the degree to which, like much modern art, they expressly set out to make a break with existing reality in order to construct a new reality, and because, like legal institutions, they appeal to ideas of justice in doing so. In the essay "What Is Enlightenment?" (1784), Kant praises revolutions for their capacity to bring down "power-seeking oppression," but dismisses the notion that they advance thought. New prejudices will come to take the place of older ones, he argues.[13] A decade later, in a famous passage from "The Conflict of the Faculties" (1795), and with the French Revolution in mind, Kant reflects on the ethics and aesthetics of the revolutionary spectacle:

> The revolution of a gifted people ... which we have seen unfolding in our day may succeed or it may miscarry; it may be filled with miseries and atrocities ... This revolution nevertheless finds in the hearts of all spectators (who are not engaged in the game itself) a wishful participation that borders closely on enthusiasm, the very expression of which is fraught with danger; this sympathy therefore, can have no other cause than a moral predisposition in the human race.[14]

Kant adds that the moral aspect of revolution comes from "the right of every people to give itself a civil constitution" and from the role of republican constitutions in promoting peace.[15] Significantly, as if anticipating the conflation of media and politics in the contemporary world, Kant touches on the slippery interval between spectatorship and participation in the face of events.

Kant's reflections on the French Revolution resonate with what is most modern in his thought – notably, his conception of the moral law, which he sometimes simply calls "the law." Gilles Deleuze has noted the structural affinity between Kant's "revolutionary" moral philosophy and the events that took place in his lifetime.[16] As with the new French Republic, the law, according to Kant, can no longer claim a higher authority or principle. It too must be understood as self-grounded – as an empty or pure form, the terms of its application indeterminate and its object "by definition unknowable and elusive."[17] Kant situates law and ethics in a close yet differential relation.[18]

The chain of non-sequiturs describing the pattern of international responses to the events in Egypt in 2011 might recall Kant's changes of outlook in response to the events in France. In the case of Egypt, however, media commentary focused on the pressing topic of who had seized control of – or "owned" – the narrative. The focus in global news outlets on the role of brands like Facebook and YouTube helped to domesticate the event. Yet even these shifts echo the rapid reframing of history during and after the French Revolution, particularly with Hegel's *Phenomenology of Spirit* (1807). Unlike Kant and at a greater distance from the event, Hegel saw the Revolution as *one* thing.[19] In Hegel's gripping narrative, the Tennis Court Oath exemplifies the Revolution's pervasive atmosphere of "unreality," its deathly power of negation, and overarching abstraction. Hegel's allusion to the Festival of the Supreme Being, organized by David and others in June 1794, is particularly damning. The "stale gas" of the "vacuous *Être suprême* ... hovers over the corpse of the vanished independence of real being," and over the "corpse of faith."[20] Yet this is a chapter in a grander story. For Hegel the shortcomings of the Revolution lead to a more concrete form of moral consciousness that seeks to function in a harmonious relation to nature and reality. The Revolution serves the narrative that Hegel wants to tell in the *Phenomenology of Spirit*, where its failings will be grasped and resolved by speculative philosophy.[21]

Hegel's commentary on the Revolution and his identification of the Terror with Kantian ethics have left their mark. Yet there are signs that this is not all there is to the Revolution or the thought and art associated with it. In *The Ethics of the Real*, Alenka Zupančič observes that the real pertinence of Kant's ethics lies in its interruptive character, its way of *not* fitting in with prevailing models. As she argues, Lacanian psychoanalysis can be allied with Kant's philosophy in this respect. In both cases ethics is structured around a radical absence – the empty form of the law (Kant), desire as lack of being or as the Other (Lacan) – whose defining characteristic is its non-assimilability into familiar understandings of selfhood, humanity, or community, or any substantive notion of the good.

In contrast to Hegel's system, where ethics is a matter of results and where judgments unfold retrospectively through a periodized accounting of historical progress, ethics retains an emphatically practical dimension in Kant's and Lacan's writings. As with the law in its most concrete and institutional manifestations, the question of what it is to act – and, in Kant's case, the agency of the will – lies at the heart of their rethinking of ethics. This absence or empty form becomes central to the ethical domain insofar as ethics entails an encounter with a law that *prescribes* nothing (Kant). On the subjective side of this encounter, the law in Kant, like Lacanian desire, is in principle universal yet it is also always idiomatic, a fiction whose content anyone subject to it must continually reinvent for him- or herself. From the side of objects and appearances, Lacan's notion of the Real describes a failure of symbolization, a "traumatic nothing" that shatters the reality principle that in everyday life constitutes the symbolic universe.[22] Events like the Tennis Court Oath, the execution of Louis XVI, the 2008 financial crisis, and much else besides, may seem inconceivable even after they have occurred. The Real correlates with the *impossible*. Zupančič writes:

> The Real happens to us (we encounter it) *as impossible*, as "the impossible thing" that turns our symbolic universe upside down and leads to the reconfiguration of the universe. Hence the impossibility of the Real does

> not prevent it from having effect in the realm of the possible. This is when ethics comes into play, in the question forced upon us by an encounter with the Real: will I act in conformity to what threw me "out of joint," will I be ready to reformulate what has hitherto been the foundation of my existence?[23]

As Zupančič notes, the radical movement implied in this encounter dissolves any clear demarcation between "subjective" and "objective" dimensions. The act or event in question eclipses any subject who could lay claim to it. Her point is relevant to the aporetic situation of symbolic and artistic authority in the event of revolution. These arguments concerning ethics and the event throw a different light on the imbrication of law, visuality, and revolution in the case of David's activities before and after 1789. What is taking place with the motif of "negative" presentation in his paintings and other works in the critical years beginning with *The Oath of the Horatii* in 1784, until 1794, the year of his arrest and imprisonment? What is it to look at David's artistic and cultural production today, long after its moment has passed?

Path of a Space

Empty space is a vital part of the studies and other remaining fragments of the largest pictorial project ever undertaken by David, an immense contemporary-history painting commemorating the Tennis Court Oath of 1789, commissioned in 1790 by the revolutionary Convention. The painting was supposed to mark the advent of a new revolutionary subjectivity in the form of the vow taken by all but one of the Third Estate's 577 deputies to continue meeting in defiance of the king. In a letter written to the president of the National Assembly in February 1792, David praised "our happy revolution" and remarked: "Never has any people's history offered me something as grand, as sublime, as this Tennis Court Oath, which I must paint."[24] The painting was never finished. While the ambition and failure of the venture leave many questions, it is particularly useful to investigate the place (or non-place) of empty space in two of the most important remnants of David's project – a pen-and-ink drawing of the planned painting, exhibited at the Salon of 1791 and widely circulated as a print, and a cut-down fragment of the unfinished canvas, showing a small fraction of the scene David had envisaged.

David's drawing offers the clearest indication of his overall conception of the picture. It also reveals the difficulty of his task. Jean

Starobinski has commented that in this scene an "abstract" tension between the pictorial whole and its parts displaces the dramatic tension of David's pre-revolutionary paintings due to the sheer number of figures.[25] The sea of deputies becomes a sprawling Hobbesian body trapped in an atmosphere oscillating awkwardly between enthusiasm and calm, according to Antoine de Baecque.[26] Yet the expansive space in the top half of the picture and the figural energy around its edges, where disparate groups witness the moment, lifts the tableau beyond these limitations. The curtain billowing into the deep interior from the top left, and the ray of light that accompanies it, bring a baroque dynamism into the tableau. The light reveals the building's wear and tear and at the same time creates a hallowed space. The wind, once again, is a sign of destiny. The unadorned architecture offers a contemplative reprieve from the activity on the ground, suggesting, perhaps, that mundane, unlikely locations like this are where true events occur. The scaled-up space encourages ideas of liberty and emancipation. Like a blank canvas or screen, the space at the top and back of the picture seems to refract the disparate attitudes of the actors and onlookers in the tableau. Through this outward orientation, with this wall that faces us, David draws the viewer in turn into the vortex of revolutionary enthusiasm that is the real subject of the scene.

The best-known fragment of David's unfinished painting of the *Oath* (dated 1791–2) was cut out of the original seven-by-ten-metre canvas in 1826 and is now in the collection of the Château de Versailles.

Here empty space takes on a different complexion. Meticulously executed portraits of several deputies float in a vast, ghostly, sepia- and cream-coloured world. Thirteen faint, partially sketched bodies are visible. They are clothed and unclothed, sometimes idealized and classicized, sometimes depicted with unsparing realism, as if the picture's parodic subject were the Revolution as a missed appointment. By mid-1792, many of the deputies featured in the picture had been discredited and the revolution David wanted to celebrate was no longer "happy," to use his word. A pervasive blankness – an absence of work – underscores the asynchrony between the painstaking, incremental time of academic history painting and the disjunctive tempo of revolution. The picture in this way anticipates the provisional view of reality and art that informs the work of painters like Manet or Cézanne. Yet David's differences from these later artists – and notably the peculiar degree to which he was imbricated in the events he painted and at their mercy – are significant. In August 1792, parts of his canvas

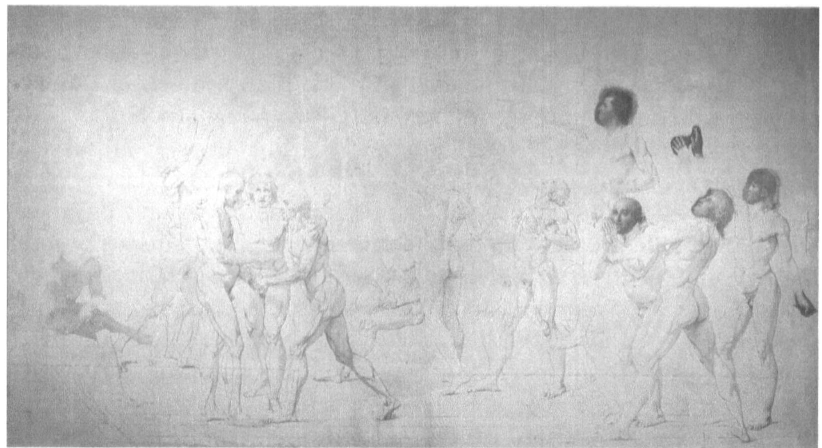

Figure 4.2 Jacques-Louis David, *The Oath of the Tennis Court* (unfinished), 1791. Châteaux de Versailles et de Trianon. © RMN-Grand Palais / Art Resource, NY.

were peppered with bayonet holes after a face-off between revolutionaries and Swiss Guards in his studio. Here it is interesting to think of the Italian post-war artist Lucio Fontana, who famously cut holes and slashes in his work to underscore its spatial existence. The different status of David's canvas – punctured with holes not by design but force of circumstance – becomes apparent. Unlike Fontana's fully realized work, it comes alive as a series of accidents which are scarcely willed or authored. It is an event even before it is an artwork.

Popular engravings were crucial models for David when he worked on his Tennis Court Oath project. In this sense the project marks a critical shift in the operation of his authorship and signature during the Revolution. That signature is no longer the sign of something individual. It has become, as Norman Bryson notes, "an incidental nomination, an inflection of *public* visuality."[27] The shift is particularly marked in the case of the revolutionary festivals that David staged, where it is clearly not a question of artworks but one of events attracting animated crowds in the hundreds of thousands. Classicism was still the leitmotif. In the first of his festivals, the Festival of Liberty (15 April 1792), participation took precedence over spectatorship, in keeping with Rousseau's view that such events should follow the Greek model. David made the popular procession the centrepiece of his festivals. Another trademark was his use of emblems whose meanings were relatively accessible – statues of Liberty, the *bonnet rouge*, tables of law (among them the Declaration of the Rights of Man). David's great success as a propagandist seems to have been driven by the relatively pragmatic, realist, and relational orientation of his festival aesthetics, as opposed to the allegorical symbolism favoured by his monarchist political adversary, Quatremère de Quincy.[28] As a riposte to David's very popular and apparently disorderly Festival of Liberty, in June 1792 Quatremère, also using tables of law as props, staged a call for a "return to order" in the form of a Festival of Law. The Festival of Law did not win crowds. The most notorious of David's festivals, the Festival of the Supreme Being (8 June 1794), incorporated a procession of 200,000 people, an artificial mountain (a Jacobin emblem), and the inauguration of a new civic religion (another Rousseauian trope). In a key moment, Robespierre set a giant papier-maché statue of Atheism alight and called for the disappearance of "all the miseries and evils of the world." This festival was the "apex of the Jacobin regime [and] the most brilliant and popular of all the fêtes of the Revolution," according to David Dowd.[29] It is not difficult to see why, fifteen years later, Hegel saw it as a sign of the Revolution's fatal negativity. Yet David was apparently sanguine about the ridicule his festivals attracted. He countered criticisms by alluding to the festival as a popular genre that worked through clarity, not subtlety.

In truth the revolutionary festival relocates the soul of contemporary life – not through the institution of any new religion, but in the rituals that it invents, rituals that set out to constitute a new body politic.[30] Ludicrous as the festival's staged disappearing act may have been, it instituted a new type of public space that contributed to a larger venture. Empty space acts here to quell fears and stir the collective imagination, succeeding as a paradoxical form of civic spectacle. David's capacity to stage-manage large-scale events may have motivated Napoleon's later efforts to recruit him to his promotional entourage. According to Dowd, the rhetorical power and mass mobilization of David's festivals created a template for the aestheticized politics of twentieth-century fascism and communism.[31] Their regenerative neoclassicism prefigures the modes of presentation that remain pervasive in the populist staging of politics today.

David's best-known empty space appears in his picture of the dying Jean-Paul Marat. Less well known is the close connection between this painting and David's work as an elected deputy at the revolutionary Convention and his work orchestrating popular festivals. His *Marat assassiné*, which now occupies the pristine environment of the Musée Modern Museum in Brussels, was painted in 1793 for the hall of the Convention, as a pendant to David's portrait of another revolutionary martyr, Michel Le Pelletier. David had visited Marat at the request of the Convention shortly before his assassination and later staged an elaborate funeral for him at the deconsecrated Church of the Cordeliers in Paris over three days, between 14 and 16 July. These events are central to the painting's genealogy. The details that David reportedly saw during his visit – bath, writing accoutrements, wooden box – are pictured with a quasi-hallucinatory realism. The painting was carried in Marat's funeral procession. Its sublime effect acts particularly through the contiguity of these intimate, nearly tangible "facts" and another reality – the space above the dying figure. The empty yet painterly upper section of *Marat assassiné* perpetuates the improvisational character of the scumbled grounds (*frottis*) in many of David's portraits. The "bottom floor" of the painting offers a partisan, moralizing narrative detailing the exemplary generosity and virtue of its subject in a normative mode. Its "upper floor" drifts away from this normativity, departicularizing and universalizing it. The painting embodies a movement, an inflection, *between* the particular and the universal, between visual representation and an empty yet ineluctably material state of indeterminacy.

Here David's classicism cedes to a baroque pictorialism looking for a communication between incommensurable zones of finite and infinite, as if the affective intensity and proselytizing energy of Caravaggio or Bernini has invaded the picture. There is the foregrounding of two systems of measuring time, a style of dating (*1793*, which appears twice) newly coded as old and another (*l'An II*) that has barely begun. There is the painting's interweaving of modes of address: more than a recitation of contemporary history, the painting speaks impossibly in the second person ("À MARAT, DAVID") at the same time that it performs an act of testimony. There is David's presentation of the dying Marat, not only on the threshold of life and death, neither definitively alive nor dead, but also, in contrast to his usual practice, as an androgynous, almost feminized figure. David's related painting of another martyr, the young, nude Joseph Bara, begun shortly after his *Marat*, exhibits a similar but more eroticized androgyny. With their prone, unconscious or barely conscious bodies, these paintings are as close to Bernini's *Ecstasy of Saint Theresa* as to Caravaggio's *Entombment*, with which the *Marat* is sometimes compared. Not a hero or a historical subject in the mode of the Horatii, neither dead nor alive, Marat's fragile person becomes an unconditional figure of evanescent presence. The relationship between the material, fluid, quasi-infinite space of the upper section and the relative realism of the rest of the painting correlates with these other manifestations of a threshold that is simultaneously historical, spatial, and corporeal. The relation between the finite and the infinite becomes the picture's critical point of tension and its subject.

Like David's use of forms of direct address in this and other works (*À Marat*, *À Lepelletier*), the non-representational space in his *Marat* exposes the time of the work's making to the viewer's time, drawing the viewer into the constitution of the work in a new way. The painting does not vacillate between realism and idealism so much as tie the infinite and the finite into a fast knot. It cultivates an out-of-joint temporality where, to use Zupančič's expression, the infinite *parasitizes* the finite. The infinite is now an element of reality, a fact of life. In this painting, like the fictive *as if* of Kant's categorical imperative, it is an "ineradicable stain," a thing "that ceaselessly pursues us."[32] David's blank, painterly space institutes a conception of the world of the picture, and, by implication, the world outside it, as one that is constitutively incomplete.

Unlike the alignment of empty space with emancipatory ideals in the *Oath of the Tennis Court* project, the muddy – as well as empty – space of David's *Marat* may appear suspect, to use the idiom of the time. T.J. Clark has claimed *Marat assassiné* – which was painted very fast – as the first modernist painting on account of its rhetorical deployment of material abstraction as a sign of revolutionary good faith. Perhaps David's more informal mode of painting was meant to suggest freshness and currency, like the Rousseauian trope of naturalness inspiring the vogue for quasi-rustic attire among the well-to-do. But the antecedents to the space in David's *Marat* lie his grand history paintings of the previous decade.

Writing of David's *Oath of the Horatii* (1784) as the most revealing expression of a subject that consumed late-eighteenth-century life and politics, Jean Starobinski notes the contradictions inherent in the modern oath as a common utterance aiming to institute sovereignty and future law "in the exaltation of a moment."[33] The oath is a contract, a kind of binding promise that sets its sights on the future but makes use of mythic, ritualized forms hypothetically deriving from ancient models. It places civic duty and a generalized will before any pleasure, care, or interest. With this first *Oath*, drawing on Livy's account of the founding of Rome, David invents a moment that exemplifies these things. The young Horatii, on one side, resemble freeze-frames of a single body in motion. They look to the swords that their father, in the centre, raises in the air. The grieving women on the other side embody what the brothers have renounced. No one in the picture makes eye-contact with anyone else. In 1785 the non-communication of the groups was seen as a departure from conventions of pictorial unity. Its repercussions persist in recent readings where David's composition represents "virile will" or, alternatively, offers a "tragic image" of the violence of patriarchal law. Yet the critical lesson is perhaps this deadlock – and the clinical precision with which the point of maximum tension between the figural groupings and what they metonymize is presented.

Just as its pictorial classicism refuses the blandishments of rococo art, the players in the drama remain oblivious to the spectator. David, like Diderot, seems to espouse an anti-theatrical, almost dream-like philosophy of painting. The world of the picture is a world unto itself. *The Oath of the Horatii* thus breaks with current models and claims a certain autonomy vis-à-vis its audience. Furthermore, to recall Bryson's account of the painting, the strangeness of the *Oath*'s pictorial space seems to result from a conflation of two scarcely compatible spatial systems. As Bryson writes, here it is as if the planar space of the sculptural frieze associated with classical art has been pasted over the perspectival depth of the Renaissance *veduta*.[34] Everything happens in the foreground of a shallow, stage-like space, yet the focal point of the scene, the flash of the clasped swords, opens onto a troubling darkness, triggering an effect like horizontal vertigo. The deep void at the back of the *Oath*, like the dark tunnel in David's *Death of Socrates*, painted shortly after it, opens a space of radical invisibility. Whether or not David in the 1780s deliberately adopted Diderot's precept that paintings should be blind to the presence of their public, the dark matter at the back of this painting is one of the great exemplifications of the blind, inhuman gaze in art. Here the void which conveys the force of an unconscious law is also the picture's vanishing point. It is the source of the scene of induction into modern subjectivity playing out in the foreground, yet it also cuts into the scene, making it less than whole.[35] Even without overt political motivation or reference to contemporary events, *The Oath of the Horatii* is, in a way, the most revolutionary of David's paintings.

When it was exhibited in 1785, the *Oath* instituted a change in how things appeared. In the 1790s it became a symbol of revolution. Acting on its moment as well as through a mode of deferred action, the painting illuminated the pivotal place of an absence, a blindness, at the centre of things. If the *Oath* is seen as marking the beginning of modern painting or as a truly "revolutionary" event,[36] it is not only because it challenged taste, but because it profoundly altered taste – tying aesthetics to modern subjectivity and ancient law – and because its new vision of law contributed in incalculable ways to a new order of thought.

The last space that I shall consider does not actually appear. David painted his *View of the Gardens of the Luxembourg Palace* in late 1794, during a term of imprisonment following the fall of the Jacobins in July of that year. David completed several smaller-scale works in jail. A mute first-person testimony seems to surface in this work. The painting is small. We look down on what could almost be a pastoral scene, showing gardens, paths, and lines of trees, a semi-ordered nature. The autumnal colours couple dullness with chromatic intensity. The large expanse of a fenced-off field – an almost empty space – occupies the foreground. Two stray figures, and a group tilling the ground in the middle distance, almost disappear into their surroundings. The scene is usually thought to have been painted from a prison window; the high viewpoint has a disorienting effect. The uneventfulness and prosaic vacancy of the scene, coupled with its odd vantage-point, almost seem designed to turn our attention around 180 degrees towards what is outside the frame – to the space that, outside the view, constitutes the view. We sense something that resists symbolization, yet which is all the more real for that – a desolation, or, to recall David's self-characterization at this time, a state of "total abandonment."[37] Made in the immediate aftermath of the Revolution, the painting evokes a state of subjective destitution yet maintains the fundamental structure of the encounter that runs through David's painting in this period.

In painting the fact of his captivity and punishment, David seems to assent to the "reality principle" and to concede the failure of his dream of revolutionary freedom and justice. But to look at the painting is to think precisely of what it does *not* show: the legally prescribed restriction of the space of visibility, the unwavering gaze of the exterior facing the cell's occupant. To paint this is also to puncture a hole in it. The void thus turns vertiginously outward. It encircles the viewer as much as the painter, as if "infinitizing" this captive condition. The so-called reality of the prison view, determined by law, is now a fiction. It is not only a punishment but a threshold, to be encountered and shared by all of us.

Acts

The abject version of David's legacy was already under way with Hegel's excoriation of the Festival of the Supreme Being. In 1837 Thomas Carlyle took up the theme, dwelling particularly on David's speech impediment and facial disfigurement in connection with his move from art to acts of legislation during the Revolution. Similarly, T.J. Clark's text on *Marat assassiné* embeds the painting in the micropolitics of the Jacobins' strategic investment in the Marat cult and the particularly "chilling" and "horrifying" aspects of David's activities.[38] In Clark's reading, David's strictly Jacobin painting strained to brand a bourgeois Revolution with a popular mandate. Ewa Lajer-Burcharth classifies her account of David's paintings in the late 1790s and beyond as psycho-cultural, dealing with "gender, not class." She investigates the operations of narcissism and of a disavowed femininity concealed in the paintings' heroic mythologies. Jean-Claude Lebenstejn has argued, however, that her framing of David constitutes a "partial depoliticization of an important cultural phenomenon."[39] Lajer-Burcharth's reading is not neutral, he argues. It appears in precise locations, namely, the privileged and safe arenas of elite academic institutions. The same could perhaps be said of Clark's use of social history in his account of David. In the wake of Hegel, art history has difficulty escaping modes of narration in which it is assumed that the narrator, in the present, has the better of the past. It still feels compelled to master its objects.

David became a pivotal figure because he was exceptionally receptive to the momentum of events. Close attention to his paintings and projects of this period indicates the possibility that this receptivity was, if only in part, propelled by a desire for justice and a new system of laws. The best exemplification of the infectious wave of enthusiasm that captured David's thought is his work for the unfinished *The Tennis Court Oath* and the enthusiasm in the picture as he conceived it. An aesthetic intensification overtakes his paintings between 1784 and 1794, but hardly outlives this period. The void that runs through his paintings and other projects during the Revolution, however, inscribed differently each time, can be identified with the ethical notion of an irruption of the infinite *in* the finite – whether this takes the form of the oath, a papier-maché sculpture in flames, the hiatus of death, the vanishing point behind vision, or, most starkly, a marking of the exterior to a place of confinement. The motif of the void in David's work underscores the constitutive place of a lack, a failure, a frailty, at the centre of every scene of (visual, legal, political) representation with a singular vividness.

The *View of the Gardens of the Luxembourg Palace* appears different because of the seemingly candid testimony it offers of its time and place. Yet is not this equally true of a painting like the *Marat*, *The Oath of the Horatii*, or the various versions of *The Oath of the Tennis Court*? In each case, no matter how far each departs from so-called reality, whether through rhetorical manoeuvres, elements of abstraction, idealization, stage props, or classical references, the work bears witness to its moment, and specially to the "unreal" aspects of that moment. David's participatory revolutionary projects, suspending conventional notions of artistic authorship, also play out a logic of encounter. The question becomes one of the relation between the act of testimony and the form of the encounter that is taking place.

In Hegel's philosophy, the post-revolutionary moment, marked by a distrust of the distancing effects of vision and of aesthetics in general, demanded a full imbrication in community. It left "no room for spectators," Rebecca Comay writes.[40] By contrast, in his political writings Kant points to sometimes subtle, sometimes confusing distinctions between looking, wishing, and acting in the event of revolution, sliding between a spectatorship "bordering closely on enthusiasm" and a "wishful participation" in the event on the part of those who are "not engaged" in it. Today these hesitations have a certain pertinence with regard to the ambiguous place of many artists and non-artists, whose thinking, curiously, is closer to David's, with its shuffling and elision of roles, its play of distances, absences, visibility and invisibility, and empty spaces.

When eight members of the anonymous Russian feminist collective Pussy Riot began to perform their "punk prayer" against the rule of Vladimir Putin at the altar of a Moscow cathedral of in 2012, they adopted a protective form of camouflage, including bright balaclavas that masked their faces. The video of the performance, which quickly captured worldwide attention – a sign of the group's courage, or evidence of its criminality – used less than a minute of footage of their action in the cathedral, spliced together with footage recorded later in another church. A photograph of Ahmed Basiony in 2011 shows him fully camouflaged, wearing goggles and protective clothing, for one of his last visits to Tahrir Square. Basiony's background as an artist had been in painting, but he was also a musician, and his recent work combined performance with abstract screen-based video installation – investigating the interface between physical movement and the abstraction of digital transcriptions of movement. Messages left by Basiony on social media, invoking ideas of peace and dignity, attest to his "wishful" participation in the protests. He went to Tahrir Square with the purpose of filming the event, probably for a future artwork, at a time when he would have known that filming the event was a dangerous way to participate in it.

It is difficult to draw clear lines between testimony, spectatorship, and participation, wishful or otherwise, in these cases. There is an intertwining, yet not a dissolution, of these categories. Some of the members of Pussy Riot have spoken of the liberating anonymity that came with their masks and costumes. Like the empty spaces in David's paintings, their camouflage opens an aporetic space in which the stakes of justice can be thought, in which questions of ethics – before and against the law – infiltrate of the scene of aesthetic judgment. Looking at Basiony's posthumous video of the events in Cairo, we are intensely aware of what is missing from the frame. Like David's nearly innocuous landscape, Basiony's testimony is overtaken by a mute force – an obscurity, a silence, yet also a brutal reality – at the limits of law and the limits of the image. Across these moments, what is constant is an act that, practising a form of testimony with regard to the present, draws the aesthetic, ethical, and legal senses of the word into a productive tension. In each case a certain nothingness, attesting to an encounter between art and ethics, acts to revolutionize law and thought.

NOTES

1 In English the word "motif" refers to a repeated figure or pattern. *Le motif* in French conveys the notion of a desire or motivation.

2 This is noted in Richard Shiff, "Sensation, Movement, Cézanne," in Terence Maloon, ed., *Classic Cézanne*, exh. cat. (Sydney: Art Gallery of New South Wales, 1998), 21.

3 Cézanne to Émile Bernard, letters of 1905 (undated) and 23 October 1905, cited in Shiff, "Sensation, Movement, Cézanne," 27 n. 21.

4 Paolo Viola, "What Revolution Means and What It Meant in 1789," *History of European Ideas* 14 (1992): 39.

5 See Simon Critchley, *Infinitely Demanding: Ethics of Commitment, Politics of Resistance* (New York: Verso, 2007), 7, and Alain Badiou, "Considerations on Law, Revolution, and Mathematics," in *Controversies: A Dialogue on the*

Politics and Philosophy of Our Times, ed. A. Badiou and Jean-Claude Milner (Cambridge, UK, and Malden, MA: Polity, 2014), 124–5.

6 See Carolyn Christov-Bakargiev, "Revolutions – Forms That Turn: The Impulse to Revolt," in *Revolutions – Forms That Turn: 2008 Biennale of Sydney*, exh. cat. (Fishermans Bend, Vic.: Biennale of Sydney and Thames and Hudson, 2008), 33.

7 Badiou, "Considerations on Law, Revolution, and Mathematics," 124.

8 See "Ahmed Basiouny – Thirty Days Running in the Place," FACT, Liverpool, 2011, https://www.youtube.com/watch?v=T2GRpvn6-OM.

9 I keep to the tradition of ascribing the flag's redesign to David, although the attribution, which goes back at least to Alphonse de Lamartine's legal measures to protect the tricolour in 1848, is unproven. See also Elodie Derdaele, "Le Drapeau tricolore, un symbole constitutionnel dans tous ses états (du droit)," *Politéa* 19 (Spring 2011): 415–506, and Michel Pastoureau, *Les emblèmes de la France* (Paris: Bonneton, 1998), 105–15.

10 Yet an alternative reading of the French flag might place less emphasis on the dramatic, destinal implication of the red field in the redesigned version and instead (in a more Hegelian mode) accent the negative force of the white field, which takes centre-stage in both 1790 and 1794 versions.

11 Georges Didi-Huberman, *Confronting Images: Questioning the Ends of a Certain History of Art*, trans. John Goodman (University Park: Penn State University Press, 2005), 264.

12 Immanuel Kant, *Critique of Judgement* (Oxford: Clarendon Press, 1989), 127–8.

13 Immanuel Kant, "An Answer to the Question: What Is Enlightenment?" in *Kant's Political Writings*, trans. H.B. Nisbet (Cambridge: Cambridge University Press, 1970), 55.

14 Kant, *The Conflict of the Faculties*, trans. M.J. Gregor (New York: Abaris Books, 1979), 153.

15 Ibid.

16 Gilles Deleuze, "Coldness and Cruelty," in Gilles Deleuze, *Masochism: Coldness and Cruelty & Venus in Furs* (New York: Zone Books, 1991), 83. See also Rebecca Comay, *Mourning Sickness: Hegel and the French Revolution* (Stanford: Stanford University Press, 2010), 44.

17 Deleuze, "Coldness and Cruelty," 83.

18 See Alenka Zupančič, *Ethics of the Real: Kant, Lacan* (London: Verso, 2000), 12: "In relation to legality, the ethical always presents a surplus or excess." For another view of the relation between justice and law, see Peter Goodrich, "The Iconography of Nothing: Blank Spaces and the Representation of Law in Edward VI and the Pope," in *Law and the Image:*

The Authority of Art and the Aesthetics of Law, ed. Costas Douzinas and Lynda Nead (Chicago: University of Chicago Press, 1999), 112–14.
19 Comay, *Mourning Sickness*, 74.
20 G.W.F. Hegel, *Phenomenology of Spirit*, trans. A.V. Miller (Oxford: Oxford University Press, 1976), 358.
21 Ibid., 605.
22 Zupančič, *Ethics of the Real*, 235.
23 Ibid.
24 Jacques-Louis David, letter dated 5 February 1792, in Philippe Bordes, *Le Serment du Jeu de Paume de Jacques-Louis David: Le peintre, son milieu et son temps de 1789 à 1792* (Paris: Réunion des musées nationaux, 1983), 164–6.
25 See Jean Starobinski, *1789: The Emblems of Reason*, trans. Barbara Bray (Cambridge, MA: MIT Press, 1988), 110.
26 Antoine de Baecque, "Le Serment du Jeu de Paume: Le corps du politique idéal," in Régis Michel, ed., *David contre David*, vol. 2 (Paris: Louvre, 1993), 778–9.
27 Norman Bryson, *Tradition and Desire: From David to Delacroix* (New York: Cambridge University Press, 1984), 87.
28 See the differing accounts of David Lloyd Dowd, *Pageant-master of the Republic: Jacques-Louis David and the French Revolution* (Freeport, NY: Books for Libraries Press, 1948) and Mona Ozouf, *Festivals and the French Revolution*, trans. Alan Sheridan (Cambridge, MA: Harvard University Press, 1988).
29 Dowd, *Pageant-master of the Republic*, 123.
30 On this question, see Bryson, *Tradition and Desire*, 86.
31 This is Dowd's claim: see *Pageant-master of the* Republic, 123.
32 Zupančič, *Ethics of the Real*, 248. David's painting seems to place Marat as a hostage to the vision of morality and justice to which many republicans, Marat and David included, upheld at this time, as much as to the reactionary politics of their foes.
33 Starobinski, *1789: The Emblems of Reason*, 102.
34 On this, see again Bryson, *Tradition and Desire*, 76–80.
35 Michael Fried, "David et l'antithéâtralité," in Régis Michel, ed., *David contre David*, vol. 1 (Paris: Louvre, 1993) 207. Fried and Bryson dispute one another's accounts of David, yet their readings of the paintings are closer and more complementary to one another than they initially appear.
36 See Michael Fried, *Absorption and Theatricality: Painting and Beholder in the Age of Diderot* (Berkeley: University of California Press, 1980), 136–7, and Starobinski, "Lecture – Interprétation des images de 89," *Art Press*, Hors série no. 9: Révolution culturelle française, December 1988: 97.

37 David's phrase in a letter dated 8 November 1794 (no. 1143 in Daniel and Guy Wildenstein, *Documents complémentaires au catalogue de l'oeuvre de Louis David* (Paris: Fondation Wildenstein, 1973), 116.

38 See T. J. Clark, "Painting in the Year 2," in T.J. Clark, *Farewell to an Idea: Episodes from a History of Modernism* (London and New Haven: Yale University Press, 1999), 52. For a critique of discourses on the Terror and its "intolerability," see in particular Sophie Wahnich, *In Defence of the Terror: Liberty or Death in the French Revolution*, trans. David Ferbach (London and New York: Verso, 2012). Wahnich's case recalls arguments for the use of military power against Germany leading into the Second World War.

39 Jean-Claude Lebensztejn, review of Ewa Lajer-Burcharth, "Necklines: The Art of Jacques-Louis David after the Terror," *The Art Bulletin* 83, no. 1 (2001): 156.

40 Comay, *Mourning Sickness*, 138.

5 Legal Imagery on the Edge of Symbolism: The Decoration Projects for the Belgian Cour de Cassation[1]

STEFAN HUYGEBAERT

For over half a millennium, courtrooms in the Low Countries have been artistically decorated and, as such, their walls document many transitions in both art and law. This article is concerned with the Belgian fin de siècle around 1900, which constitutes a transitional era in art, with the rise of symbolism, and law, with a legal avant-garde advocating for new law. The focus lies on the Cour de Cassation, Belgium's supreme court, and the decoration projects and plans for its two main rooms inside the enormous Palais de Justice (1866–83) in Brussels, designed by architect Joseph Poelaert. On the left side of the Palais's impressive façade, a projecting part conceals the huge Solemn Room of the Cour de Cassation, used only for its yearly opening session and other ceremonial activities.[2] A hallway filled with busts of lawyers connects it with the smaller Ordinary Session Room of the Cour, where day-to-day sessions are held. The decoration history of both rooms so far has only been looked at fragmentarily, whilst much can be drawn from the letters kept at the General Archives of Belgium.

This paper questions what courtroom decoration is for, and what it should *do*. Belgium's fin-de-siècle artistic, political, and legal world presents an interesting case study for two reasons. First, its legal, political, and artistic avant-garde scenes were headed by one and the same group of lawyers; and second, wall decoration was treated in two very different ways, each of which linked its own objective to the decoration type and its use in courtrooms. The more traditional historical-realist wall painting aimed at national education by looking at the past, through (legal) history. Contrarily, symbolist wall painting, such as the works commissioned for the Commercial Court and the Cour d'Assises, also housed in the Palais, aimed at a spiritual education or mental edification by depicting an ideal of law and justice.

Scrutinizing the arguments and actors within the debate on the decoration of the two rooms reveals the relationship between artistic and aesthetic change and law's ambition. The argument between historical realism and symbolism is one between old and new, between cautious conservatism and determined modernism, and ultimately between two different views on law's ambition.

Tracing the debate and history of these courtroom decorations tells us about law and its representation as apotropaic and archaic, on the one hand, and affective, on the other hand. The resulting compromise, as can still be seen today, reveals the balanced cautiousness in a country's supreme court, where even absent images and gaping voids tell more than their decision makers intended.

A Call for Symbolist Courtroom Decorations ... and New Law

When will we see our rooms and vestibules filled with scaffoldings of artists working on the site, like the old masters? ... Nothing arouses artistic temperament more than great works of art. It is the best national education.[3]

It is hard not to recognize the spirit of Edmond Picard (1836–1924) in this call for national education through the decoration of Brussels's Palais de Justice, anonymously published in the *Journal des Tribunaux* in 1899. Picard's importance for the Belgian legal and artistic world can hardly be overemphasized. He was a leading figure of both the legal and artistic scene in Belgium: he was an *avocat* and since 1880 a member of the bar of the Cour de Cassation, a senator for the socialist party from 1894, a novelist, and a patron of the arts. Among his numerous initiatives were the founding of both the *Journal des Tribunaux* and *L'Art Moderne* in 1881, key periodicals in law and art, respectively.[4] Both journals had more or less the same group of artistically interested lawyers on their editorial board.

Writing about Belgian fin-de-siècle lawyers such as Picard and Henri Carton de Wiart, Debora Silverman uses the term "juridical modernism," but omits to define this neologism. Bart Coppein's research on Picard's legal thinking is clarifying for the matter – although Picard's views should not be overly generalized. Picard's call for new law was threefold, as suffrage required generalization, justice needed socialization, and the law needed vulgarization. This meant a fight against the old threshold system and the general multiple suffrage installed in 1893, in favour of a "one man, one vote" principle. He interpreted the social situation of the working class as a legal issue, arguing that the government should intervene legally in order to defend the weak and emancipate the working class. This would bring change in the paternalistic old order, and, ultimately, "socialize" justice, to use Picard's words. In order to do so, the law had to be explained and spread, and the *Journal des Tribunaux* was thus both a practitioner's journal and a vulgarizing legal periodical for the broad audience, or this was at least the objective.[5]

What's important to emphasize in this paper is that Picard and his like-minded professional colleagues interpreted the vulgarization of art in the same way.[6] Although emanating from a bourgeois background themselves, they did not care for art for art's sake. Likewise, these lawyers closely followed the Palais de Justice's construction. In 1911, Picard founded Les Amis du Palais (The Friends of the Palace), which promoted the decoration of Belgium's courthouses. One of their main objectives was improving the Palais de Justice's artistic and aesthetic condition. The building's interior decoration had been a concern for many years.[7] When the 1899 article was published, the Ordinary Session Room of the Cour de Cassation had already been decorated with tapestries, while the decoration of the Solemn Room was still being debated.

The discussions on courtroom decoration uncover an intriguing history of the connection of art and law in a transitional era. With the rise of symbolism, the artistic vision on the decoration of a public building, such as Poelaert's Palais de Justice, shifted. Picard's 1899 article referred with approval to the commissioning of Xavier Mellery (1845–1921) to decorate the Commercial Court inside the Palais. Mellery was one of Belgium's principal symbolist artists and Picard's protégé. Already in 1892, an article in *L'Art Moderne* called for Mellery to decorate the Palais de Justice, since he alone was seen fit to express the ideal of justice. In the eyes of *L'Art Moderne*, the artist's task was twofold, as his decorations had to soften, light, and complete the austere, dark, and unfinished *Palais*, while the artist himself needed to guide the beholder to sublime ideals, which were to be found in the lofty domains of the mind or soul.[8] Mellery's symbolist allegory for the Commercial Court, entitled *The Genius of Trade*, was never realized, but its conception was similar to a poster he designed and reused for an international gathering of lawyers in Brussels in 1894.[9] Both portrayed evocative interacting personifications within an allegory of ideal law.

A similar kind of allegory was used by Jean Delville (1867–1953), another Belgian symbolist heavy-weight, in his decorations for the Cour d'Assises in Poelaert's building. In line with Delville's idealist principles, his decorative paintings featured a double juxtaposition. A terrifying image of Moses stopping two men from killing each other ("Thou shalt not kill") hung opposite an image of Christ visiting convicted felons. Equally, *Old Law* was evoked by means of an enthroned and hooded man torturing a convict, in contrast to *New Law*, a modern magistrate with the face of a former minister of justice, Jules Le Jeune (1828–1911), accompanied by a personification of science. In the central allegory, titled *Ideal Justice*, on the wall opposite the judges, a winged Justice was flanked by Compassion and the Law.[10]

These kind of decorations were, according to the *Journal des Tribunaux*, far from redundant. On the contrary, they served a specific purpose:

> The *décor* acts so profoundly upon us. There is a mysterious link between the minds and their familiar retreat. What comes about in a beautiful and complete environment comes out beautiful and complete. And for those who desire for all things the correction of a perfect justice, they must start by educating their mind. The *décor* in which they will live is the first of these duties and worries. By persistently harmonizing the very environment and themselves, making it more beautiful and perfect, they themselves will come out more noble and just.[11]

By means of this call for decorative art to serve didactic ends, the author of the 1899 article was not proposing an entirely innovative idea. Half a millennium earlier, indeed, in a description of local customary law in a small Dutch town called Den Briel, Jan Matthijssen wrote how courtrooms should be decorated. "The courtroom will be made clean inside and filled with paintings and written with good old wise words, from which one can acquire wisdom and cleverness, as one says: to see is to think."[12] Thus, the goal of these two types of courtroom decoration, paintings and words, was to provoke wisdom and insight by means of visual confrontation. The citation refers to late-medieval and early-modern use of *exempla justitiae*, artworks commissioned by aldermen and magistrates as courtroom decorations. In 1525, for example, Jan Provoost (c. 1465–1529) painted a Last Judgment, one of the key subject matters of such exempla, for the courtroom in the town hall of Bruges. The accompanying Renaissance frame by Lanceloot Blondeel (1498–1561) features Latin biblical quotations, such as "Videte quid faciatis: non enim hominis exercetis judicium, sed domini" ("Consider carefully what you do, because you are not judging for mere mortals but for the Lord," 2 Chronicles 19:6).

The two types of courtroom decoration mentioned by Matthijssen help distinguish between the two sides of the debate over the Palais de Justice's decoration. In her extensive work on Belgian wall painting, Judith Ogonovszky-Steffens emphasizes an opposition within the history of wall painting as an art form in the fin de siècle. During the last decades of the nineteenth century, historical wall painting depicting episodes from national history, collided with a more recent kind of idealist wall painting, referring to symbolist principles about a superior world and the essence of human being.[13] The first type includes portraits of great men and realist paintings depicting historical events, offering choice selections from national legal history. This is what Valérie Hayaert and Antoine Garapon, in their analysis of the fin-de-siècle courtroom decorations in Besançon, describe as making history into a *véhicule*, a vector by means of which civic virtues are exalted.[14] Historical wall painting could be interpreted as the descendants of Matthijssen's paintings or "portraiture" in old Dutch. Within the dichotomic scheme, Matthijssen's "old wise words" become synonyms for the idealists' allegories about law and justice, which sought to evoke universal, everlasting principles, the symbolist wall paintings as Ogonovsky-Steffens's second type. For example, Mellery's 1894 poster even literally included "wise words," maxims such as "Brotherhood is the basis of law" and "Without goodness, Justice fails in her task." In 1907, Carton de Wiart, the president of the Young Bar Association suggested that words, maxims, verse and prose – dating back as far as Solomon – should be written on the interior walls of the Palais de Justice. These words expressed ideals which were meant to inspire the upholders of justice.[15] The dichotomy can be synthesized as follows:

Matthijsen's instructions (1405)	Portraits	Good old wise words
Type of wall painting	Historical realist	Symbolist
Type of representation	Portraits and history scenes	Allegories
Typical subject matter	Local (legal) history, *in casu* ancient lawyers and courts	Personifications; heroes and stories drawn from biblical, mythological, literary, and historical sources
Objective as interpreted by Picard's legal *avant-garde*	National education	Edification of the mind

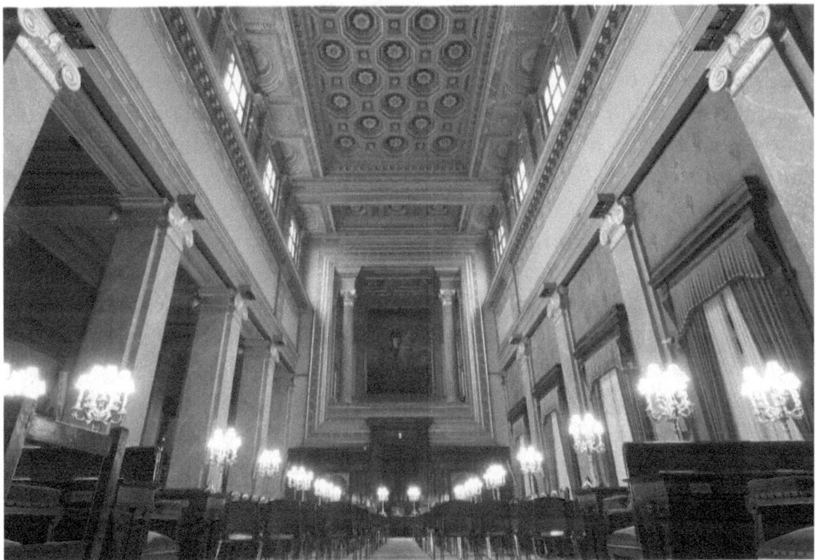

Figure 5.1 The Solemn Room of the Cour de Cassation, with the equestrian portrait of Leopold I by Eugène Van Mierlo, installed c. 1954. © Tchorski.

The Decoration of the Solemn Room of the Cour de Cassation

Each side of the Solemn Room features an empty one-and-a-half-metre-high frieze, divided into three – one long piece measuring thirteen metres flanked by two shorter fragments of three metres. A huge frame of over 30 square metres hangs at both ends of the room. These frames and friezes had remained empty since the Palais's inauguration on 15 October 1883.

Six years later, in 1899, the first recorded proposal to fill these voids came from Alfred Cluysenaar (1837–1902), a late Romantic painter and decorative artist. In his letter to Jean-Baptiste Rousseau (1829–91), the director-general of the Belgian government's fine arts department, Cluysenaar expressed his preference for a uniformly gold-coloured background, in keeping with the surrounding marble. The most appropriate subject matter, according to the artist, was to be found in the Cour de Cassation's history. Cluysenaar was an established history painter, who could rely on a career of historical wall paintings of the official, academic kind.[16]

Cluysenaar, however, was an artist, not a legal historian. His choice of dates and even words makes it possible to reconstruct his sources. For the larger part of his proposal, Cluysenaar drew on a book from 1866 about the Cour de Cassation written by Camille Scheyven (1838–1913), who later became first president of that court. Scheyven wrote that the Cour de Cassation "is also and foremost, on our soil, the successor in direct line of the Great Council of Malines." The way Scheyven had it, his contemporaries could learn from the intellect of the medieval and early-modern Malines lawyers, as well as from their interpretation of organizational and procedural laws, since "the customs and the character endure the ages and outlive their laws."[17]

On the basis of Scheyven's historical overview, Cluysenaar picked and listed some of the crucial events from the Great Council's history as well as from the history of those courts that were interpreted as its successors. He suggested to fill the friezes with scenes of the foundation of the court (Burgundian era), an ordinance by Emperor Charles V (Habsburg era), a French revolutionary ordinance from 1795 (French era), and the opening session of the actual Cour de Cassation on 15 August 1832 (Belgian era). As for this event, Cluysenaar repeated Scheyven's comment that, in 1832, the Cour de Cassation's judges wore black gowns. For the sake of the decorative ensemble, however, he proposed to dress them in red. This tiny adjustment demonstrates how historical realism in wall painting, formerly characterized by an almost archival attention to detail and authenticity, had started to give way to more personal aesthetic considerations – for art's sake – marking its transformation into an allegorical or symbolist kind of wall painting.

Cluysenaar's suggestion for the two large frames on each side of the courtroom are equally revealing. As an alternative to more historical scenes, Cluysenaar advanced the use of painted allegories of universal, eternal principles. "They should, according to me, represent general ideas of Justice … Equality of Justice for all … Justice is limited in its action … Justice is free of charge."[18] Cluysenaar, however, did not succeed in defining the actual content of these principles. He merely stated that they should be fitting "to the level of the destination." Despite this vagueness, all those involved in the decision-making process agreed that the decorations had to be in line with the solemn and lofty character of the court.

One important voice was that of the president of the Royal Committee for Monuments, François Wellens (1812–97), an engineer and the administrative head of the Palais de Justice's construction. Already in

1881 he had written that the Palais's architect had provided numerous spaces in the interior "where painting and sculpture one day will be called to reproduce the memory of the country's illustrious legislators and lawyers, who did their country honour, as well as those historical events that have strongly contributed to assure Belgium's high rank amongst the civilized nations."[19] This somewhat dated view in favour of historical realism and wall painting would prove incompatible with most of the commissioned artists' ideas and designs for both rooms of the Cour de Cassation. For instance, in contrast to Cluysenaar's proposals for the Solemn Room, Wellens had in mind a historical scene in which Leopold I, Belgium's first king, approved the plans for the Palais de Justice.[20] Whilst financial issues were still being debated, the inspector for fine arts, Émile Leclercq (1827–1907), suggested that Cluysenaar be allowed to start the large painting, but employing Wellens's preferred subject matter, and so avoiding the apparently problematic symbolist aspects of the artist's initial design.

However, even this compromise did not pass. In 1908, some twenty years after Cluysenaar's letter, Émile Fabry (1865–1966), one of Belgium's leading symbolist painters, presented a new proposal to decorate the Cour de Cassation's Solemn Room. Fabry had demonstrated a clear interest in the worlds of dreams, Platonic ideas, and Nietzschean philosophy, creating allegories whose heroes were drawn from Greek mythology, the Bible, or Wagnerian operas. By the time he started the Cour de Cassation project, Fabry had obtained the commission to decorate the staircases of the Monnaie opera house, a highly prestigious job. He worked on the Monnaie commission in different stages until 1933, and painted symbolist compositions such *The Poet Adoring Beauty*. Fabry's plans for the Cour de Cassation shared much of the hermeneutist character and mythological references of this work. Key figures for his Cassation projects were biblical and mythical: Moses, Christ, and Prometheus, each of whom had pleaded for the destiny of man before their respective gods, and had fought against some kind of repression.[21]

Art critic Edmond Louis de Taeye wrote in 1911 that Fabry's work "talks to the soul, makes you think and realizes, as such, one of the major goals of great art."[22] It is not surprising that Edmond Picard and his art-minded colleagues of Les Amis du Palais welcomed Fabry's initial project. These were more or less the same people who authored the 1892 and 1899 articles, asking for art which addressed and educated the mind and soul. In 1912, Les Amis du Palais even stated that it was one of their main goals to have Fabry's projects realized.[23]

In his earliest known version, dating from 1908, Fabry wished to fill the two large frames with the expulsion of Adam and Eve from paradise and Christ's crucifixion. This opposition seemed fitting for a *Cour de Cassation*; the latter episode quashed the first, much like the councillors' decisions quashed previous judgments. "God has expelled Adam and Eve from earthly paradise, after their offence, but he has reformed his first judgment by means of the baptism [of Christ] and has quashed his verdict by means of the death of Jesus Christ."[24] The opposition is also analogous with the Lutheran understanding of the Old and New Testament and the evangelical theme known as Law and Gospel, or Law and Grace. Painters such as Lucas Cranach the Elder (1472–1553) had used the biblical scenes Fabry intended to depict, within didactic evangelical images. A similar opposition between Old and New Testament Gods, between justice and mercy, would be used by Jean Delville in his decorations for the Cour d'Assises.[25]

Originally, Fabry considered having the long friezes feature a chained Prometheus, one of the symbolists' favourite heroes. By 1913, the fire thief had disappeared from the projects and the Fall of man and the baptism had been added. The room would feature a double juxtaposition, with the Fall opposite the crucifixion, and the expulsion from Paradise opposite Christ's baptism. However, after having shown his project to Les Amis du Palais in 1913, Fabry lost their support.

> The subject which he chose did not please all, and specifically the occupants – the judges and members of the Public Ministry of Cassation – did not show themselves enthusiastic about these decorations. However, it is recognized by all that the panel which surmounts the entrance door of this sumptuous room asks for something else than the drapery that is currently hanging there. Some suggest that an art work of great allure should be hung there, representing our great king Leopold II. It is certain that, if a great work of art would feature this figure, it would be admirably placed in the sumptuous frame of the Cour de Cassation.[26]

At a time when decoration commissions for public buildings in Brussels welcomed symbolist, allegorical wall paintings, the decision makers opted for a far more traditional subject matter for the Cour de Cassation. Despite Fabry's alternative and revised projects from 1925 (in which a chained Prometheus reappeared, in combination with the Fall of man) and 1941, and despite the approval of Procurator General Collard, Fabry's plans were never executed, due to the lack of sufficient budget.[27] Eventually, in the 1950s, an equestrian portrait of Leopold I by Eugène Van Mierlo (1880–1972) was put in the frame of honour above the heads of the country's highest judges. Several Belgian buildings, including the Antwerp and Tournai cathedrals and the Liège *perron*, are featured within a fictional background. Opposite Leopold, on the other end of the room, a standing portrait of Philip the Good by the same painter fills the frame. In a piece of teleological and patriotic history writing bridging four centuries, the late-medieval *conditor Belgii*, who brought most of the "Belgian" territories under one and the same rule for the first time, almost looks into the eyes of the first king of Belgium.

The friezes, however, remain empty, and their remaining voids remind us of the difficulties of courtroom decoration in general and the Belgian fin de siècle and Cour de Cassation in particular. Here is a Solemn Room of which newspapers such as *L'Indépendance Belge* emphasized the apotropaic and archaic nature, and whose decoration's function they compared to the military's gaudery: to arouse an irrational fear.[28] Indeed, the only consensus that can be found in the debates is one about the lofty nature of the Cour. The eventual compromise consists of two half-hearted historical reconstructions nothing close to the symbolist allegories of law's ideals, advocated for by Picard's avant-garde circle. Quite the contrary, in their emptiness the 1950s portraits of Leopold and Philip hardly seem to fill their frame's void, but remind us only of a lack of judgment and decision in favour of compromise.

The Decoration of the Cour de Cassation's Ordinary Session Room

Ironically, the Cour de Cassation's Ordinary Session Room, used on a day-to-day basis, stimulated far more sumptuous and prestigious projects. Braquenié et Cie, a French company with a branch in Malines, which produced tapestries for European royal courts including Napoleon III, proposed a series of tapestries to decorate the blank spaces of wall between the windows, and at both ends of the room.[29] Due to their high production costs, tapestries traditionally had a higher prestige than murals. Many of the original "cartoons," as tapestry designs are called, were drawn by Willem Geets (1838–1919). Among his commissions were the tapestries for Brussels's town hall and the senate's smoking room, which featured historical scenes such as *Philip the Good Receives the Eastern Ambassadors*. For the Cour de

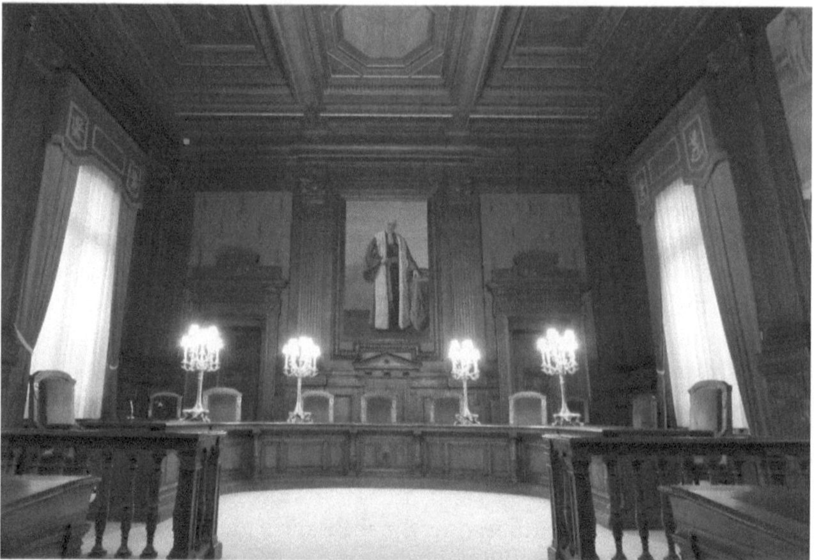

Figure 5.2 The Ordinary Session Room of the Cour de Cassation, with the central portrait tapestry of Eugène de Gerlache by Willem Geets, installed in 1895. © Tchorski.

Cassation, as opposed to their earlier historical material, the firm proposed allegorical tapestries, including *Justice*, *Law*, *Jurisprudence*, *Equity*, *Eloquence*, *Roman Law*, and *Customary Law*.[30]

The Administration for Fine Arts seemed favourably disposed towards Geets's decoration project, on the condition that the artist made some changes and submitted new cartoons. Following the adjustments to the designs for *The Law* and *Force* – a new theme – the minister in charge approved the changes, as did the members of the Cour de Cassation. Their president, Guillaume De Longé (1815–90), had been member of the jury deciding on the Palais de Justice's construction back in 1860. He wrote that the allegorical subjects were perfectly appropriate for the building's decoration, but that the court was not competent to decide on aspects "that [are] a matter of art and tradition."[31] As to the suitability of allegorical treatments, the court stated, "It [the *Cour de Cassation*] considers allegories to be more decorative and thinks that otherwise a modern portrait would be surprising amidst ancient portraits."[32]

François Wellens's Royal Committee for Monuments reacted far more negatively:

> Although the artist's [Geets] decoration program seems to us acceptable in principle, the Committee would prefer that the subject matter of the decorations would be somehow different than purely allegorical. We then consider that these subjects have not been treated with the necessary severity, given the special destination of this decoration ... [I]t would be far more preferable to replace these allegorical subjects proposed by the artist with portraits of illustrious lawyers.[33]

At once, the committee drew up a list of lawyers from "Belgian" legal history, including their historical merits. All the selected lawyers had already been part of a larger list drafted by Jacques Britz (1806–67). A lawyer and legal historian, in 1847 Britz composed a list of men whom he thought had earned a portrait, bust, or statue. The purpose of this kind of glorification of legal scientists was, according to Britz, to "make science itself progress, to arouse sentiments of nationality, to conserve glorious traditions and to satisfy a legitimate desire of the country."[34] In addition, the modern portraits had to link Belgium's past with its present, and thus they explain what national education through historical wall painting would aim at.

Earlier decorations in the Palais de Justice were clearly in line with this particular kind of "national education" pantheon. In 1885, when the walls of both rooms of the Cour de Cassation were still vacant, there were already reports of an "avalanche of busts" in the Palais.[35] Wellens's committee clearly wanted to continue this tradition in the Ordinary Session Room, at the expense of the allegorical designs. They argued that tapestries in general (and with them, Geets's allegorical program) would not fit the walls of the room, and that busts would be preferable. However, after a try-out with existing busts, the idea was abandoned.[36]

Despite the approval of the Cour de Cassation's president for Geets's tapestry program, and much to the surprise of the Fine Arts administration, in 1893 Geets was commissioned to design five portrait tapestries. The earliest was of fifteenth-century lawyer Filips Wielant, who was a councillor at the Parlement de Malines immediately after its founding in 1473 and served the courts of Mary of Burgundy, Maximilian of Austria, and Philip the Handsome. Geets included these three sovereigns in the tapestry's background. Wielant also wrote vernacular publications on civil law (*Practyke civile*) and criminal law (*Practycke criminele*), which gained international fame due to Latin translations by Joos de Damhouder.[37] Damhouder (1507–81) also got his woven portrait in the Cour de Cassation. Most probably, Geets referred to Damhouder's writings, *Praxis rerum civilium* and *Praxis rerum criminalium* by means of the books featured next to the lawyer, dressed in a black gown and standing in front of a wall with wainscoting and gold leather.[38] The third tapestry shows a baroque interior with Pieter Stockmans (1608–71), a clergyman who lectured as a humanist at the *collegium trilingue* and was rector of Leuven University. The committee eventually opted for Eugène Defacqz (1797–1871) for the fourth tapestry. Defacqz's portrait, too, had sculptural precedents within the building. It was preceded by two busts, both by Charles Van Oemberg. One showed Defacqz in his civil clothes as a politician and co-founder of the Belgian liberal party (1846); the other was meant for the Palais de Justice and showed him as a magistrate and president of the Cour de Cassation. A legal historian, Defacqz had written – among others topics – about the Council of Malines in his *Ancient droit belgique* (1873).[39]

What remained was the central and most honourable space, directly above the seat of the first president of the Cour de Cassation. Originally, Wellens's committee preferred a portrait of Leopold I signing the organic law concerning the legal order, one year after his inauguration as Belgian king. Since plans existed to include Leopold in the Solemn Room, the committee eventually proposed Étienne-Constantin de Gerlache (1785–1871). De Gerlache was Belgium's *man of firsts*. He was the first president of the country's Constitutional Assembly, the Chamber of Representatives, and the Cour de Cassation. Despite his advocacy for a strict separation of the *trias politica* in his days as a Belgian revolutionary, de Gerlache came to symbolize the politically influenced appointments of the early Belgian years. He became first president of the Cour de Cassation without any magistracy experience, thanks to his Catholic political connections.[40] No doubt, in a country where the political landscape for over half a century was dominated by the quarrel between liberals and Catholics, de Gerlache's portrait was thought to balance that of Defacqz.

From the many letters between the different administrations, the Cour de Cassation, and the artist, it is hard to find a real argument in favour of the portraits. However, some of the arguments against Geets's allegorical designs could just as well be read as a disapproval of symbolist art and wall painting. A letter to Bracquenié asked him to exclude "the nudity and small child figures" and rejected his "black backgrounds, in the manner of Pompeian decorations."[41] Symbolist art frequently featured nude, idealized, athletic bodies – often of children and *ephebes* – in front of decontextualized monochrome backgrounds. The decorations by Albert Ciamberlani (1864–1956) in the Court of Appeal in the Palais de Justice, started in 1902, were covered up immediately after their inauguration in 1957, due to the abundant presence of nudes. Mellery, too, was associated with a certain degree of eroticism evoked by nude bodies, and perhaps this was the reason his design for the Commercial Court, featuring a naked breastfeeding woman, was never realized.[42]

Thus, the final execution of the Ordinary Session Room's decoration confirms the opinion that respect for a country's supreme court is better found in its history than in wise words or symbolic lessons. Here, the interpretation of the Cour de Cassation's sumptuousness dominated the committee's aesthetic judgment, which was essentially iconoclastic, as in their view representing or allegorizing the law on such a level as the supreme court was unfit and impossible, unless by means of history. Contradictorily, in their determined demand for historical portraits, the committee unconventionally quashed the judgment of those at the top of the judicial hierarchy, a hierarchy they were so anxiously protecting.

Conclusion

The two massive portraits of the first "Belgian" ruler (Philip the Good) and the first Belgian king in the Solemn Room of the Cour de Cassation are the result of a non-judgment, a weak compromise. The five woven portraits drawn from the country's pantheon of illustrious lawyers in the Cassation's Ordinary Session Room originated in a firm belief in authority through hierarchy and history. In both cases, litigants, lawyers, magistrates, and visitors are confronted with a distant past. This distance is no different than the one criticized by Robert Jacob in his survey on legal imagery. According to Jacob, legal imagery in general and courtroom decorations in particular feature something of a downward evolution. First, the great and gruesome medieval *exempla justitae* depict good or bad judgments and legal practices using biblical episodes, antique stories, myths, and local legends, in a time when justice was executed in the centre of society. The distance, alienation if you will, started with the allegorization of Justice into a single figure, that of the lady with the sword and scales, and met its climax with the apotropaic temples of the law constructed in the nineteenth and twentieth centuries – perhaps most of all in the world's biggest building at the time, Brussels's Palais de Justice.[43]

To many, the men featured in the Cour de Cassation decorations were – and still are – as anonymous as the many products of the period's *statuomania*, and thus their project of national education through art missed its goal. For how was one to draw lessons from a portrait of a long-forgotten and de facto anonymous man?[44] Arguably, the only lesson would be one in the history of design. In his backgrounds Geets included a textbook overview of historical wall decorations, from the medieval tapestries behind Wielant, past Damhouder's sixteenth-century Spanish gold leather and Stockman's heavy baroque curtain, to Defacqz's early-nineteenth-century wall painting. The same could be said about the lawyers' uniforms. It is not legal history but aesthetic history that is most clearly articulated here.

However, in this light, symbolist allegories could hardly be seen as a better alternative, given their equally illegible nature – despite Picard's wish for the vulgarization of art. It is therefore reasonable to state that the *via media* was reached in the tapestry of Étienne de Gerlache, of which a review quoted by *Journal des Tribunaux* wrote: "One cannot help but feel a kind of respect in the presence of the stately appearance of this representative of law and order. The sumptuous tone of the long red gown bordered with ermine is of a most fruitful decorative effect, and forms, with the colour of the oak wainscoting, an opulent harmony."[45]

This is where the lesson in the history of design stops. The background is largely monochrome and gold, against which the icon-like portrait looks decontextualized and sacral – the intended effect of many symbolist backgrounds. The judge's gown does what it is made for: it is sumptuous, expensive looking, and marks the "representative of law and order." At the same time, authority for Belgium's supreme court is found in history, its own history, with a depiction of its first president, its founding father. Even when national education was lacking and the visitor or beholder is unaware of de Gerlache's identity and history, an edification of the mind is achieved, one that asks for respect for the court's authority, and the legal system's hierarchy. The gold and gown of man and building form "an opulent harmony": they are eclectic, archaic, and apotropaic. Time and again, journalists from the liberal newspaper *L'Indépendance Belge* characterized the Solemn Room, too, as excessive, lavish, "gilded, salmoned, chocolated and marbled," "naturally lacking this sober and adequate simplicity needed for a courtroom,"[46] a courtroom which "create[s] a certain superstitious fear."[47] Moreover, its ceremonies were "fustian we would way, if we dared to," and the *Cour de Cassation* was a place "where modernism has no hold over respectable and conventional traditions."[48]

In this court, the ideals of one and the same group of lawyers, headed by Picard, advocating for symbolist wall paintings and supporting the idea of new law and progressive political changes, in one and the same avant-garde quest, met resistance. Thus, most of the walls of the Cour de Cassation's Solemn Room remained empty, and our story becomes one of visual images that never were, in a time of important legal debate and transition. However, in their absence – an absence revealed through the study of archival sources – these non-images remain important signposts of conservatism.

Although the Solemn Room was unknown to many citizens, *L'Indépendance Belge* thought people should know of it, since it demonstrates the country's degree of civilization. Here again, national education of the people came to the foreground. Likewise, as in the case of de Gerlache's portrait in the Ordinary Session Room, the judges themselves were enough of a spectacle, a decoration.[49] In the absence of actual paintings, these old men literally became a tableau, an image, a history painting: "As we know, the members of the Cour de Cassation are, for the most part, men of very advanced seniority, whose spry old age and venerable appearance add to the prestige of the assembly. The spectacle for the eyes is not to be despised … [Like a] tableau of a past age, which would tease the pencil of a painter of … historical reconstructions."[50]

NOTES

1 This contribution is the shortened, adapted, and translated version of a part of the book chapter by Stefan Huygebaert, "'Le décor au milieu duquel ils vivront': Beeldhouwkunst en decoratie in het Justitiepaleis," in *Genius, Grandeur en Gêne. Het Fin de Siècle rond het Justitiepaleis te Brussel en de controversiële figuur van Edmond Picard*, ed. Willy Van Eeckhoutte and Bruno Maes (Gent: Knops, 2014), 117–83. I owe my gratitude to Dirk Heirbaut, Georges Martyn, Bruno De Wever, Sebastiaan Vandenbogaerde, Nathalie Tousignant, Matthias Van der Haegen, Judit Beke-Martos, Jana Wijnsouw, Desmond Manderson, and Jan Caudron. This article was realized with the support of the IAP "Justice & Populations" (PVII/22),

Interuniversity Attraction Poles Programme – Belgian Science Policy; and the Research Foundation – Flanders (FWO).

2 On the Cour de Cassation see Georges Martyn, "Belgium, the Netherlands and Luxembourg since 1800," in *European Supreme Courts: A Portrait through History*, ed. R.C. Remco Van Rhee and Alain Wijffels (London: UK Third Millennium Publishing, 2013), 218–27. Françoise Muller, *La cour de cassation belge à l'aune des rapports entre pouvoirs* (Bruges: La Charte, 2011).

3 "La décoration du Palais de Justice," *Journal des Tribunaux*, 1899: 142. Quotes are translated from French by myself unless stated otherwise.

4 On Picard and the other artistically interested lawyers, see Jane Block, ed., *Belgium, The Golden Decades 1880–1914* (New York: Peter Lang, 1997); Bart Coppein, *Dromen van een nieuwe samenleving: Intellectuele biografie van Edmond Picard* (Brussels: Larcier, 2011); Paul Aron and Cécile Vanderpelen-Diagre, *Edmond Picard (1836–1924): Un bourgeois socialiste Belge à la fin du dix-neuvième siècle. Essai d'Histoire Culturelle* (Brussels: Musées Royaux des Beaux-Arts de Belgique, 2013) ; Debora Silverman, "'Modernité sans Frontières': Culture, Politics, and the Boundaries of the Avant-Garde in King Leopold's Belgium, 1885–1910,' *American Imago* 68, no. 4 (2011): 707–97.

5 Silverman, "'Modernité sans Frontières,'" 709.

6 Stefan Huygebaert and Sebastiaan Vandenbogaerde, "Êtes-vous Justice, Minerve ou Thémis? Een tijdschriftlogo als numen mixtum en symptoom van de versmelting van kunst en recht in het Belgische fin de siècle," *Pro Memorie. Bijdragen tot de rechtsgeschiedenis der Nederlanden* 16, no. 2 (2014): 244–58.

7 "Constitution des Amis du Palais," *Journal des Tribunaux*, 1911: 1142; "Les Amis du Palais," ibid., 1275.

8 "La décoration du Palais de Justice," *L'Art Moderne*, 1892: 401–2.

9 Anne-Marie Geerinck, "De Decoratie van het Justitiepaleis te Brussel," in *Poelaert en zijn Tijd*, ed. Richard Vandendaele (Brussels: Gemeentekrediet, 1980), 300–2.

10 Emilie Berger, "Jean Delville et l'enjeu du 'Monumental,'" in *Jean Delville (1867–1953) Maître de l'Idéal*, ed. Denis Laoureux (Paris: Somogy, 2014), 106–14.

11 "La décoration du Palais de Justice," *Journal des Tribunaux*, 1899: 142.

12 Quote translated from Middle Dutch. Jan Matthijsen, *Het Rechtsboek Van Den Briel, Beschreven in Vijf Tractaten*, ed. J.A. Fruin, and M.S. Pols ('s-Gravenshage: Nijhoff, 1880). Georges Martyn, "Inspiring Images for Judges. Late Medieval Court Room Decorations in the Southern Netherlands," in *The Iconology of Law and Order (Legal and Cosmic)*, ed.

Anna Kérchy, György E. Szönyi, and Attila Kiss (Szeged: JATE Press, 2012), 37–49. Stefan Huygebaert, Georges Martyn, Vanessa Paumen, and Tine van Poucke, *The Art of Law: Three Centuries of Justice Depicted* (Tielt: Lannoo, 2016).

13 Judith Ogonovsky-Steffens, *La peinture monumentale d'histoire dans les édifices civils* (Brussels: Académie Royale de Belgique, 1999), 354–7. Judith Ogonovszky-Steffens, "Un idéal de mur," in *Splendeurs de l'Idéal: Rops, Khnopff, Delville et leur temps*, ed. Michel Draguet (Gent: Snoeck-Ducaju, 1996), 179–97.

14 Valérie Hayaert and Antoine Garapon, *Allégories de Justice: La grand'chambre du Parlement de Flandre* (Abbeville: F. Paillart, 2014), 100.

15 Henri Carton de Wiart, "Décorum judiciaire," *Journal des Tribunaux*, 1907: 404–5.

16 Judith Ogonovszky-Steffens, "Cluysenaar, Alfred," in *Nouvelle biographie nationale* (Brussels: Académie Royale de Belgique, 1999), 58–60. Ogonovszky-Steffens, *La peinture monumentale*, 325–51; General Archives of Belgium (GAB), Fine Arts Records (FAR), no. 368.

17 Camille Scheyven, *Traité pratique des pourvois en cassation, de l'organisation et des attributions diverses de la cour suprême* (Brussels: Bruylant-Christophe & compagnie, 1866), 6–7, 23.

18 GAB, FAR, no. 368.

19 François Wellens, *Le nouveau Palais de Justice* (Brussels: H. Leys, 1881), 19.

20 GAB, FAR, no. 368.

21 Jacqueline Guisset, *Emile Fabry (1865–1966)* (Brussels: Fonds du patrimoine de Woluwe-Saint-Pierre, 2000), 9, 11, 32, 81, 108–10.

22 Ibid.

23 "Les Amis du Palais. Assemblée générale de 18 mai 1912," *Journal des Tribunaux*, 1912: 635; "Les Amis du Palais," ibid., 1197 ; "Les Amis du Palais," *Journal des Tribunaux*, 1913: 811.

24 "Les Amis du Palais. Un projet de décoration de la Salle des Séances Solennelles de la Cour de Cassation," *Journal des Tribunaux*, 1913: 323.

25 Bonnie J. Noble, "'A Work in Which the Angels Are Wont to Rejoice': Lucas Cranach's 'Schneeberg Altarpiece,'" *The Sixteenth Century Journal* 34, no. 4 (2003): 1018–25.

26 "Les Amis du Palais," *Journal des Tribunaux*, 1913: 1292.

27 Guisset, *Emile Fabry*, 83–9.

28 *L'Indépendance Belge*, 11 October 1910, 3.

29 Wim J.J. Mertens, "Meubeltapisserieën in de Nederlanden en Frankrijk vanaf de Late Middeleeuwen tot 1900," PhD diss. (Leiden University, 2008).

30 GAB, FAR, no. 368.
31 Ibid.
32 Ibid.
33 Ibid.
34 Jean Britz, *Histoire de la jurisprudence et de la législation des Pays-Bas et des Principautés de Liège, de Bouillon et de Stavelot* (Brussels: 1846), xi.
35 Aude Hendrick, "Des mots de circonstance: Les discours de rentrée de la haute magistrature belge au XIXe siècle," PhD diss. (USL Brussels, 2012), 274.
36 GAB, FAR, no. 368.
37 Jos Monballyu, ed., *Filips Wielant verzameld werk I* (Brussels: Paleis der Academiën, 1995), 7–27.
38 Egidius Strubbe, "Joos de Damhouder als criminalist," *Tijdschrift voor Rechtsgeschiedenis* 37 (1970): 1–65.
39 Philippe Godding, "Defacqz Eugène," *Nouvelle biographie nationale*, 6 (Brussels: Académie Royale de Belgique, 2001), 106–11.
40 Jean-Pierre Nandrin, "L'acte de fondation des nominations politiques de la magistrature: La Cour de cassation à l'aube de l'indépendance belge," *Belgisch Tijdschrift voor Nieuwste Geschiedenis* 2 (1998): 158.
41 GAB, FAR, no. 368.
42 Geerinck, "De Decoratie van het Justitiepaleis te Brussel," 304. Vincent Vanhamme, *Xavier Mellery: De ziel der dingen* (Amsterdam: Van Gogh Museum, 2000), 60.
43 Robert Jacob, *Images de la Justice: Essai sur l'iconographie judiciaire du Moyen Âge à l'âge classique* (Paris: Léopard d'Or, 1994).
44 On the exegesis of historical imagery in courtrooms, see Hayaert and Garapon, *Allégories de Justice*, 93, 103–6.
45 "Of law and order" is my translation of the French "de la loi et du droit": "Le portrait de de Gerlache," *Journal des Tribunaux*, 1896: 726.
46 *L'Indépendance Belge*, 17 March 1903, 2 and 12 May 1911, 3.
47 Ibid., 11 October 1910, 3.
48 Ibid., 2 October 1896, 1.
49 Ibid., 11 October 1910, 3.
50 Ibid., 12 May 1911, 3.

6 The Visual Force of Justice in the Making of Liberia

SHANE CHALMERS

This essay is concerned with a particular image – that of "Liberia" – and a particular history – the "making of Liberia." My intention in the brief narrative that follows is to show how this image and this history are implicated in each other. At the same time, the essay is concerned with the relation of justice and force, and how "Liberia," as an image of justice, has been made visible in the most forceful ways in consolidating it as a nation state. This draws on Pascal's *pensée*: "*Justice, force.* – ... Justice without force is impotent; force without justice is tyrannical. Justice without force is contradictory, as there are always the wicked; force without justice is accused of wrong. And so it is necessary to put justice and force together; and, for this, to make sure that what is just be strong, or what is strong be just."[1] As I show, force not only fortified the justice of "Liberia" in west Africa, but it also fortified the image of "Liberia" there – although not without altering image, justice, and history in material ways.

There are four parts to the essay. (1) I begin by theorizing the image as a transitional phenomenon that is both *of* history and *in* history, making history visible whilst simultaneously making history. This provides the framework for my analysis of the making of Liberia. (2) I begin the analysis by showing how "Liberia" was conceived at the start of the nineteenth century as a racialized vision of justice. (3) I then turn to the image of the young African-American settler "Matilda Newport," created and deployed in the nineteenth century as an image of the making of the black republic. As I show here, the image of "Matilda Newport" made "Liberia" visible in the most forceful ways in the attempt to realize the republic's jurisdiction in west Africa. This forceful visualization of "Liberia" cut deep into the lands and peoples it was required to signify under international law (or else lose to competing colonial powers, Britain and France), whilst both the lands and peoples signified by "Liberia" continued to elude the jurisdiction of this sovereign image. (4) I bring the narrative to a close by considering how "Liberia" has managed to stay afloat despite the revolution and wars that swept away "Matilda Newport" and the colonial Americo-Liberian regime it represented. The question this poses, and which I consider in conclusion, is where it leaves "Liberia" as an image *of* and *in* history, at a time when the nation state is being remade with the assistance of an international peace-building intervention post-war.

Images in Transition

Two types of image pervade history, one tracking across its surface, the other coursing through its middle.

The first type is the image *of* history, corresponding with what Desmond Manderson in the introduction to this collection refers to as *representation*, providing ways of seeing and revealing, but also of overlooking. Images of this type are media of meaning making – of making sense, by making visible; but also of ideology, the sense that is made superimposed upon the sensed at the risk of the image being mistaken for its object. Such images are the "mobile signifiers" of myth,[2] providing a plurality of ways of imagining and representing what is being signified.[3] Like the wake of a ship that courses historically, they signify the history aft, a history that is only ever known through the traces that have been left behind, as waves tracking across the surface, signifying the passage of what has come before.

The second type is the image *in* history, corresponding with what Manderson refers to as a *technology*. This is about the physical force of visualization: if images of history are about how history is *made visible*, then this is about how making visible *makes history*. In contrast with the first type of image – as a fluid signifier that alters around its object – this is about how "the image" is itself an object, with a constancy that brings it into contact with a world that alters around *it*.[4] Images of this type course through history with a physical force that brings them into collision with other objects, altering them in the encounter, but also, and more critically, being ignored or defied. Like waves coursing through the ocean, they have a depth and energy that can capsize ships, wash away shorelines, but also be sailed right over or surfed as a plaything.[5]

In sum, those are the two different types of image I consider here: the first implicated in how history is *visualized*, the second implicated in how history is *made*. And yet it is also clear that these two "types" cannot be so neatly distinguished.

Thus, the imaginative process of seeing and revealing, and overlooking, also makes history, with what "is" history, unknown apart from its images, always altering with its altering images. Just as a ship cannot be entirely separated from its wake – the one always pointing to the other – the ship that has coursed by also can never be definitely known from the traces left in its wake, any more than the traces of its course can provide a definite vision of what has passed. The ship remains as fluid as the waves that remain to tell its story.

But this also points to a certain constancy of both the image and its object. The ship that has coursed by might remain as fluid as the waves that remain to tell its story, but a *ship* has passed on its course, and it has created a wake that now makes *its* own course. As much as the two remain fluid, there is a solidity to both as separate objects that course through history. Likewise images in history: just as there is an objectivity to history apart from its images, every visual technology is also always historical, binding the image in material ways to its historical production.

The result is four aspects to the image cutting across the two types: (1) as representation, images provide a fluid medium for seeing and revealing, and overlooking, their object; but (2) as representation, images also create their object through visualization – making visible what would remain otherwise unseen; and (3) as technology, images are a product of history, bound to their own objectivity; but (4) as technology, images also course through history, whilst being defied or ignored by a world that shifts around them.

These four aspects are not standpoints. No image is simply an imaginative medium to visualize an object, as in (1), any more than an image is simply a historically bound object, as in (3). An image is always in transition between these four points: always objectively *in* history, images course through its middle as much as they are its product; always subjectively *of* history, images track across its surface, constantly revised as everything shifts around them, and constantly revising what would remain otherwise insignificant.

"Liberia"

Light appeared in the horizon: a triumph was before this Society such as the wisest man might envy, and the most virtuous man long to realize. They would triumph, not as conquerors, binding bleeding nations to their chariot wheels; but as liberators, who came not to destroy but to save ... Their march would be surrounded by the songs of the grateful, the blessings of the free; their triumph would be recorded in two hemispheres, and its lasting memorial would be written in heaven.[6]

Imagine this. The year is 1821, the month is winter, and the day is stretched out radially between the unbroken circumference of the horizon, as the US brig *Nautilus* courses across the Atlantic Ocean in the direction of Africa. Aboard are thirty-three free black women, men, and children, under the command of two white officers of the US government and two white agents of the American Colonization Society,[7] a philanthropic organization established with the aim of transporting "the free people of color of the United States" to Africa.[8] The *Nautilus* is bound for the British colony of Sierra Leone, where it is to join another band of black colonists who departed the United States a year earlier aboard the *Elizabeth,* before continuing to search for their promised land along the Windward Coast.

But all of that is to come. Out at sea for now, there they *are*: coursing across the Atlantic, gazing beyond the railings of the *Nautilus* at an apparently limitless expanse of sky and ocean, cut only by the horizon. And the light on the horizon holds out a promise: *imagine,* Africa ahead! A land of justice to come!

This scene is part of another great transition: the United States of America at the turn of the nineteenth century – a newly independent republic, emerging from revolution, struggling with the institution of slavery. In 1819 the US government enacted a law authorizing its armed vessels to patrol the coast of Africa to intercept slave traders, with the aim of stopping the "importation" of any "negro, mulatto, or person of color" and returning them to Africa.[9] The US government's need for a place of return coincided with the establishment of the American Colonization Society, which used the opportunity created by the 1819 slave trade act to secure funding from the federal government to support its colonizing mission.[10]

To begin with, the American Colonization Society was dominated by slaveholders, and there is little doubt about their motivations: to secure the institution of slavery still foundational in the south of the country, as well as the whiteness of the United States.[11] The answer to a visible contradiction was to make it less visible, in this case by deporting "the free people of color," whose very presence threatened the security and purity of whites and the docility of their slaves.[12] However, the idea of colonizing these "free people of color" in Africa was also seen by some, both white and black, as a promise of liberty, equality, and fraternity.[13] Colonization would, it was said, make black people free in a way they could never be in the United States. What is more, the establishment of an African-American colony in Africa would, it was said, provide a model of African civilization that would lead to the emancipation of all of Africa's peoples.[14] This was the great humanitarian mission of the day: to make Africans free from enslavement to their traditional ways – or as one of the founders of the American Colonization Society proclaimed in an initial meeting of the organisation: "It is the hope of redeeming many millions of people from the lowest state of ignorance and superstition."[15] Through this colonization mission, "civilization and the Christian religion would be introduced into that benighted quarter of the world."[16]

This was the colour of justice to come: the flourishing of the United States as a white homeland, and the flourishing of Africa as a black homeland; and both would be simultaneously achieved by the transit of the free people of colour of the United States to Africa. On one side this vision was propagated by slaveholders and white supremacists; on another side it was championed by radical black nationalists, along with pragmatists, black and white; whilst the views of the Africans who were to be made civilized were nowhere to be seen. And this troubled vision literally underwrote "Liberia." To quote the slave-owning member of the American Colonization Society General Harper, who proposed the name in 1824:

> Our Colony has at present no name. It is situated, indeed, near a Cape called Montserado, and has hitherto taken its only designation from this circumstance; but that is a name not appropriate to its object, a name that means nothing. In reflecting on this circumstance, I have thought of a name that is peculiar, short, and familiar, and that expresses the object and nature of the establishment – it is the term LIBERIA; and denotes a settlement of persons *made free*: for our Colony may with truth be called the home and country of freedmen, in contradistinction to the slaves of whom they once formed a part.[17]

And so the colony, which had been referred to simply by its geographical indicator – Cape Montserado – and therefore by a name that "meant nothing," by a name that signified no more than the outcrop of rubble that history had piled at the place where the settlers now stood, was named "Liberia," expressing the "object and nature" of the American Colonization Society's vision, not simply of liberty, but of the kind of liberty that comes with being made free.[18] *This* was the justice of "Liberia" to come, just over the horizon.

"Matilda Newport"

Cape Montserado, November 26th, 1822, (morning.) Sir: I had the honour of writing you by the Shark, on the 9th ultimo, and, subsequently, by the "Strong," in a very weak and sickly condition. We are now engaged in a bloody and perilous war with all the native tribes around us. On the morning of the 11th, were attacked by eight hundred, who were repulsed, after doing us some injury, with the loss of nearly one hundred killed on the spot. Subsequently, we have been employed in a negotiation for peace, which I fear will fail. We expect another assault to be made on us in two or three days ... I have the honour, sir, to be, your most obedient servant,

J. ASHMUN,
Acting Agent for liberated Africans

November 26th, (evening.) Sir: Our negotiation with our perfidious enemies seems to have entirely failed of its object. They are bent on our ruin.[19]

Now imagine this. It is December 1822, mere months after the *Nautilus* was at sea, and the tiny colony erected on Cape Montserado is on the brink of ruin. Without food or adequate shelter, its fifty-odd residents, already sick and dying from disease, are under attack from an alliance led by the Dey, who are demanding the return of land "purchased" from them by the two white American agents with the assistance of a cocked pistol.[20] Two battles ensue. The first, in late November, is described by the American Colonization Society's "Acting Agent for liberated Africans" in the letter to the secretary of the US Navy quoted above. The second assault, foreseen by the agent in his letter, occurs five days later. During this battle, an estimated fifteen hundred soldiers led by the Dey attack the settlers. The settlement barely avoids destruction. Its survival is attributed to cannon fire, forcing the Dey to retreat. This war will be memorialized as the Providential beginning of Liberia. Half a century later, the president of the Republic, J.J. Roberts, will recall it as "that signal triumph of freedom over the implacable enemies of human progress and the rights of man" – a triumph "which permanently established on this hill the foundations of our present political fabric."[21]

Shortly after the second battle, a US Navy ship arrives at the Cape. The captain offers his assistance in constructing a fort – or as he describes it later, "a tower of strength." This, the captain notes, "I conceived well suited to effect the object in view": to make an "impression on the minds" of those who might threaten the colony and its just claims.[22] He describes the construction of this "tower of strength" in a letter to the secretary of the US Navy: "In fifteen days, a circular massive work of stone, measuring one hundred and twelve feet in circumference, eight feet in thickness, and ten feet in elevation, was seen to tower above the surrounding heights, commanding the site for the town, and a wide range of the circumjacent country."[23]

The result, he writes, is "*formidable to any eye.*"[24] And indeed the captain is left with no doubt about "its effect in neutralizing, in no small degree, the menacing designs of the natives. Every day brought me additional proof of a change in their intentions ... I was happy in perceiving this revolution in their sentiments, this change in their designs."[25]

Not long after the settlers declared "Liberia" a free, sovereign, and independent republic in 1847,[26] accounts began to circulate that it was a young settler woman, Matilda Newport, who had fired the cannon that saved the colony during the Providential "battle of Fort Hill."[27] Whether she did or not is unknown; but that fact is insignificant to this history. What is significant is that she came to be represented as if she had. What is significant is that this image of "Matilda Newport" substituted for a woman whose trace in history is little more than the name that would give birth to "Liberia" as a republic. As another Liberian woman proclaimed admiringly almost a century later, "It was ... our noble Matilda, seeing the handful of men dispirited, observing the shattered condition of affairs and the gloom which the menacing advance of the natives had cast upon the lives of the pioneers, stepped forth, lighted the cannon ... and the existence of the Republic became a possibility."[28]

And the existence of the Republic became a possibility. There she stands: on public monuments and commemorative stamps,[29] in children's schoolbooks,[30] in poems, parades,[31] and civic names,[32] her heroism retold and re-enacted – "Matilda Newport," always behind the cannon with a hand raised to its fuse, a figure both just and formidable to any eye.

The timing of the emergence of the image of "Matilda Newport" is important. In the second half of the nineteenth century, the European

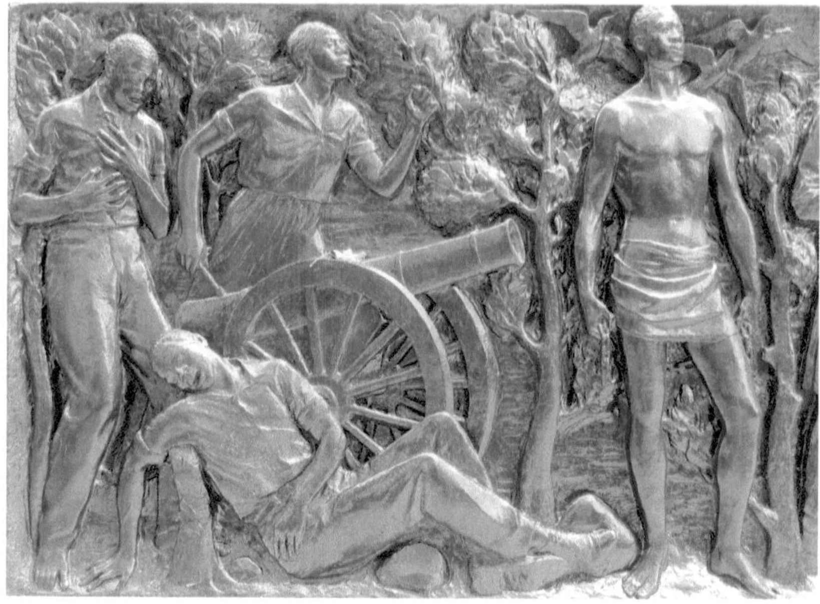

Figure 6.1 This panel forms part of a relief depicting the origin myth of Liberia, set at the base of a monument on Cape Montserrado that stands next to a replica of the cannon. Source: Shane Chalmers.

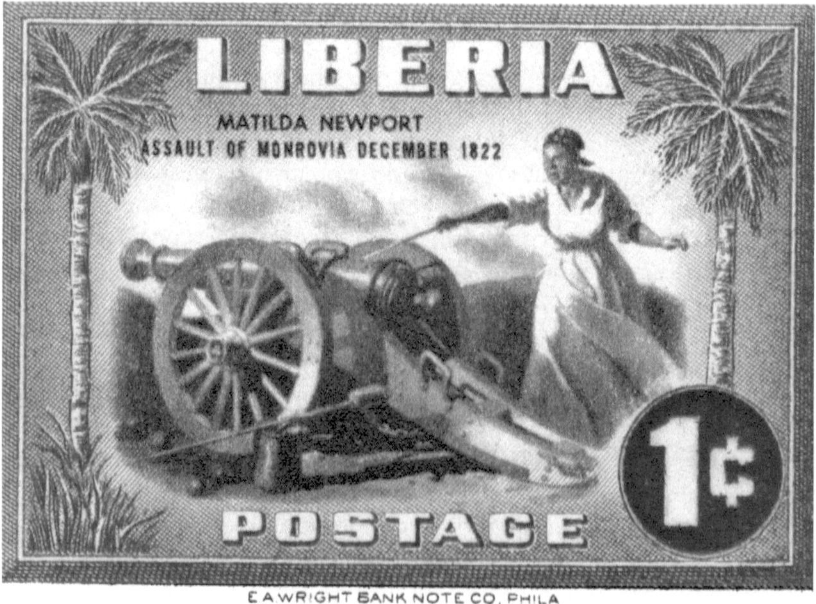

Figure 6.2 Stamp issued in 1947 for the 125th anniversary of the "battle at Fort Hill." Source: Manfred Beier, Philately of Liberia, philib.org.

"scramble for Africa" was accelerating, and the government of the black republic was under intense pressure to secure both its external sovereignty against the incursions of France and Britain, and its internal sovereignty against the African peoples who were rebelling against, or simply ignoring, the claims of the Americo-Liberian government.[33] In this situation of colonial nation-state building the name of Matilda Newport was given to a company of the republic's first militia.[34] Around the same time, December 1 was proclaimed a public holiday – to be named Matilda Newport Day – in honour of the 1822 battle of Fort Hill and the birth of the nation.

In this way, and very importantly at this time, when the existence of the republic was once again imperilled by its "perfidious enemies," both the militia created to secure the future presence of "Liberia" and the holiday created to commemorate the battle that secured the past presence of "Liberia" were drawn together in the image of "Matilda Newport."[35] Thus, "Matilda Newport" emerged as an image *in* and *of* history, connecting what was behind – the Providential battle for "Liberia's" past – with what was ahead – the Promise of "Liberia's" future – through an image that legitimated and propagated the legality and force of this history. Where "Liberia" remained an abstraction even after its declaration as a republic in 1847 – with an uncertain presence in international law and an uncertain presence on the ground in west Africa, outside its littoral settlements – "Matilda Newport" came to consolidate a place for "Liberia" both as an image of justice and as a historical reality.

The body of the settler woman, now the body of the republic, thus gave birth to "Liberia" in two ways. As a representation, an origin myth, "Matilda Newport" came to signify the history of "Liberia," visualizing – making visible – its providence as a settlement of pioneers under a banner of liberty. And as a technology, a tool of colonial nation-state building, the image of "Matilda Newport" was deployed to make this history. In these two ways, not only did "Matilda Newport" come to represent the past and the future of "Liberia" in west Africa – and thus a narrative *of* history that placed "Liberia" *in* history – but she also combined the justice of "Liberia" with the force that had and would secure its very presence as a Republic in Africa and the world.

"Lady Justice"

Finally imagine this. Standing in the entrance hall of the Peace Palace in The Hague is a marble statue entitled *Peace through Justice.* The statue depicts a figure who appears at once female and male, merging feminine and masculine types.[36] This is the figure of a "modern Lady Justice" – of *Justitia* bulging with strength.[37] Force ripples through her limbs, pulses through her veins. The wind blowing aside her gown reveals not the typically feminine legs of justice but brute trunks of force. Resembling Michelangelo's marble statue of David poised for battle against Goliath – and as the very embodiment of Pascal's *pensée* – this image poses a disturbing truth: "peace" needs a forceful justice.

The image of "Matilda Newport" suggests a Liberian version of this "Lady Justice." Conjugating woman and cannon in the act that gave birth to the republic, the image unites feminine justice with phallic force to make its vision of "Liberia" manifest. There is nothing rigid, nothing timeless, nothing placeless, about "Matilda Newport." Like Bernini's version of David,[38] she is tensed in action, a bandana keeping her hair and sweat from blinding her vision, the barrel of the cannon directed in no uncertain way at whatever would deny her place in the promised land – this is not an anaemic figure of *Justitia* for all times and for all places; she is active, determined, *forceful*.

And this is precisely why the image of "Matilda Newport" was eventually condemned as a representation of "Liberia." In the second half of the twentieth century, Liberia underwent a revolution that culminated in 1980 with the overthrow of the Americo-Liberian regime that had ruled Liberia for a century and a half. African-Liberians, whose ancestors knew the lands of "Liberia" long before the republic was an idea, finally took control of the government. The celebration of Matilda Newport Day was swept away, and the image publicly denounced for glorifying "the defeat of one group of citizens by another group of citizens."[39] The image that had represented, and that had deployed to achieve, the consolidation of "Liberia" as a nation state, through the forceful seizure of the lands and the institution of control over the peoples of this place, was too deeply implicated in this history. Where "Liberia" retained its mobility as a signifier, surviving the revolution to remain, as it does today, a wholly acceptable image of this country and its peoples, "Matilda Newport" had become too bound to the bloodied chariot wheels of its own historical production and its technological intervention in history.[40] In the four-cornered interplay of the image, "Matilda Newport" had sunk too deeply into a specific history to remain viable as a dynamic image of a revised, post-colonial republic.

But the very floating quality that kept the image of "Liberia" from sinking into history has also kept it from providing a solid basis for remaking the nation state after the revolution and wars of the 1990s and early 2000s. The abstract image of "Liberia" that required "Matilda Newport" to ground it in history has kept it on the surface of history. It remains a disembodied ideal, *still* a promise of justice to come, signifying, from a great height, nothing and everything on the ground. What it means to "be" Liberian in the second decade of the twenty-first century remains as fluid and plural as the peoples who inhabit this country. "Liberia" remains a state without a nation, and more than that, a state without a definite image of itself as a nation. Like the image of "Matilda Newport," the official symbols of the republic – its flag, patterned on the US flag, its coat of arms, with its colonial motifs, and its motto, "The love of liberty brought us here" – are of a nation that was, a nation of Americo-Liberians that a violent history has submerged.

And yet "Liberia" is being remade, with the assistance of an international "peace building" intervention led since 2003 by the United Nations Mission in Liberia.[41] The mandate of this UN mission reflects the statue that stands in The Hague: to bring about "peace through justice"; and like that modern statue of *Justitia*, the justice that is to secure this state of peace is indistinguishable from force. In the first decade of the remaking of "Liberia," new fortifications are being erected and new military and police forces commissioned, as a new vision of transitional justice is brought within the logic of building and strengthening the state "security sector."[42] "Decentralization," to diffuse the administration of democratic government throughout the interior, and thereby strengthen the government's control of the interior; "reconciliation," to foster national unity; "human rights," to ensure dignity for all; "legal system reform," to strengthen the institution of state law, and above all, the property, contract, and investment rights necessary to open the country's lands up to economic development: these, among other pillars of the post-war state-building and development agenda, have come to represent the official vision of "Liberia" as a modern, liberal, democratic nation state integrated into a global corporate-capitalist economy.[43]

Conclusion: "Liberia" in Transition

Recall the four aspects of the image I set out in the first part of the essay: as representation, the image provides a fluid medium for seeing and revealing, and overlooking, its object, whilst creating its object through visualization; and as technology, the image is a product of history with a definite materiality, whilst altering the course of history at the same time as it is ignored or defied by a world that shifts around it. What I have sought to show through the essay is how "Liberia" was made and is being remade in this four-cornered interplay of "image" and "object," leaving it in a state of perpetual transition.

Thus, whereas "Liberia" was conceived by the American Colonization Society as an image of justice to come – its birth foreseen as the light on the horizon that would save Africa from darkness – its consolidation in west Africa was achieved through the most visible show of force, a conjugation of justice and force that was represented most strikingly in the image of "Matilda Newport." And this transition from "Liberia" as an image of justice for all of Africa, to the forceful justice of "Matilda Newport" directed at securing the liberty of a few, occurred because the African peoples who would be made Liberian, as well as the European states who would have to recognize the black republic under international law, were opposed to the consolidation of "Liberia" from the first moments of its settlement.

And yet, whereas "Matilda Newport" sunk under its concrete weight as an image *in* history, the image of "Liberia" has stayed afloat despite the tumultuous currents that have washed over the lands and peoples it came to signify. As an image *of* history, "Liberia" has proved agile, capable of signifying new meanings as everything shifts around it. Now, after the revolution and wars that destroyed the First Republic of "Matilda Newport," "Liberia" is being made once more. As its history is revised, from a narrative of liberation to one of violent colonial incursion into west Africa, its image is likewise being revised, providing new ways of seeing this history, and new ways of imagining its future presence as a post-colonial republic.

And yet again, this new "Liberia" does not have a concrete image of itself. The very quality that has enabled the image of "Liberia" to remain afloat – its high abstraction as a promise of justice – continues to make it a weak technology for influencing the course of history, just as the very quality that made "Matilda Newport" such a force in history made it sink with the weight of the colonial Americo-Liberian regime that it so concretely represented. Post-revolution, post-war, "Liberia" remains an abstraction, still a promise of justice to come, just over the horizon.

In this light, both government and international interveners are working to recast "Liberia," this time as a liberal, democratic nation state integrated into the global economy. At the same time as the justice of this post-war "Liberia" is being proclaimed, new fortifications are being built and new forces are being trained to make it concrete. Whilst the image of "Liberia" has changed, the irreconcilable separation of "image" and "object" – of Liberia and its place in the world – has not. And so, as the justice of the new "Liberia" takes forceful form, as it always must, and as its peoples continue to defy the liberalization of their lands, the authority of the central government, and the laws of its parliament, but also as they change under its influence and contribute to the remaking of this "Liberia," two things seem clear. As an image *of* history, "Liberia" remains open to multiple, contradictory visions of justice, its meaning shifting along with the peoples who care enough to use it to make sense of their place in west Africa and the world. And as an image *in* history, "Liberia" continues to take concrete forms that cannot avoid the histories, both past and future, of the peoples and places it represents. While some of these forms continue to be backed with more force than others, even the greatest force cannot keep control of a troubled vision of justice.

Thus, two types of image can be seen to pervade the history of the making of Liberia, one tracking across its surface, the other coursing through its middle. And perhaps the genius of "Liberia" is its capacity to be both types at once: whilst it remains a mobile signifier, an abstract image of justice that floats over the tumultuous movements of history, it does so by marshalling an army of constant signifiers, such as the image of "Matilda Newport," to represent it, and to create it, in history.

NOTES

1 Blaise Pascal, *Pascal's Pensées* (New York: E. P. Dutton & Co., 1958), 85. This translation is from Jacques Derrida, "Force of Law: The 'Mystical Foundation of Authority,'" *Cardozo Law Review* 11 (1989–90): 937. See also Marin's consideration of this: Louis Marin, *Portrait of the King* (Minneapolis: University of Minnesota Press, 1988), 17–23.

2 See discussion and critique in Desmond Manderson, "The Metastases of Myth: Legal Images as Transitional Phenomena," *Law Critique* 26 (2015): 207–23.

3 As *representation*, such images are transitional, involving a repositioning of history, which continues to exist only in its imprints, which are constantly being reframed. As Marin writes, "representation" always involves this double act of substitution and authorization: Marin, *Portrait of the King*, 5–6. Thus, the passport photo substitutes your image in place of you

and at the same time authorizes that image as if it *were* you. When the immigration officer checks your credentials, she looks at your passport photo first, and then checks whether you conform with your image. In this, you have become the trace of your image, and not the other way round. Through the act of representation, your image is now *before you*, signifying your existence.

4 For a discussion of these two different approaches, see Manderson, "The Metastases of Myth," 208–9. In sum, Manderson contrasts "the search for constant signifieds beneath mobile signifiers" (as "a pretty succinct characterization of structuralism") and "the search for mobile signifieds beneath constant and iterable signifiers" (as "a pretty succinct characterization of post-structuralism").

5 With thanks to Desmond Manderson for suggesting the metaphor of the ship and its wake.

6 George Washington Park Custis, address to the Annual Meeting of the American Colonization Society in support of their colonization mission: American Colonization Society, *Seventh Annual Report of the American Society for Colonizing the Free People of Colour of the United States* (Washington: printed by Davis and Force, 1824), 15–16.

7 Charles Henry Huberich, *The Political and Legislative History of Liberia* (New York: Central Book Co., 1947), 143. See also Frederick Starr, *Liberia: Description, History, Problems* (Chicago: [no publisher] 1913), 57.

8 Constitution of "The American Society for Colonizing the Free People of Color of the United States," in *A View of Exertions Lately Made for the Purpose of Colonizing the Free People of Color, in the United States, in Africa, or Elsewhere* (Washington, DC: printed by Jonathan Elliot, 1817), 11–12.

9 "An Act in Addition to the Acts Prohibiting the Slave Trade," 3 March 1819, in *Statutes at Large of the United States of America, 1789–1873*, vol. 3 (1845), 532–4.

10 See Eric Burin, *Slavery and the Peculiar Solution: A History of the American Colonization Society* (Gainesville: University Press of Florida, 2005).

11 See ibid. For a history of the origins of "Liberia," see also: Amos J. Beyan, *African American Settlements in West Africa: John Brown Russwurm and the American Civilizing Efforts* (New York: Palgrave Macmillan, 2005); James Ciment, *Another America: Story of Liberia and the Former Slaves Who Ruled It* (New York: Hill and Wang, 2013); Claude A. Clegg III, *The Price of Liberty: African Americans and the Making of Liberia* (Chapel Hill: University of North Carolina Press, 2004); William Jay, *An Inquiry into the Character and Tendency of the American Colonization and American Anti-Slavery Societies*, 4th ed. (New York: R.G. Williams, 1837); Tom W. Shick, *Behold the Promised*

Land: A History of Afro-American Settler Society in Nineteenth-Century Liberia (Baltimore: Johns Hopkins University Press, 1980).

12 See, e.g., the discussion at one of the first meetings of the American Colonization Society, in *A View of Exertions Lately Made*, 4–11, and see in particular the statement of John Randolph at 9–10. On the connection between the colonization mission and the desire to secure the purity of white America, see also the "Memorial of the President and board of Managers of the American society for colonizing the free people of color of the United States" submitted to Congress, in *A View of Exertions Lately Made*, 14.

13 See, e.g., Burin, *Slavery and the Peculiar Solution*, chap. 1.

14 See, e.g., ibid., 13–14.

15 Statement of Elias Caldwell, in *A View of Exertions Lately Made*, 7. See also Ciment, *Another America*, 9.

16 *A View of Exertions Lately Made*, 7. On the aims of the colonization mission, see also American Colonization Society, *Seventh Annual Report*, 7.

17 American Colonization Society, *Seventh Annual Report*, 5–6 (emphasis in original).

18 Thanks to Desmond Manderson for pointing out this unusual situation of a country named after an idea rather than an ethnic or geographic indicator.

19 Letter from the acting agent of the American Colonization Society at Cape Montserado, J. Ashmun, to the secretary of the US Navy, in American Colonization Society, *Seventh Annual Report*, 49–50.

20 See, e.g., "Extract of a letter from Captain Robert T. Spence to the Secretary of the U.S. Navy," in American Colonization Society, *Seventh Annual Report*, 58–9. See also generally references, *supra* note 11.

21 Cited in Svend E. Holsoe, "Matilda Newport: The Power of a Liberian-Invented Tradition," *Liberian Studies Journal* 32, no. 2 (2007): 30.

22 American Colonization Society, *Seventh Annual Report*, 55 and 60 (my italics).

23 Ibid., 60.

24 Ibid. (my italics).

25 Ibid.

26 Declaration of Independence of Liberia (1847).

27 See Holsoe, "Matilda Newport."

28 Ibid., 34.

29 In addition to the depiction of "Matilda Newport" in the relief reproduced here, there is a plaque in her honour at the Centennial Pavilion in Monrovia, alongside a cenotaph erected on the 100th anniversary of the

battle of Fort Hill, known as the Matilda Newport Monument: see also ibid., 34.

30 Ibid., 38.

31 "The Story of Matilda Newport – Liberian Heroine," *AFRO Magazine*, 3 February 1953, 8.

32 A main street and a school in central Monrovia are named after Matilda Newport. An act to establish an interior township named Matilda Newport, "in honor of the heroine Matilda Newport," was also passed by the Liberian legislature in 1854: see American Colonization Society, *The African Repository*, vol. 30 (Washington, DC: American Colonization Society, 1854), 241.

33 See, e.g., Monday B. Abasiattai, "European Intervention in Liberia with Special Reference to the 'Cadell Incident' of 1908–1909," *Liberian Studies Journal* 14, no. 1 (1989); Harrison Akingbade, "The Pacification of the Liberian Hinterland," *Journal of Negro History* 79, no. 3 (1994); Raymond Leslie Buell, *Liberia: A Century of Survival, 1847–1947* (Philadelphia: University of Pennsylvania Press, 1947); Yekutiel Gershoni, *Black Colonialism: The Americo-Liberian Scramble for the Hinterland* (Boulder: Westview Press, 1985); Yekutiel Gershoni, "The Formation of Liberia's Boundaries, Part I: Agreements," *Liberian Studies Journal* 17, no. 1 (1992); Yekutiel Gershoni, "The Formation of Liberia's Boundaries, Part II: The Demarcation Process," *Liberian Studies Journal* 17, no. 2 (1992).

34 Holsoe, "Matilda Newport," 33.

35 Thus a historian, writing in 1926, claimed that Matilda Newport's heroic deeds contributed to securing Liberia's independence from external powers, France and Britain: see Siahyonkron Nyanseor, "Putting to Rest the Matilda Newport Myth – Part 2," *The Perspective*, 7 January 2004, http://www.theperspective.org/2004/jan/matildanewportmyth.htm.

36 For an image of the statue, see "Piece of the Palace," http://pointsoflight.pieceofthepalace.com/PTJvert.pdf.

37 US Department of State, "Sites Relating to US History in the Netherlands," 20 August 2013, http://photos.state.gov/libraries/netherlands/328666/pdfs/Sites%20of%20memory%20Ranked%20by%20Theme%202013-8.pdf, 35.

38 With thanks to Desmond Manderson for drawing my attention to the comparison with the statues of David by Michelangelo and Bernini.

39 Holsoe, "Matilda Newport," 37–8.

40 "Chariot wheels" is a reference to the passage at the beginning of the section on "Liberia": see note 6 above.

41 For the initial mandate, see UN Res. 1509 (19 September 2003).

42 For an extended analysis, see Shane Chalmers and Jeremy Farrall, "Securing the Rule of Law through UN Peace Operations in Liberia," *Max Planck Yearbook of United Nations Law* 18 (2014).

43 See, e.g., Republic of Liberia, Agenda for Transformation: Liberia's Medium Term Economic Growth and Development Strategy (2012–2017), http://cdcliberia.org/The_Agenda_for_Transformation_AfT.pdf.

PART TWO

Technologies – Excesses of Legal Modernity in the Twentieth Century

7 "You Will See My Family Became So American": Race, Citizenship, and the Visual Archive

SHERALLY MUNSHI[1]

One morning in October 1932, Dinshah Ghadiali was at his home in New Jersey, eating breakfast with his family when, as he later wrote, "a dignified looking gentleman entered the living room and announcing himself as Deputy United States Marshal Buck, presented me with a paper marked *subpoena*."[2] As Ghadiali soon learned, the government was seeking to cancel his citizenship, on the grounds that it had been "illegally procured."[3] The complaint against him alleged that "Dinshah P. Ghadiali by reason of his not being a free white person or a person of African nativity or descent is, and was, ineligible racially for naturalization."[4] Upon reading the complaint, Ghadiali reflected: "So I was not a White man and not a Black man either. *What then was I?* ... I looked ruefully at my skin, that unfortunate covering which had brought me into Court once more. I rubbed it to see what was underneath, but do what I could, no color ... that I could recognize as other than White shone forth."[5]

A Parsi Zoroastrian, born and raised in Bombay, India, Ghadiali immigrated to the United States in 1911. He became a naturalized citizen in 1917, the same year that Congress passed a law barring further immigration from Asia. He made his home in Malaga, New Jersey, where he hoped to establish himself as an important inventor, but instead earned notoriety as a charismatic and irrepressible quack. Over the course of his career, Ghadiali had been arrested several times for violating laws regulating the practice of medicine.[6] But after he married a white woman, in 1923, he had become the target of increasingly racialized scrutiny.

Thus, when Ghadiali learned of the government's attempt to cancel his citizenship – more than fifteen years after his naturalization ceremony – he assumed that he was the victim of "medico-political conspiracy."[7] As he explained to the judge at his denaturalization trial, "It is a *persecution*, Your Honor."[8] In fact, as he would soon discover, Ghadiali had not been singled out for persecution; he had been caught in a much broader campaign to denaturalize citizens of Indian origin after the Supreme Court, in *United States v. Thind*, determined that "Hindus" were "racially ineligible" for naturalization.[9] The court explained that although individual immigrants from India had proven themselves capable of cultural assimilation, as a group, Indian immigrants were disqualified from citizenship because they were *visually* inassimilable.[10] Unlike their European counterparts, who "quickly merge into the mass of our population,"[11] Indians retain their "physical group characteristics … [which] render them readily distinguishable."[12]

By the time Ghadiali appeared before a judge, he had already been living in the United States for more than twenty years, most of them as an American citizen. He had established a business, bought a home, and married an American woman, with whom he had five sons. He studiously avoided the political organizations and mutual aid societies established by other Indians in the United States, choosing to pursue a life of middle-class respectability instead. When the United States entered the world war as an ally of British imperialists, hundreds of Indians in the United States left to return home, hoping the war would bring an end to British rule in India. Ghadiali, by contrast, hoping to prove his loyalty to the United States, volunteered his service.

But after *Thind*, the relevant qualification for citizenship was neither assimilation nor loyalty; it was racial appearance. Thus, at his denaturalization trial, Ghadiali found himself in the peculiar position of having to defend his citizenship by convincing the judge that he *looked* white. Ghadiali submitted into evidence more than a dozen photographs, depicting himself, his children, and his property. As he submitted these, he assured the judge, "You will see my family became so American. We live just like American people. Here is one of my babies' rooms, to show how we live inside. The Honorable Justice Sutherland said in the *Thind* case, 'The Hindus are not assimilable.' I am NOT Hindu. I am European and I shall give you the proofs presently."[13]

How do these photographs purport to show that Ghadiali and his family had become "so American"? In this essay, through a close reading of Ghadiali's photography, I explore the tension between the visualization of race – a practice at once institutionalized by law and inextricably bound with the medium of photography – and the performance of national belonging. By assuring the judge that his photographs would prove his identity, Ghadiali appealed to the contemporary confidence that photography offered a true and unmediated view of reality.

Scholars of visual culture relate the evidential force of photography to its indexical character, or the material connection between the photographic image and the person or thing that it represents. It was photography's indexical character that rendered it so immediately attractive to race scientists who used the camera to study and record human variation in the nineteenth century. The supposed transparency of the camera eye lent habits of racial regard the air of scientific objectivity. In the hands of race scientists, Coco Fusco has argued, early photography did not just record "the existence of race"; instead, it played a critical role in "producing race as a visualizable fact."[14] The observation and recording of racial difference was not confined to race scientists. The methods of race scientists also informed the criminological uses of photography in the late nineteenth century. Francis Galton used composite images to visualize criminal types; Alphonse Bertillon introduced photography to policing practices in Paris to identify recidivists. By fixing the criminal to his image, photography proved especially effective at "literally arresting" its subject.[15] In the United States, it was the photograph's superiority over the supposedly duplicitous speech of Chinese immigrants that rendered the medium critical to the administration of new immigration controls.[16]

But as critics have argued, photography's authority to represent reality is not primarily a function of its indexical properties but the effect of social conventions, reflecting prevailing social relations.[17] In the United States, racial order has been maintained not only through the repressive force of law, but through law's organization of the perceptible world. In *Thind*, for instance, the Supreme Court constructed a new racial category, one that would provide the basis for excluding large groups of peoples from the United States. But the court went further to construct the racial reality it sought to govern – purifying the landscape of foreign elements, marking certain bodies with racial difference, investing others with powers of racial surveillance, cultivating in them new forms of racial knowledge and instinct. The visual realm remains a particularly useful site for locating racial knowledge because it appears self-evident, transparent to the eye, prior to and thus innocent of the effects of law. Law's complicity in producing forms of racial difference, affiliation, and aversion disappear into the apparent givenness of the visible world. Regimes of power dissolve into the regime of senses.

The photographs that Ghadiali submitted at his trial do not reveal the truth of his identity so much as the regime of racial looking of which it is a part. They betray both the violence of racial inscription as well as the burdens of self-discipline and compliance borne by Ghadiali and his family. But they also demonstrate to us that the visual is not merely coextensive with either the real or what is seen.[18] Instead, it is mediated through social categories and historical processes that continuously reconstitute reality. How can we engage Ghadiali's photographs, then, without reproducing the terms of difference, the self-evidence or facticity of race? How might we produce an alternative framework for addressing the question "*What then was I?*"

Thind and the Legal Construction of Racial Difference

The Naturalization Act of 1790, one of the first laws enacted by the United States Congress, restricted citizenship to "free white persons."[19] The law was amended in 1870, after the abolition of slavery, to extend citizenship "to aliens of African nativity and to persons of African descent."[20] The law posed few hurdles to immigration or naturalization until the turn of the twentieth century, when a great diversity of peoples began immigrating to the United States.[21]

With the arrival of these "new immigrants," American courts found themselves under pressure to administer a more restrictive interpretation of the Naturalization Act – especially the words "white persons."[22] Ian Haney López, in his widely influential study of immigrant racialization in the United States, observed that around the turn of the twentieth century, courts interpreting the racially restrictive language of the Naturalization Act generally followed one of two lines of reasoning to determine racial identity.[23] The first appealed to "common knowledge," or popular conceptions of race and racial classifications. The second turned to "scientific evidence," or the expertise of race scientists – anthropologists, ethnologists, and linguists. In most cases, common knowledge and scientific evidence tended to point to the same conclusion – individuals who *looked* "white" often belonged to groups that scientists identified as Caucasian or Aryan. But confusion would arise in cases involving immigrants from India and "Arabia": to most Americans, Indians did not belong to any category of persons they recognized to be white, but race scientists maintained that these immigrants were Aryan or Caucasian, descendants of the same ancestors as European Americans.[24] The confusion eventually reached the Supreme Court.

In 1923, in *United States v. Thind*, the court was asked to determine whether Bhagat Singh Thind, "a high-caste Hindu, of full Indian blood, born at Amritsar, Punjab, India is a white person within the meaning of [the Naturalization Act]?"[25] In a similar case, decided the year before, the court determined that Japanese immigrants were not "white persons" for purposes of naturalization, and were thus racially ineligible for citizenship.[26] In that case, *Ozawa v. United States* (1922), Takao Ozawa argued that he *was* a "white person" because his skin, like the skin of most Japanese, *looked* white.[27] The court declined to adopt the skin-colour test Ozawa proposed, finding that skin colour was not a reliable indicator of race. Instead, it ruled that the words "white person" were meant to indicate persons of "Caucasian race."[28] Confronted with the variability of forms of visual identification, the court appealed to the supposed certainty of racial scientific discourse.

A few months later, when Thind argued that, as an Indian, he belonged to the category of persons that race scientists called "Caucasian," the Supreme Court did not disagree. But Thind's argument forced the court to revise its appreciation of race science as well as its ruling in *Ozawa*. That most experts considered Indians to be Caucasian, the court explained in *Thind*, "does not end the matter."[29] The court emphasized that in *Ozawa* it had held that the words "white person" should accord with "what is *popularly* known as the Caucasian race."[30] Justice Sutherland, writing for a unanimous court, further explained: "What we now hold is that the words 'free white person' are words of *common speech*, to be interpreted in accordance with the understanding of the common man ... As so understood and used, whatever may be the speculations of the ethnologist, it does not include the body of people to whom [Thind] belongs."[31]

The court conceded that among ethnologists, the words "Caucasian" and "Aryan" had come to embrace a wide swathe of humanity, peoples as diverse as Europeans and Indians. But in embracing such diverse peoples, the language of race scientists no longer reflected "the understanding of the common man." Indeed, the court reasoned, the "average well-informed white American would learn with some degree of astonishment that the race to which he belongs is made up of such heterogeneous elements."[32] In the court's opinion, science had proved a less than discriminating judge of difference, and the "common knowledge" shared by average white Americans was the preferable litmus test for determining who qualified for naturalization.

Haney López, whose analysis of the racial bar to naturalization remains influential and authoritative, argues that *Ozawa* and *Thind*, read together, reveal the role that law plays in the construction of racial categories.[33] He argues that the court's recourse to the language of race science in *Ozawa* and its sudden disavowal of the same language in *Thind* only a few months later betray the court's understanding of the essential instability of race as a social construction. In Haney López's analysis,

> The Supreme Court abandoned scientific explanations of race in favor of those rooted in common knowledge when science failed to reinforce popular beliefs about racial differences. The Court's eventual embrace of common knowledge confirms the falsity of natural notions of race, exposing race instead as a social product measurable only in terms of what people believe.[34]

But how does the average white American come to share in a common knowledge about racial difference? In Haney López's analysis, the court toggles between two racial epistemologies or abstract knowledge-forms – namely, race science and "common knowledge" – ultimately betraying the arbitrariness, contingency, and instability of both. I want to suggest that what is perhaps most remarkable about the court's movement between *Ozawa* and *Thind* is its attempt to shift the location of racial knowledge from racial episteme to racial ontology, from racial reasoning to racial sensibility, from "what people believe" to what they *feel* "instinctively." In other words, the law is implicated in not only the formalization of racial categories but in the institutionalization of racial regard and the cultivation of racial aversion.

For Justice Sutherland, Hindus were inassimilable in a peculiar sense. They were *visually* inassimilable not only because they looked different from white Americans, but because their differences impeded white Americans' recognition of identity. As he explained, Hindus' "racial difference" was "of such character and extent that the great body of our people *instinctively* recognize it and reject the thought of assimilation."[35] It was only from the supposed perspective of a white majority that Hindus were inassimilable. Hindus could not be naturalized, in Justice Sutherland's view, because their appearance could not be reconciled with a white majority's *vision* of citizenship.

What is striking about the language in *Thind* is the way in which race appears not just as an abstract form of *common knowledge* but as a more deeply embodied *common sense*. While in *Ozawa* the court sought to fortify a dubious construction – "white persons" – with the supposed rigour of racial scientific discourse, in *Thind* the court began its analysis by pointing out the "flexibility" of words like "Caucasian" and "Aryan." The court expressed its impatience with the "speculative processes of ethnological reasoning" that had conjured a kinship between the European and Hindu.[36] "It may be true," the court acknowledged, "that the blond Scandinavian and the brown Hindu have a common ancestor in the dim reaches of antiquity, but the average man knows perfectly well that there are unmistakable and profound differences between them today."[37] But what are these "profound" differences, both "unmistakable" and *unnamed*? Where ethnologists and linguists had developed their discourse to bridge supposedly unfathomable difference, the court favoured the mute, inarticulate certainty of the common man, who *perceives* without naming what distinguishes him from others. Here, the authority to designate racial qualification for citizenship is withdrawn not only from the language of race experts but from language altogether.

The authority to identify racial difference, in turn, is reinvested in the perceptual capacities and racial instincts of the average American. After conceding that the European and Hindu may have descended from a common ancestor, the court announced that the relevant test for racial identity was not common ancestry but contemporary resemblance. It went on to offer this curious illustration: "It is not impossible, if that common ancestor could be *materialized in the flesh*, we should discover that he was himself sufficiently differentiated from both of his descendants."[38] Apart from the ghoulishness of the thought-experiment, the test the court announced was not merely one of physical resemblance but "visceral resonance."[39] We hear the demand for visceral resonance amplified in the court's claim that the original drafters of the Naturalization Act intended to limit citizenship to only those immigrants whom they would have recognized to be white – "*bone of their bone and flesh of their flesh.*"[40]

In the court's analysis, the statutory language limiting citizenship – "white persons" – gains a flesh and corporeality, not only through repeated references to the body, but through the force of the ruling itself. At its heart, the holding in *Thind* might be understood to assert that the right to interpret the meaning of the words "white persons," and thus the power to define the national body, is itself the natural right of "white persons." The court explained that, at the time the Naturalization Act was drafted, immigration "was almost exclusively from the British Isles and Northwestern Europe, whence they and their forbearers had come." As such, "when [the drafters] extended the privilege of American citizenship to 'any alien'; being a free white person," it was these immigrants and their kind whom they must have had affirmatively in mind.[41] Thus, acting the part of a dutiful heir, the court described itself as constrained to interpret the words "white persons" in accordance with the intention of the founding fathers, from whom they descend, almost as hereditary title, to restrict the inheritance of the nation to members of the same racial family.

To be clear, the argument advanced here is not that the court in *Thind* provided us with an accurate representation of what average Americans actually *saw* or *felt*. Instead, the argument is that, through its rhetoric and reasoning, the court participated in rendering race a visualizable fact. It participated not only in the construction of the "Hindu" other but of the national body itself. The court's repeated references to the supposed "common understanding," "knowledge," and "instinct" of the "average ... white American" participate in the conjuring of a visible national body. So does the refusal to identify with and coexist alongside the Hindu become constitutive of national identity. The court's opinion is not a passive description of a given reality, but an assertion that transforms the reality it describes. It does this most obviously by transforming the status of both the raced Hindu and the white American. But it also does this more subtly by rendering "racial difference" a visual fact, given in nature, fixed and unchanging.

Naturalization and the Visual Archive

Ghadiali was one of few Indian immigrants to survive a challenge to his citizenship in the early part of the century. But his case was never reported. Like the trials of others who faced denaturalization, Ghadiali's is absent from the official legal archive.[42] His case is known to us only because he memorialized his ordeal in a slim volume entitled *Dinshah Naturalization Case Clearing Contested Citizenship* (hereinafter *Naturalization Case*).

Early in his career, Ghadiali bought a printing press to promote his discoveries. As he became the target of professional and increasingly racialized persecution, he gradually repurposed the press to archive the many injuries and affronts that he suffered at the hands of professional organizations, immigration officials, police officers, judges, juries, and journalists. Ghadiali published *Naturalization Case* in 1944 and gifted copies to libraries, attorneys general, and anyone whom he thought might be willing to give him a fair hearing. It is an unusual record, a heterogeneous collection of official documents – legal briefs, trial transcripts, newspaper clippings, mug shots – interrupted by his own editorialization and counter-narration.

Ghadiali's *Naturalization Case* is compelling not only because it records a history that has long escaped the attention of legal scholars. His narration and photographs exceed and call our attention to the limits of the "official" legal record. For instance, in one especially startling moment in his text, Ghadiali interrupts the usual transcription of trial argument to narrate an incident to the reader. Frustrated by so many questions about his racial identity, Ghadiali suddenly lifted his pant leg to reveal the skin underneath. As he wrote, "at this point, I laid bare my left leg and requested the judge to look at it as well as to feel it and note the texture."[43] The judge did so, evidently to the satisfaction of both men, as they thanked one another before the judge allowed Ghadiali to continue with his argument.

What are we to make of such an episode? Visual inspection of the body was not entirely new to the American courtroom – Ariela Gross, in her study of race trials in the antebellum south, describes it as something of a shameful commonplace.[44] The respondent in at least one other race naturalization case, an Afghani immigrant of "dark complexion" and "delicate" features, is reported to have been asked to "pull up [his] sleeves" to reveal not only that the skin covered by his clothing was "several shades lighter than his face and hands," but that it was "sufficiently transparent for the blue color of his veins to show very clearly."[45] What did Ghadiali expect to communicate by exposing his skin not only to visual inspection but to *touch*? What in turn, did the judge, *feel*? And when we speak of the judge's feeling, do we restrict ourselves to the notion of a tactile exchange of information, or does the scene compel us to imagine another kind of exchange, of *feeling* as affect?

These are not questions that we can pretend to answer, but the narrative aside directs our attention beyond the text of the law and into the realm of embodied experience – the worlds of sight, sound, and sensation in which racial meaning is so often lived and contested, made and unmade. Ghadiali's narration allows us to consider the ways in which race is made to appear *and disappear* within the legal text. But for Ghadiali's narration, how would we know, for instance, that the government attorney in this case, Assistant United States Attorney Oliver Randolph, was African American?[46] And when Ghadiali characterized his case not as "open and shut" but as "black and white," was he inviting the judge to make a visual comparison between Randolph and himself?[47] Do his words amplify a visual choreography that would otherwise escape the legal record?[48]

The photographs that Ghadiali submitted at his trial and reproduced in *Naturalization Case* foreground racial embodiment and modes of racial reasoning that often elude legal analysis but nonetheless animate it. What do photographs disclose that is not already disclosed by the legal text? Roland Barthes suggested that the rhetorical power of photography lies in its capacity to make the connotative appear denotative – photography has a way of naturalizing the artifice of culture.[49] Do Ghadiali's photographs "naturalize" the racial difference that, according to the *Thind* court, "our people instinctively recognize … and reject"? Or do the stubborn denotations of race impede his connotative claim to Americanness? Looking at Ghadiali's photographs, did the judge – do we – even in these black and white images, see the imprint of race?

"The Hopeful Immigrants in America"

Photography played an essential role in the visualization of "criminal" types; it also played a critical, if less acknowledged, role in constructing a racialized image of the American family.[50] The relatively low cost of photography beginning in the late nineteenth century gave middle-class Americans new opportunities to present themselves in ceremonial guise. Commercial photo studios drew upon conventions of self-representation rehearsed by elites, but were also careful to distinguish commercial portraits from the repressive forms of photography developed in scientific and criminal contexts.[51] In commercial portraits, distinctions of race and class were not dissolved in the common medium of photography, but heightened through representational conventions. While commercial portraits drew the middle class into conformity, standardizing the appearance of the respectable American family, administrative photography precipitated deviant types – the criminal, the immigrant, the industrial worker, the urban poor – as objects of scrutiny, knowledge, and control.[52]

MANEK — DINSHAH

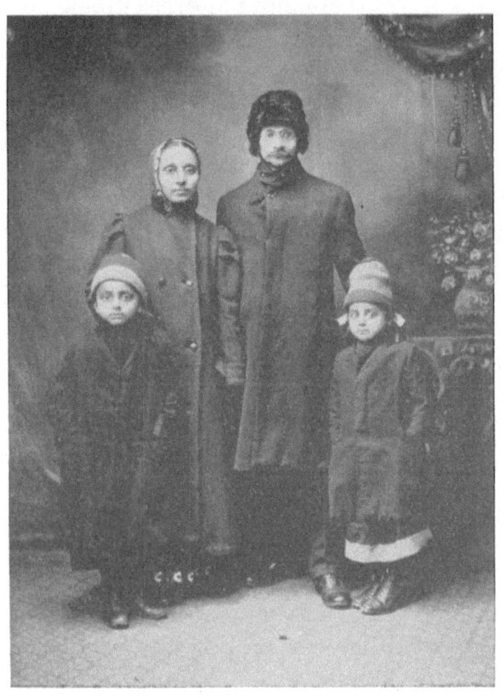

KHUSHCHEHER KASHMIRA

The Hopeful Immigrants In America
As They Looked in January, 1912.

Figure 7.1 A family portrait (1912). Reproduced with permission of Darius Dinshah.

In figure 7.1, a studio portrait representing the Ghadiali family as "Hopeful Immigrants in America," we recognize the projection of middle-class aspirations. In the photograph, a portrait of Ghadiali, his first wife, Manek, and their two young children, Kashmira and Khushcheher, are positioned in front of a painted backdrop, representing a domestic scene. The draped curtains and gilded table, topped with an arrangement of flowers, signify an American middle-class respectability and comfort that is not yet theirs but perhaps awaits them. The caption helps us to situate the image at the beginning of a familiar narrative of immigrant uplift and assimilation. But, insofar as captions often appear when images fail to speak for themselves, the caption also indexes uncertainty, the possibility of failure – a failure in the unfolding of the plot, a failure to look the part, a failure to project their own futurity.

We might situate our own view of the "Hopeful Immigrants" alongside other, administrative and regulatory modes of looking – inspection, spectatorship, surveillance – that begin but do not end at the border.[53] At the turn of the century, Asian immigrants entering the United States from San Francisco's Angel Island were routinely subject to physically invasive inspection.[54] European immigrants, mainly entering through Ellis Island, were spared invasive inspection but were nonetheless subject to what Anna Pegler-Gordon describes as medical and social "observation."[55] From the elevated galleries in Ellis Island, physicians scanned the mass of entering bodies for signs of irregularity, as other officials surveyed the scene for signs of disorder.

The galleries themselves attracted ordinary New Yorkers who came to witness the mass of people streaming through the gates. Pegler-Gordon aligns this form of spectatorship with visiting ethnographic exhibitions at one of the world's fairs or "slumming" – practices of observing structured by social distance and affirming the superiority of the observer over the observed.[56] The scene at Ellis Island also attracted professional and amateur photographers who wanted to capture the parade of difference on display. As Pegler-Gordon argues, describing it as "ethnographic honorific,"[57] their photographs are tinged with nostalgia, reflecting a desire to memorialize old-world differences (winged bonnets and long beards, for instance) before they disappeared entirely in the process of Americanization. The respectful presentation of these passing types confers a dignity on their subjects, mainly European, but it also bespeaks the confidence – expressed by Justice Sutherland in *Thind* – that the same subjects would eventually disappear into a homogeneous American population.[58]

Does the Ghadialis' portrait lay the same claim to assimilability as that of their European counterparts, for whom the signs of difference are erased with a change of costume? Or does the appearance of racial difference impede assimilation? Curiously, the hopeful Ghadialis arrive wearing none of the old-country clothing that featured so prominently in Ellis Island photography. Instead, they are shown wearing dark overcoats, worn boots, and plain head-coverings. The Ghadialis' clothing is unremarkable but for the striking incongruity between the appearance of defensive outerwear and warm intimacy suggested by the painted backdrop. How do we account for this incongruity, which seems only to exaggerate their status as outsiders?

Perhaps the coats themselves were worth putting on display. Before arriving in the United States, Ghadiali had applied for residency in Canada.[59] Though he was a subject of the British Empire, he was denied entry under new regulations restricting the migration of Indian subjects to the country.[60] Among the reasons Canadian officials cited for the regulation was the "humanitarian" concern that the "transfer of any people from a tropical climate to a northern one … [would] result in much physical suffering and danger to health."[61] If, as Canadian officials seemed to argue, the possibility of cultural assimilation was precluded by the supposed "climactic incompatibility" of Indians, then we might imagine that the Ghadialis' coats are shown to assert cultural assimilation as environmental adaptation.

I want to venture here another, related hypothesis. Perhaps Ghadiali and his family appear in coats and boots to disguise the fact that they were also covering their heads – not from the cold but in religious observance. At his denaturalization trial, Ghadiali recounted to the judge that in 1917 he had been thrown out of his naturalization oath ceremony for refusing to remove his *topi*.[62] As he testified, "the authorities lifted me and threw me out bodily."[63] The incident was also reported in the *New York Times*:

> One hundred and five aliens, representing seven nations of Europe, renounced their allegiance to their former Governments and were made American citizens … A little excitement was created when Dr. Dinshah P. Ghadiali of Hillsdale, N.J. … appeared in the court room wearing a turban hat, which he refused to remove when ordered by the court, and was ousted.[64]

Ghadiali was allowed to return to the oath ceremony, but his application was put aside until March of that year, after additional witnesses had testified in support of his application. Ghadiali explained to the judge, "It is a religious principle and a respect to the Honorable Court … We never make an Affirmation without a cap."[65]

What Ghadiali wore on top of his head was not a turban but a *topi*, the head-covering traditionally worn by Parsi Zoroastrians in India more closely resembling a skullcap, but the newspaper's mislabelling is telling of the way in which the turban had become a particularly "sticky signifier" by 1917.[66] Earlier in the century, the turban was still an object of benign fascination, a picturesque ornament, so inert a signifier that it had become a staple in women's fashion. But as Indian immigration to the United States increased, inciting animus from unions and anti-immigrant groups, particularly in the west, the turban became an object of suspicion, associated with excessive religiosity, deviant masculinity, and a lack of cleanliness. The turban – especially the refusal to remove it – came to signify unruly difference, a resistance to assimilation, defiance.

Thus, while the distinctive dress of Europeans features in Ellis Island photography as an object of mourning, a quaint difference lost to the process of Americanization, the turban appears as a stubborn sign, flickering between the cultural and the immutably corporeal, and hence, as Jasbir Puar suggests, between "that which can be disciplined and that which must be outlawed."[67] Here, perhaps, Ghadiali smuggles into the frame a sign of religious attachment that exceeds what the American family portrait can accommodate.

Naturalization as Discipline and Reform

At his denaturalization trial, Ghadiali produced a second family portrait, one that he had printed on a publicity card announcing his citizenship in 1917. As he explained to the judge, "I was so proud of my citizenship, I put this before the public with the remarks, 'The only Parsee Zoroastrian Citizen of the United States of America – America Always.'"[68]

In his *Naturalization Case*, the two family portraits, showing the Ghadialis first as new arrivals then as full-fledged citizens, appear one after the other, loosely conforming to the conventions of the familiar "before-and-after sequence." The before-and-after sequence, Laura Wexler argues, had become something of a staple in reformist propaganda by the late nineteenth century.[69] Reformists used the convention to demonstrate their capacity to turn others – emancipated slaves, pacified natives, raced immigrants – into citizens. How is citizenship represented in Ghadiali's announcement? If the previous photograph, showing the Ghadialis as they looked upon arrival, situates the family at the beginning of a narrative of assimilation, how is assimilation represented in the announcement photograph? Apart from the striking absence of Ghadiali's wife – an absence to which we will return in a moment – what sort of development does the photograph purport to represent?

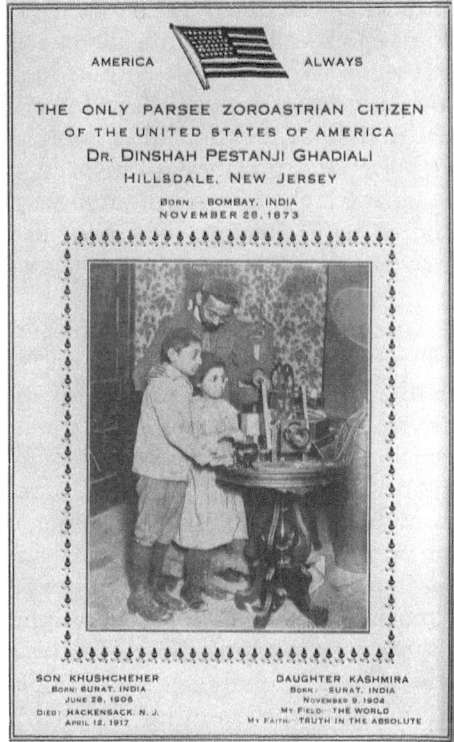

Figure 7.2 A publicity card announcing citizenship (1917). Reproduced with permission of Darius Dinshah.

In the photograph, Ghadiali and his two children are positioned beside a projector. His gaze is directed not at the camera, as before, but at his children, upon whom he looks with paternal authority and affection. The photograph is supposed to attest to Ghadiali's fulfilment of his civil duties as a patriarch. The children, in turn, appear cooperative, pliable. Because assimilationists recognized the children of immigrants to be more malleable than their parents, Ghadiali's claim to assimilability would rest, in part, upon his children's performance.

One cannot help but notice the artifice of the image, the contrived choreography of the bodies depicted. One hand rests on his son's shoulder while the other handles the projector. The hands of both children are riveted to the machine. Within the conventional grammar of photography, the machine represents forms of modernity, progress, and value that perhaps the bodies themselves cannot. Then there is the curious triangulation of looks: the children direct our gaze towards the projector, which seems to confront us with its look more directly than the subjects depicted. But our eyes return to bodies of the children, torqued as if to display, beyond their compliance with the photographer's instructions, openness to inspection generally – the kind of inspection made a routine part of immigrant processing and selecting, the kind of inspection into which we, like the judge, are drawn. It is an image of compliance, conformity, and spectacularized self-discipline.

The tension between the appearance of racial difference and the performance of citizenship can be further traced in the temporal framing of the photograph, the strangeness with which the image purports to capture development by *arresting* activity. But in the photographer's stilling of the image, we recognize the violence of the imposed order, the stultifying demand for self-discipline. Opponents of Indian immigration argued that Indians were lazy and unemployable, likely to become public charges; but the photograph purports to demonstrate that Ghadiali and his children were hard workers, willing and able to provide for themselves. And yet, while in much of his autobiographical writing Ghadiali represented himself as a zealously aspiring individual, here the promise (or threat) of upward mobility is carefully contained. While the previous image allows us to project "hope" onto the Ghadiali's future, the same bodies depicted in figure 7.1, in their uncomfortable state of suspended animation, here disclose their precarious liminality, the threat of deportation and statelessness that looms in the event of poor performance.

Becoming American

Figure 7.3 depicts Ghadiali's five sons from his second marriage. The youngest are perched on tricycles, the eldest on a bicycle, the sentimental appurtenances of a middle-class American childhood well displayed. Though all of Ghadiali's children were schooled at home – at a time when Asian-American children in some parts of the country were prevented from attending white public schools – their matching uniforms seem to place them within a metonymic sequence that extends from brotherhood to membership within the national community.[70]

In *Thind*, the court determined that no amount of education or discipline could incorporate the children of Ghadiali's first marriage into

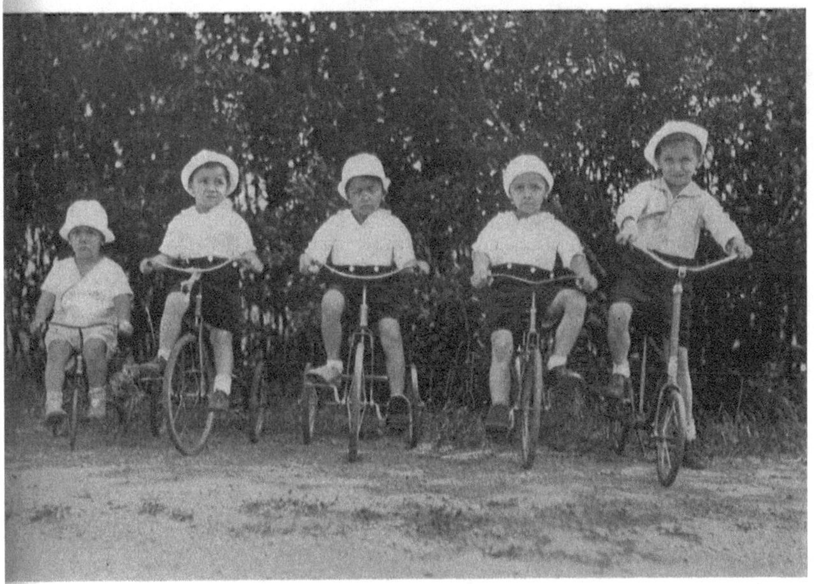

Figure 7.3 Ghadiali's sons from his second marriage (1929). Reproduced with permission of Darius Dinshah.

the national body. As Justice Sutherland explained, "The children … of Hindu parents would retain indefinitely the clear evidence of their ancestry … of such character and extent that the great body of our people instinctively recognize it and reject the thought of assimilation."[71] Compare the representation of the children from Ghadiali's first marriage to those of his second. In the earlier image, the children are pictured in training. Here, we are invited to imagine the children at play. In the earlier photograph, Ghadiali's children fix their gaze narrowly upon the projector, the symbol of progress in the photograph; they hold their bodies open to display. Here, Ghadiali's mixed-race children look directly into the camera, eliciting what Marianne Hirsch has described as "familiality," a recognition of the continuity in the domestic arrangements that extend from subject to spectator – in this case, the judge, who seemed far more captivated by Ghadiali's family album than he was by any other evidence of racial identity.[72] Here, Americanness is represented by the children themselves, their lighter skin, the relative comfort with which they seem to inhabit their environment – a natural setting, in this photo – and their own bodies. The contrast between the two images, I think, vivifies the differing claim to citizenship enjoyed by the natural-born and naturalized. For the natural-born citizen, rights and privileges flow naturally; for those who appear otherwise, or marked by racial difference, citizenship is conditioned upon performance – spectacular displays of self-discipline and mirroring of American social forms.

Vanishing Women

While figure 7.3 gestures at a continuity between Ghadiali's family and the nation, what is noticeably absent from Ghadiali's family album is any impression of racial discontinuity within the family. The photographs assemble as family either the Parsi Ghadialis (Dinshah, Manek, and their two children) or the mixed-race Ghadialis (the sons from his second marriage), but in none of these photographs are Ghadiali and Irene Grace pictured together. The suppression of the mixed-race couple of course signals the limits of the family portrait, or at least what Ghadiali understood as the limits of what the American gaze could familialize or naturalize.[73]

I have come across only one published photograph in which Ghadiali and his second wife, Irene, are pictured together. Though they are shown together alongside Ghadiali's daughter from his first marriage, Kashmira, it was framed as a scandal. The photograph was published in the *Dearborn Independent*, a newspaper known to reflect the anti-Semitic and xenophobic leanings of its owner, Henry Ford. The caption to the photograph reads, "Dinshah P. Ghadiali … who has come out of the Orient to heal the ills of mortal man … and his wife, Irene Grace Ghadiali, who *claims* to be an American."[74] Behind the rhetorical withholding of any recognition of national identity lay the real threat of expatriation. While the citizenship of wives generally followed that of their husbands, the Expatriation Act of 1907 provided that "any American woman who marries a foreigner shall take the nationality of her husband."[75]

In 1922, in response to an outcry by newly enfranchised women voters, Congress passed the Cable Act, generally repealing the marital expatriation provisions, but with an important exception: American women who married "aliens ineligible for citizenship," a category reserved for Asian immigrants, might yet lose their citizenship.[76]

At his denaturalization hearing, as the judge scanned the images of Manek and Irene Grace, Ghadiali pointed out the awful irony of his situation. He explained that he was deserted by his first wife "because I would *become* a Citizen. Now America throws me out and my second wife will desert me because I did *not* become a Citizen. The government puts me in a funny position."[77]

Conclusion

After both parties made their final arguments, as Ghadiali narrated, "there was a tense silence pervading the Court ... The Honorable Judge was seated on his bench, with his hands folded behind his neck, for a few short moments, gazing steadily into space."[78] The judge finally spoke, somewhat uneasily:

> The real issue, I suppose, laying aside all the technicalities, is as to whether or not the Respondent was and is a White Person, as contemplated in the Statute. The ... question is rather difficult, in view of the fact that the Races of the Earth are considerably mixed at the present time ... and that there is no tracing of the descent of this Respondent, excepting in his own recollection or tradition.[79]

Throughout the trial, the judge, John Boyd Avis, seemed reluctant to engage in any analysis of Ghadiali's racial identity. And in the end, rather than apply the rule announced in *Thind*, Judge Avis decided the case on procedural grounds. In his view, the question of Ghadiali's eligibility for citizenship had been litigated once before, more than fifteen years earlier, and *res judicata* precluded its reopening. As he said,

> I am inclined to think ... that the Respondent is a White Person, in the contemplation of the Statute. But regardless of that, here is a man who was naturalized after a hearing ... authorized to be admitted as a Citizen ... either on its own motion or with the assent, consent, and approval of the Government, [which] authorized, found, concluded and decided that the

> Respondent was a White Person, entitled to be naturalized under the Statute which is now in question ... I think that in the instant case, the case we are now trying, that it is *Res Adjudicata* ... that the Court has not the power at present to grant the Prayer of the Bill of Complaint and cancel the Naturalization Certificate, now held by the Respondent, and as a result, I feel it my duty to dismiss the Bill of Complaint.[80]

Ghadiali's victory did little to unsettle prevailing white supremacy. The *New York Times*, in an editorial, supported Ghadiali's claim to citizenship – but on grounds of the "scientific evidence" he presented to the court. "The defendant contends that he is not a Hindu but a Parsee of the Indo-Iranic or Indo-European family to which all the leading racial white strains belong. But even if he were a Hindu, the argument from ethnology and philology would carry force. If anybody was entitled to an Indo-European club it ought to be a native of India."[81] The *Times* called for only the slightest enlargement of "club" membership to embrace those belonging to "leading racial white strains." Beyond that marginal expansion of the definition of "white," it did little to challenge the colour line.

Moreover, as Ghadiali's case conveys, the nation maintains its identity not only through practices of immigrant exclusion but by narrowing the terms and conditions of inclusion. Immigrant naturalization renders apparent the conventionality of birthright citizenship, the peculiar manner in which political membership becomes attached to the raw process of birth, grafting certain peoples to certain places while rendering the newcomer an "alien." Naturalization, as the legal process that turns "aliens" into citizens, also renders apparent the social and cultural prerequisites of national identity.[82] Ghadiali's photographs reflect an Americanness conceived narrowly in terms of respectable family formation and entrepreneurial self-reliance. In other photographs, Ghadiali's Americanness is displayed through military patriotism and material acquisition. His practices of self-representation thus reveal how the nation maintains its self-image – not only by excluding others but by conscripting bodies capable of serving as a narcissistic mirror reflecting its superiority and universality.

The Supreme Court, in *Thind* as in other cases of racial assignation, institutionalized a particular way of looking at others. But the court's view, of course, does not foreclose our capacity to generate alternative visions. Though the court asserted, again, that "Hindus" were distinguished by a racial difference instinctively recognized and rejected by the "great body of our people," we can imagine otherwise. By limiting itself to the official record, legal scholarship often resigns itself to the perspective of the state. But by engaging with unofficial records, the unauthorized and sometimes unconscious reflections of immigrant others, we might begin to critically re-examine naturalized assumptions about the nation state and its defining social and cultural institutions.

Ariella Azoulay suggests that we might regard the set of exchanges occasioned by photography – their taking, their viewing, their circulation – as a new form of civil contract.[83] But by "contract," she refers not to the static form that binds the subject to his state or fixes the relation between contracting parties, but to the dynamic social conditions that bind subjects to one another. That condition is the fact of our coexistence and co-presence – a fact that *precedes* the inscriptions and intermediations of law. Rather than rehearse prescribed ways of looking – inspecting for colour, appraising worthiness – how else might we answer the gaze of "hopeful immigrants"? We should regard the visual archive not as a supplement to the authoritative legal record, but as a crucial register through which we collaborate in reconstructing forgotten histories, projecting alternative futures, and re-envisioning the meaning of citizenship.

NOTES

1 I am grateful to Tina Campt, Saidiya Hartman, Marianne Hirsch, Desmond Manderson, Allegra McLeod, Julie Peters, Patricia Williams, and Franz Werro for their insightful comments and suggestions, and to Darius Dinshah for his generosity. I am also indebted to the editors of the *American Journal of Comparative Law*, in which an extended version of this essay appeared. Any errors are my own.
2 Dinshah P. Ghadiali, *Dinshah Naturalization Case Clearing Contested Citizenship: Entertaining Narrative of How a Lawfully Naturalized Citizen of the United States of America, Defeated a Medico-Political Plot to Deprive Him of His Citizenship and Making of Him a "Man without a Country"* (Malaga, NJ: Dinshah Spectro-Chrome Institute, 1944), 1.
3 Ibid., 3 (citing government complaint).
4 Ibid. (citing government complaint).
5 Ibid. (emphasis added).
6 Ghadiali was the proud originator of the Spectro-Chrome, a projector of coloured lights, consisting of an aluminum box on a stand, a light bulb,

and several coloured gels. Ghadiali claimed that the body was composed primarily of seven elements, each of which corresponded to one of the seven colours of the prism. In a healthy body, the colours are balanced; in an unhealthy body, they are out of balance. Thus, the unhealthy body may be cured by administering colours that are lacking or by reducing colours that have become too brilliant. For example, green light may be applied as a pituitary stimulant, red to energize the liver, and so on. In 1920, before an audience of twenty-seven students in New York City, Ghadiali unveiled his invention. But as he would write, "from the day I presented [my] work to the World … untold privations, miseries, and inconceivably illogical, heartbreaking opposition followed me at every step." Dinshah P. Ghadiali, *Triumph of the Spectro-Chrome: Attuned Color Waves Vindicated in New York Supreme Court* (Malaga, NJ: Dinshah Spectro-Chrome Institute, 1944), 334, A17.

7 Ibid., 54.

8 Ibid.

9 *United States v. Bhagat Singh Thind*, 261 U.S. 204 (1923); see Joan M. Jensen, *Passage from India: Asian Indian Immigrants in North America* (New Haven, CT: Yale University Press, 1988).

10 *Thind*, 261 U.S. at 215.

11 Ibid.

12 Ibid. at 215.

13 Ghadiali, *Dinshah Naturalization Case*, 38.

14 Coco Fusco, *Only Skin Deep: Changing Visions of the American Self* (New York: International Center of Photography, 2003).

15 Allan Sekula, "The Body and the Archive," *October* 39 (Winter 1986): 27.

16 Anna Pegler-Gordon, *In Sight of America: Photography and the Development of U.S. Immigration Policy* (Berkeley: University of California Press, 2009).

17 John Tagg, *The Burden of Representation: Essays on Photographies and Histories* (Amherst: University of Massachusetts Press, 1980); Jennifer L. Mnookin, "The Image of Truth: Photographic Evidence and the Power of Analogy," *Yale Journal of Law & the Humanities* 10 (1998).

18 I am grateful to Desmond Manderson for his helpful suggestions on this point.

19 Naturalization Act of 1790, ch. 3, 1 Stat. 103, 103, repealed by Naturalization Act of 1795, ch. 20, 1 Stat. 414.

20 Naturalization Act of 1870, ch. 254, 16 Stat. 254, 256. Rather than simply eliminate the language restricting citizenship to "free white persons," Congress decided to add language to extend citizenship only to emancipated African Americans. It did this for the express purpose of preventing "Asiatics" from becoming naturalized citizens. *Thind*, 261 U.S. at 214.

21 Ian Haney López, *White by Law: Legal Construction of Race* (New York: New York University Press, 1996), 27–55.
22 See ibid.; see also Roland Tataki, *Strangers from a Different Shore: A History of Asian Americans*, rev. ed. (Boston: Little Brown, 1998), 295–300.
23 López, *White by Law*, 56–76.
24 See, e.g., *In re Balsara*, 171 F. 294, 295 (C.C.S.D.N.Y 1909) (holding that Congress intended to restrict citizenship to "white persons belonging to those races whose emigrants had contributed to the building up ... [of the] nation"); *United States v. Balsara*, 180 F. 694 (2d Cir. 1910) (reversing lower-court decision, citing scientific evidence that suggested that as a Parsi Zoroastrian, the petitioner, though a native of India, belonged to a class of people scientists considered "white"); *United States v. Dolla*, 177 F. 101 (5th Cir. 1910) (upholding the determination of a naturalization court, based on examination of skin, that the petitioner, a native of India, looked white). For a summary of published cases adjudicating the racial eligibility of Asian and "Arabian" immigrants for naturalization, see López, *White by Law*, 163–8.
25 *Thind*, 261 U.S. at 206.
26 *Ozawa v. United States*, 260 U.S. 178 (1922).
27 Ibid. at 197. In a brief he submitted to the court, Ozawa cited experts who observed that "in Japan the uncovered parts of the body are also white"; "the Japanese are of lighter color than other Eastern Asiatics, not rarely showing the transparent pink tint which whites assume as their own privilege"; and "they are whiter than the average Italian, Spaniard or Portuguese." Brief for Petitioner at 55, 57, 71, *Ozawa v. United States*, 260 U.S. 178 (1922), cited in López, *White by Law*, 58.
28 *Ozawa*, 260 U.S. at 197.
29 *Thind*, 261 U.S. at 208.
30 Ibid.
31 Ibid. at 214–15 (emphasis added).
32 Ibid. at 211.
33 *See* López, *White by Law*, 56.
34 Ibid.
35 Ibid. (emphasis added).
36 Ibid., 210.
37 Ibid., 209.
38 Ibid. (emphasis added).
39 As Jaspbir Puar explains, "It is not just that the blond Scandinavian cannot *see* himself in the brown Hindu. Rather, the bodies inhabit different tactile and affective economies [such that] touch, texture, sensation render the

impossibility of resonance, of appearing to *feel* the same." Jasbir Puar, *Terrorist Assemblages: Homonationalism in Queer Times* (Durham: Duke University Press, 2007), 107. While most scholars devote little attention to the physical markers that so distinguished Thind from his American counterparts, Puar draws our attention to his beard and his turban, with which he must have appeared before the court. Puar's analysis focuses on the particular way in which those markers of difference impede recognition of commonality between Americans and others. The turban and beard, she argues, appear before Americans as an especially troubling marker of difference, flickering between the immutably corporeal and culturally defiant – or, as she writes, "that which can be disciplined and that which must be outlawed." Ibid.

40 *Thind*, at 213 (emphasis added).

41 Ibid., at 214.

42 All that remains on file with the New Jersey court is an order dismissing the complaint against Ghadiali on 8 May 1934. The order and correspondence with the archivist at the National Archives at New York City are on file with the author.

43 Ghadiali, *Dinshah Naturalization Case*, 47.

44 Ariela J. Gross, *What Blood Won't Tell: A History of Race on Trial in America* (Cambridge, MA: Harvard University Press, 2008), 46.

45 *United States v. Dolla*, 177 F. 101, 102 (1910) (5th Cir. 1910).

46 See Bernard Freamon, "The Origins of the Anti-Segregation Clause in New Jersey's State Constitution," *Rutgers Law Journal* 35, no. 4 (2004): 1267. Oliver Randolph would go on to become an important figure in the civil rights movement. The first African American member of the New Jersey Bar Association, and the second African American elected to that state's legislature, Randolph was a delegate to New Jersey's constitutional convention in 1947. He is credited with not only authoring a constitutional provision banning discrimination in public schools and the militia – unique among constitutions at the time – but also convincing an otherwise all-white convention to ratify the provision.

47 Ghadiali mentions in *Naturalization Case* that he arranged to meet with Randolph before his trial. According to Ghadiali, both men were surprised to find one another on opposing sides of a race case. "Judge of my surprise when, in a Black and White case, I found an Assistant United States Attorney, Oliver Randolph, a full-blooded Ethiopian!" Ghadiali followed this exclamation with an assurance to the reader that he himself harboured no racial prejudice: "Being a … firm believer in Brotherhood of Man, it made not the slightest bit of difference to me." Randolph, after giving

Ghadiali a "patient hearing," declared sportingly – at least in Ghadiali's account – "I don't know how I am going to prove you are *not* a White man." How should we interpret these expressions of surprise? Is the surprise that an African American should be the enforcer of a racial bar to citizenship? Is it one of presumed if unspoken solidarity? Is it one of an unexpected advantage: if an African American was capable of representing the government, so then could the government accommodate a Hindu foreigner. Or perhaps the advantage took another form, as Randolph's question would indicate: How could Ghadiali appear as anything but "white" while standing before this "Ethiopian?" Ghadiali, *Naturalization Case*, 15.

48 During his trial, Ghadiali argued that the government has acted in "bad faith" when it identified him as an "Indian born in Bombay." "Bad faith," Ghadiali argued, "on the obvious ground that an Englishman born in Africa does not become a Negro." By analogy, "the Respondent although born in India is a Free White person and racially eligible for citizenship under the law." While the analogy distances Ghadiali from the category of "Negro," it also identifies Ghadiali with the colonial Englishman, the free white person, and impliedly, the judge, in whom, Ghadiali seemed to suggest, even the thought of mistaking an Englishman for a Negro should produce an outrage, enough to sustain the charge of "bad faith." Ghadiali, *Naturalization Case*, 11. To be clear, though Ghadiali's narrative calls our attention to moments of embodied reasoning that seldom enter the legal record, I do not mean to suggest that his representation of race somehow transcends the racial reasoning of his time or our own. His representation of Oliver Randolph is illustrative. Randolph enters and exits Ghadiali's narrative primarily as a figure of racial difference, the African American other that confirms his own eligibility for citizenship.

49 Roland Barthes, *Image, Music, Text* (New York: Hill and Wang, 1977), 12

50 Shawn Michelle Smith, *American Archives: Gender, Race, and Class in Visual Culture* (Princeton: Princeton University Press, 1999), 3.

51 Sekula, "The Body and the Archive," 7.

52 See ibid.

53 See Pegler-Gordon, *In Sight of America*, 104–73. Though the practices I describe here are specific to the late nineteenth and early twentieth centuries, it is not hard to recognize the persistence of immigrant surveillance in contemporary laws such as those modelled after Arizona's Senate Bill (S.B.) 1070, 49th Leg., 2d Reg. Sess. (2010). For an analysis of the harm caused by racial profiling in immigration policing,

see Kevin R. Johnson, "The Case against Racial Profiling in Immigration Enforcement Contexts," *Washington University Law Quarterly* 78, no. 3 (2000): 675.

54 Asian immigrants, suspected of carrying parasites, were routinely forced to strip and surrender their waste for inspection. Immigration officials in San Francisco, intent on preventing Indian immigrants from entering although no federal ban had been enacted, administered exhaustive medical exams, finding, as one headline reported, "Hookworm Is More Potent than Laws." See Nayan Shah, *Contagious Divides: Epidemics and Race in San Francisco's Chinatown* (Berkeley: University of California Press, 2001), 179–203; Amy L. Fairchild, *Science at the Borders: Immigrant Medical Inspection and the Shaping of the Modern Industrial Labor Force* (Baltimore: Johns Hopkins University Press, 2003), 132–9.

55 Pegler-Gordon, *In Sight of America*, 104–73.

56 Ibid., 112.

57 Ibid., 126.

58 Naomi Mezey, "Erasure and Recognition: The Census, Race, and the National Imagination," *Northwestern University Law Review* 97, no. 4 (2003): 1701. Mezey writes of the paradoxical character of the census, at once a national ceremony and surveillance technology that presents us with "a portrait of the whole nation" through a formal process of differentiation, "emphasizing the discrete units and different identities that make up (or do not make up) the whole." Ibid., 1713.

59 Dinshah P. Ghadiali, *Railroading a Citizen; Diabolic Perjury, Branded Innocent As White Slaver; Supernatural Powers, Hypnotism, Mesmerism, Mysticsm, Astral Projection, Flying Through Space, Otherwise Salem Witchcraft, Vilely Adduced in Portland, Oregon, Federal Court, To Convict A Reputable American … Fearlessly Exposing Flagrant Injustice In America* (Malaga, NJ: Dinshah Spectro-Chrome Institute, 1926), 13.

60 Radhika Viyas Mongia, "Race, Nationality, Mobility: A History of the Passport," *Public Culture* 11, no. 3 (1999): 533. Mongia describes how reviewing telegrams, confidential memoranda, and reports exchanged between government officials in Britain, Canada, and India in 1906, led to "race-neutral" policies to restrict further migration.

61 Ibid., 534 (citing Memorandum: Re: Immigration of Hindoos [*sic*], in Canada, Department of Commerce and Industry, *Emigration Proceedings A*, May 1907, no. 7, ser. no. 1).

62 Ghadiali, *Dinshah Naturalization Case*, 38.

63 Ibid.

64 "105 Aliens Made Citizens: Flag Decks Hackensack Courtroom – Oriental Wears Green Skull Cap," *New York Times*, 20 January 1917.
65 Ghadiali, *Dinshah Naturalization Case*, 31.
66 Puar, *Terrorist Assemblages*, 187.
67 Ibid., 171.
68 Ghadiali, *Dinshah Naturalization Case*, 35.
69 Laura Wexler, *Tender Violence: Domestic Visions in the Age of U.S. Imperialism* (Chapel Hill: University of North Carolina Press, 2000), 127–76.
70 See *Lum v. Rice*, 275 U.S. 78 (1927) (state laws providing separate educational facilities for white children and coloured children – "brown, yellow, and black" – did not violate the Fourteenth Amendment rights of an American-born child of Chinese descent).
71 *Thind*, at 215.
72 Marianne Hirsch, *Family Frames: Photography, Narrative, and Postmemory* (Cambridge, MA: Harvard University Press, 1997), 48.
73 For critical analyses of the range of restrictions imposed on cross-racial intimacy and marriage, see Kevin Noble Maillard and Rose Cuizon Villazor, eds, Loving v. Virginia *in a Post-Racial World: Rethinking Race, Sex, and Marriage* (New York: Cambridge University Press, 2012); Peggy Pascoe, *What Comes Naturally: Miscegenation Law and the Making of Race in America* (New York: Oxford University Press, 2009); Leti Volpp, "American Mestizo: Filipinos and Antimiscegenation Laws in California," *U.C. Davis Law Review* 33, no. 4 (1999): 795–835; Kerry Abrams, "Polygamy, Prostitution, and the Federalization of Immigration Law," *Columbia University Law Review* 105, no. 3 (2005): 641–716; Robin A. Lenhardt, "Forgotten Lessons on Race, Law, and Marriage: The Story of *Perez v. Sharp*," in *Race Law Stories*, ed. Devon W. Carbado and Rachel F. Moran (New York: Thomson Reuters/Foundation Press, 2008), 343–79; Rose Cuizon Villazor, "The Other Loving: Uncovering the Federal Government's Racial Regulation of Marriage," *New York University Law Review* 86, no. 5 (2011): 1361–443.
74 Morgan Robert, "Colored Glass Now Cures All Our Ills," *Dearborn Independent*, 15 March 1924 (emphasis added).
75 Expatriation Act of 1907, ch. 2534, § 3, 34 Stat. 1228, 1228 (1907), repealed by Naturalization and Citizenship of Married Women (The Cable Act), ch. 411, §§ 3, 6–7, 42 Stat. 1021, 1021–2 (1922).
76 Naturalization and Citizenship of Married Women (The Cable Act), ch. 411, § 4, 42 Stat. 1021, 102 (1922).
77 Ghadiali, *Dinshah Naturalization Case*, 36.

78 Ibid., 85.

79 Ibid.

80 Ibid., 78.

81 "Fights Racial Ban on His Citizenship: New Jersey Resident, Naturalized in 1917, Says He Is a Parsee-Zoroastrian, Not a Hindu," *New York Times*, 25 January 1933.

82 Indeed, as Ghadiali asked at his own trial, "What is naturalization?" How can anyone or anything that is not already natural be *made natural*? The paradoxical character of naturalization is figured in the word itself. The word invokes, all at once, conceptions of "nature" and its opposites – nature as prior to law, nature as innocent of artifice, the natural as opposed to the unnatural. Naturalization, like immigration itself, unsettles our understanding of citizenship and national identity because it renders apparent the conventionality of political and legal processes usually ascribed to nature. In other words, naturalization exposes the conventionality of birthright citizenship, the relative arbitrariness with which fundamental rights and recognition are determined by place of birth rather than by belonging. In the United States, laws recognizing birthright citizenship, laws delimiting racial eligibility for immigration and naturalization, laws restricting sociability and sexual intimacy across racial boundaries – all of these have effectively produced, reproduced, and naturalized whiteness as the embodiment of citizenship. For racialized others, as Ghadiali argued at his trial, citizenship is conditioned upon performance. To his own question, "What is naturalization?" Ghadiali answered, "It is a contract," one that obliges the racialized other to satisfy the demand of social conformity and ideological mirroring.

83 Ariella Azoulay, Rela Mazali, and Ruvik Danieli, *The Civil Contract of Photography* (New York: Zone Books, 2008).

8 From Sentimentality to Sadism: Visual Genres of Asylum Seeking

HONNI VAN RIJSWIJK

Human rights take their shape as a moral discourse centred on pain.

Wendy Brown, "Human Rights and the Politics of Fatalism"[1]

I have lived in war zones, with bombs and explosions. I have never experienced what I am experiencing here with the uncertainty we face.

If we had died in the ocean that would have been better.

Iraqi refugee, 43 years old, Amnesty International[2]

Precarity, Terror, and Suffering

Fury Road, the fourth Mad Max film, is directed by the Australian George Miller and also co-written by him in collaboration with Nico Lathouris and comic-book creator Brendan McCarthy. Since its release in mid-2015, the film has grossed over $300 million. The film begins with Max (played in this film by Tom Hardy) surveying the empty expanse of the Australian centre, haunted by visions of violence, in particular the loss of his child. *Fury Road* is motivated by the same post-apocalyptic trope as the earlier Mad Max films[3] – driven by a nihilistic Australian Gothic[4] – but thirty years on since the last film, this trope has been updated. As in the past films, *Fury Road* suggests a quintessentially Australian world-end entailing endless drag races across the eviscerated landscape of the desert centre: road-trains of hotted-up V8 Holdens, war-trucks with skulls attached to them, and everything on fire. All the Mad Max films have emphasized the significance of masculinity and violence to the Australian imaginary.[5] *Fury Road*, like the earlier films, is so buff and masculine that it tips over into camp – the mascot of the road-train in this film is a flamboyantly dressed, heavy metal guitarist playing a flamethrower-machine-gun-guitar who is chained to an enormous truck. But what is most striking about *Fury Road*, and what distinguishes it from the earlier Mad Max films, is that the dominant experience of watching the film, alongside the exhilaration of a two-hour-long car chase, is an uncomfortable, ever-constant awareness of vulnerability – of a pervasive texture and aesthetic of dangerous, painful precariousness. The road trains of giant trucks roar through the desert, and their stoushes are exhilarating, but the viewer is also anxious: always conscious of, and waiting for, things to fall apart. The vehicles shudder as much as they roar, and the plot is driven by the threat that they will not make it: they are roughly patched together and need constant repair. The camera focuses on the jerky, side-to-side motion of the vehicles, which threaten to break or tip over. Similarly, the machine-bodies of the main villain, Immortan Joe (Hugh Keays-Byrne), and his descendants, are inherently vulnerable. The sovereign body is bloated, aged, and ill, and his descendants have such deep genetic flaws that they require constant blood transfusions to stay alive. The heroes are also vulnerable, physically and mentally: Imperator Furiosa (Charlize Theron) is missing an arm; Max is hooked up as a "blood bag" for the sovereign's heirs. Both have survived terrible trauma. Roaring along the eviscerated landscape, cars, trucks, motorcycles, and people fly into the air and shatter – everyone and everything struggles against the centrifugal forces of entropy.

Fury Road spectacularly stages the imaginary driving Australia's current immigration policies, an imaginary driven by the anxious desire to assert sovereignty in the face of precariousness. An allegory of precarity and terror in the Australian landscape, reading *Fury Road* alongside Australian asylum-seeker policy reveals how fantasies of sovereign self-sufficiency are shored up by the spectacle of real or imagined violent strikes against foreign others. The comic-book style of *Fury Road* foregrounds the significance of the image in generating the affective realm of authority. The Australian government also self-consciously uses images to convey authority, and these images reveal this authority to be sado-masochistic, driven by anxiety over a loss of control in the world. Each of these representations, however, have different end-effects. Julia Kristeva suggested in *Powers of Horror* (1982) that when the subject is confronted with its own vulnerability, there are only two responses: the fascist response (violence directed at the other to maintain an illusion of wholeness) and the abject response (which entails embracing the state of vulnerability and compromise). In *Fury Road*, the sovereign villains sadistically torture the wretched of the earth; but their fascist fantasies of a whole sovereign body are consciously staged and continuously undone, revealing both villains and heroes as not fascist but rather as abject, in the Kristevan sense. The boundaries of the subject are compromised through wounds, corrupt surfaces, and amputation. Here, technology is not utopian, it does not enhance the subject, but rather emphasizes its fragility: the characters are not Terminators but fragile cyborgs. In contrast, Australia tries to keep itself whole through territorial excision. Current Australian discourse around the figure of the asylum seeker deploys the image of suffering, and in particular, the face of suffering, to assert a fantasy of a separate and impermeable sovereign self (in Kristeva's formulation, the fascist subject). Successive Australian governments have used visual languages to promote their framing of the asylum-seeker issue, and have gone to great trouble to control images of arrivals and of the conditions of detention, especially managing images of suffering at these sites. Since 2012, the federal government has controlled media access to detention centres through a deed of agreement that journalists must sign,[6] while at the same time carefully using its own images to produce and then punish a guilty foreign other. This sadistic tableau must be constantly restaged as the (imagined) deserved suffering of this guilty other, which momentarily assures the sovereignty, coherence, and agency of the subject. The government tries to engage this popular aesthetic in its propaganda, but in an unknowing way, which nevertheless reveals its fascism.

Australia is not the first or only nation to subjugate others in the name of an impossible safety. After 9/11, not only the United States but also a number of Western nations proclaimed their terrible vulnerability, emblemized by the photograph of tiny human figures falling from the twin towers, an image that was reproduced again and again. This trope purported to justify an irrational brutality and aggression towards Afghanistan and other ill-chosen targets, as well as the introduction of violent "security" measures within domestic legal systems.[7] In Australia, the figure of the asylum seeker is conflated with that of the terrorist. This conflation was made literal in recent changes to government departmental structures, with customs, immigration, and security matters now being administered together under the Australian Border Force Act 2015 (Cth). We are in a "postmodern" era in the sense that Bill Brown uses the term – a post-Enlightenment era characterized by various refusals of rationality, animated by both neoliberalism and new fundamentalisms.[8] Rationality is refused by governments in their various, shifting iterations of "wars on terror." Instead, claims of national vulnerability and precarity drive legal interventions and politics. Anxiety and fear have become dominant political affects.[9]

The government's discourse of authority arises out of anxiety, and the images it produces as part of its immigration policies are a prime way of observing the operation of these affects in political life. Australia's obsession with maritime arrivals is irrational, and the rule of law is subjugated in the name of security: refugees who have legitimate grounds for asylum can be indefinitely detained without judicial orders, any knowledge of the grounds for their detention, or the opportunity to seek judicial review.[10] The Australian government controls media access to certain heightened sites involving asylum seekers, and has produced an effective blackout of images from detention centres.[11] The government has thematized the absence of images and of information – justifying secrecy in the name of security, invisibility in the name of safety. This tactic not only prevents the circulation of unwanted images but also strengthens the fantasy of authority through what is *not* shown – the fantastic elements intensified by these blank spaces. But at the same time, the government has produced images of asylum seekers which assert a particular authority. In this chapter, I argue that Australian governments have used images of suffering surrounding these policies to communicate a sado-masochistic relationship with asylum seekers – images that engage and then punish the asylum seeker. Images do this work through the language of pain. In Elaine Scarry's formulation, the language of pain entails the translation of pain's components "into the insignia of power, the conversion of the enlarged map of human suffering into an emblem of the regime's strength. This translation is made possible by, and occurs across, the phenomenon common to both power and pain: agency."[12]

Scarry's argument is based on the fact that pain has an amorphous quality that can be captured by different forms in the service of creating relationships of power.[13] The infliction of pain, then, and its representation, are both highly political acts. In the context of one person inflicting pain upon another, the experience of pain is that it is "world destroying" and so brings about, symbolically, the shrinkage of the sufferer's world and an expansion of the world of the person who inflicts that suffering.[14]

The Politics of Representing Suffering

Pain and its representation are central to the government's response to asylum seekers. Amnesty International reports that 2000 people have been sent to Manus Island since 2012, but only one person has been processed.[15] "So if Manus Island isn't about processing asylum seekers," Amnesty International asks, "what is it about?" The excess being produced beyond the purportedly lawful processing of asylum seekers, is suffering. Pain is instrumentalized by Australian migration law – suffering is not incidental or collateral, but one of its main, intended effects. Pain is didactic, and its representation is carefully managed as propaganda for both prospective asylum seekers and the Australian public. The images not only communicate the sado-masochistic relationship between the government and asylum seekers, but constitute authority itself as legitimated sadism.

In representing and adjudicating suffering, visual codes become part of, in Guy Debord's formulation, the "spectacular means" through which otherness is made and managed.[16] This spectacle is a social relationship created through capitalist and imperial economies.[17] The spectacle also determines what is visible and invisible – forming part of the practices that determine what Jacques Rancière terms "the distribution of the sensible."[18] Although the representation of physical and psychological pain comes up against problems that are phenomenological,[19] it is important to pay attention to the significance of politics in the representation of pain, and not to take the representation of suffering for granted. There is nothing "natural" about suffering or its representation, and the ways in which suffering comes to matter legally, morally, and politically have significant consequences to the phenomena of pain.[20] Whose suffering counts, and how, become questions of law and politics, as well as of representation. The production of bodies in law, the production and recognition of pain in the body, and the capacity to use the body to communicate, are political and legal issues, as well as cultural issues. Pain is made sense of through a number of visual and textual genres – from medical discourses to pornography – with clearly different political, ethical, and legal effects. While Rancière focuses on the relationship between constructions of the aesthetic and constructions of class, we can use his formulation to consider how the distribution plays out in the highly racialized context of humanitarian practices and refugee law.

Australia's policies on asylum seekers rely heavily on narratives, tropes, and images of suffering. Specifically, these policies rely on a visual vocabulary in which the government makes asylum seekers suffer. In turn, asylum seekers try to use their own suffering, and representations of that suffering, as the basis of legal claims and political protest. Hunger strikes by asylum seekers in both onshore and offshore detention centres have occurred continuously since 1992, but have become increasingly invisible.[21] The act of hunger striking has powerful potential: it occurs at the limits of law's jurisdiction, and is an act that both demands law's jurisdiction, but at the same time refuses it. At this site, the subject asserts the right to harm herself, but also uses the scene of self-violence to make demands on law. The visibility of this harm, and the difficulty of law's preventing it, has historically provoked violent responses from the state. Hunger strikes have been used in a number of political contexts – by Gandhi, at Long Kesh Prison in 1981, recently by Turkish prisoners and supporters, and also in Guantanamo Bay. Images of these strikes have registered in different genres, and have been the subject of power struggles. In Long Kesh Prison, for example, photos were released of those who died as a result of hunger striking, lying in state, as martyrs – solemn and Christ-like.[22] Images of hunger striking suffragettes in the early twentieth century, however, were very different. Hundreds of women in England were forcibly fed between 1909 and 1914.[23] Sketches of forced feeding were published with the aim of supporting the suffragettes, and evoking outrage, in pro-suffragette papers such as *The Suffragette*, *Votes for Women*, and the *Women's Dreadnought*. But the images were "double-edged." In fact, because of the composition of these images, feminist scholars such as Lisa Tickner note that the viewer is actually invited to experience a covert pleasure in the spectacle of suffering.[24]

Asylum seekers have little control over their bodies and their ability to protest through hunger striking is contested; they also have little control over representations of these acts. The image of sewn lips is arresting: the lips are bloodied and swollen, and the makeshift instruments they have used make the stitches frayed, uneven, and the wound infected.[25] There are, under the current regime, fewer images of hunger strikes and other protests now, compared to the years of the Howard government (1996–2007), when images of protesting asylum seekers with sewn lips led to protests against government policies by the public and by journalists, as well as human rights groups.[26] Images that are obtained now tend to be limited to distant shots of detention centres. In 2015, an image of hunger striking shows a detention centre with police officers surrounding the periphery.[27] There are reports that asylum seekers have been sent offshore after talking to the media[28] and, on 2 June 2014, that a sit-in hunger strike on Christmas Island was violently broken up by Serco (a private company contracted by the federal government), leaving at least eight asylum seekers injured.[29] Forced feeding is also taking place.[30] Information on the numbers of people who have participated in hunger strikes, the incidence of the use of the power under Regulation 5.35 of the Migration Regulations 1994 (Cth), and the policy regarding treatment of people on hunger strike is not publicly available, and the policy on managing hunger strikes in detention centres is treated as a "commercial in confidence" document between Serco and the government.[31] The Turnbull/Abbott/Coalition government elected in 2013 has been especially careful about the release of images and information, at one point ceasing to give regular briefings regarding boat arrivals,[32] and more recently introducing legislation that brings together immigration and security issues, and purports to make doctors and others criminally liable for disclosing matters occurring at offshore processing sites and detention centres.[33]

The Human Rights Genre of Suffering

Different genres of suffering make claims to different forms of authority. Since the second half of the twentieth century, the default genre for the political representation of mass suffering has been the humanitarian genre, which relies on a particular narrative of power and vulnerability. The international human rights community, including organizations such as the United Nations and Amnesty International, asserts jurisdiction through this genre. They use the fact of suffering to make claims that directly affect the sovereignty of nations – claims that demand nations to change their laws and policies in response to rights that adhere in the person, and that are administered by an international community. Images of humanitarian intervention rely on representing an encounter with the other as a spectacle of suffering – as an encounter with a vulnerable being in pain who is in need of rescue, this scene also frequently relies on the tropes of colonial rescue and racialized inferiority. In Hannah Arendt's critique of humanitarianism,[34] this kind of empathic connection can as easily generate terror as compassionate action: "Pity, taken as the spring of virtue, has proved to possess a greater capacity for cruelty than cruelty itself."[35] For Arendt, pity is close to cruelty because it is invested in the persistence of suffering:

> Pity, in contrast to solidarity, does not look upon both fortune and misfortune, the strong and the weak, with an equal eye; without the presence of misfortune, pity could not exist, and it therefore has just as much vested interest in the existence of the unhappy as thirst for power has a vested interest in the existence of the weak. Moreover, by virtue of being a sentiment, pity can be enjoyed for its own sake, and this will almost automatically lead to a glorification of its cause, which is the suffering of others.[36]

In *After Evil*, Robert Meister suggests that we can think of the genre of human rights discourse as "melodrama," interpellating an audience "that regards itself as *sensitive* to human suffering in just the way melodramatic fiction does."[37] This genre produces an affective texture of justice that encourages the viewer to feel, rather than to take political action.[38]

In the context of migration law and policy, Australia is refusing the authority of the sentimental, humanitarian genre of suffering, and in doing so, is also refusing the authority of organizations such as the United Nations. Australia has redrawn its map of legal and political responsibility, excising itself from the human rights frameworks which provide asylum seekers with forms of legal and political protection. The policy of territorial excision was first introduced in Australia in 2001, following 9/11. This policy designates certain parts of Australian territory as "excised" from Australia's migration zone.[39] Legislation regulating migration classifies any person who reaches an "excised offshore place" by sea without authorization as an "unauthorised maritime arrival."[40] Unauthorized maritime arrivals are held to be outside Australia's migration zone and, importantly, may not apply for a visa under Australia's existing onshore visa application process, as set out in the Migration Act 1958 (Cth).[41] In May 2013, the policy of excision, which at that time applied to 4891 of Australia's outlying islands and territories, was expanded to include the entire Australian mainland.[42] As a result, an "unlawful non-citizen" entering Australian territory "at any place" by sea becomes an "unauthorised maritime arrival."[43] Australia has thereby prevented asylum seekers from gaining access to Australia's legal system, circumventing its obligations under international human rights law, and undermining international comity.

Australian governments have prevented the circulation of images of the suffering of asylum seekers from building a sentimental, humanitarian discourse. If human rights are figured as a moral or sentimental narrative, then the refusal of Australia to engage with human rights, and with organizations such as the United Nations and Amnesty International, suggests that we are inhabiting not only a different genre of suffering, but also a different form of authority. Then Prime Minister Tony Abbott stated in March 2015 that Australians were "sick of being lectured to by the United Nations,"[44] after the United Nations Special Rapporteur on Torture released a report that stated Australia was in breach of the Convention Against Torture and Other Cruel, Inhuman or Degrading Treatment or Punishment. In June 2015, the UN again condemned Australia for its "hostility and contempt" towards asylum seekers.[45]

In the human rights genre, suffering forms the basis of the affective connection between viewer and sufferer, and suffering is the basis of a political or legal claim. Here, suffering is viewed as immeasurable, and the fact of suffering is taken for granted. By contrast, the Australian government's sadistic framing of its response to asylum seekers relies on quantifying and even instrumentalizing suffering. Here, the suffering of asylum seekers forms only one part of a wider economy of pain, and is thematized as both measurable and relative. The figure of the victim is splintered into a lexicon of competing figures in narrative and visual tropes. These tropes rely on the victim being revealed as another figure: the "economic refugee," the "queue jumper," and "the terrorist." A calculus of suffering organizes these figures: the economic refugee does not suffer enough, and is not forced to migrate but chooses to do so; the queue jumper denies the rights of other suffering subjects that are following the proper processes; and the terrorist sneaks into Australian territory by taking advantage of asylum laws, thereby making Australia the victim. Suffering is also seen to be produced by a perpetrator external to Australia – the "people smuggler" – who is prepared to risk lives for profit, sending people across the seas in leaky boats. These narrative and visual responses support political and legal responses. Suffering is presented as self-inflicted, an act of folly from which people (especially children) need to be protected. Australia's policies, which involve "turning back the boats" and incarcerating asylum seekers, are thereby justified through careful calculation: the suffering of one particular asylum seeker is necessary to protect the rest, their pain instrumentalized for the greater good.

In the context of securitized responses to migration, the refugee applicant appears as an already criminalized subject, as "an illegal," "an illegal immigrant," or an "undocumented migrant."[46] He or she is already in the category of the criminal, necessarily abject as defined by Kristeva.[47] Abjection, following Kristeva, designates an "intrinsically corporeal" phenomenon that operates through both a binary logic of othering and a self-constitutive practice of exclusion. For "abjection," Kristeva remarks, "is a precondition of narcissism. It is coexistent with it and causes it to be permanently brittle."[48] From this perspective, the sovereign nation becomes a psycho-political project, built on a founding exclusion that must be constantly policed in order to confirm its legitimacy. Nauru, Manus Island, and Christmas Island are abject spaces of suffering and punishment that shore up a precarious national fantasy of sovereignty.

Jurisdictions of Suffering

Successive Australian governments have tried to use images of suffering in support of their policies.[49] In July 2013, the Department of Immigration and Citizenship (DIAC) released videos and photographs, which, they said, showed eighty-one Iranian asylum seekers being processed on Christmas Island. This highly orchestrated event depicted neither the boat nor the offshore detention centres where the refugees were sent, but the processing centre. The news release issued by the government was headlined: "81 Iranians get the new message: You will not settle in Australia."[50] The photograph that became emblematic of this event depicts a woman, sitting, with her head in her hands, clearly distressed, and is captioned by DIAC: "A female asylum seeker comes to terms with the fact she won't be settled in Australia."[51] No journalists were allowed at the Christmas Island location to produce alternative versions of this event or to verify what took place.

The minister for immigration at the time, Tony Burke, stated that "getting this message out is critical to stopping people from drowning at sea and I make no apology for maximising that opportunity."[52] A pain metric is applied: the pain of arriving "illegally" needs to be greater than the pain of staying overseas, or arriving "properly." The implied narrative is that the excessive demands of the asylum seeker are being thwarted. The asylum seeker is granted an excessive will in this drama – she comes to us with too much force and intention. The image purports to capture the moment of the thwarting of this will: the moment when the asylum seeker is told that her unfair demands will not be met. The agency of asylum seekers coming to Australia is thematized as the problem, rather than the broader context of underlying political or economic conditions. But beyond its instrumental logic, we are also in the realm of scopophilic sadism, where pleasure lies in ascertaining guilt, asserting control, and subjecting the guilty person through punishment or forgiveness.[53] "Sadism demands a story," Mulvey argues, and "depends on making something happen, forcing a change in another person, a battle of will and strength, victory/defeat, all occurring in a linear time with a beginning and an end."[54] Power lies in subjecting another person to the will sadistically or to the gaze voyeuristically. The Iranian woman's suffering represented in the photograph was clearly designed to invite a satisfaction, even sadistic pleasure, in the act of refusal. Australia's fantasy and Australia's pleasure are thereby indulged. These photographs led to protests against the policy and also against the government's use of images of suffering to promote its policy domestically, and as deterrence internationally.[55]

The governments' efforts to circulate images to promote their policies are noteworthy mainly for their failure, and for what exceeds their intention. The instability of the images shows how easily the fantasy of the coherent sovereign authority is undone, and how fragile and therefore vulnerable is this particular fantasy of Australia. In 2013, the Rudd Labor government commissioned an eighteen-page graphic novel which was published and then distributed on the Customs and Border Protection website from November that year.[56] Written in Dari and Pashto, it appears to specifically target Afghani asylum seekers, and tells the story of a young Hazaran man.[57] The reader of the graphic novel is the prospective asylum seeker, and also the Australian public. It is significant that the government chose the genre of the graphic novel rather than photography or another more realist genre of representation – we are clearly in the domain of a highly stylized fantasy. The graphic novel tells the story of the "economic" refugee who chooses to suffer for potential gain and fails. The first image shows a poor family with a young son. The parents dream of a brighter future for their son, and approach someone – presumably a "people smuggler" – telling him of their dream. A "thought bubble" appears above the father's head, picturing a bright, wealthy city (Perth). The next page shows money changing hands, and the father saying farewell to the son, who travels to a wharf, where he boards a crowded, wooden boat. The following page depicts perils at sea, and then the boat being rescued/intercepted by an Australian government vessel. The most intriguing part of the graphic novel follows, which shows the asylum seeker being searched, processed, and then sent to an offshore detention centre. Here, the

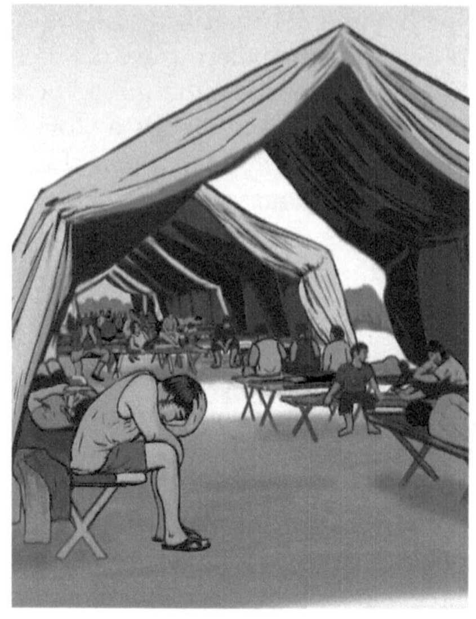

Figure 8.1 Detention facility, panel from the comic by Department of Customs and Border Protection, http://www.customs.gov.au.

Australian government, represented by the intercepting ship, the customs official, and the detention centre, is clearly the agent of the harm, which – according to the first half of the comic – the asylum seeker has voluntarily engaged. In the illustration of the detention centre, the asylum seeker is bent over in a position of despair, alongside other prostrate and suffering bodies.

The next page depicts his face in anguish, and his memories of a much happier life at home. The text on the following, and last page (which is also on the first page), translates from Dari and Pashto as: *If you go to Australia without a visa/You will not be established there.* On the last page of the comic, the agent of suffering is no longer a person, a zone, or a place. The last page shows only the Commonwealth Coat of Arms, the formal symbol that signifies Commonwealth authority and ownership, and a large image of the asylum seeker's face, which has an expression of anguished suffering. The viewer's gaze is drawn to his eyes, one of which is crying red tears. Although the "people smuggler" figure has often been used as a proxy for the fury aimed at government policy, here the government takes full ownership of the suffering. It is the government who owns the position as the perpetrator, who will make the asylum seeker suffer. The visual lesson to asylum seekers presents a stark choice: you *will* suffer/we *will make you suffer*, if

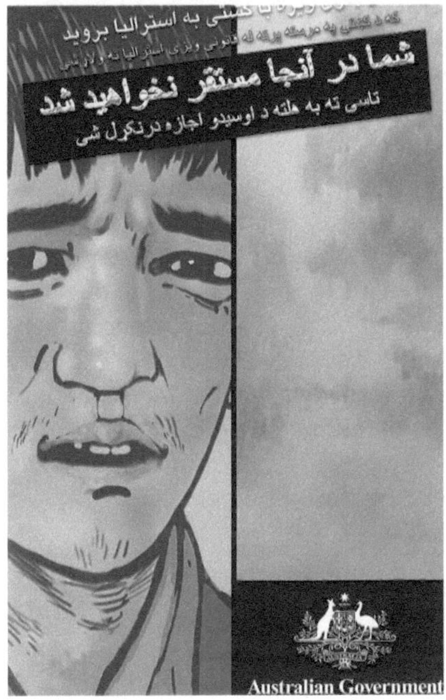

Figure 8.2 Final page, panel from the comic by Department of Customs and Border Protection, http://www.customs.gov.au.

you choose this path. Once again the sado-masochism of migration law is evident, construing the asylum seeker as a figure who consensually engages with the state's infliction of pain. Both the figure of the asylum seeker and the geographic zone that attracts Australia's migration laws are sites of a number of intersecting laws and authorities. But Australia instrumentalizes the suffering of asylum seekers in order to assert its jurisdiction and exercise its pleasure, as against international law and other national laws.

Conclusion: Fascist Sovereignty

These images constitute the national fascist body against the abject other: a relation of authority and subjection established through contract, subservience, and calculation. With its stylization and framing of images, this Australian comic invokes the end of Pier Paolo Pasolini's controversial final film *Salo, or 120 Days of Sodom* (1975). *Salo* makes very clear the connection between torture and the fascist state. That this torture is also necessarily a *spectacle* of torture is emphasized as the viewer sees the final horrific scenes unfold, as if through binoculars. (The audience of the comic is, after all, the Australian public, as well as potential asylum seekers.) The despots in *Salo* deliver the following speech to their victims: "You herded, feeble creatures, destined for our pleasure. Don't expect to find here the freedom granted in the outside world. You are beyond reach of any 'legality.' No one knows you are here. As far as the world goes, you are already dead."

The Australian government's constitution of the asylum seeker through sado-masochistic images allows us to understand the affective realm of authority and how authority is deployed through specific genres. These images reveal the changing discourses of legal authority post 9/11 – from sentimental humanitarianism to an emergent, blatant fascism. These images help us to understand not only how legal authority is transforming in the post-9/11 era, but also how that authority constitutes new affective and aesthetic modes of being.

NOTES

1 Wendy Brown, "'The Most We Can Hope for …': Human Rights and the Politics of Fatalism," *South Atlantic Quarterly* 103, no. 2/3 (2004): 453.

2 "The Hidden Truth about Manus Island," Amnesty International Australia, http://truthaboutmanus.com.

3 *Mad Max*, directed by George Miller (1979, Australia); *Mad Max 2: The Road Warrior*, directed by George Miller (1981, Australia); *Mad Max: Beyond Thunderdome*, directed by George Miller and George Ogilvie (1985, Australia).

4 Ross Gibson, "Yondering: A Reading of Mad Max Beyond Thunderdome," *Art & Text* 19 (1985); David Carter, "Crocs in Frocks: Landscape and Nation in the 1990s," *Journal of Australian Studies* 20 (1996): 89–96; Kieran Tranter, "Mad Max: The Car and Australian Governance," *National Identities* 5 (2003): 67–81; Meghan Morris, "Fear and the Family Sedan," in *The Politics of Everyday Fear*, ed. Brian Massumi (St Paul: University of Minnesota Press, 1993), 285–306; Christopher Sharrett, "The Hero as Pastiche: Myth, Male Fantasy, and Simulacra in Mad Max and The Road Warrior," *Journal of Popular Film and Television* 13 (1985): 80–91.

5 Katherine Biber, "The Threshold Moment: Masculinity at Home and on the Road in Australian Cinema," *Limina* 7 (2001): 26–46; Morris, "Fear and the Family Sedan," 285–306; Sharrett, "The Hero as Pastiche"; Rose Lucas, "Dragging It Out: Tales of Masculinity in Australian Cinema, from

Crocodile Dundee to Priscilla, Queen of the Desert," *Journal of Australian Studies* 22 (1998): 138–46.

6 Australian Border Protection media access policy states: "The department's media access policy provides opportunities for accredited media representatives to enter immigration detention facilities for the purposes of general reporting on the facilities' operation and status. Deeds of agreement must be signed by both the media entity (editor, executive producer or similar) and each of the media representatives seeking to enter the detention facility. Not all requests can and/or will be met, for a range of reasons including operational and security priorities … The Media Entity acknowledges that standard DIAC policy prohibits visitors from photographing, filming, audio recording or in any other way recording the Detainee Clients or Protected Parties in the IDF." See "Deed of Agreement: Media Access," the Commonwealth of Australia represented by the Department of Immigration and Border Protection, at http://www.border.gov.au/about/news-media/access-to-detention-facilities. It exists as "policy" rather than being authorized through any specific legislation.

7 Judith Butler, *Precarious Life: The Powers of Mourning and Violence* (London: Verso, 2004).

8 Bill Brown, "The Dark Wood of Postmodernity (Space, Faith, Allegory)," *PMLA* 120 (2005): 735.

9 On the connection between anxious affect and the latest iteration of capitalism, see "Six Theses on Anxiety & the Prevention of Militancy," *Critical Legal Thinking*, http://criticallegalthinking.com/2014/04/17/six-theses-anxiety-prevention-militancy.

10 The policies are irrational, also, because the majority of asylum seekers in Australia come by plane, rather than by boat. Those who arrive by plane come on visas (tourist, student, or business) and then seek asylum after clearing immigration. In contrast, those who arrive by boat generally do not have visas, and may not even have passports or other documentation. Boat people do not "queue in line" waiting for their visas, or wait to be chosen. Marr and Wilkinson suggest there is continuity in current policies from the anti-Chinese sentiments of the 1880s. They qualify a more recent attitude of generosity regarding immigration, from the European refugees following the Second World War to the treatment of Vietnamese refugees in the 1970s by arguing that, in these contexts, Australia accepted refugees by means of a process of selection in offshore camps, in which Australian officials were in complete control of the process, so that "ever since then, in Australian eyes, refugees are people who wait patiently in camps far away

for us to come and select them." See David Marr and Marian Wilkinson, *Dark Victory* (Sydney: Allen & Unwin, 2004), 45.

11 Because of this media blackout, the critical position of the political left also tends not to be expressed through photographs or realist drawings, but rather through stylized cartoons and graphics. See, for example, "A Guard's Story," *The Global Mail*, http://tgm-serco.patarmstrong.net.au. The comics of *First Dog on the Moon* are also a popular site of critique: http://firstdogonthemoon.com.au.

12 Scarry, *The Body in Pain: The Making and Unmaking of the World* (New York: Oxford University Press, 1985), 56.

13 Ibid., 37.

14 Ibid.

15 "The Hidden Truth about Manus Island," Amnesty International, http://www.truthaboutmanus.com.

16 Guy Deboard, *The Society of the Spectacle*, trans. Donald Nicholson-Smith (New York: Zone Books, 1994), 37.

17 Ibid.

18 Jacques Rancière, *Dissensus: On Politics and Aesthetics*, trans. Steven Corcoran (New York: Continuum International Publishing Group, 2010), 54.

19 Scarry, *The Body in Pain*.

20 See Cathy Caruth, *Unclaimed Experience: Trauma, Narrative and History* (Baltimore: Johns Hopkins University Press, 1996); Dori Laub and Shoshana Felman, *Testimony: Crises of Witnessing in Literature, Psychoanalysis and History* (New York: Routledge, 1992). Dominick La Capra queries the universalization of trauma as history in *Writing History, Writing Trauma* (Baltimore: Johns Hopkins University Press, 2001) and *Representing the Holocaust: History, Theory, Trauma, History and Memory after Auschwitz* (Ithaca: Cornell University Press, 1996). On the day-to-day versus the "event" of trauma, see Ann Cvetkovich, *An Archive of Feelings: Trauma, Sexuality and Lesbian Public Cultures* (Durham: Duke University Press, 2002).

21 A review of reports by official bodies including the Australian Parliamentary Joint Standing Committee on Foreign Affairs Defence and Trade, the Australian Human Rights Commission, the United Nations Working Group on Arbitrary Detention, and the United Nations High Commissioner for Refugees along with media reports and a review of academic literature reveals that hunger strikes lasting from a few days to several weeks have consistently occurred in Australian detention centres since 1992. See Juss S. Satvinder, *The Ashgate Research Companion to Migration Law, Theory and Policy* (Surrey and Burlington: Ashgate, 2013);

Mary Anne Kenny and Lucy Fisky, "Regulation 5.35: Coerced Treatment of Detained Asylum Seekers on Hunger Strike: Legal, Ethical and Human Rights Implications," in *The Ashgate Research Companion to Migration Law, Theory and Policy* (Surrey and Burlington: Ashgate, 2013), 423–42. See also Lucy Fiske, Mary Anne Kenny, and Nicholas Procter, "Comment: Manus Island Hunger Strikes Are a Call to Australia's Conscience," *SBS News*, 20 January 2015, http://www.sbs.com.au/news/article/2015/01/19/comment-manus-island-hunger-strikes-are-call-australias-conscience.

22 See for example Irish Hunger Strike 1981, http://www.irishhungerstrike.com.

23 The first suffragette to strike was Marion Wallace Dunlop, a Women's Social and Political Union (WSPU) member who was in prison for pasting a passage from the Bill of Rights on the wall of St Stephen's Hall. Dunlop began a hunger strike on 5 July 1909, protesting her "third-division" criminal status. She argued that as a citizen engaged in a political war, suffragettes should be awarded the privileges of political status, which was "first-division" status. After refusing food for ninety-one hours, she was released. The hunger strike became a strategy for the WSPU after that, and by August thirty-seven women had been able to terminate their sentences in this way. On 24 September 1909, Gladstone, the home secretary, ordered tube feeding, and on 29 September, informed the House of Commons of his decision to do so. He stated that forcible feeding was the only way to preserve the "sacred" lives of women. See Midge Mackensie, *Shoulder to Shoulder: A Documentary* (New York: Alfred A. Knopf Inc., 1975), 130.

24 This effect was heightened by the anti-suffragette images that were circulating at the same time – published in satirical journals such as *Punch* and also as postcards and posters, which relied on similar visual vocabularies, so that sometimes it is difficult to tell at first whether the image is "pro" or "anti." Further, viewers were also trained in a visual vocabulary of caricature that did not deal specifically with force feeding but determined their interpretation. These images appeared in *Punch*, newspapers, posters, and postcards which had been circulating since the nineteenth century. Most of this material was not intentionally anti-suffragist (see Lisa Tickner, *The Spectacle of Women: Imagery of the Suffrage Campaign 1907–1914* [Chicago: University of Chicago Press, 1988], 162), but its effect was to mobilize stereotypes of femininity, and misogynist images, drawing on the rich heritage of misogynist caricature. George Orwell said comic postcards were "as traditional as Greek tragedy, a sort of sub-world of smacked bottoms and scrawny mothers-in-law which is part of western European consciousness," and concluded that between half and three-

quarters of them were devoted to sex jokes, hen-pecked husbands and stock characters, among them the suffragette who was "too valuable to be relinquished" (see "The Art of Donald McGill," *Horizon* [London: Horizon, 1941], 21, cited in Lisa Tickner, *The Spectacle of Women*, 162, 306). The use of humour adds layers of pleasure and cruelty, scrambling the pedagogical message. Images of both the exaggerated, caricatured noses and mouths of *Punch* and the sado-masochistic images of the forcibly fed body are evoked.

25 There are a handful of images from Manus Island in 2015 (Liam Cochrane, "Hundreds of Asylum Seekers Stage Protest on Manus Island, Detainees and Advocates Say," *ABC News*, 15 January 2015, http://www.abc.net.au/news/2015-01-14/manus-island-asylum-seekers-protest-png/6016126), from Nauru in 2014 (Thea Cowie, "Nauru Asylum Seekers Reportedly Sewing Lips Shut OVER Visa Denial," *SBS News*, 3 October 2014, http://www.sbs.com.au/news/article/2014/09/30/nauru-asylum-seekers-reportedly-sewing-lips-shut-over-visa-denial), and from the Broad Meadows Detention Centre Melbourne, showing the limits of physical, psychological, and political endurance. In a letter released via refugee advocates at the Tamil Refugee Council, detainees said they planned to continue to starve themselves until "there is solution, one way or the other" (Jane Lee, "Release Us or Kill Us: Asylum Seekers on Hunger Strike," *Sydney Morning Herald*, 8 April 2013, http://www.smh.com.au/federal-politics/political-news/release-us-or-kill-us-asylum-seekers-on-hunger-strike-20130408-2hg1q.html). "If the Australian government does not release us, we ask that they kill us mercifully" (Lee, "Release Us or Kill Us").

26 See Richard Bailey, "Strategy, Rupture, Rights: Reflections on Law and Resistance in Immigration Detention," *Australian Feminist Law Journal* (special issue: Law, Crisis, Revolution) 31 (2009): 33–56.

27 Chris Wahlquist, "Iranian Asylum Seeker on 38-day Hunger Strike Believed to Be Close to Death," *The Guardian*, 1 April 2015, http://www.theguardian.com/australia-news/2015/apr/01/iranian-asylum-seeker-on-38-day-hunger-strike-believed-to-be-close-to-death.

28 Michael Coggan, "Asylum Seekers in Darwin Sent to Offshore Detention after Talking to Media," *ABC News*, 1 November 2013, http://www.abc.net.au/news/2013-11-01/asylum-seekers-who-spoke-to-media-sent-offshore/5062622.

29 There is a blackout of images and also, increasingly, a refusal by the government to provide information regarding "operational issues": see "Labor Blasts 'Stalinist' Silence over Reports That Government Will Buy Lifeboats to Send Asylum Seekers Back to Indonesia," *ABC News*,

4 February 2014, http://www.abc.net.au/news/2014-01-08/government-considers-plan-to-buy-lifeboats-to-ferry-asylum-seek/5189722; Alan Leigh, "Australian Authorities Violently Suppress Refugee Hunger Strike," World Socialist website, 17 June 2014, http://www.wsws.org/en/articles/2014/06/17/refu-j17.html.

30 Regulation 5.35 of the *Migration Regulations 1994* (Cth) authorizes the treatment of a person in immigration detention. It authorizes the use of "reasonable force" to administer medical treatment, including the reasonable use of restraint and sedatives. See Kenny and Fiske, "Regulation 5.35," and Fiske, Kenny, and Procter, "Comment."

31 The source of the power to make this regulation comes from s. 273 of the Migration Act 1958 (Cth), which refers only to the power to make regulations regarding the conduct and supervision of detainees and the powers of those performing functions in connection with the supervision of detainees. It could be argued that the power contained in regulation 5.35 is ultra vires in that it goes beyond such a function, but this has never been tested in a case.

32 "Labor Blasts 'Stalinist' Silence."

33 The Australian Border Force Act 2015 (Cth), which came into effect on 1 July 2015, could see workers at onshore and offshore detention facilities risk up to two years in jail if they speak out about what they see. Any doctor, healthcare worker, or member of staff working at Nauru, Manus Island, or other detention centres who reports on child abuse, sexual assault, or other forms of harm is breaking the law and can be imprisoned for up to two years. The legislation was passed with the support of the federal Coalition and Labor.

34 Hannah Arendt, *On Revolution* (New York: Viking, 1965).

35 Ibid., 85.

36 Ibid.

37 Robert Meister, *After Evil: A Politics of Human Rights* (New York: Columbia University Press, 2010), 23 (emphasis in original).

38 Ibid., 63–4.

39 Section 5 of the Australian Migration Act 1958 (Cth) defines the "migration zone" as "the area consisting of the States, the Territories, Australian resource installations and Australian sea installations."

40 Ibid., s. 5AA.

41 Ibid., s. 46A.

42 Migration Amendment (Unauthorised Maritime Arrivals and Other Measures) Act 2012 (Cth), sch. 1, item 8, inserting Migration Act 1958 (Cth), s. 5AA.

43 Ibid.
44 Danuta Kozaki, "Abbott Says Australians 'Sick of Being Lectured by the UN' after Scathing Report on Asylum Policies," *ABC News*, 9 March 2015, http://www.abc.net.au/news/2015-03-09/tony-abbott-hits-out-united-nations-asylum-report/6289892; "Australians Sick of UN Lectures: Abbott," *SBS News*, 9 March 2015, http://www.sbs.com.au/news/article/2015/03/09/australians-sick-un-lectures-abbott.
45 Human Rights Law Centre, "UN Human Rights Chief Condemns Australian Government's 'Hostility and Contempt' towards Refugees," 16 June 2015, http://hrlc.org.au/un-human-rights-chief-condemns-australian-governments-hostility-and-contempt-towards-refugees.
46 See generally Catherine Dauvergne, *Making People Illegal: What Globalization Means for Migration and the Law* (Cambridge: Cambridge University Press, 2008) and Audrey Macklin, "Disappearing Refugees: Reflections on the Canada-U.S. Safe Third Country Agreement," *Columbia Human Rights Law Review* 36 (2005): 365.
47 Also the foreigner in Julia Kristeva's sense, as the "hidden face of our identity" (see *Strangers to Ourselves* [New York: Columbia University Press, 1991], 264), a universal sense of alienation within the self, or, in the Derridean sense, as the policed other who is "first of all foreign to the legal language in which the duty of hospitality is formulated" (ibid., 15). In these articulations, the foreigner remains a pawn in the politics of difference, always required to carry a particular identity.
48 Julia Kristeva, *Powers of Horror* (New York: Columbia University Press, 1982), 13.
49 Most notoriously, close-up photographs of the arrival of a boat off Christmas Island, *The Tampa*, led the Howard government to falsely narrate that children had been thrown overboard by their parents in an attempt to strengthen their chances of being picked up, claims that were later disproven. See for example Michael Gordon, "The Boat That Changed It All," *Sydney Morning Herald*, 20 August 2011, http://www.smh.com.au/national/the-boat-that-changed-it-all-20110819-1j2o2.html.
50 Helen Davidson, "Release of Footage of Distressed Asylum Seekers Angers Advocates," *The Guardian*, 22 July 2013, http://www.theguardian.com/world/2013/jul/22/release-footage-disterssed-asylum-seekers.
51 Ibid.
52 Ibid.
53 Laura Mulvey, "Visual Pleasure and Narrative Cinema," in *Issues in Feminist Film Criticism*, ed. Patricia Erens (Bloomington: Indiana University Press, 1990 [1975]), 22.

54 Ibid., 20, 40.

55 See, for example, Lexi Metherell, "Immigration Department Under Fire for Photos of Asylum Seekers Being Told of PNG Policy," *ABC News*, 23 July 2013, http://www.abc.net.au/news/2013-07-22/government-under-fire-for-asylum-seeker-photos/4835940; Davidson, "Release of Footage"; Bianca Hall, "All at Sea," *Sydney Morning Herald*, 27 July 2013, http://www.smh.com.au/federal-politics/political-news/all-at-sea-20130726-2qpp9.html.

56 The comic book has been removed from the DIAC site, but plates can be viewed here: "The Federal Government Uses a Comic Book to Stop the Boats," News.com.au, 12 February 2014, http://www.news.com.au/national/the-federal-government-uses-a-comic-book-to-stop-the-boats/story-fncynjr2-1226824447746.

57 The comic book also appears to contain the first official concession that the Australian Navy had been ordered to turn back the boats.

9 Images of Victims: The ECCC and the Cambodian Genocide Museum

MARIA ELANDER[1]

Photographs, Mourning, and Interruption

In a scene in a film[2] made by the Public Affairs Section (PAS) of the Extraordinary Chambers in the Courts of Cambodia (hereinafter the ECCC, also known as the Khmer Rouge Tribunal), a woman stands at the Tuol Sleng Genocide Museum. In front of her is a board of photographs that were taken as mug shots when the place was the Khmer Rouge security centre S-21. The film, narrated in Khmer but with English subtitles, is a short documentary about the ECCC's outreach work and the impact it has on Cambodian society to – as the ECCC slogan says – "move forward through justice." In the scene, Ou Chearm tells the ECCC's press officer Dim Sovannarom that by accident she has spotted the photo of her brother. The camera closes in on her face as she says she wishes the court "to bring justice for my brother's death." While the camera zooms in on the photograph, depicting a young man with a fringe hanging to the side, she describes how she "remember[s] when he left, he was 15 years old but I recognized him straight away." The camera turns to another woman, Sa Rim, who says that she found photos of her brother and her uncle's family. "I do not know how suffering they got [*sic*]. When I think of this, I feel so painful and have pity on them. I do not know how he was beaten, and starved." After the women's statements, the camera turns again to Press Officer Dim Sovannarom, who is standing before another camera crew. "The Khmer Rouge Tribunal," he states to that camera, "does not only provide justice to the victims, but the truth that victims found their missing relatives like today."

The film documents the ECCC's work with outreach, a component of international criminal courts that is increasingly being presented as key for a successful transitional justice endeavour. By engaging communities that have been affected by the crimes adjudicated by the court, outreach acts as a mechanism to produce a lasting legacy, linking court proceedings to community transitions. Through outreach, victims and communities are interpellated as participants not simply of criminal trials but, just as importantly, as engaged participants of transitional justice.[3] At the ECCC, an internationalized court set up to try senior leaders and those most responsible for the crimes committed during the Khmer Rouge regime,[4] the aspirations go beyond finding an individual guilty or innocent. As the court began to operate, its Public Affairs Section decided on how to express the "objective and hope for what the work of the court can bring to Cambodia. It chose 'Moving Forward Through Justice.'"[5] The ECCC slogan makes the transitional justice enterprise explicit. It represents the ECCC as partaking, or perhaps even initiating, in a *movement*, one that is directed *forward*. And it is by its programs of outreach that what happens inside the chamber is connected with those outside.

The film and in particular the scene described above appear to represent the form of movement forward the ECCC strives to initiate: the two women, when partaking in a study tour organized by the court to view the Tuol Sleng photographs, identify lost relatives. The women's act of identification ensures that the men represented in the photographs – the mug shots – are named and remembered. The losses are recognized, the humans are remembered. Meanwhile, the women partake in a particular ritual of commemoration, facilitated and institutionalized by a criminal law institution, yet operating beyond the material site of the courtroom. Through this ritual, the women are constituted as particular subjects, namely, as victim-survivors. The movement generated by the photographs is for the women one from a state of ignorance to, in the words of the ECCC press officer, knowing "the truth." For the men depicted, it's a move from silent anonymity to being named and thereby mourned.

Law as a process of transition or movement is central to this collection. In this chapter, I focus on the photographs at the Tuol Sleng Genocide Museum and the ways in which they "move forward" justice. I explore why, in these contexts, law and justice are understood to depend on an idea of transition or movement for their legitimacy. In this process, visual images are key to not only the construction of law and justice but also to subject formation. In the following, I unfold the way that the photographs instigate a movement, but in doing so, I question the narratives of which this movement partakes.

The Legal Response: ECCC and Outreach

On 6 January 1979, Vietnamese forces ousted the Khmer Rouge from the capital Phnom Penh, bringing an end to the three year and nine month–long regime of the Khmer Rouge, officially known as the Communist Party of Kampuchea and their state as the Democratic Kampuchea.[6] Almost four years earlier, the public had met the Khmer Rouge with a hope that they would bring peace and an end to years of civil war. They were wrong. In the face of real and imagined internal and external threats, the Khmer Rouge became paranoid, establishing an elaborate security apparatus. The epicentre of this apparatus was security centre S-21, where between twelve and seventeen thousand persons were brutally killed.[7] By the time Vietnamese forces entered the capital, between 1.7 and 2.2 million people[8] had perished in purges, or of disease and famine.

The ECCC was set up in 2004 after years of intense negotiations between the UN and the Cambodian government.[9] To date, it has completed two trials. In the first, the former chairman of S-21, Kaing Guek Eav, *alias* Duch, was found guilty of crimes against humanity and grave breaches of the Geneva Conventions.[10] The second trial was part of a larger case against the now two (originally four) surviving leaders of the Khmer Rouge. In August 2014, Nuon Chea and Khieu Samphan were found guilty of crimes against humanity for forced evacuations from the cities and the execution of soldiers of the previous regime.[11] The case is ongoing at the time of writing.[12] Two more cases have been opened, but it is contentious whether these will ever go to trial.[13] While scholars like Lawrence Douglas have pointed to the didactic function of trials, the ECCC has made explicit its didactic functions to educate the public about the Khmer Rouge and Democratic Kampuchea.[14] For this aim of education, the "flagship"[15] is a study tour that takes participants to, inter alia, the Tuol Sleng Genocide Museum.

If numbers count, the tour has been immensely successful. Every week, the ECCC brings around 600 villagers and students on the tour. Within a year, villagers from all of Cambodia's twenty-four districts had partaken in the tour, and by April 2014 there had been over 86,000 participants.[16] To further expand its reach, some of the tours are directed towards perceived "multipliers" – persons of influence whose views are locally respected and who can further spread the court's messages.[17] While the ECCC's outreach program also includes stops at the Choeung Ek Killing Fields and the ECCC compound, my interest here lies in the way photographs, as visual technologies, are used to teach participants of the tour about the past and call on them to participate in a "move" "forward."

These tours are openly didactic. According to the Public Affairs Section that organizes them, they are intended to help "improve understanding about what happened during Democratic Kampuchea, especially among the young people."[18] The tour is meant to stimulate knowledge and create the possibility of closure. In one court report, the tour is described as "educational for many participants as well as cathartic for some." On one particular tour, "many participants found their relatives and friends in the mugshots at Tuol Sleng."[19] And as former chief of PAS Reach Sambath explained, "I hope this Study Tour

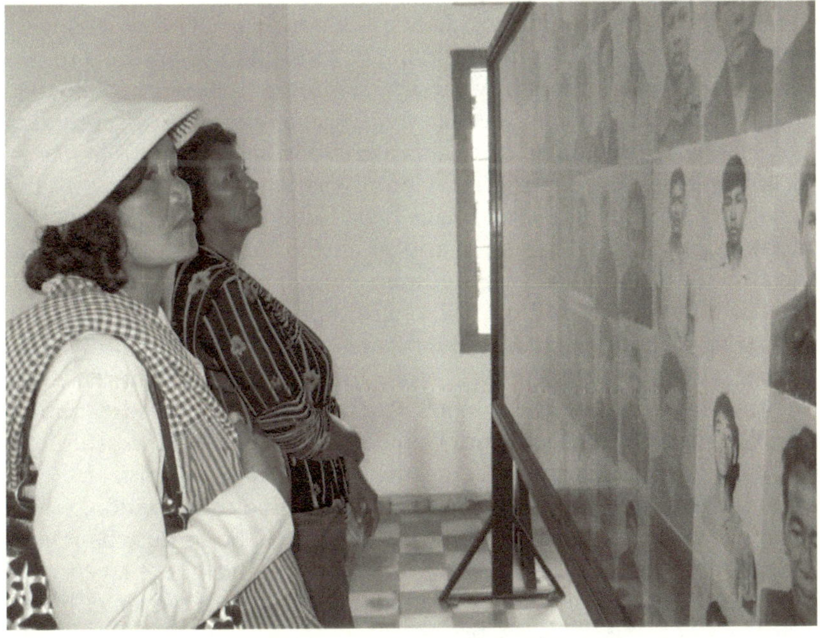

Figure 9.1 Participants in the ECCC Study Tour at the Tuol Sleng Genocide Museum, November 2010. Photo credit: ECCC/Kalyan Sann.

helps them understand the history of their own country better so that they can help to prevent the regime reoccurring."[20] While the wording in English-language articles suggests a need for a certain self-representation in an international climate, where the continuation of the tour relies on external donors, the repeated references to education are striking. So how is this meant to be achieved? How do these photographs act as a medium between the court and the public, how do they facilitate a transition forward, and how are they didactic?

Encountering the Photographs

The Tuol Sleng photographs are iconic. Since they were taken during the Khmer Rouge regime, they have moved across contexts and genres.[21] Originally taken as mug shots at S-21, they functioned as records within a paranoid criminal-law institution with the purpose of producing knowledge about the population and its traitorous elements. The mugshot produced a criminal. After the fall of the Khmer Rouge, the photographs were discovered by two Vietnamese journalists. S-21 became the Tuol Sleng Genocide Museum and the photographs went from being mug shots in a criminal-law institution to portraits of victims in museum exhibits. The preserved photographs were catalogued and became an archive used as evidence of the regime's brutality and its own criminality. Today, this archive is held in multiple places, including an online depository.[22] Controversially, the photographs also appear as art in galleries, and have been published in art and photography books.[23] They regularly appear in the West as illustrations of the atrocities committed by the Khmer Rouge, in particular the purges against intellectuals and oppositional figures.[24] With the ECCC, they appear in yet another context. But before I examine the way they figure in this particular legal context, I turn to the museum itself. The Tuol Sleng Genocide Museum is what Patrizia Violi has called a trauma site: "neither real museums nor cemeteries, nor places of worship, nor monuments – [it is] all of these together, and perhaps even more."[25] The museum is distinguished by an almost obsessive conservation, where most has been left intact to stand as "evidence." So in this chapter on visual technologies of legal transformation, I ask, how does an encounter with the museum and the photographs trigger a movement "forward" and proceed as a practice of subject formation?

The visitor arrives at a compound comprised of several buildings. On entering, s/he is soon surrounded by the photographs; they hang on the walls as well as on free-standing boards. The many photographs appear as masses. Most are displayed as part of larger collectives – in rows of six by twelve or more photos – arranged by a common trait. At first, they appear indistinguishable: the men and women become a mass of faces or what Sontag called "an aggregate of victims."[26] Anonymous for most visitors, the mass of images is difficult to take in. They remain what Barthes called a *studium*, horrible "scenes" that require the "rational inter-mediary of an ethical and political culture."[27]

If one looks closer, the individual traits of each person begin to appear. Most photographs hold a single individual in a typical mug-shot manner: a single man, woman, or child sitting down and photographed chest up and facing the photographer. In a few, the person is chained to a bystander, and in others, a mother is holding her infant child. There is a board with young girls, one with young boys; out of context they could have been pictures for a school catalogue. It is, to continue with Barthes's terminology, the *punctum* that draws the viewer in. Something in the pictures punctures you, compels you to look closer.[28] One person stares with disbelief, another is terrified, a third smiles as if in contempt, and a fourth smiles as if pleading with the onlooker. They are old men and women, teenagers looking as if coming direct from battle, women and men thin with starvation, women carrying their babies, young girls and young boys.

The mug shots are horrifyingly striking in their simplicity. Today's visitor enters what appears to be the very same room and sees the very same walls, windows, and trees as those killed in the 1970s. In a context that has been conserved almost entirely, the photographs are presented as remnants from the past. Their apparent lack of manipulation – a grainy photograph, a black spot here and lack of light there – make the pictures appear more real, adding to a perception of authenticity.[29] It is as if the poor quality of the photos both strengthens their documentary status and intensifies the affective encounter[30] with them.[31]

The encounter prompts questions over one's being in a position of visitor, a viewer. What does it mean to view photographs produced under such horrendous circumstances? How does one face the photograph, or perhaps, face the eye of the person depicted? How does one respond *responsibly*?[32] The position of the visitor, of viewer, is problematic at Tuol Sleng. The visitor meets the prisoner's eye from the same position as the photographer and with the same superior knowledge of their imminent death. In this way, the people photographed are, in the words of Sontag, "as in Titian's *The Flaying of Marsyas*, where Apollo's knife is eternally about to descend – forever looking at death, forever about to be murdered, forever wronged."[33] The visitor's gaze in this way not only witnesses the scene but does so from the position of the former perpetrator.

The faces are impossibly many, too many for the visitor to face, too many to address.[34] In their plurality, they look at you, the visitor, they call on you, probing you with questions of responsibility. The blur between the "you" in the photographic moment and the "you" as a visitor to Tuol Sleng makes the encounter powerful, an interpellative act that arrests the visitor to bear witness to the perpetual flaying. The encounter holds an affective dimension that cannot be dismissed simply as cheap sentimentality. Rather, as affective encounter, it holds a potential to open up a space for relations between viewers,[35] connecting the visitors, facilitating a community. In viewing the photographs, the visitors become part of a community held together by having born witness to a loss and a wrong. This possibility of creating something new through an affective encounter seems to tie into the ECCC assertion of a "move forward."

Learning

Irrespective of this affective dimension, the ECCC study tour has the explicit aim of educating the public. So how is it that the visitor *learns* by viewing the photographs? The museum has always had a didactic aim and has always functioned as a medium of information. In its early days, Tuol Sleng played an important part in proving to foreigners that atrocities had occurred. In the year following its discovery, Tuol Sleng was only open for foreigner delegations who were guided through the museum. Many of these visitors noted in the museum guestbook that while they had been sceptical of the scale of the atrocities at first, they had now been convinced.[36] In the first four months after opening to the general public in 1980, a staggering 320,000 people (309,000 Cambodians and 11,000 foreigners) visited the museum.[37] A report from the Cambodian Ministry of Culture, Information, and Propaganda states that by opening on Sundays, the museum played an "important element in educating the masses."[38] Senior curator Mai Lam later explained that "for seven years I studied ... to build up the Museum ... for the Cambodian people to help them study the war and the many aspects of war crimes ... For the regular people who cannot understand, the museum can help them."[39] For him, the intention was that the museum would, "in a very literal sense [stand as] 'evidence' of the crimes of the Khmer Rouge."[40] So too, in one of its court reports, the ECCC quotes a participant of the tour who explains that the visit had provided evidence to support stories that previously they had only heard.[41]

Barthes envisioned that photographs hold a unique status as medium, as a transfer and transport of the past. While "language is, by nature, fictional," the photograph "is indifferent to all intermediaries: it does not invent; it is authentication itself ... Photography never lies."[42] For him, the photograph is a gateway, "at once the past and the real."[43] Barthes suggests that the power of a photograph is formed by one's cleaving to this experience of the past. It is not that photographs reflect a "real," but instead the eventuality – the event – of the photography takes place as a return of a past real. As he put it, "the Photograph does not necessarily say *what is no longer*, but only and for certain *what has been*."[44] In this way, the past forcefully comes into the present, demanding our attention. Tuol Sleng seems to assume this self-evident power, that alongside their location at the site where they were taken, their evidentiary force lies in the photographs themselves, resuscitating the past. In line with this rationale, information at the museum is remarkably scarce. That is, there are few *words* at Tuol Sleng; very few signs explain or provide further information and context. Initially, guides accompanied all visitors through the museum, but this is far from the case now.[45] The ECCC study tour usually consists of two or three hundred villagers, accompanied by a single guide. Picture upon picture, man, woman, child, stare at the visitor, in what seems to be a return of the real, bringing back the past unmediated with self-explicatory evidence.

In line with this reliance upon the images' self-explicatory force, most of those photographed appear anonymous to the viewer, and only a handful of prominent people are explicitly named. This withholding of identity was a deliberate act by the curator, and stands in contrast to the practice of many other atrocity memorials across the globe.[46] While the identity of some remains unknown, others are only anonymous for the visitor. During the first years, visitors who identified their loved ones would write their name directly on the photo. Eventually this practice was disallowed, "as the photos were 'evidence' and the cost of replacing damaged photos were high and at times not even possible."[47] The ban suggests, as Rachel Hughes notes, that the authorities did not consider the museum an appropriate site for personal memorialization and mourning.[48] It also suggests that for the museum authorities, the form of silence that comes with anonymity was not problematic but rather preferable. In the sense then that Tuol Sleng is a trauma site – neither or perhaps both museum and memorial[49] – it seems that its status as memorial stands in tension with its status as an archive. Here, it is as if memorialization is competing with archiving, as if a practice of memorialization stands at odds with that of preserving artefacts as evidence. Rather than engaging with this tension, the photographs are left to stand independently, as if self-evident.

So what is self-evident in the photographs? Although the photographs were taken as mug shots, it is not the criminality of those depicted that is on display at Tuol Sleng. Nor does the force of the photographs lie in what they depict. Rather, their force lies in *existing*. It is the fact that there are masses of mug shots produced in conjunction with the killings of masses of Cambodia's population that is meant to stand as the evidential link between the regime and the deaths. While the photographs are images depicting persons, they are also objects, "physical things that have survived actual events as evidence, although they cannot directly 'show' those events."[50] It is the photograph – its organization and presentation – and not what is depicted in any one of them that is the remnant of atrocity. If for purposes of clarity, a distinction is made between remnant and artefact where remnants are understood to encompass more than physical objects, the photographs as a remnant hold a cleavage between what the photographs "show" and the artefact.

Yet even so, it is necessary to interrogate this status as remnants. It is difficult to keep the image and the artefact separate. Photographs are not equivalent to memories and may just as well act as counter-memory, in that they can block and replace what is remembered,[51] "not through recollection but through projection, investment, and creation."[52] The same photograph may very well come to represent multiple and conflicting pasts. Barbie Zelizer found in her study of Holocaust photographs that photographs were republished and reprinted in later decades "not necessarily because they supported a photo's original publication but because they helped launch new rhetorical arguments."[53] Photos anchor arguments in a (represented) past, and appear to the contemporary viewer mediated by both this representation and contemporary contexts. The distinction between image and artefact collapses, and the force of the image is reinforced by its status as artefact.

A space for interpretation opens when photographs are assumed to "speak for themselves." Without prior knowledge of the Khmer Rouge regime, the visitor to Tuol Sleng learns little. For someone like

Sontag, this should come as no surprise: "Whether the photograph is understood ... its meaning – and the viewer's response – depends on how the picture is identified or misidentified; that is, on words."[54] Without texts accompanying the photographs at Tuol Sleng, they remain caught in a tension between their presentation as evidence and as remnants that rely on memories created elsewhere.

This tension is also evident in the ECCC activities. As a way to pay tribute to the victims who perished at the centre, the court, as part of its non-judicial measures aimed at benefiting victims of the regime, decided in 2014 to build a Buddhist *stupa* in the courtyard of the museum. This memorial would replace one that was destroyed in a storm, but would also hold the names of all those who were killed at the site.[55] In this way, the status of the site as a memorial is strengthened while the photographs are left intact.

Narration

The presentation of the photographs as self-explicatory and self-evidential leaves the visitor relying on external context in order to interpret them. The danger, as Sontag points out, is that "eventually, one reads into [the] photograph what it *should* be saying,"[56] whatever it is that the context frames it as saying.

As the Tuol Sleng photographs have moved across genres and contexts, they have also appeared in a number of narratives. In the West, they often appear as representatives of all the victims of the Khmer Rouge, at times with comparisons to Nazi crimes and the Holocaust.[57] In Cambodia, the museum and the photographs played an important part in the production of a state narrative about the Khmer Rouge during the 1980s. In this narrative, a "glorious revolution" was "hijacked" by a "handful of sadistic, genocidal traitors" – the "Pol Pot Ieng–Sary clique."[58] This account presents a regime that killed for the sake of killing. The experiences of suffering at S-21 come to stand for suffering nationwide. At the museum, this narrative of a responsibility that lies only with a few collapses time and space, and effectively silences any differences of experience or motivation among areas or groups.[59] A few of the enlarged photographs are accompanied by signs in Khmer, the English and French translations of which attribute guilt exclusively to the "Pol Pot–Ieng Sary clique." By identifying only a few "prominent" victims and claiming them as "martyrs" for the (future) regime, the public could safely identify a relative as having been purged at S-21, without raising questions or suspicions about their loyalties during the DK period.[60]

The ECCC study tour enters into a pre-existing narrative and context. Its status as an international court positions the photographs in yet another narrative, with its own logic and rationale. Students are invited to "learn" about the country's past;[61] villagers find their loved ones; and citizens are given "the opportunity to confront a dark chapter of the country's history."[62] What is significant is not so much the question of who the persons in the photographs were, but rather the movement that the encounter is expected to trigger. Through the Tuol Sleng photographs, the court interpellates the visitor – a Cambodian who lived through the regime or is a child of the regime – as a participant in the transitional justice endeavour. They are represented as a figure who was somehow "stuck"[63] – in personal suffering, in not knowing the fate of loved ones, in ignorance about the past – but who, thanks to the study tour, can now "mov[e] forward through justice." Indeed, as the ECCC's Outreach Film describes it, this takes the court's work beyond the legal developments inside the chamber.

Victims and Perpetrators

Visiting the museum means becoming part of the court and of its judicial process. Although the study tour is designed and carried out by a public affairs section, it cannot avoid its close association with an institution devoted to criminal law and to the binary determination of guilt and innocence. Within this logic, there is only room for perpetrators and victims, which creates a dichotomy of subjects. And so, while carrying previous and existing contexts of the photographs at Tuol Sleng with it, the study tour furthers the representation of those depicted and those viewing the photos in terms of international criminal law.

The anonymous appearance of these photographs has meant that fewer questions are asked about the people who were killed at S-21. Consequently, it has also meant that fewer questions have been asked about why the regime killed so many of its own, including many who were more or less devoted Khmer Rouge. In his testimony at the ECCC, former S-21 chairman Duch explained that those who were taken to S-21 came in two waves. Before April 1976, they were soldiers and supporters of the former Lon Nol regime. After this, the focus was directed at internal enemies. Notwithstanding the narrative of martyrdom we saw above, almost 10,000 of the 12,273 prisoners whose files have remained were lower- and middle-ranking Khmer Rouge cadres.[64] Around 500 of these had held positions of responsibility, and were rightly or wrongly accused of treason.[65] Many fell victim to internal purges, attempts by the regime to eliminate any suspected traitors. In addition (although these were allegedly not photographed), 155 of those who were killed at S-21 were former staff,[66] victims of the paranoia of the regime, but at one time also part of it. This aspect has been mostly silenced or brushed over. For some, this "masking" of the background of those killed even ensures the site as an "authentic marker of the genocide."[67] In this logic, there are only perpetrators and victims, no one in between and no one both.

This silencing of the complexity of the victim-perpetrator dynamic is essential to the work carried out by the ECCC. As a criminal-law institution, it is committed to finding and allocating responsibility. But its jurisdiction is strictly limited. Its mandate only covers *senior leaders* and *those most responsible*.[68] This focus on only a few is one of the most persistent messages repeated by the ECCC, particularly in its outreach work. "Ordinary Khmer Rouge have nothing to fear";[69] responsibility lies only with a handful of men and women and no one else needs to worry. In this vein, people in former Khmer Rouge strongholds like Pailin have been encouraged by ECCC representatives during the study tour to file complaints or become civil parties, emphasizing that many former Khmer Rouge cadres were also victims.[70] In the rush to victimhood, previous participation as Khmer Rouge is not repressed, but since it cannot be narrated by the ECCC as evidence of responsibility, it must therefore be disavowed – or perhaps even reinscribed as victimhood.[71] In this vein, the ECCC initiative to inscribe the names of all those who were killed at S-21 on a *stupa* was opposed by at least one survivor, Chum Mey, who did not consider it appropriate to have the names of victims alongside those of Khmer Rouge cadres. For him, it was inconceivable to "take the names of some who kills and put it on a stupa."[72] While his protest did invoke conversations about the blurring of victimhood and perpetration, the *stupa* – with all known names inscribed – was inaugurated in March 2015.[73]

Reliance upon the anonymous photographs at Tuol Sleng then is not surprising: rather than complicate or encourage questions on how and why people not only fall victim to but also participate in atrocities, the ECCC reinforces a narrative – imposed on it by its own legal structure – in which responsibility and guilt lie only with a few of the leaders, architects, or "masterminds," and everyone else is a victim.

This articulation of mass victimization is close to the state narratives produced during the 1980s, where the responsibility of a few "traitors" caused the victimization of all.

Conclusion: Mourning and Interruption

Loss and victimization shatter communities, disturbing our ties to one another. During the Khmer Rouge period, there were so many losses, so many victims. The ECCC strives to help the country "move forward through justice" by holding senior leaders and those most responsible to account, and by teaching the public about the crimes they committed.

Mourning is important, Judith Butler writes in *Precarious Life*, as "without a capacity to mourn, we lose that keener sense of life we need in order to oppose violence."[74] Mourning furthers the process initiated by loss that has made, in her words, "a tenuous 'we' of us all."[75] It is our common exposure to loss that holds us together, generating community, establishing new attachments. The Tuol Sleng photographs are used to trigger an "us" by representing a universal victimhood in the transitional justice endeavour of the ECCC. The losses are *seen* through the photographs. The identification of those depicted in the mug shots ensure that they are named and remembered, that they do not constitute or remain what Butler calls "ungrievable lives." Meanwhile, those who participate in the tour, like the two women in the introduction, are called upon to *learn* by seeing for themselves. They are called upon to act – or enact – the role of victim-survivors. In this way, the photographs are used to reflect *and instigate* a particular transitional justice endeavour.

Yet, as I have demonstrated here, the way these photographs are currently presented does not question their highly adventitious reasoning. The way the study tour turns to the photographs does not question assumptions or interrupt the pre-existing structures that constitute society. Rather, the pre-existing is reasserted wherein a community (and a legal system) stipulates whom to mourn. By not addressing the complex and manifold subject identities of perpetrators and victims it is possible to perpetuate a Manichean division of bad perpetrators and innocent victims. To Butler's insight on the importance of mourning I wish then to add Bonnie Honig's assertion[76] that it is not enough to call for mourning without also paying attention to and *interrupting* the structures that undergird society and may even have caused the loss in the first place. Instead of turning to photographs to "move forward," as the ECCC slogan has it, we should allow the photographs to interrupt us, allowing their stories to be fully told rather than conveniently silenced. Then we can talk about responsibility.

NOTES

1 I'm grateful to Rachel Hughes, Peter Rush, and Des Manderson for helpful comments. Part of this chapter was published in "Education and Photography at Tuol Sleng Genocide Museum," in Peter D. Rush and Olivera Simić, eds, *The Arts of Transitional Justice: Culture, Activism, and Memory after Atrocity* (New York: Springer, 2014), 43.
2 ECCC, *Moving Forward Through Justice* (ECCC, August 2010). Available at the ECCC website under "Outreach," https://www.youtube.com/watch?v=gbRX4khXp_0.
3 Janine Natalya Clark, "International War Crimes Tribunals and the Challenge of Outreach," *International Criminal Law Review* 9 (2009): 99; Marlies Glasius, "'We ourselves, we are part of the functioning': The ICC, Victims, and Civil Society in the Central African Republic," *African Affairs* 108, no. 430 (2008): 49; Peter Manning, "Governing Memory: Justice, Reconciliation and Outreach at the ECCC," *Memory Studies* 5, no. 2 (2011): 167; Peter Manning, "Legitimacy, Power and Memory at the Extraordinary Chambers in the Courts of Cambodia," in Nicola Palmer, Phil Clark, and Danielle Granville, eds, *Critical Perspectives in Transitional Justice* (Intersentia, 2012), 217; Diane F. Orentlicher, *That Someone Guilty Be Punished: The Impact of the ICTY in Bosnia* (New York: OSJI & ICTJ, 2010), 102; Norman Henry Pentelovich, "Seeing Justice Done: The Importance of Prioritizing Outreach Efforts at International Criminal Tribunals," *Georgetown Journal of International Law* 39 (2008): 445; Victor Peskin, "Courting Rwanda: The Promises and Pitfalls of the ICTR Outreach Programme," *Journal of International Criminal Justice* 3 (2005): 950; Jaya Ramji-Nogales, "Designing Bespoke Transitional Justice: Pluralist Process Approach," *Michigan Journal of International Law* 32 (2010): 1; Eric Stover and Harvey M. Weinstein, eds, *My Neighbour, My Enemy: Justice and Community in the Aftermath of Mass Atrocity* (Cambridge: Cambridge University Press, 2004).
4 The ECCC was set up through an agreement between the Cambodian government and the UN that came into effect in 2004. It operates within the Cambodian domestic system but applies both domestic and international law and has both national and international presence through staff and funding. Its jurisdiction is limited to "senior leaders"

and "those most responsible" for the crimes committed during the time Cambodia was known as Democratic Kampuchea and ruled by the group mostly known as the Khmer Rouge. See, e.g., http://www.eccc.gov.kh/en/.

5 Helen Jarvis, chief of public affairs, "Moving Forward Through Justice" (presentation at conference "Dealing with a Past Holocaust and National Reconciliation: Learning from Experiences," Phnom Penh, Cambodia, 28–9 August 2006), 2.

6 The literature on the Khmer Rouge period (1975–9) is extensive. See, e.g., Elizabeth Becker, *When the War Was Over: The Voices of Cambodia's Revolution and Its People* (New York: Simon and Schuster, 1986); David Chandler, *Voices from S-21: Terror and History in Pol Pot's Secret Prison* (Berkeley and Los Angeles: University of California Press, 1999); Alexander Laban Hinton, *Why Did They Kill? Cambodia in the Shadow of Genocide* (Berkeley: University of California Press, 2005); Ben Kiernan, *The Pol Pot Regime: Race, Power, and Genocide in Cambodia under the Khmer Rouge 1975–79*, 3rd ed. (New Haven: Yale University Press, 2008); Ben Kiernan, *Genocide and Resistance in Southeast Asia: Documentation, Denial and Justice in Cambodia and East Timor* (New Brunswick: Transaction Publishers, 2008).

7 The *Duch* judgment notes a revised prisoners' list that provides a figure of 12,273 prisoners, but given that children were not registered and many records have been lost, "the numbers are likely to be considerably greater than indicated." *Duch Trial Judgment* [143], see also [141]. Historian David Chandler has suggested that since the logbooks from 1978 are incomplete and children were not registered, some 17,000 persons may have been killed at S-21. Chandler, *Voices from S-21*, 6.

8 Historian Ben Kiernan estimates 1.671 million, demographer Marek Sliwinski 1.8 million, and Patrick Heuveline 2.52 million. Summarized by Tom Fawthrop and Helen Jarvis, *Getting Away with Genocide? Elusive Justice and the Khmer Rouge Tribunal* (London and Ann Arbor: University of New South Wales Press, 2005), 3–4.

9 On the negotiation history, see in particular the accounts by David Scheffer and Helen Jarvis, both of whom participated actively. Fawthrop and Jarvis, *Getting Away with Genocide?*, 234; David Scheffer, *All the Missing Souls: A Personal History of the War Crimes Tribunals* (Princeton, NJ: Princeton University Press, 2012), chap. 12. It should be noted that this is not the first attempt to hold those responsible for the crimes to account. In 1979, a People's Revolutionary Tribunal found Pol Pot and Ieng Sary in absentia guilty of genocide. See Rachel Hughes, "Ordinary Theatre, Extraordinary Law at the Khmer Rouge Tribunal," *Environment and Planning D: Society and Space* 33, no. 4 (2015).

10 *Prosecutor v. Kaing Guek Eav alias Duch (Judgment)* (Extraordinary Chambers in the Courts of Cambodia [ECCC], Trial Chamber, Case no. 001/18–07–2007/ECCC/TC, 26 July 2010), 567. Upon appeal, he was sentenced to life imprisonment. See *Prosecutor v. Kaing Guek Eav alias Duch (Appeal Judgment)* (ECCC, Supreme Court Chamber, Case no. 001, 3 February 2012) ("*Duch Appeal Judgment*").

11 *Prosecutors v. Nuon Chea and Khieu Samphan (Judgment)* (Extraordinary Chambers in the Courts of Cambodia, Trial Chamber, Case no. 002/01, 7 August 2014).

12 The trial hearings began on 17 October 2014, and are ongoing at the time of writing, November 2015.

13 The national co-investigative judge considers Case 003 to be closed, while the international counterpart finds it open. See Office of the Co-Investigative Judges, *Statement by the Co-Investigating Judges regarding Case 003* (28 February 2013), http://www.eccc.gov.kh/en/articles/statement-co-investigating-judges-regarding-case-003.

14 See, e.g., "Pailin Residents Visit ECCC & Tuol Sleng," *ECCC Court Report* 31 (November 2010): 4; ECCC, *Moving Forward Through Justice*.

15 "KRT Study Tours Mark 29,000 Visitors from Across Cambodia in 2010" (January 2011), 32; *ECCC Court Report* 1.

16 "ECCC at a Glance" (Factsheet, April 2014), http://www.eccc.gov.kh/en/about-eccc/introduction.

17 See, e.g., "KRT Study Tours Extend to Commune Leaders in 2011," *ECCC Court Report* 33 (February 2011): 4.

18 "Pailin Residents Visit ECCC & Tuol Sleng."

19 "KRT Study Tours Mark 29,000 Visitors."

20 Reach Sambath quoted in "Pailin Residents Visit ECCC & Tuol Sleng."

21 I discuss this movement further in Maria Elander, "Education and Photography at Tuol Sleng Genocide Museum," 43; also see Michelle Caswell, *Archiving the Unspeakable: Silence, Memory, and the Photographic Record in Cambodia* (Madison: University of Wisconsin Press, 2014).

22 See Yale University, Cambodian Genocide Program, CTS Database Search Form, http://cgp.research.yale.edu/cgp/cts/ctssearch.jsp.

23 Exhibitions include that at MOMA in 1997 and the photo festival *Rencontres photographiques d'Arles.* For discussion on these, see Thierry de Duve, "Art in the Face of Radical Evil," *October* 125 (2008): 3; Rachel Hughes, "The Abject Artefacts of Memory Photographs from Cambodia's Genocide," *Media, Culture and Society* 25 (2003): 23.

24 E.g., *Year Zero: The Silent Death of Cambodia* (presented by John Pilger, directed by David Munro, 1979); *Scream Bloody Murder* (CNN documentary, 2008).

25 Patrizia Violi, "Trauma Site Museums and Politics of Memory: Tuol Sleng, Villa Grimaldi and the Bologna Ustica Museum," *Theory, Culture & Society* 29, no. 1 (2012): 36.
26 Susan Sontag, *Regarding the Pain of Others* (New York: Picador, 2003), 61.
27 Roland Barthes, *Camera Lucida: Reflections on Photography* (Vintage, 2000 [1980]), 26.
28 Ibid., 27.
29 On authenticity and art, see Sontag, *Regarding the Pain of Others*, 26–7.
30 Alison Young has written extensively on the affective dimensions of art and photographs. See, e.g., "From Object to Encounter: Aesthetic Politics and Visual Criminology," *Theoretical Criminology* 18 (2014): 159; *The Scene of Violence: Cinema, Crime, Affect* (Abingdon: Routledge-Cavendish, 2009); *Judging the Image: Art, Value, Law* (Abingdon: Routledge, 2005).
31 Compare this with the United States Holocaust Memorial Museum, where "curators found that they preferred so-called dirty photographs – those marred by scratches, dust, dirt, and generations of copying – that gave the photograph a badge of authenticity." See Barbie Zelizer, *Remembering to Forget: Holocaust Memory through the Camera's Eye* (Chicago and London: University of Chicago Press, 1998), 195.
32 De Duve, "Art in the Face of Radical Evil," writes about his struggle in the encounter with the photographs, struggling to reject an impossible aesthetic judgment and an initial reaction of cheap sentimentality. As he sees the photographs in an art exhibition in France, he encounters them in a different context than at Tuol Sleng.
33 Sontag, *Regarding the Pain of Others*, 61.
34 For a discussion on singularity and "being-with" through a reading of the photographs alongside Derrida and Nancy, see Jenny Edkins, "Exposed Singularity," *Journal for Cultural Research* 9, no. 4 (2005): 359.
35 See Alison Young, "The Scene of the Crime: Is There Such a Thing as 'just looking'?" in Keith J. Haywar and Mike Presdee, eds, *Framing Crime: Cultural Criminology and the Image* (Abingdon and New York: Routledge, 2010), 84–5.
36 Judy Ledgerwood, "The Cambodian Tuol Sleng Museum of Genocidal Crimes: National Narrative," *Museum Anthropology* 21, no. 1 (1999), 89.
37 Ibid., 88.
38 Ibid.
39 Interview by Sara Colm in 1995, quoted in Chandler, *Voices from S-21*, 8.
40 Ledgerwood, "The Cambodian Tuol Sleng Museum," 89.
41 Quoted in "KRT Study Tours Mark 29,000 Visitors," 3.
42 Barthes, *Camera Lucida*, 87.

43 Ibid., 82.
44 Ibid., 85 (italics in original).
45 An audio tour is currently being prepared for Tuol Sleng by the company Narrowcasters, similar to the one already existing at Choeung Ek. See Helen Jarvis, "Powerful Remains: The Continuing Presence of Victims of the Khmer Rouge Regime in Today's Cambodia," *Human Remains and Violence: An Interdisciplinary Journal* 1, no. (2015): 35.
46 Violi, "Trauma Site Museums," 49.
47 Rachel Hughes, "Fielding Genocide: Post 1979 Cambodia and the Geopolitics of Memory," doctoral thesis (University of Melbourne, 2006), 189.
48 Ibid.
49 See Violi, "Trauma Site Museums."
50 Hughes, "The Abject Artefacts of Memory Photographs from Cambodia's Genocide," 28.
51 Barthes, *Camera Lucida*, 89.
52 Marianne Hirsch, "Projected Memory: Holocaust Photographs in Personal and Public Fantasy," in Mieke Bal, Jonathan Crewe, and Leo Spitzer, eds, *Acts of Memory: Cultural Recall in the Present* (Lebanon, NH: Dartmouth College Press, University Press of New England, 1999), 2, 8.
53 Zelizer, *Remembering to Forget*, 187.
54 Sontag, *Regarding the Pain of Others*, 29 and 89.
55 Kevin Ponniah and Meas Sokchea, "Stupa to Be Built for KR Victims," *Phnom Penh Post*, 10 July 2014, http://www.phnompenhpost.com/national/stupa-be-built-kr-victims.
56 Sontag, *Regarding the Pain of Others*, 29 and 89.
57 I have discussed this in Maria Elander, "The Victim's Address: Expressivism and the Victim at the Extraordinary Chambers in the Courts of Cambodia," *International Journal of Transitional Justice* 7 (2013): 95, 115; and Elander, "Education and Photography at Tuol Sleng Genocide Museum," 43.
58 Ledgerwood, "The Cambodian Tuol Sleng Museum," 82 and 91.
59 Ibid., 82–3, 93, with reference to Vickery's Standard Total View.
60 Hughes, "Fielding Genocide," 141.
61 See, e.g., "Study Tour in Cooperation with Peace Corps," *ECCC Court Report* 47 (April 2012): 4.
62 ECCC, *Moving Forward Through Justice*.
63 See Alexander Laban Hinton, "Transitional Justice Time, Uncle San, Aunty Yan, and Outreach at the Khmer Rouge Tribunal," in Deborah Mayersen and Annie Pohlman, eds, *Genocide and Mass Atrocities in Asia: Legacies and Prevention* (London: Taylor and Francis, 2013).

64 "5,609 entries are members of the RAK [Revolutionary Army of Kampuchea] and 4,371 are DK [Democratic Kampuchea] cadres." *Duch Trial Judgment* [141].
65 Chandler, *Voices from S-21*, chap. 3.
66 *Duch Trial Judgment* [141].
67 For example, Lisa M. Moore, "(Re) Covering the Past, Remembering Trauma: The Politics of Commemoration at Sites of Atrocity," *Journal of Public and International Affairs* 20 (Spring 2009): 53.
68 Law on the Establishment of the Extraordinary Chambers, with inclusion of amendments as promulgated on 27 October 2004 (NS/RKM/1004/006) (unofficial translation by the Council of Jurists and the Secretariat of the Task Force, revised 26 August 2007) ("*ECCC Law*").
69 See, e.g., ECCC Outreach Poster with the English text "Only the senior Khmer Rouge leaders and those most responsible for committing serious crimes will be tried. Ordinary KR soldiers have nothing to fear."
70 Manning, "Governing Memory," 174.
71 Disavowal is, according to Lacanian psychoanalysis, the fundamental operation in perversion, distinct from repression in neurosis and foreclosure in psychosis. While something *repressed* is expelled from the conscious but buried in the unconscious, and something *foreclosed* is expelled even from the unconscious, a subject who *disavows* simply refuses to recognize the reality. See Dylan Evans, *An Introductory Dictionary of Lacanian Psychoanalysis* (London and New York: Routledge, 1996), "disavowal."
72 Poppy McPherson, "Memorial Plan Prompts Debate about Victims and Perpetrators of Genocide," *Phnom Penh Post*, 9 May 2014, http://www.phnompenhpost.com/7days/memorial-plan-prompts-debate-about-victims-and-perpetrators-genocide.
73 Jarvis, "Powerful Remains," 45.
74 Judith Butler, *Precarious Life: The Powers of Mourning and Violence*, 2nd ed. (London: Verso, 2006), xviii.
75 Ibid., 20.
76 Bonnie Honig, *Antigone, Interrupted* (New York: Cambridge University Press, 2013) , passim, and esp. p. 2.

10 The Exceptional Image: Torture Photographs from Guantánamo Bay and Abu Ghraib as Foucault's Spectacle of Punishment

CONNAL PARSLEY[1]

Two striking elements of the Bush administration's "war on terror" were its use of torture and the publication of related images. This chapter considers two of these images together in order to think through the fraught relationship between images of torture emanating from a liberal democratic state and that state's strategies for maintaining its governmental power. The two publicly available images of torture I will address in this chapter will be instantly recognizable to most readers, drawn as they are from the most iconic groups of photographs made during the "war on terror." The first comes from a series made by Navy Petty Officer Shane McCoy at Camp X-Ray, Guantánamo Bay, in January 2002.[2] Deliberately released shortly afterwards by the US Department of Defense, these images were, for most who saw them, the first glimpse of the ephemeral "enemy" of the USA-led "coalition of the willing": those accused of involvement in the 9/11 attacks, famously dubbed by then Secretary of State Donald Rumsfeld as "the worst of the worst."[3] The second image is from the "Abu Ghraib archive": a now-notorious series of "279 images and 19 videos from the [US] Army's internal investigation" into detainee torture and abuse over a three-month period at Abu Ghraib prison in Iraq.[4] These images, made by personnel on their own cameras, were never intended for official release. In the example shown below, taken by Specialist Harman, two military personnel (Corporal Graner and Private First Class England) pose with a human pyramid of naked detainees. Both sets of images attracted significant scholarly attention,[5] though perhaps unsurprisingly the Abu Ghraib images have been treated much more extensively.[6] Whilst both sets of images garnered both support and opprobrium for the Bush regime,[7] and catalysed an intense new debate on torture,[8] the photographs from Abu Ghraib provoked nothing short of a crisis for the United States,[9] reportedly prompting some of even the most conservative media voices to change their minds about the war.[10]

The importance of these images to political and visual culture guarantees that much more will be said about them in the years to come. Indeed, they constitute something of a *mise-en-abyme* for the problem of sovereign power in the age of liberal democracy and the digital image. Yet surprisingly, no attempt has been made to read the two images together.[11] This is especially interesting given the documented connection between the practices of interrogation and torture at Abu Ghraib and Guantánamo Bay.[12] In this chapter, rather than pursue the rich lines of inquiry connected to one or the other of these images – nor the ongoing debate on torture to which they are tightly connected – my modest aim is to propose a connection between them. Drawing on Michel Foucault's famous description of the "spectacle of the scaffold" in *Discipline and Punish*, I contend that the spectacle of public torture has not disappeared as Foucault claimed, but has in our age been "exceptionalized," splitting into two images which continue to have a function in relation to political power. In accounting for some of the material and historical conditions in which this spectacle appears, I will suggest that the "theatre" of punishment, once unified in space and time, has been disaggregated by contemporary political conditions and the material conditions of images and visual culture. Like the picture obtained by Walter Benjamin's cameraman-surgeon, this theatre has ceased to be "total" and instead "consists of multiple fragments ... assembled under a new law."[13] As a result, we must be attentive to an "element of continuity" persisting despite a different "organization of the visual":[14] alongside Foucault's "micro-physics of power," I suggest, we should acknowledge the micro-*theatrics* by which sovereign political power still renews itself.

The pursuit of this hypothesis implicates three particularly relevant strands of contemporary scholarship. First, studies in law, politics, and visual culture, which now offer a great plurality of approaches through which to address the role of images in constituting the public, structuring political subjectivity in relation to power, and dramatizing (and thus making liveable) legal relations and law's authority. Second, post-Foucauldian scholarship, which has emphasized the evolution and intensification of what Foucault called "governmental rationality"; in many cases with specific reference to the penal paradigm of Bentham's panopticon, or in any case the question of the gaze in relation to the production of subjectivity and power relations. Third, visual culture, image studies, and art history, which have emphasized the importance of the material conditions of image production and viewing: not only in interpreting this or that image, but in understanding "what is an image"[15] – a question that takes on special political significance at certain historical moments. In combination, I suggest, these approaches at least call into question Foucault's own historical narrative as to the relationship between sovereign power and spectacular force. At their strongest they beg a new theory of that relationship capable of accounting for the survival, reproduction, or re-emergence in the digital image of the spectacle of sovereign power.

Points of Departure

Such a new theory is beyond the scope of this chapter. Instead, I will situate a reading of the two images in question in terms of two more specific points of departure. The first is the claim that the images of shackled detainees at Camp X-Ray were "a sign of successful vindication."[16] As Patrick Lenta writes, "spectacular torture" may have "the potential to resurface in a contemporary form as an instance of what Blackstone labels "an engine of the state."[17] This chapter moves away from the language of "purpose," objective, or function that undergirds Lenta's account.[18] Such language assumes that political torture has no *necessary* connection with visibility, and the decision to document it visually or make it visible to the public is rationally motivated.[19] My account proceeds from the possibility that now and in eighteenth-century Paris, torture is *intrinsically* concerned with a kind of political dramatization that is not only "irrational" but is always in tension with so-called rational forms of governmental power.

My second point of departure is the paradigm adopted by Thomas Mathiesen in "The Viewer Society." Mathiesen maintains that the "creation of human beings who control themselves through self-control ... is a task which is actually fulfilled" by what he terms the "synopticon," in which it is the *many* who watch the *few* via a "total system of the modern mass media"[20] – rather than the few who (at least theoretically) watch the many, as in Bentham's panopticon. Mathiesen's focus on viewing practices runs counter to the dominant trajectory of post-Foucauldian scholarship, which embraces Foucault's rejection of an "optical epistemology,"[21] thus turning vision into a mere metaphor for the epistemic conditions of "visibility"[22] within a regime of power and knowledge.

In emphasizing visibility rather than actual seeing, this work denies the mass spectator any role, conclusively accepting that the panopticon broke the seeing/seen dyad.[23] Mathiesen, then, helpfully reminds us that media consumption retains a potential role in the production of political power relations.

Yet Mathiesen, like others who emphasize the "power of the public gaze,"[24] falls short of acknowledging the potential *heterogeneity* of the spectacle to the paradigm of discipline. In short, although some scholars have attempted to move beyond the organizing metaphor of the panopticon,[25] surveillance-discipline has remained the sole paradigm through which to approach the contemporary relationship between practice and power. In foregrounding the recrudescence of the spectacle, my intention is not to call into question Foucault's persuasive argument about the rise of discipline. What I hope to provoke is a finer-grained reflection on whether and how the spectacle of torture-punishment mobilizes a distinct, less "rational" strategy of power *precisely in relation to this dominant governmental paradigm.* Drawing on an analysis of two publicly available images of torture, this chapter rejects the mutual exclusivity of discipline and spectacle, arguing that political torture has a tendency to display itself, but that the prevailing governmental rationality offers important contextual complications.[26]

The "Spectacle of the Scaffold"

What did Foucault mean by the "spectacle of the scaffold"? In answering this question, great emphasis is typically given to the first three pages of *Discipline and Punish*, which opens with the famous graphic example of the *amende honorable* made in 1757 by Robert-François Damiens. The last person to be "drawn and quartered" in France, Damiens was brutally tortured to death in public (at the Place de Grève), for having attempted the life of Louis XV. The account is particularly gruesome and has often been retold, and it seems unnecessary to do so again here. We should however linger on certain key elements of Foucault's description of the event, since it is there that we find articulated the paradigm of the spectacle that Foucault claimed was to disappear.

The sovereign power that spectacular torture enabled was "exalted and strengthened by its visible manifestations."[27] But public torture was never something straightforwardly visible. The public destruction of the body of the convicted prisoner was not the beginning of the penal process's operation on the body. The accused was first judicially tortured as part of a private yet carefully measured interrogation aimed at gathering information surrounding the crime, amassing evidence, and if possible, obtaining a confession. Yet any proof obtained in this way – which Foucault describes as a complex and precarious strategy – had to be repeated before the judges, as a "'spontaneous' confession,"[28] and then again for the benefit of the public. If, for Foucault, the scene of violent punishment should be understood as theatre for an audience of would-be sovereign subjects, then its "backstage" elements were indispensable. Here, we must pay attention to Foucault's crucially important insight that it was "as if investigation and punishment had become mixed,"[29] and acknowledge that what was at stake was not merely a public spectacle, but an economy of display and concealment. Concealed torture *stricto sensu* (the infliction of pain to produce speech in order to double the voice of the regime, as Scarry famously put it)[30] formed the basis for the juridical conviction by which the crime became "notorious and manifest."[31] Yet this speech lacked confirmation and authenticity, which could only be granted through repetition in the public ritual of punishment.

Crucially, considering Foucault's object and method, this process culminated in the production of the "truth of the crime," which could only be achieved through a *theatrical* performance, in which an assembled crowd witnessed the power of the sovereign.[32] This theatre, emphasizes Foucault, had its place within a juridical logic, but it also served a complex and resolutely political function: it "justif[ied] justice" and confirmed its veracity.[33] It also addressed a personal attack on the sovereign, rectifying this attack in both honouring the sensibilities of those who abide by the law, and restoring the *im*balance of power and authority in favour of the sovereign – from whom the law was said to emanate.[34] Foucault goes on to say, drawing on Muyart de Vouglans, that the right to punish must be understood as "an aspect of the sovereign's right to make war on his enemies."[35] The body of the condemned was central to this theatre. It was the sight of the excessively destroyed body that "produced and reproduced the truth of the crime,"[36] and "established the reality of what one punished"[37] – but only through a crowd of public witnesses acting as that truth's "guarantors."[38] This body punished beyond pain[39] was the meeting place between public and private, investigation and punishment, and "the judgment of men and the judgment of God."[40]

What was essential to the Foucauldian "spectacle of punishment," then, was not punishment in the modern sense. It was a theatrical performance for a public audience in which pain visited on a body produces that body as the political enemy of the sovereign, and restores the imbalance of power in his favour. These features, along with torture's dynamic of concealment and display and the blurring of war with crime and investigation with punishment, are what return in the images under consideration.

The Limits of Governmental Rationality

Foucault's purpose in describing Damiens's punishment in detail is to establish a paradigm of sovereign penal power that overlapped with two alternative paradigms in the second half of the eighteenth century, and was later entirely supplanted. Foucault attributes the demise of the public theatre of punishment to the perceived complicity of excessive sovereign violence with the "atrocity" of the original crime, in time provoking the disaffection of the crowd. Although this excess confirmed the "truth of the crime" and its punishment within the rules and obligations belonging to a personalist form of sovereignty, Foucault suggests that it came at the cost of the sovereign being seen to have "soiled his hands," which conflicted with the emerging call for a more "humane" use of the power to punish.[41] But equally important for Foucault is that the crowd was itself the central character at public executions. The crowd was an active participant in the spectacle – once chanting "give us back our gallows" – well into the eighteenth century, and the stance it might take to the execution was an unpredictable element that could even sometimes disrupt the sovereign's intentions. Indeed, this manifestation of the crowd's power could turn on the punisher. Protecting the convict, or more quickly killing him, was not unknown,[42] and there were even sometimes direct attacks on the executioner.[43] Executions, moreover, were sometimes the beginning of more general "social disturbances"[44] arising from the solidarity that people were inclined to feel with the condemned.[45]

Foucault thus suggests that the turn to a more "humane" practice was motivated by innovation in the stability, efficiency, and rationalization of penal power. The famous transition through successive paradigms that Foucault narrates, however – in which governmental power becomes ever less "discontinuous, irregular and above ... its own laws"[46] – also charts the demise of the visual. Binding the spectacle to sovereign force (with its marked bodies and ceremonial theatre), Foucault claims the legal reformers introduced a new visual logic:

an economy in which punishments were rationally proportional to the crimes they "represented." And with the rise of the disciplinary paradigm, innovations in power's efficiency see the sovereign become more or less invisible – in penal power and, we might observe, within Foucault's methodology – and reduced to an omnipresent, abstract gaze, a mere trace manifesting in the trained body of the individual.

As valuable as this narrative was to the development of Foucault's historical account and the emergence of the field of governmentality studies, it can equally be seen as containing two severely limiting factors. Punishment, population, and the "criminal" (rather than enemy) become special objects of analysis,[47] but are severed from the juridical representations of power that might have offered another plane of power's historical continuity and transformation.[48] Concomitantly, image and vision become increasingly metaphorical. As Véronique Voruz has observed, Foucault tends to convert vision into the principle of the intelligibility of discursive power. Through Foucault's methodology, Voruz suggests, "we do not see things but visibilities."[49]

Foucault's disavowal of sovereignty and juridical models of power has attracted a great deal of attention. Yet his "eclipse of vision" – the emphatic rejection of the so-called hegemonic "optical epistemology" that was associated, since Plato, with the paradigms of thought Foucault sought to critique[50] – is an equally important methodological constraint. Critically, these two factors are related. For Foucault, the importance of visuality decreases in inverse proportion to the evolution of superior and more stable forms of governmental rationality, but it is precisely this mutual exclusivity between the two that requires challenge. The generality of Foucault's claim that surveillance "extinguishes spectacular manifestations of power" and is the "perfection" of power's exercise,[51] must be tempered, that is, by his "failure to pursue the question of transformation in the form of representation of sovereign power,"[52] and by his subversion of the visual in favour of a focus on governmental rationality. Certainly, examples of mutual exclusivity could be found: contemporary spectacles of violent "punishment" of the enemy abound in regimes that are not characterized by modern disciplinary governmental rationalities; for example, the Islamic State, a medieval-styled caliphate, with its gruesome execution videos. But how should we understand a spectacle of torture that emanates from a Western liberal state? Herein lies the problem: fully accepting the cogency and value of Foucault's insights in accounting for major innovations in governmental power (and indeed those of later authors who have pointed to the intensification of this rationalizing improvement of power, as "control"[53] or as "optimization" rather than discipline),[54] what to do with the survival of the spectacle? Whether understood in terms of the importance of "theatre" as a paradigm in twentieth and twenty-first century war,[55] or specific examples of spectacles of violence manufactured by liberal democratic governments, the spectacle seems too important to discount.

"Hidden" Tortures

Rather than propose a new paradigm to succeed that of discipline, my approach is to ask how such different paradigms of power might coexist.[56] Political torture, I suggest, is the "ground zero" of this question, because it always entertains a negotiable and problematic relationship with the visibility that seems to offer it its public-ity and thus its political efficacy. For instance, Henry Shue suggests that torture has a "terroristic" or "deterrent" function; the intimidation of would-be opponents.[57] From this point of view, we could point to a similar logic of display that belongs to the *amendes honorables* of eighteenth-century France, the Chinese practice of *lingchi* that survived into the twentieth century, and the Islamic State's propaganda videos (which not only feature violent execution but sometimes also the "confessions" of the victims). In liberal modernity, then, torture is fundamentally paradoxical, since it tends to want to display and ritualize what must, according to the contemporary political order, be excluded from the politico-legal sphere. The question thus becomes how torture's tendency to appearance, in any specific time and place, negotiates the prevailing political and visual culture and thus configures its dynamic of concealment and display.

The Bush administration's frequent insistence that "we do not torture"[58] demonstrates how antithetical is the relation between torture and the dominant liberal rationality of the rule of law, the rise of whose penal paradigm Foucault accurately described. Indeed, this mutual exclusivity is a "self-defining feature of liberal democracies" in both state rhetoric and liberal theory.[59] Whilst it is true that post-9/11 debates have again seen a defence of torture to rival the more dominant arguments against it,[60] Foucault's key claim about the rise of modern penal regimes remains astute: the administration of modern justice "no longer takes public responsibility for the violence bound up in its practice."[61] The key to this disavowal lies not in a rejection of violence, but in the refusal to take responsibility for it – and of course it contains no suggestion that Western liberal democracies do not in fact torture. As Darius Reijali's impressive 2007 study notes, such states not only torture but deliberately pioneer "clean" torture techniques, either because of the inherent nature of power within these regimes, or simply to evade public monitoring for human-rights abuses.[62] According to Amnesty International, torture was as prevalent in 1999 (even before the "war on terror") as it was in 1972 when they launched their first Campaign Against Torture.[63]

In the war on terror, the spectacle of punishment was "exceptionalized" in relation to the dominant or paradigmatic rationality that was presaged by Foucault and proclaimed by Bush, producing not one but two kinds of "hidden torture." On the one hand, there were the

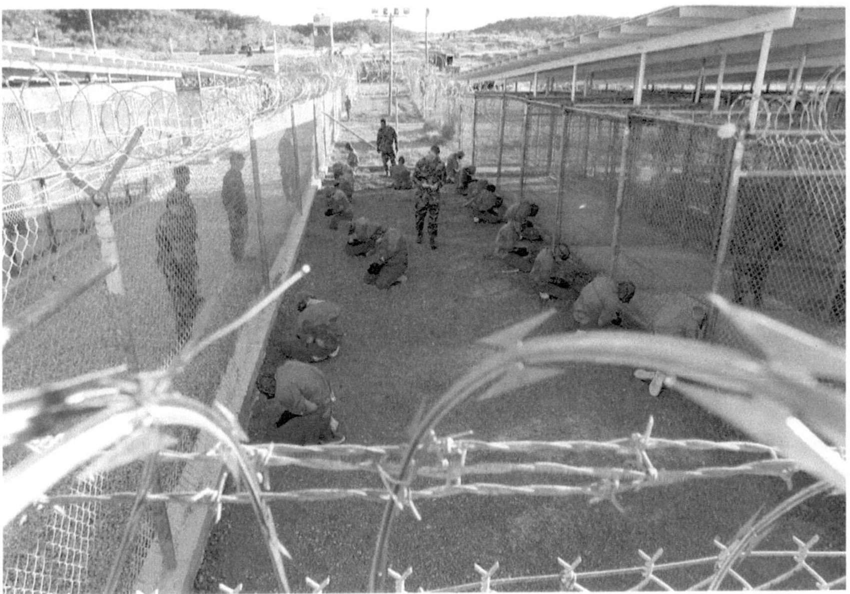

Figure 10.1 Taliban prisoners in orange jumpsuits sitting in holding area under the watchful eyes of military police at Camp X-Ray at Naval Base Guantánamo Bay, Cuba, during in-processing to the temporary detention facility on 11 January 2002. The detainees will be given a basic physical exam by a doctor, to include a chest X-ray and blood samples drawn to assess their health. Photo by Shane Mccoy/Mai/Mai/The LIFE Images Collection/Getty Images.

legally authorized "enhanced interrogation techniques." As evidenced in memoranda relating to the interrogation of specific detainees like Abu Zubaydah, these included practices such as insult-slapping, facial holds, cramped confinement, forced standing, stress positions, and waterboarding.[64] Designed to survive public scrutiny and fall outside the legal definition of torture, the advice regarding these practices was marked by the impression of rational motivations, legality, scientific precision and restraint, and regard for the subject's physical and mental health. Despite the view of the US Office of Legal Council, however, these techniques were eventually shown to amount to tortures: tortures, we could add, that tried to imagine their own display.[65] On the other hand, driven by changes in White House policy after 2002, formal "top secret" orders for interrogation by the military and CIA were issued. Now well known, these then-secret interrogations made extensive use of extraordinary rendition, so-called black sites (e.g., in Thailand or Poland), and highly physical, brutal, bloody torture. According to Captain Ian Fishback, in 2005 standard practice included beatings, exposure to extremes of hot and cold, sleep deprivation, starvation, protracted naked confinement in empty pitch-black concrete rooms, and stacking in human pyramids. The Abu Ghraib prison in Iraq was the site of literally hidden prisoners – "ghost prisoners" – who did not officially exist and were sometimes tortured to death,[66] not always in the course of interrogations but merely to "soften up" the detainee.

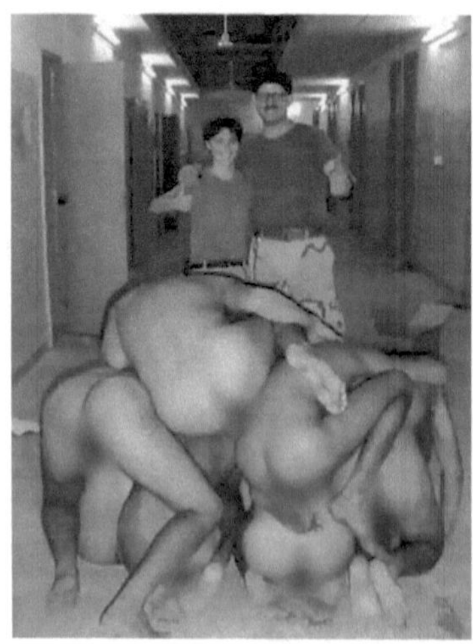

Figure 10.2 11:51 p.m., Nov. 7, 2003. The detainees were brought into the hard site for their involvement in a riot. The seven detainees were instructed to remove their clothing. Detainees were placed into a human pyramid. CPL GRANER and PFC ENGLAND posed for the picture, which was taken by SPC HARMAN. [Detainee name deleted] is detainee with writing on leg. SOLDIERS: CPL GRANER AND PFC. Caption from Salon.com.

Exceptional Images

These two kinds of hidden torture are intimately related – and not only because the techniques used at Abu Ghraib were developed at Guantánamo Bay. Both tortures relied on a common paradigm of exceptionalism, whether in the Schmittian sense of the sovereign's suspension of the regular legal order in general, or in the more specific technical sense of legal loopholes, interpretations of the definition of "torture," and the use of Guantánamo as an offshore base considered beyond the writ of US courts. To these two hidden tortures, paradoxically, belong two *exceptional images* of torture, precisely because of torture's tendency to make itself visible. But in what sense are these images exceptional? Jasbir Puar notes that what is exceptional at Abu Ghraib is not the violence of the acts, but their capture on film.[67] Despite being perfectly common – indeed a historical and factual constant – state violence *is* sometimes exceptional: when it ruptures rational norms of appearance and display. These norms, then, are *inherently* and not secondarily about the relationship between state force and public display. This is helpful because it lets us think about the relation of torture to its display, and that display's role in the functioning of the exception. Referring particularly to the culturally specific sexualized and racialized nature of the abuse at Abu Ghraib,[68] Puar claims that these images "reproduce the [cultural] power dynamics that made the acts possible in the first place,"[69] and to this extent, they help to *constitute* the norms of political culture. At a different level, Smith and Dionisopoulos suggest that they disrupted the public discourse shaped by Bush's Manichean frame – "us (good) vs them (evil)."[70] The exceptional image mediates between these two apparently contradictory observations. It is the disruption of the liberal democratic frame *made visible* in the image which, in *performing* its own exceptionality, both confirms the necessity of an exception to the liberal norm, and underwrites the normative (raced, gendered) order.

One should not simply see the images from Guantánamo Bay as the confirmation of Foucault's claims about the disappearance of the spectacle, and those from Abu Ghraib as their rupture, or repressed consequence. Rather, we could say that in each display of the tortured enemy, the same tension is negotiated between liberal-democratic display values and those of the "alternative" paradigm of the spectacle of torture, albeit in unstable and contrary ways. The image of Camp X-Ray at Guantánamo Bay articulates a rational and controlling captor, and a subdued enemy in an almost penitent stress position, securely contained by storm fencing and military personnel. At Abu Ghraib, there is an excess of violence, of domination, of subjugation. Other images in this series show army personnel smiling over corpses, cowed and bleeding bodies, people on leashes. The first presents us with a composed, rational, and unitary sovereign, but this presentation is incompatible with the destroyed body of the enemy. The second gives us a spectacular torture that ostentatiously mixes investigation and punishment, but crucially, it does so at the expense of the sovereign's *public* self-image (which cannot merely be victorious, but must also seem "humane"). Each evidences aspects of the sovereign paradigm of the spectacle of punishment that belongs to the scene of political torture. We might say that the theatrical display described by Foucault has been split and made visible in different images, which can be recomposed as one spectacle. Together, these images put into effect the spectacle of a guilty, dangerous, and unruly enemy, and affirm the necessity of a sovereign legal order whose entire conduct – legislative, interrogatory, military – is thus vindicated and endowed with the legitimacy it needs in order to re-establish its political power over that enemy. As Foucault remarked, a "war ... between the criminal and the sovereign" is thus decided by restoring the proper *imbalance* of power in favour of the sovereign.[71] Whilst retaining echoes of its older, personalist flavour, in Bush's war on terror what is re-established – however unstably – is also the "invisible empire"[72] of a moral and cultural order.

The Disaggregated Spectacle and the Micro-theatrics of Power

This account points out a deeper connection with the Foucauldian spectacle of punishment, whilst subjecting it to important historicizations. When read together as the contrary expressions of torture's attempt to become visible within a political culture whose governmental rationality is, as Foucault argues, inimical to its display, these images produce a subjugated Arab body as the political enemy by mixing investigation and punishment, by recourse to the sovereign's right to make war on its enemies, and by the presentation of that body in the role of the condemned. It is well known that Bush's war on terror blurred the paradigms of war and crime, challenged the rule-of-law paradigm, and attempted to display its force to enlist the support of its audience (with similarly contrary and unpredictable results in the twenty-first century as in the eighteenth).[73] An interrogation of the spectacular image, however, directs our attention to contemporary material practices, for example, within global news media culture, by which the guilt of the enemy – the political truth of the crime – is produced theatrically within a visual drama of political power and legitimacy.[74] It may be, as Mathiesen suggests, that the consumption of these images is, in the end, also part of the production of disciplined individuals. I have sought, however, to argue for the value of recognizing the survival of a heterogeneous paradigm of power.

To recompose the Foucauldian spectacle through these two images, it may be objected, means to overlook the provenance of the Abu Ghraib photographs. After all, unlike those from Guantánamo Bay, these were no official army production. They were not deliberately released, and their publication precipitated a great crisis for the regime from which they emerged. As I have already suggested, however, even hidden torture is always in tension with its own publicity. This publicity is itself conditioned historically, and this invites us to rethink the material configuration of the Foucauldian "theatre" as the vehicle of the spectacle in the age of the image.[75] Whereas the theatre of punishment is marked by unities of time and place – and, crucially, the unity of sovereignty in the person of the monarch – the twenty-first century has disaggregated each one of these elements. In the era of the digital image and the Internet, the potential audience for the spectacular image is global, and the dissemination of that image[76] ensures its consumption is asynchronous with its generation. Moreover, as several scholars have noted, the production of an enduring, shareable image of torture is not separate from but rather *part of* the infliction of humiliation.[77] In the era of the image, taking a photograph of torture is a kind of micro-publicity, or potential publicity – for the victim, a material gaze that shames, ridicules, and humiliates with an efficiency to rival the panopticon's. Alongside this disaggregation, then, there is an equally important process of conflation: not only of torture and its documentation, but of the *personae* that make up the theatre's staging. It has been noted that personnel at Abu Ghraib were not only soldiers, but also journalists, and, we might add, their own first audience.[78] Is it important that these images were never intended for the public eye if we live, as Puar notes, at a time when it is becoming implausible to separate "participant from voyeur," or to distinguish "production and consumption, image and viewer"?[79] In the modern age, some kinds of torture are performed by a paradoxical figure: an agent of sovereign power who acts in secret, armed with a digital camera. Abu Ghraib thus shows us the material evolution of the tension between concealment and display inherent in torture, compressed into a new logic of publicity, conditioned equally by norms of the display of state violence and the new possibilities of imaging technology.

The limitations in Foucault's historical framework have failed to properly account for the resurgence of the irrational theatre of sovereign display and dominance. Neither confined to a past era nor constituting an ahistorical element, the spectacle must, in any age, be configured in relation to dominant rationalities of governance, which inherently involve norms about the concealment and display of state violence. In *Discipline and Punish* Michel Foucault frames a history of the "micro-physics" of power. The changes brought by political and visual culture in the twentieth and twenty-first centuries push us to think also about its micro-*theatrics*. This micro-theatrics of power attempts to name a specific historical counter-rhythm of the evolution of the rationality of governmental power and culture, made visible in these publicly available images of torture.

NOTES

1 Thanks to Maria Drakopoulou, Peter Goodrich, Hyo Yoon Kang, Sara Kendall, Cristina Martinez, Lisa Radford, and Alison Young for precious conversations and comments on this paper; additional thanks to Nicholas Croggon for a helpful reference suggestion, and particularly to Des Manderson for invaluable suggestions that have clarified and improved the argument. Errors, omissions, and obscurities remain my own. I would also like to thank Jose Bellido and Elspeth Van Veeren for their helpful collegiality.

2 Carol Rosenberg, "Photo Reverberates 6 Years Later," *Miami Herald*, 12 January 2008, http://www.santafenewmexican.com/news/national_and_world_news/guant-namo-photos-reverberate-around-the-world/article_ac063984-3351-511a-999b-d2374b775bbb.html.

3 See Ken Ballen and Peter Bergen, "The Worst of the Worst?" *Foreign Policy*, 20 October 2008, http://foreignpolicy.com/2008/10/20/the-worst-of-the-worst-4, for an example of the media reaction to statistics establishing that the "vast majority of prisoners detained … [at Guantánamo Bay] never posed any real risk to America at all."

4 The archive of Abu Ghraib files can still be found at Salon.com: http://www.salon.com/topic/the_abu_ghraib_files.

5 See, for example, Judith Butler, *Precarious Life: The Power of Mourning and Violence* (New York: Verso Books, 2006); Elspeth Van Veeren, "Captured by

the Camera's Eye: Guantánamo and the Shifting Frame of the Global War on Terror," *Review of International Studies* 37, no. 4 (2011): 1721–49.

6 The images from Abu Ghraib have generated an overwhelming response, including monographs (Stephen F. Eisenman, *The Abu Ghraib Effect* [London: Reaktion Books, 2007]), W.J.T. Mitchell, *Cloning Terror: The War of Images, 9/11 to the Present* [Chicago: University of Chicago Press, 2010]), films like Errol Morris et al., *Standard Operating Procedure* (Sony Pictures Home Entertainment, 2008), numerous artworks, and innumerable academic articles.

7 Like the public spectacles described by Foucault, the images of torture discussed here had unpredictable effects. Support for torture increased; see Andrew Sullivan, "The Truth about Torture, Revisited" (2014), available at http://dish.andrewsullivan.com/2014/12/10/the-truth-about-torture-revisited. Yet as Giroux describes, the Abu Ghraib scandal in particular both galvanized "radical extremists" and "legitimate opposition to the American occupation" like calls to close Guantánamo Bay. See, e.g., Henry A. Giroux, "Education after Abu Ghraib," *Cultural Studies* 18, no. 6 (2004): 779–815.

8 See, e.g., Sanford Levinson, ed., *Torture: A Collection* (New York: Oxford University Press, 2004); Jinee Lokaneeta, "Torture Debates in the Post-9/11 United States: Law, Violence and Governmentality," *Theory and Event* 13, no. 1 (2010).

9 See the discussion in Christina Smith and George Dionisopoulos, "The Abu Ghraib Images: 'Breaks' in a Dichotomous Frame," *Western Journal of Communication* 72, no. 3 (2008).

10 The Abu Ghraib images renewed scepticism about the USA's interrogation practices in Andrew Sullivan, British-born USA-based "conservative" author, and led to him reversing his earlier support for the war: see Sullivan, "The Truth about Torture, Revisited."

11 Few writers even discuss both, as does Anne McClintock, "Paranoid Empire: Specters from Guantanamo and Abu Ghraib," *Small Axe: A Caribbean Journal of Criticism* 13, no. 1 (2009): 50–74.

12 Josh White, "Abu Ghraib Tactics Were First Used at Guantanamo," *Washington Post*, 14 July 2005; see also Judith Butler, "Torture and the Ethics of Photography," *Environment and Planning D: Society and Space* 25, no. 6 (2007): 957.

13 Walter Benjamin, "The Work of Art in the Age of Mechanical Reproduction," in *Illuminations* (Glasgow: HarperCollins, 1982), 233–4. Thanks to Des Manderson for drawing this connection.

14 Jonathan Crary, *Techniques of the Observer: On Vision and Modernity in the 19th Century*, October Books (Cambridge: The MIT Press, 1992), 2.

15 See W.J.T. Mitchell, "What Is an Image?' *New Literary History* 15, no. 3 (1984): 503.
16 Butler, *Precarious Life*, 77–8.
17 Patrick Lenta, "The Purposes of Torture," *South African Journal of Philosophy* 25, no. 1 (2006): 54.
18 The idea that states torture for some "purpose" other than gathering intelligence is intuitive, given its well-documented inefficacy. Among innumerable attestations, see David Rose, *Guantanamo: America's War on Human Rights* (London: Faber and Faber, 2004), 115; Peter Aldhous, "Here's What Actually Gets Terrorists to Tell the Truth – and It's Not Torture," *Science* (BuzzFeed, 2015), http://www.buzzfeed.com/peteraldhous/torture-doesnt-work. However, the language of purpose implies a rational calculation that is not supported by the literature on decisions regarding torture in Bush's war on terror.
19 Perhaps the clearest evidence to the contrary is that videotapes of high-value detainee interrogations, which might have otherwise been admissible as evidence if charges were brought against them, had to be destroyed because they documented "enhanced interrogation," which amounted to torture. This was the subject of a US district court ruling in 2011: *American Civil Liberties Union (& Ors) v. Department of Defence (& Ors)*, 04 Civ. 4151, 1 (2011).
20 Thomas Mathiesen, "The Viewer Society: Michel Foucault's 'Panopticon' Revisited," *Theoretical Criminology* 1, no. 2 (1997): 219.
21 Thomas R. Flynn, "Foucault and the Eclipse of Vision," in David M. Levin, ed., *Modernity and the Hegemony of Vision* (Berkeley: University of California Press, 1993).
22 See Véronique Voruz, "The Status of the Gaze in Surveillance Societies," in Ben Golder, ed., *Re-reading Foucault: On Law, Power and Rights* (Abingdon: Routledge, 2013).
23 See, e.g., Maxine Sheets-Johnstone, *The Roots of Power: Animate Form and Gendered Bodies* (Chicago: Open Court Publishing Co., 2003), 21; Judith Mayne, *Framed: Lesbians, Feminists, and Media Culture* (Minneapolis: University of Minnesota Press, 2000), 117.
24 For example, Jeffrey Edward M. Green, *The Eyes of the People: Democracy in an Age of Spectatorship* (New York: Oxford University Press, 2010), 154.
25 Some, like Doyle following Mathiesen, account for Internet technologies and resistance practices: Aaron Doyle, "Revisiting the Synopticon: Reconsidering Mathiesen's 'the Viewer Society' in the Age of Web 2.0," *Theoretical Criminology* 15, no. 3 (2011): 283–99. Elsewhere, Foucault's history is subtly displaced in a different way, by a different theme of

the "eye of the law" that eschews the panopticon model altogether: see Michael Stolleis, *The Eye of the Law: Two Essays on Legal History* (Abingdon: Birkbeck Law Press, 2008), and a wealth of literature on drones; for example, Gregoire Chamayou, *Drone Theory* (London: Penguin Books, 2015), 37.

26 Local complications remain extremely important when it comes to the configuration of political power and "visible hands-on violence," as evidenced by Feldman's work in the context of Northern Ireland: see esp. Allen Feldman, "Violence and Vision: The Prosthetics and Aesthetics of Terror," *Public Culture* 10, no. 1 (1997): 30.

27 Michel Foucault, *Discipline and Punish: The Birth of the Prison*, trans. Alan Sheridan (London: Penguin Books, 1991), 57.

28 Ibid., 39.

29 Ibid., 35–41.

30 Elaine Scarry, *The Body in Pain: The Making and Unmaking of the World* (New York: Oxford University Press, 1985), 36.

31 Foucault, *Discipline and Punish*, 38.

32 Ibid., 57–8.

33 Ibid., 44.

34 Ibid., 56.

35 Ibid., 47–8.

36 Ibid., 47

37 Ibid., 56.

38 Ibid., 58.

39 Ibid., 34, 46, 35.

40 Ibid., 46.

41 Ibid., 57.

42 Ibid., 57–60.

43 Ibid., 64

44 Ibid., 59–61.

45 Ibid., 63.

46 Ibid., 130.

47 On Foucault's modulation of enemy and criminal (vs. Schmitt's) see Gil Anidjar, "Terror Right," *CR: The New Centennial Review* 4, no. 3 (2004): 40.

48 See esp. Michel Foucault, *Society Must Be Defended*, trans. David Macey (London: Penguin Books, 2003), particularly the second lecture.

49 Voruz, "The Status of the Gaze," 137.

50 See Flynn, "Foucault and the Eclipse of Vision," and Martin Jay, *Downcast Eyes: The Denigration of Vision in Twentieth-Century French Thought* (Berkeley: University of California Press, 1993).

51 Foucault, *Discipline and Punish*, 217 and 201.

52 Paul Patton, "Agamben and Foucault on Biopower and Biopolitics," in Calarco Matthew and Steven DeCaroli, eds, *Giorgio Agamben: Sovereignty and Life* (Stanford: Stanford University Press, 2007), 216–17.

53 Gilles Deleuze, "Postscript on the Societies of Control," *October* 59, no. 1 (1992): 3–7; Mark G.E. Kelly, "Discipline Is Control: Foucault Contra Deleuze," *New Formations* 84 (2015): 148–62; Giorgio Agamben, "For a Theory of Destituent Power," *XPONOΣ* Online Magazine, http://www.chronosmag.eu/index.php/g-agamben-for-a-theory-of-destituent-power.html.

54 Davide Tarizzo, "Dalla Biopolitica all'Etopolitica: Foucault e noi," *Nóema* 4, no. 1 (2013).

55 Samuel Weber, "War, Terrorism, and Spectacle, or: On Towers and Caves," *Grey Room*, 7 (2002), 14–23.

56 Marianna Valverde has proposed a similar kind of coexistence in paradigms: remarking on the "survival" of premodern logics, she claims that at times "a particular way of seeing ... fails[,] ... leading to the sudden adoption of its opposite – but without one mode of seeing replacing the other." See Mariana Valverde, "Seeing Like a City: The Dialectic of Modern and Premodern Ways of Seeing in Urban Governance," *Law & Society Review* 45, no. 2 (2011): 277–312. See also Butler's comments on the return of premodern forms of sovereignty, in Butler, *Precarious Life*.

57 Henry Shue, "Torture," *Philosophy & Public Affairs* 7, no. 2 (1978): 132. According to Mitchell, *Cloning Terror*, 64, the "sending of a message" is what unites "non-state with state terrorism."

58 Deb Riechmann, "Bush Declares: 'We Do Not Torture,'" *Washington Post*, 28 December 2015, http://www.washingtonpost.com/wp-dyn/content/article/2005/11/07/AR2005110700521.html.

59 Lokaneeta, "Torture Debates in the Post-9/11 United States," 2.

60 See Sullivan, "The Truth about Torture, Revisited"; Levinson, *Torture*.

61 Foucault, *Discipline and Punish*, 9.

62 Darius Reijali, *Torture and Democracy* (Princeton: Princeton University Press, 2007), 7–8.

63 Erik Prokosh, quoted ibid., 21–2.

64 Jay S. Bybee (then Assistant US Attorney General), Memorandum from the US Department of Justice Office of Legal Counsel for John Rizzo, Acting General Counsel of the CIA, regarding the Interrogation of al-Qaeda Operative Abu Zubaydah, dated 1 August 2002.

65 The controversy of the US Office of Legal Counsel's advice regarding the definition and practice of torture is addressed by David Luban,

"Lawfare and Legal Ethics in Guantánamo," *Stanford Law Review* 60 (2008): 1981–2026; and *Legal Ethics and Human Dignity* (Cambridge: Cambridge University Press, 2007).

66 Josh White, "Army, CIA agreed on 'Ghost' Prisoners," *Washington Post*, 11 March 2005, http://www.washingtonpost.com/wp-dyn/articles/A25239-2005Mar10.html. See also Derek Gregory, "Vanishing Points," in Derek Gregory and Allan Pred, eds, *Violent Geographies: Fear, Terror and Political Violence* (New York: Routledge, 2006).

67 Jasbir K. Puar, "Abu Ghraib: Arguing against Exceptionalism," *Feminist Studies* 30, no. 2 (2004): 531.

68 On which, see esp. Sherene H. Razack, "How Is White Supremacy Embodied? Sexualized Racial Violence at Abu Ghraib," *Canadian Journal of Women and the Law* 17, no. 2 (2005): 341–63; Eduardo Subirats, "Totalitarian Lust: From Salò to Abu Ghraib," *South Central Review* 24, no. 1 (2007): 174–82; Nicholas Mirzoeff, "Invisible Empire: Visual Culture, Embodied Spectacle, and Abu Ghraib," *Radical History Review* 95 (2006): 21–44; and Allen Feldman, "On the Actuarial Gaze," *Cultural Studies* 19, no. 2 (2005): 218–19.

69 Puar, "Abu Ghraib," 531.

70 Smith and Dionisopoulos, "The Abu Ghraib Images."

71 Foucault, *Discipline and Punish*, 50–1.

72 Mirzoeff, "Invisible Empire."

73 See note 7 above.

74 On the importance of images in producing the political enemy of the war on terror, see Oliver Watts, "The Image and the Terrorist," *Law Text Culture* 10 (2005), 221–38. Watts draws in particular on an article by W.J.T. Mitchell later incorporated into Mitchell, *Cloning Terror*. On the production of the enemy, see Daniel Ross, *Violent Democracy* (Cambridge: Cambridge University Press, 2005), 151–2.

75 The importance of historically specific material conditions is underlined by Crary, *Techniques of the Observer*.

76 Susan Sontag, "Regarding the Torture of Others," *New York Times Magazine*, 23 May 2004: 27. Sontag notes: "A digital camera is a common possession among soldiers."

77 See esp. Carsten Bagge Laustsen, "The Camera as a Weapon: On Abu Ghraib and Related Matters," *Journal for Cultural Research* 12, no. 2 (2008): 123–42; Paul Frosh, "The Public Eye and the Citizen-Voyeur: Photography as a Performance of Power," *Social Semiotics* 11, no. 1 (2001): 43–59.

78 See Sontag, "Regarding the Torture of Others."

79 Puar, "Abu Ghraib," 531.

PART THREE

Critique – Irony and Legal Modernity in the Twenty-First Century

11 T-Shirt's Guevara: The Visual Jurisprudence of the New Man

LUIS GÓMEZ ROMERO[1]

you are our bullet-ridden conscience
they say that they burnt you
with what fire
they are going to burn the good
the good news
the irascible tenderness
that you brought and carried
with your cough
with your mud
they say that they incinerated
your entire vocation
less one finger
enough to point us the way
enough to accuse the monster
and his burning embers
to squeeze the triggers again

Mario Benedetti[2]

The Obstinate Vitality of Spectres

On 1 January 1959, Fidel Castro and his revolutionary *barbudos*[3] took over the Caribbean island of Cuba. Among the most popular *barbudos* was Ernesto Guevara de la Serna – also known as "*Che*"[4] – who would eventually become the most mythologized figure of the Cuban revolution.[5] He was an Argentinian physician who had impressive natural aptitudes to lead guerrilla forces. He was also a revolutionary theorist who deeply influenced Marxist tradition with his ideas not only about guerrilla warfare,[6] but also about the goals and nature of socialism.[7] Though radicals, neither Castro nor the majority of his comrades were originally communists. They were pushed towards communism by the dynamics of the Cold War: the Cuban revolutionary regime gained the sympathy and support of the Soviet Union as soon as it antagonized the United States – for example, by intervening in labour-management conflicts when farms were foreign owned, or limiting the legal frame for private foreign investment.[8] Moreover, the only institution that was left untouched by the revolution was the Partido Socialista Popular (PSP, Popular Socialist Party), which henceforth provided the *barbudos* the organization they required to shape the new revolutionary state.[9]

Che's ideological commitments were deeper and clearer than Castro's hazy nationalist politics. In 1954, well before Castro had discovered that both he and Cuba were to be socialist, a twenty-six-year-old Che confessed to his mother that he would join the Communist Party "sooner or later." He admired the strong sense of comradeship that distinguished its members.[10] It is no surprise then that Che would become the architect of some of the most radical and utopian economic reforms implemented in Cuba during the 1960s.[11] He also came to symbolize Cuba's commitment to internationalism and solidarity with revolutionary movements in Africa, Asia and Latin America, as he urged the peoples of the world to wipe out capitalism and imperialism by creating "two, three, many Vietnams."[12]

Che died a martyr on 9 October 1967, implementing his revolutionary theories in the mountains of Bolivia.[13] By his death, his unremitting faith in communism and magnanimous spirit of sacrifice became a symbol associated with the sense of infinite possibility of the early days of the revolution, rather than with the many compromises Castro made through decades of revolutionary power.[14] Today, in an age of global and arrogant capitalism that is largely bereft of the great ideals – liberty, equality, and solidarity – that once moved men and women to fight for a better world, Che's memory has gone from representing the revolutionary vanguard, to being the nostalgic symbol of a lost promise of justice. The political pledge that Che embodies can actually be referred to what Alain Badiou calls *the idea of communism* – that is, the idea of a society in which the principle of equality is the prevailing political truth and, as such, stirs a collective organization that aims at eliminating both the subordination of labour and the inequality of wealth.[15]

There is, however, something deeply uncanny about the way in which Che's symbolism has been perpetuated. The compelling events of Che's revolutionary biography and the story of his violent end seem insufficient to explain his afterlife as an emblem of what Álvaro Vargas Llosa contemptuously calls "revolutionary chic."[16] Che's figure walks among us: he stares out at us from T-shirts – the primary artefact of his resurrection – hoodies, baseball caps, coffee mugs, watches, sneakers, key rings, ashtrays, wallets, condoms, and practically any sort of imaginable gadgets or knick-knacks. The leftist slogan is uncannily accurate: "*¡El Che Vive!*" (Che lives!). Che did not die in Bolivia: he was literally raised from the dead in the famous photograph taken during the early years of the Cuban revolution by Alberto Díaz Gutiérrez, better known as Alberto Korda,[17] which has constituted Che's manly countenance and fierce gaze, framed by an askew beret, flowing hair and straggly beard, into a symbol of resistance in the developing world, an anti-globalization banner, and a favoured merchandizing stratagem.

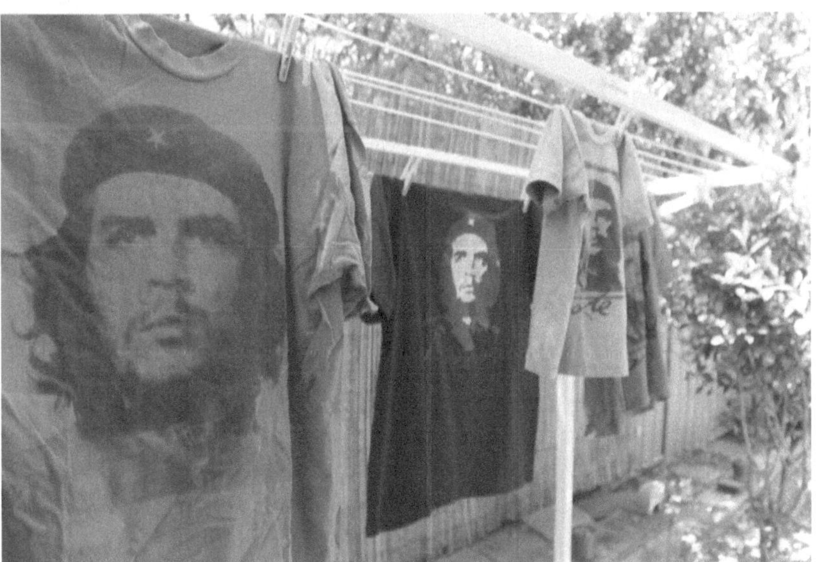

Figure 11.1 T-shirts featuring Che's portrait, Wollongong, December 2015. Photo courtesy of Luis Gómez Romero.

Korda's epochal photograph – which he simply titled "*Guerrillero Heroico*" (Heroic Guerrilla Fighter) – has given Che, as Michael Casey observes, "a purgatorial existence"[18] that commingles revolution and commerce. Luis López and Trisha Ziff aptly summarize the social history of this paradox in their 2008 documentary *Chevolution*:

> It happened in a fraction of a second. The shutter opened and closed to capture the iconic portrait of an elusive man known to most as "Che." Over time, the image has been transformed, gathering different meanings along the way. The photograph had become a graphic, the graphic turned to political statement, the statement being appropriated for art, then commerce to sell a dizzying array of products, many of which strayed from Che's ideals ... and yet, despite the commercialization, the image still recalls the life of the iconic revolutionary.[19]

Che's Mexican biographer Jorge Castañeda points out that, during his lifetime, he incarnated an "eternal refusal of ambivalence" that was "shared by too many in the generation he personified."[20] The sixties, Castañeda argues, "were based upon a wholesale rejection of life's contradictions": cross-purposed feelings, conflicting desires or mutually incompatible political goals were unacceptable in an era forged in black and white.[21] Such emphatic love for certainty, however, has apparently not survived Che and his times. The malleability of *Guerrillero Heroico* – reportedly the most reproduced photograph ever by the end of the twentieth century[22] – and its subsequent co-option by the corporate world have apparently reduced the ideals and memory of the once fearsome revolutionary to the status of a harmless icon and global brand. Under the long and terrible cultural resignation that followed the fall of the Eastern bloc, Che has become a spectre that either embodies a "visual emblem for a vague notion of dissent, rebellion and political awareness," or a "subject of kitsch and spoof makeovers."[23]

I will challenge this commonsensical contention by claiming that there is an unwavering political truth at the heart of both Che's political ideals and *Guerrillero Heroico*'s lasting power: the promise of a radical transformation of the consciousness, values, and habits of human beings that Che encapsulated in his vision of "*el hombre nuevo*" (the new man). Che may have been reduced to a spectre by the forces of the market, but spectres have frequently proved to be obstinately alive. In 1848, Karl Marx and Friedrich Engels joyfully announced that the spectre of the communist idea was haunting Europe.[24] Over a century later, in 1989, Francis Fukuyama (in)famously proclaimed that such a spectre had been crushed by the "unabashed victory of economic and political liberalism" and the "ineluctable spread of consumerist Western culture."[25] Fukuyama epitomized the ideal of good life under exultantly ubiquitous capitalism in guaranteeing "easy access to VCRs and stereos" for everyone – if only you could afford them.[26] Time, however, ultimately proved that the spectre had only temporarily retreated. Today, the word "communism" is back in circulation, as a growing literature around a concept supposedly sentenced to death thirty years ago demonstrates.[27]

The perception that capitalist liberal democracies had, for all their faults, caused the collapse of communism by the pure force of their prosperity raised a spirit of self-congratulation (not to say complacency) in the Western world after the break-up of communism in Eastern Europe. This shallow optimism failed to acknowledge that the communist idea does not put the future of capitalism into question just for the sake of social revolution, but because of the very nature of its untrammelled global operations.[28] As early as June 1989, while Fukuyama was proclaiming the end of history, Norberto Bobbio observed that capitalist liberal democracies had yet to confront the problems out of which the communist challenge was born.[29] Capitalism not only leaves the plight of the dispossessed unsolved: it purposely ignores it. The fall of the communist regimes in Eastern Europe thus did not and could not put an end to poverty and the thirst for justice it entails. Bobbio notes that the promise of emancipation of the poor and the oppressed embedded in the communist idea had led "men with a high moral sense to sacrifice their own life, to face prison, exile and extermination camps … from the Red Army in Russia to Mao's Long March, from the conquest of power by a group of resolute men in Cuba to the desperate struggle of the Vietnamese people against the mightiest power in the world."[30] Communism certainly created a secular narrative that gave purpose and meaning to individual lives. The enduring appeal of *Guerrillero Heroico* embodies this sort of continued validity of the communist idea. It is true that Korda's portrait resonates nowadays with visual irony: it is at once a merchandizing tool and a lasting symbol of resistance against the capitalist system that promotes such merchandizing. Irony, however, is a two-way street: the "real" Che, as David Kunzle suggests, has not died, but rather undergone "a tactical shift."[31]

Political and legal iconographies – not only symbols such as, for instance, the red rose for social democracy or the bird in flight for libertarianism, but also the dress, architecture, statuary, and insignia that provide visible presence to justice and law – are understood through cultural codes of connotation that introduce political, ethical, and jurisprudential values into the reading of images.[32] This is the work of ideology. In the early years of his work, Roland Barthes suggested that political connotation considerably depends on "text" as no photograph (or image) "has ever convinced or refuted anyone," though photographs (or images) can certainly "confirm" political opinions.[33] Such a view on the political – and hence normative and jurisprudential – significance of images, however, neglects the role that they have always played in preserving the prestige and memory of norms through "visual depiction or textual figures that bind, work and persist through the power of ... a vision, for example, of "neighbourhood," "reasonableness," "national security," or simple authority."[34]

Communism is, hence, more than a merely verbal phenomenon. There is a distinct political iconography – for example, the hammer and the sickle, the red banner or the five-pointed red star – that specifically upholds, promotes, and develops the communist idea.[35] *Guerrillero Heroico* became an element of such a political iconography after Che's death. From a jurisprudential perspective, the symbols in the communist iconography – as it happens with the symbols related to any other ideology – represent the way in which individuals have to *focus* both justice and prudence in political life in order to carry out the idea that inspires them: they evoke the shadings of discourse, the projections of rhetoric, and the outlines of gesture required to animate a truthfully egalitarian society.

Since their very origins in the art of heraldry, one of the key functions of political iconographies has consisted in identifying the sociopolitical views of the emitter of a visual message.[36] The rise and fall of ideologies and political regimes are most often marked by the material construction, destruction, or appropriation of symbolic buildings, statues, walls, or flags. Historical transitions have been repeatedly mediated by changes in visual environments that support, confirm, and legitimate social, political, economic, and legal changes.[37] These changes are also reflected in the configuration of the cultural codes of connotation we use to interpret images. It is not coincidental that in 1989, when communism – in the words of Ralf Dahrendorf – was presumed "gone, never to return,"[38] the triumphant capitalism cynically took over its abandoned political iconography. The communist symbols of equality, solidarity, and community were merchandized and branded to signify consumption, economic prosperity, and individual growth. At that time, this was interpreted as the ultimate cultural victory of capitalism.

Guerrillero Heroico reflects – and is somehow confined in – the moment of historical transition from a bipolar world in which two competing views of political justice (communism and capitalism) strived for achieving global hegemony, to the mammoth globalization processes that followed the apparent fall and subsequent demise of one of these views (communism). Yet the cultural reception and reproduction of this particular photograph not only sustains (and is sustained in) such a transition, but also critiques it. While Che, as Vargas Llosa contends, has metamorphosed "into a capitalist brand,"[39] his image has also appeared to function as a powerful insurgent symbol and galvanizing force among various contemporary radical movements – for example, the Zapatista rebels in Mexico; the *indignados* in Spain and the *αγανακτισμένοι* (*aganaktismenoi*) in Greece;[40] leftist artist collectives in Caracas, Vitoria or Belfast; or Palestinian nationalists in the Middle East – that radically oppose the capitalist mode of production and the powers associated with it.[41]

Both the anti-systemic movements that revere Che and the cultural industry that sells his image are emblematic of a contest over his memory.[42] In other words, Che's image has not been domesticated by capitalism – otherwise, the tension around it would not exist. The long-lasting struggle over the meanings and collective memories associated with *Guerrillero Heroico* has made this picture a simultaneous site of processes of both commodification and ideological resistance to capitalism.[43] In this sense, *Guerrillero Heroico* is the perfect icon of the current world situation: it expresses the tension between the triumph of capitalism and the desire of the poor and exploited to see their fate improved in face of a system that necessarily entails a highly unequal distribution of income and power, the exploitation or demise of vulnerable people and recurring crises that sweep thousands of individuals into unemployment and deprivation.

Che's image thus functions today as the *locus* of two interconnected conflicts in the fields of aesthetics and jurisprudence that preceded his death and now succeed it. The aesthetic conflict involves the delicate nexus between photography and morality that Susan Sontag highlighted in *On Photography*. "The camera's ability to transform reality into something beautiful," claims Sontag, "derives from its relative weakness as a means of conveying truth."[44] By placing in contention the truth embedded in *Guerrillero Heroico* – that is, the communist idea as understood and lived by Che – the jurisprudential conflict is made manifest. The unending manipulation of Che's portrait reveals clashing conceptions of justice, liberty, equality, and fairness around the necessity or contingency of the logic of class hierarchies and the rule of profit and private interest that upholds it. In other words, *Guerrillero Heroico* raises, precisely by the ambivalence and irony of the image, the question of both the political morality and (supposed) inevitability of liberal-democratic capitalism.

This chapter addresses both conflicts via an ironic close reading[45] of *Guerrillero Heroico* based on Roland Barthes's analysis of the operation of photography. My argument is divided into three parts. The first section briefly recounts the social history of *Guerrillero Heroico,* from Korda's studio to its current ubiquity. The second section delves into Barthes's elucidation of the fundamental roles of emotion and subjectivity in the experience of and accounting for the ways in which a viewer can be affected by a photograph. There is an unsettling nexus between (communist) heroic portraiture and the (capitalist) mass commodity that draws us into an ironical subversion of the final victory of capitalism that the commercial reproduction of Korda's photograph outwardly suggests. The third section relates Che's vision of a new humanity to his penetrating gaze in *Guerrillero Heroico.* As Ariel Dorfman notes, deep inside the T-shirt where Che is trapped, "his eyes are still burning with impatience."[46] Che's image interpellates us, continuing to find in injustice a million reasons to rebel and to reformulate the communist idea in such a way that constructs horizons of emancipation capable of building a better world. His image is both the symptom of a transition and a provocation to it.

The Freezing of a Gaze

On 4 March 1960, the French freighter *La Coubre* exploded while it was docked in Havana's harbour with a load of seventy-six tonnes of Belgian weapons in its cargo hold. Seventy-five Cuban dockers were killed and over two hundred were injured.[47] Outraged, Fidel Castro quickly blamed the CIA for sabotage and called for a massive memorial service at Havana's Colón Cemetery. After a funeral march along the seafront boulevard known as Malecón, Fidel Castro gave a deeply emotional oration for the fallen before an audience that included the visiting French intellectuals Simone de Beauvoir and Jean-Paul Sartre.

In his fiery speech, Castro used the slogan "¡*Patria o Muerte, Venceremos!*" (Homeland or death! We will prevail!) for the first time.[48] Among the crowd was Alberto Korda, a former fashion photographer who was working on assignment for the Cuban daily newspaper *Revolución* (Revolution). Suddenly, Che came into view for a few seconds. He let his eyes wander over the mourners for twenty seconds, looking, as Korda would later remember, "*encabronado y doliente*" (angry and sorrowful).[49] Korda snapped just two frames of him with his Leica camera before he disappeared from sight. The first photo had Che framed alone between an anonymous silhouette and a palm tree; the second had someone's head appearing above his shoulder.

The first picture, with the intruding material cropped out, eventually became Che's most famous portrait. The editor of *Revolución* decided to use only Korda's shots of Castro, Sartre, and Beauvoir, while sending Che's shot back to the photographer. Believing the image was powerful, Korda made a cropped version for himself, which he enlarged and hung on his wall next to a portrait of the Chilean poet Pablo Neruda. *Revolución* first published the portrait a year later, when it was used to promote a conference at which Che, as minister of industry, was to be the main speaker.[50] The conference, however, was suspended when 1300 CIA-supported counter-revolutionaries stormed Bahía de Cochinos in a failed attempt to overthrow Castro's government.[51]

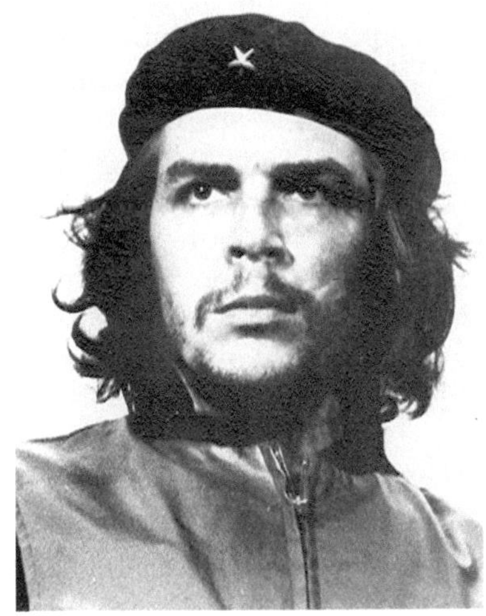

Figure 11.2 *Guerrillero Heroico*, Havana, 5 March 1960 (cropped version). Photo by Alberto Korda.

Che's portrait sat dormant in Korda's studio for seven years.[52] A print was sold (or given) to wealthy Italian publisher and intellectual Giangiacomo Feltrinelli in 1967. Feltrinelli had just returned from Bolivia, where he had hoped his fame would help negotiate the release of French journalist Régis Debray, one of his publishing house's authors who had been arrested in connection with the guerrilla operations led by Che.[53] As Che's eventual capture or death appeared to be imminent with the CIA closing in, Feltrinelli acquired the rights to publish Che's *Diario en Bolivia* (Bolivian Diary) in Italy.[54] At this time Feltrinelli asked Cuban officials where to obtain images of Che, and was directed to Korda's studio. He presented a letter of introduction from the government asking for Korda's assistance in finding a good portrait. Korda right away pointed to the 1960 shot hanging on the wall. Feltrinelli agreed and ordered a couple of prints.[55]

Upon his return to Italy, Feltrinelli mass-produced a poster using the portrait in order to raise awareness of Che's precarious situation and impending demise. The poster was basically a textless enlargement of Korda's photograph with an inscription in the lower left corner that reads "Comandante Ernesto 'Che' Guevara © Libreria Feltrinelli 1967" – with no reference to the photographer.[56] Later in 1968, after Che's execution, his *Diario en Bolivia* with Korda's photo on the cover was released worldwide.

Feltrinelli's transformation of *Guerrillero Heroico* into a poster divorced it from its photojournalistic origins. Subsequent posters, as Brian Wallis observes, "pushed this abstraction of the image further, in ways that were influenced by the contemporary penchant for both satirical caricature and pop celebration."[57] The most notable of these *"posterized"*[58] variations of Korda's photograph is Irish artist Jim Fitzpatrick's 1967 stylized design featuring Che's countenance outlined as black and white shapes that are silk-screened against a flat, bright red background. This poster was widely distributed throughout Europe – in Ireland, Spain, France, and Holland.[59] Converted into a simple graphic in this way, *Guerrillero Heroico* became an easily copied icon that quickly expanded into a central theme of youth counterculture, as Matilde Sánchez observes:

> The poster marks the freed territory in a teenager's bedroom, where *nonsense* is charged with significance. Guevara is certainly not the only foundation of this imagery of youth, but some of his features converge in its legacy: the nomadic impulse, the anti-systemic sentiment, or the ideal of

a heroic death in the splendour of early life, all embraced in the guise of a certain nocturnal façade. There is nothing trivial about this rebel *look*, considering that the lightness of icons is frequently deceptive.[60]

The poster and the inexpensive techniques of screen-printing and lith film hence provided the material means to transform *Guerrillero Heroico* into a portable symbol of the communist idea in the propitious context of youth counterculture during the late 1960s. Rolled into tubes or folded in magazines, Che's features were distributed around the world – in Paris, West Berlin, Mexico City, London, Rome, or Rio de Janeiro, among many other cities – in the turbulent year 1968. In his introduction to Che's *Diario en Bolivia*, Fidel Castro actually praised the African Americans and "progressive students" who, in the United States – the heart of capitalism – had made Che a personal model of conduct and turned his portrait into a "fighting emblem" to be hoisted "in the most combative demonstrations for civil rights and against the aggression in Vietnam."[61]

Castro, who supported the Soviet invasion of Czechoslovakia, omitted however to mention that *Guerrillero Heroico* had also been used by Alexander Dubček's supporters as a badge for advocating and endorsing political reform in the context of the Prague Spring uprising.[62] The fact that Che's portrait was actively used to symbolize the aspiration to pursue a *better* implementation of the communist idea in Eastern Europe demonstrates the unsettling power of images in both politics and law. Most viewing experiences, as Alison Young points out, "do not provoke in the viewer the joy of recognition – 'there I am,'" but they rather "arouse the shock and anxiety of an encounter with the Other – 'there I am not.'"[63] As early as 1968, Che's image signalled the absence of the communist idea not only in the capitalist world, but also under the so-called *real socialism* enforced by the ruling communist parties within the Eastern Bloc. In other words, *Guerrillero Heroico* maintained not just an ideological meaning, but also the possibility to critically challenge the very ideology that sustained it. David Kunzle, commenting on Castro's remarks, asks a question that compellingly summarizes this double-sided visual (and cultural) appeal of *Guerrillero Heroico*: "What, then, is a Che T-Shirt but an individual banner worn in the social parade?"[64]

Yet the cultural and social unrest that 1968 unleashed on both sides of the Iron Curtain is insufficient to fully explain the rapid global dissemination of *Guerrillero Heroico*. Black-letter law also played a major role in the social history of Korda's photograph, whose iconic status was ultimately secured by the approach to intellectual property adopted by the Cuban communist regime. The issue of copyright was a thorny one in the Cuban context because it revealed the most fundamental differences between capitalism and communism regarding labour, private property, individual rights, and social equality.[65] The general principles that structure Cuban copyright law thus privilege the social dissemination of culture and science over the individual rights of authors, which are limited by the interests and goals of the "Socialist Revolution."[66]

Until 1997, *Guerrillero Heroico* remained unhindered by international copyright agreements because Cuba was not a signatory to the Berne Convention for the Protection of Literary and Artistic Works. It was instead a party to the weaker Universal Copyright Convention, adopted in Geneva, Switzerland, in 1952. Nonetheless, after the statization of the cultural apparatus that followed the Revolution, the protection of intellectual property was limited to the recognition of *derechos morales* (moral rights) to authorship, but not *derechos patrimoniales* (economic rights) beyond the wages paid by the Cuban state to the authors.[67] Moreover, as Cuba stopped paying copyright fees to foreign authors, Cuban copyrights in those countries were, in return, not enforced.[68] For decades, artists and advertisers all over the world were free to use *Guerrillero Heroico* as they pleased, thus benefiting from the "frozen millisecond" of a gaze that, even today, stands for opposition to the establishment, freedom and revolution.[69] On 5 March 1960, an icon of our age emerged from Korda's camera.

The Irony of the Portrait of a Hero

Power is rooted in appearance. Kings, for example, used to accompany themselves by guards, drums, or officers in order to imprint on their subjects respect and terror.[70] Portraiture played a major role in structuring this paraphernalia of power. Portraits reinforced authority by emphasizing the uniqueness or social superiority (or both at once) of the sitter.[71] In the twentieth century – an era that Eric Hobsbawm has described as "full of charismatic figures on balconies and before microphones"[72] – portraits of political heroes took this function even further, as David Kunzle suggests, by "dignifying the idea that certain individuals are called upon to transcend the norms of humanity and that they possess superhuman (that is, supersocial) will."[73] The aesthetics of socialist realism – that is, the glorified depiction of communist values in a lifelike manner that was the dominant artistic style under communist regimes from the 1930s until the fall of the Soviet Union in 1991[74] – involve, in this sense, a return to the age of parable.[75]

Parables (from the Greek παραβολή, that is, analogy or comparison) are moral narratives that condense a normative progression from ignorance to insight, wickedness to virtue, or darkness to light. Medieval hagiography, for example, is a parabolic genre in which a Manichaean struggle between the forces of good and evil was closely tied to events unfolding in historical time that were presented as instantiations of greater events described in the scriptures. Socialist realism likewise conceived both society and history as "a hierarchy of "fathers," or highly "conscious" members of the [communist] vanguard," and "'sons,' or highly 'spontaneous' positive figures who were nurtured to political consciousness by the 'fathers.'"[76] This narrative pattern symbolically confirmed the purity of the modes of political awareness and moral discipline that strictly followed the line of succession from those individuals that were identified as the *original fathers* of the communist idea – for example, Lenin, Stalin, or Mao.

The parabolic structure of socialist realism hence made the "positive hero" a key aesthetic element for illustrating how to develop within the mundane realm of history the necessary public virtues for the moral and political transformation of the entire society into a communist one – a transition that was assumed as the unavoidable destiny of humanity.[77] Public political portraiture operated in this context as a powerful instrument of propaganda through which communist regimes introduced into the tradition of hero imagery the idea of the individual as a representative of the masses who functions as human embodiment of, or emissary from, a higher moral and political order.[78]

Cuba was not a stranger to this parabolic aesthetic framework. The official propaganda that has been constructed around Che instituted him as the universal and permanent hero of the Cuban revolution. Cuban schoolchildren chant, "¡Seremos como el Che!" (We will be like Che!) to begin their school day.[79] *Guerrillero Heroico*, however, agitates the aesthetic conventions of socialist realism. There is a major difference between Che's modes of portraiture and those that were applied, for example, to Lenin in the Soviet Union or Mao in China. Lenin and Mao were consistently and uniformly idealized in manifold portraits. In other words, the multiple depictions of Lenin or Mao result in a single fetishized image of these *fathers* of the communist idea. Che's singular image, by contrast, is both stereotypical and diverse: it has undergone myriad modifications that fluctuate from simplifications of line and contour to colouristic embellishments and tonal contrasts.[80] A single portrait resulted in countless derivative works. This is the visual magic of *Guerrillero Heroico*: Korda's high-contrast photograph provides a kind of image much prized not only among Cuban artists, but also in Western (capitalist) graphic art, for its powers of immediate visual impact and symbolization. The derived versions of the original matrix photograph of Che Guevara's face taken by Alberto Korda have been displayed by various authors in different media, colours, and sizes, but they always recognizably refer back to the original.

Che's spectral afterlife is thus uniquely tied to Korda's portrait-photograph. On the one hand, portraits always allude to individual human beings who exist *outside* the artwork. In this sense, the word *portrait* reflects its etymological roots in the Latin *prōtrahere* (present infinitive of the verb *prōtrahō*), which can be translated as to disclose, reveal, or bring forth. The portrait ensures presence while its subject

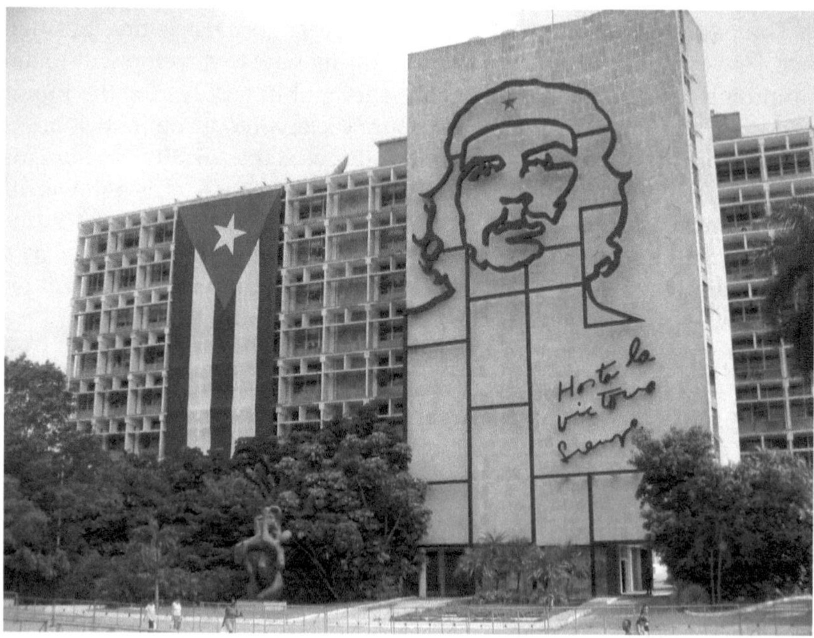

Figure 11.3 Monumental image on Cuban Ministry of the Interior, based on Jim Fitzpatrick's graphic of *Guerrillero Heroico*, Havana, 2003. Photo by Mark Scott Johnson.[81]

is absent, thus bringing the past into the present and the dead back to life.[82] On the other hand, portrait-photographs, as Roland Barthes observes, instantiate contemporary cultural processes that transform subjects into objects. The portrait-photograph hence entails a micro-experience of death or, paraphrasing Barthes's words, the act of *becoming a spectre*.[83]

The tensions between multiple readings and appropriations – both political and commercial – of Che's portrait thus exemplify the distinctive dialectic between what Barthes calls *νόημα* (*noema*, i.e., that which is perceived) and *εἶδος* (*eidos*, i.e., the form or constitutive nature) of photography. The *noema* (or content) of a photograph is "*ça-a-été*" (that-has-been), that is, the specific photographic referent that is *necessarily* constituted by the real thing that was placed before the lens.[84] This real presence is potentially obliterated by the very nature of photography as a visual medium and art form. The *eidos* of photography involves the *death* of its *noema*, that is, its alteration and disposal as an object.[85] *Guerrillero Heroico* ratifies that Che once existed, but at the same time composes him as an object susceptible of being transmuted into virtually anything that is envisaged by those who manipulate his image.

A double meaning and a double function can therefore be assigned to the portrait-photograph, which makes an absence present while exhibiting its own presence as image, thus constituting the sitter as object and the person who looks at it as the looking subject. Barthes provides a whole new vocabulary to explain the interaction between these constitutive elements of photography: the photographer becomes "the *Operator*," the subject of the photograph is "the *Spectrum*" (who, by virtue of the "little simulacrum" inscribed in photography, acquires the uncanny ability to "return" from death), and its viewer is "the *Spectator*."[86] These three elements mirror the three practices embedded in photography: to do, to undergo, and to look.[87] The third practice is the most important in Barthes's view. In the same way that Barthes moved from the study of how literature makes meaning possible to that of how the reader makes sense of the text,[88] in his analysis of photography he placed the emphasis primarily on the viewer. Drawing on this account of photography, the story of *Guerrillero Heroico* is a story about how *we* (i.e., society in general) transformed Che's portrait into a repository of our collective fears, hopes, and desires.

From the perspective of the spectator, Barthes elaborates a distinction between two planes of the image. The first, which he calls the *studium*, is the manifest subject, meaning, and context of the photograph. The *studium* is "a kind of education" – that is, "knowledge and civility" – that allows the viewer to discover the operator and "experience the intentions which establish and animate his practice."[89] In other words, *studium* is what we perceive familiarly as a consequence of our knowledge or our culture or the range of photographic meanings available and obvious to everyone through the existing codes of connotation that we use to interpret images. The second plane of the image he calls the *punctum* (in Latin, a sting, a cut, or a puncture): that aspect (often a detail) of a photograph that holds our gaze without condescending to mere meaning or beauty.[90] The *studium* functions to inform, to represent, and to signify. In contrast, the *punctum* is beyond the order of form. It is uncoded and unnameable: it *acts*.[91] The *punctum* is more powerful and compelling to the spectator than the *studium*. It is a detail that disturbs, arousing all kinds of feelings – for example, sympathy, recognition, or disgust – which are difficult to analyse beyond their sheer intensity. The *studium*, in sum, is the order of *liking*, whereas the *punctum* enters into the domain of *loving*.[92]

The power of *Guerrillero Heroico* both in politics and law lies precisely in its ability to endorse social conformity (*studium*) and *at the same time* to undermine it by forcing a critique of the *statu quo* (*punctum*). It is true that Korda's portrait-photograph is inscribed in the canon of Cuban socialist realism, but it also became, as I explained in the previous section, an inspiring image for the supporters of Dubček's *socialismus s lidskou tváří* (socialism with a human face) during the Prague Spring in 1968. John Storey evidences a similar tension between these two aesthetic elements of Che's portrait-photograph under the aegis of capitalism through an apparently simple textbook question. "In the 1960s," Storey writes, "a bedsit without a poster of Che Guevara was hardly furnished at all. Was the poster a sign of commitment to revolutionary politics or a commitment to the latest fashion (or was it a complicated mixture of both)?"[93]

The only way to fruitfully approach this question, I think, consists in exploring the third option. *Guerrillero Heroico* is both a fetishist commodity and an anchor of rebellious hope in a just world. It is undeniable that Che's image has been appropriated by capitalist ideology (just as it was originally used for communist propaganda), but at the same time it has not been entirely *contained* within an ideological frame. *Guerrillero Heroico* not merely communicates a concept that can be apprehended – that is, the portrait of an Argentine-Cuban revolutionary (Che-*studium*)[94] who can either be considered a faultless hero to emulate (communism) or a defeated foe whose derision is the righteous spoil collected by the victors of the Cold War (capitalism). Che's image also *acts* upon individuals (Che-*punctum*)[95] by connecting, as Peter McLaren suggests, "if only in [a] whimsical way, people who share a common resolve to fight injustice and to liberate the world from cruelty and exploitation."[96] McLaren argues that even admitting that there is no way of knowing the politics of those who wear a Che T-shirt and how seriously they identify with his life and teachings, "Che's image brings out the promise of such a connection" and the "political fecundity" of actually hoping it.[97]

The historical reception of *Guerrillero Heroico* has therefore flung Che's countenance between *studium* and *punctum*. In the field of *studium*, from 1960 to 1997 Che's portrait effectively roamed the world copyright-free as artists, satirists, and political commentators exploited it without paying any fees.[98] Some of them have been faithful to the Cubans' *official* representations of Che, others not. The famous image has therefore been globally parodied, exploited, and distorted. In Mexico, for example, *Guerrillero Heroico* has been blended for over a decade with the features of a popular clown named *Cepillín* (Little Brush) in order to create the comic derivative *Che-Pillín* (Che-Little Scoundrel).[99] In 2003, Streets, the brand under which Magnum ice cream is sold in Australia and New Zealand, brought out a limited edition series known as *The Sixties Nine* featuring sixties-related names. Among them was "Cherry Guevara," a flavour whose tasting experience was brazenly described as "the revolutionary struggle of the cherries ... trapped between two layers of chocolate."[100] Korda's portrait appeared in the wrapper, with a cherry replacing the star in Che's beret.

A few years before, in 2000, *Guerrillero Heroico* was used, along with a pattern of hammers and chilli-pepper sickles and the slogan "Hot Fiery" – a stereotype usually associated with "Latin lovers and revolutionaries" – to promote a new spicy line of Smirnoff Vodka.[101] Korda successfully extracted a £50,000 payment from ad agency Lowe Lintas and picture agency Rex Features for *this* unauthorized use of Che's portrait. The agreement was ratified by the British judiciary,[102] but there was no official ruling on whether the depiction constituted a violation of copyright.[103] Korda dutifully donated his settlement money to the Cuban health system.[104] When asked why he had targeted Smirnoff over other abusers of *Guerrillero Heroico*, Korda answered that "to use the image of Che Guevara to sell vodka" was "a slur on his name and memory."[105] The Smirnoff affair was interpreted by Che's admirers as the beginning of a crusade for their fallen hero's integrity. Unfortunately, it seems hardly coherent with the communist idea that drove Che's feats to take revenge on capitalism through the out-of-court settlement of a copyright claim. Che, as Michael Casey suggests, had not beaten capitalism by bringing the traffickers of his image to justice: he had actually joined them.[106] Casey is not alone in this reading of *Guerrillero Heroico*'s destiny. The commercial use of the image has been interpreted by many as a sign of the ultimate defeat of Che's ideals. Trisha Ziff, for example, ingeniously renamed him as *Ch€* for an exhibition on the iconography around *Guerrillero Heroico* that was displayed in Barcelona in 2007.[107] The replacement of the "e" in *Che* with a euro sign speaks of a thoroughly betrayed ideal. This is, however, a deeply commonsensical interpretation of Che's portrait. Common sense, as Richard Rorty claims, simply assumes that there is a definitive language in which to express our interpretations of any given situation.[108] A commonsense reading of *Guerrillero Heroico* thus necessarily presupposes the triumph of capitalism and assumes the finality of the transformation of his portrait into a nameless icon without regard to the complexities of Che's legacy.

Irony, however, seems a more accurate method to approach *Guerrillero Heroico* given the ambiguities and paradoxes in both its reproduction and reception that I have previously discussed. Susan Sontag famously chastised moralists for demanding from photographs what they cannot ever do: speak moral truths. According to Sontag, because the photograph is always "an object in context," its moral meaning "is bound to drain away."[109] Nonetheless, while it is hard to contend that the moral weight of a photograph depends on the context in which it is inserted, there are specificities of the portrait-photograph that escape Sontag's general assessment of photography. In order to overcome this blind spot in Sontag's theses, Barthes's distinction between *studium* and *punctum* can be supplemented with Walter Benjamin's remarks on the ultimate irreducibility of portrait to complete commodification. Benjamin notes that, even though photography as a whole fatally entails the decline of the *aura* of the work of art, the aesthetic "cult value" of human countenance survives in the portrait. The visage is the last repository of the indefinable – though evanescent – beauty of the human being. "The cult of remembrance of the loved ones, absent or dead," writes Benjamin, "offers a last refuge for the cult value of the picture."[110]

The *punctum* perspective hence acquires utter importance for ironically considering *Guerrillero Heroico* as a visual testimony of Che's passage through earth. In my view, the *punctum* which attracts Che's admirers or repels his detractors towards *Guerrillero Heroico* is his bittersweet gaze, which is at once pensive, determined, and defiant. The fact that *Guerrillero Heroico* is precisely a portrait facilitates ironic readings of Che's countenance even in the current context of the supposedly unbeatable hegemony of capitalism. Irony reflects both the tensions between levels and registers of meaning within any cultural artefact and the juxtaposition of intentional meaning against a particular context.[111] In this sense, irony highlights the *contingency* of the meaning of our most central beliefs and desires. These contingencies and ironies are part of the critical potential of the image. The instability they generate is not, as Derrida points out, a problem for interpretation but, on the contrary, "a stroke of luck for politics."[112]

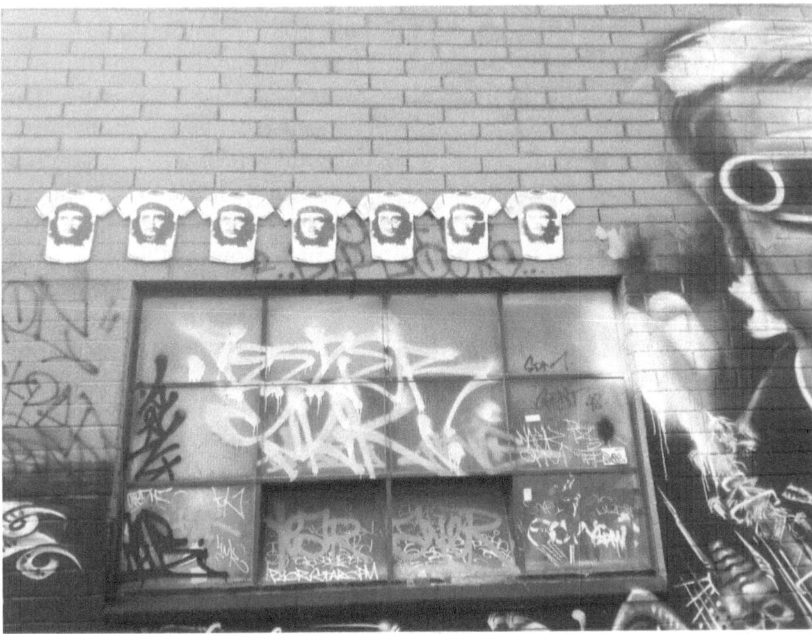

Figure 11.4 Che's T-Shirts (part of the "not aNOTher street art CliChé!" series), by street artist Phoenix, on Fitzroy Street (Melbourne), August 2014. Photo by Alison Young.

Ironists, Rorty claims, get out from under inherited contingencies and make their own contingencies.[113] In other words, ironists subvert old vocabularies, languages, and world views, and fashion new ones of their own. Today, capitalism is our inherited contingency. By absorbing Che into its gutters, capitalism has ironically contributed to maintaining the memory of his ideals and achievements. Che's expression in his stereotyped portrait, *encabronada y doliente*, continues to call for radical dissatisfaction with the current state of the world. Capitalism cannot escape Che's accusing gaze. In the Swatch watch colour catalogue for spring/summer 1995, for example, a watch with the face of Che derived from a René Burri photograph (Korda refused permission to use his) and the word "*Revolución*" (Revolution) on the strap, was advertised with the following exhortation: "The true revolutionary is the one who never stops – even after success has been reached, and who continues wanting to change the world, beginning with himself. With the 'Che Guevara' Swatch doesn't pay homage to a man or to an ideology but to the courage and freedom of thought that make true revolutions."[114]

Swatch's publicity shows what survived of the communist idea after the debacle of the Soviet Union in 1991: dissatisfaction with things as they are, and the vague feeling that we are responsible for making them better. This has been possible partly because *Guerrillero Heroico* culturally sits as a bridge that ensures the permanence of Che's dreams of deliverance in disenchanted times.[115] Che's vision of the new man will not die as long as he continues embodying a promise of liberation from any oppressive force and a general and romantic fantasy about change and revolution.[116] It was irony that, in the first place, transformed *Guerrillero Heroico* into a global brand. And it is irony that, in the deeply subjective domain of *punctum*, still binds the specificity of Che's communist ideals and revolutionary struggle to Korda's portrait.

El Hombre Nuevo

Alain Badiou conceives of communism as a pure Platonic Idea of equality that has historically enabled the practice of emancipatory politics.[117] As soon as mass action opposes unjust coercion in the name of egalitarian justice, rudiments or fragments of the communist idea begin to surface in human history. One of the key features of such an idea is its reference to the "infinity of the people."[118] Consequently, in order to be properly comprehended, the communist idea also needs "the finitude of proper names."[119] The "glorious Pantheon" of "revolutionary heroes" who have fought for the communist idea – for example, Spartacus, Thomas Müntzer, Robespierre, Toussaint-Louverture, Blanqui, Marx, Lenin, Rosa Luxemburg, Mao, and, of course, Ernesto "Che" Guevara – simply symbolizes the "rare and precious network of ephemeral sequences of politics as truth."[120] Che and his revolutionary ilk, Badiou argues, are the historical proof of what ordinary individuals can achieve whenever they force their temporal and situational finitude or, in other words, whenever they dare to step outside their personal biography – with its conventional mediations of family, work, the homeland, religion, and so forth – in order to embrace *hic et nunc* emancipatory politics as "a truth in the making" (*vérité en devenir*) that proclaims that "we are not doomed to lives programmed by the constraints of the [capitalist] State."[121]

Che certainly forced his historical situation far beyond his bourgeois Argentine origins, by placing himself at the centre of a world-changing outrage whose trace still haunts *Guerrillero Heroico*'s gaze. This is precisely what he required from everyone else: to transform themselves into new men and new women who would ultimately be selfless, just, and courageous, thus echoing a venerable tradition of Latin American socialist thought that sought in the pervasive and chronic inequality of the region a resonating *local* ground for a *universally* significant upsurge of the communist idea. Anticipating Che, José Carlos Mariátegui, a Peruvian political philosopher and Marxist, wrote in 1928 that socialism in Latin America should not be "an imitation or a copy," but a "heroic creation" in consonance with Latin American realities.[122] Che's ideas on the construction of socialism are precisely an attempt at such *heroic creation* of something new, a distinct model of socialism that was radically opposed in many respects to its bureaucratic implementation in Eastern Europe and Asia.

Almost forty years after Mariátegui, in his celebrated 1965 essay "El Socialismo y el Hombre en Cuba" (Socialism and Man in Cuba), Che rejected the possibility of implementing socialism through capitalist fetishes such as money, commerce, and credit. This essay constitutes Che's major theoretical effort to formulate an alternative path towards socialism – one that was more radical, more egalitarian, more fraternal, and more consistent with the communist ethic than the models that had been put into practice in the Soviet Union and the People's Republic of China. In Che's view, "the pipe dream that socialism can be achieved with the help of the dull instruments bequeathed to us by capitalism (the commodity as the economic cell, profitability, individual material interest as a lever and so on) can lead into a blind alley."[123] Che considered that in order to build communism, it was necessary to build *"el hombre nuevo"* (the new man) simultaneously with the new society. He believed that the new man (and woman) was called upon, by the entire history of human suffering under capitalism, to overcome the selfishness that he despised and (naively) assumed was uniquely characteristic of individuals in capitalist societies.[124] In his own words:

> The true revolutionary is guided by great feelings of love. It is impossible to think of a genuine revolutionary lacking this quality. Perhaps it is one of the great dramas of the leader that he or she must combine a passionate spirit with a cold intelligence and make painful decisions without flinching. Our vanguard revolutionaries must idealize this love of the people, of the most sacred causes, and make it one and indivisible. They cannot descend, with small doses of daily affection, to the level where ordinary people put their love into practice.[125]

The *hombre nuevo* was a *communist* individual: the dialectic negation of those men and women that capitalism has transformed into merciless predators who, living under the law of the jungle, can only conceive success through the defeat and marginalization of others.[126] The ultimate factor to ensure the success of a revolution aimed at fulfilling the communist idea was therefore not material, but affective – *love*. "Socialism," Che declared at the Afro-Asian Conference celebrated in Algeria in 1965, "cannot exist without a change in consciousness resulting in a new fraternal attitude toward humanity, both at an individual level, within the societies where socialism is being built or has been built, and on a world scale, with regard to all peoples suffering from imperialist oppression."[127] In other words, the new man demanded a concrete universal brotherhood aimed at constituting what Karl Marx called "socialized humanity" (*vergesellschaftete Menschheit*),[128] that is, a human society that has transcended the division between private and public, particular and general interests, or the individual and the community.[129] "For us," Che claimed, "there is no valid definition of socialism other than the abolition of the exploitation of one human being by another."[130]

Che tried to lead the conversion of Cubans to the moral standards of the new man by providing himself as its example, working endlessly at his official positions in the Cuban government, in construction, and even cutting sugar cane on his day off.[131] Unfortunately, he was blind to the fact that the practice of the values that structure the ideal of the new man involved a high degree of voluntarism that clashed not only with the existing capitalist legal and political institutions, but also with cultural practices deeply embedded in our current social structures. Jon Lee Anderson correctly highlights Che's constant failure to understand the enormity of attempting "to alter the fundamental nature of others and get them to become 'selfless communists.'"[132] This fatal lack of understanding of the role that persuasion and deliberation play in the transformation of both culture and institutions, I believe, is essential to understand Che's exasperated emotional response towards the fragility of human will after the triumph of the Cuban revolution.

He conceived of the revolutionary as an individual guided by deep love for humanity and justice,[133] yet driven, at the same time, by "a relentless hatred"[134] of the capitalist/imperialist enemy. For Che, a truthful revolutionary should hence become a compassionate "killing machine."[135] Che's love rituals did not reach out to others with communion or understanding, but were engraved with violence, battle, and, when necessary, death. He deservedly gained a reputation as a skilled, egalitarian, and courageous leader, but he was also a stern disciplinarian who could be merciless with those who did not satisfy his high moral standards.[136] Anderson comments that, as an official of the rebel army during the revolution, "his trail through the Sierra Maestra was littered with the bodies of *chivatos*, deserters, and delinquents, men whose killings he had ordered and in some cases carried out himself."[137] The *barbudos* dreamt of a just, free, egalitarian, and prosperous Cuba. Che's utopian vision was a step ahead of them – ahead of Castro himself, who always maintained a harshly pragmatic sense of political reality.[138]

Che had a total faith in the power of will to achieve a moral transfiguration of human beings. The violence he deployed to impose his ideals on the new man over those he judged too self-interested, too weak, or too greedy for the victory of the communist idea has led critics such as Álvaro Vargas Llosa to accuse him of having "a lot more in common with the regimes he fought than would seem conceivable."[139] This superficial appraisal of Che's revolutionary practice and legacy, however, obscures and misses the reasons that drove him to sacrifice himself on the altar of rage for the emancipation of "the hungry indigenous masses, the peasants without land," and "the exploited workers" of Latin America and beyond.[140] Che can only be understood by seriously considering the impact that the painful history and unjust realities of

Latin America had over him. A single story among the many he collected during his travelling along the region will illustrate the extent and depth of such influence. In 1955, Dr Guevara – he was not yet Che at that time – worked as a medic in the allergy section of the General Hospital in Mexico City. One of his patients was an elderly asthmatic washerwoman named María who, regardless of her illness, worked practically until the last day of her life to provide for her grandchildren. Che's first wife, Hilda Gadea, would later remember that Che did everything he could to cure and comfort her.[141] Despite all his efforts, she died, asphyxiated by her asthma. He was at her bedside when she took her last gasp.[142] The experience drove him to write a poem in which he poured out his anger over the social neglect he felt had brought about her death:

Old María, you are going to die
I want to talk seriously:
your life was a complete rosary of agonies.
There was no loved man, no health, no wealth,
just hunger to be shared …
don't pray to the inclement god that denied your hopes
your whole life
don't ask for clemency from death,
your life was horribly dressed with hunger,
and ends dressed by asthma.
But I want to announce to you,
in a low voice virile with hopes,
the most red and virile of vengeances
I want to swear it on the exact
dimension of my ideals
Take this hand of a man which seems like a boy's
between yours polished by yellow soap,
scrub the hard calluses and the pure knots
in the smooth shame of my doctor's hands.
Rest in peace, old María,
rest in peace, old fighter,
your grandchildren will all live to see the dawn.
I SWEAR IT[143]

María personifies all the wasted, browbeaten, and poor lives of disenfranchised individuals not only in Latin America, but in the entire world. She stands for the people who starve in Africa, for the unemployed youth in southern Europe, for the asylum seekers held in indefinite detention in Australia. Che was wrong for trying to heal the pain inflicted by capitalism by causing more pain. Nobody can force another human being to be virtuous: the communist idea is a guide for ethical action, not an imperative that must be obeyed with a gun pressed to our heads. He, however, was right in his rage against the unnecessary grief that capitalism causes. Economic growth should not be paid for with the misery of those who cannot afford dignity. He was also right in denouncing who should be made responsible for the victory of injustice in our times. We – you, reader of these pages, and I – are the ones who keep capitalism alive through our social, moral, political, and legal agency. There is authentic compassion in Che's youth poem, along with a rising rage that announces the violence to come. This is the same sorrow and wrath reflected in *Guerrillero Heroico*'s eyes. The *punctum* of the portrait-photograph pierces our humanity, evidencing the obscene absence of justice in the world, and cuts into our comfortable existence, denouncing the extreme difficulty – if not the impossibility – of indifference towards the pain injustice causes.

Guerrillero Heroico ultimately proves that human faces cannot be entirely reduced to commodities. Some trace of Che's concentrated fury and generous empathy is ineradicable from the T-shirts, key chains, posters, and analogous gadgets that display his features. This provides Che's image with a tension and an irony that becomes the more acute, the more we reflect on it. The power of *Guerrillero Heroico* lies in its capacity not just to record a social and legal transition towards globalized capitalism, but at the same time and with the same means, to critique and deride it. Irony does not recede with time: Che will continue emerging in the midst of social protests and demonstrations, gazing out from placards and banners, energizing resistance against inequality and turning the forces of capitalist common sense against themselves.

Epilogue: Revolution Is (Still) One T-Shirt Away

"*C'est elle!*" (There she is!), I exclaim, with Roland Barthes, as my avid eyes scrutinize the beloved face of my daughter.[144] The moment is gone, frozen forever in the photograph. I remember her sleeping after playing with an old Cuban souvenir: a beret with a patch featuring the Cuban flag and *Guerrillero Heroico*. Che, *encabronado y doliente*, kept watch over her *animula* – the "little individual soul," ageless but not timeless, of

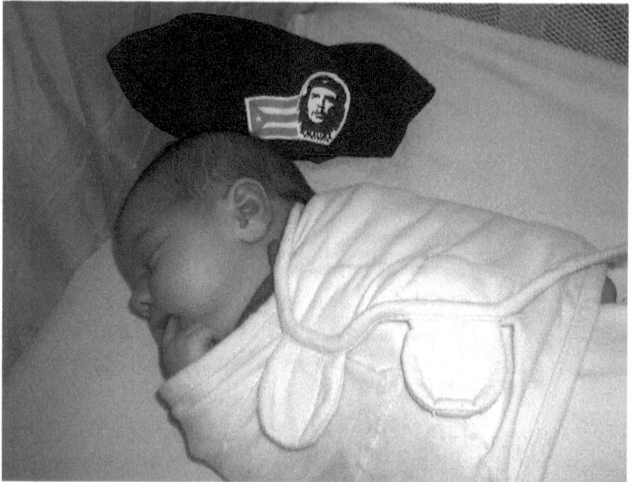

Figure 11.5 Mariana and Che, Montreal, May 2011. Photo by Luis Gómez Romero.

the being I love.[145] I know that those who are reading these lines, or looking at this photograph, cannot feel it as I do: it is pure *studium* for you. In my case, by contrast, it has acquired the sharp cutting edge of *punctum*. Che will continue haunting my daughter's dreams because I have failed to quench his thirst of justice. It was I who turned Che's compassion into raging madness: I accept my part in the wreckage of decency and hope. Che's gaze accuses my selfishness, my cowardice, my ambiguous compromises, and the multiple times that I gave up and sold out myself to injustice. Those terrible eyes keep staring at me in pain, in rage. I promise myself that I will change. I will do my best until my daughter grows up. She will become a woman; she will have her own capacity for discernment. And, when the time comes, the spirit of revolution will still be one T-shirt away, inviting her to keep up the struggle for equality, liberty, and justice. The legacy of the image is ambivalent and complex, but its time will come.

NOTES

1 I am indebted to Desmond Manderson for his generous and enlightening comments on previous drafts of this work.

2 *Troubled, Furious* (October 1967). "[E]res nuestra conciencia acribillada/ dicen que te quemaron/ con qué fuego/ van a quemar las buenas/ buenas nuevas/ la irascible ternura/ que trajiste y llevaste/ con tu tos/ con tu barro/ dicen que incineraron/ toda tu vocación/ menos un dedo/ basta para mostrarnos el camino/ para acusar al monstruo y sus tizones/ para apretar de nuevo los gatillos." Mario Benedetti, "Consternados, Rabiosos," in Mario Benedetti, *Inventario*, 14th ed. (Mexico City: Nueva Imagen, 1991), 434–6. All translations are mine unless noted otherwise.

3 *Barbudos* means "bearded men." The term was coined to describe the rebel combatants of the Cuban Revolution, who did not shave while they were fighting in the Sierra Maestra. The beard was later perceived as the emblem of the rebels. See Hugh Thomas, *Cuba: The Pursuit of Freedom* (1971) (Basingstoke and Oxford: Pan Books, 2001), 692.

4 I will use the Argentinian colloquialism *Che* – which can be roughly translated into English as *mate* or *bro* – to name *Comandante* (Commander) Guevara throughout this essay because his correspondence proves that he willingly adopted this friendly moniker when he referred to himself. See, for example, the famous farewell letter that Fidel Castro read aloud, on 3 October 1965, before the central committee of the Cuban Communist Party after Che had departed to his final destination in Bolivia, in Ernesto Guevara, *Escritos y Discursos*, 9 vols. (Havana: Editorial de Ciencias Sociales, 1977), 9: 393–5.

5 For a comprehensive account of Che's life, see the three major biographies that were published in 1997, the thirtieth anniversary of his death in Bolivia: Jon Lee Anderson, *Che Guevara: A Revolutionary Life* (1997) (Revised edition, New York: Grove Press, 2010); Jorge Castañeda, *La vida en rojo: Una biografía del Che Guevara* (1997) (Mexico City: Suma de Lectura, 2002); and Paco Ignacio Taibo II, *Ernesto Guevara, también conocido como El Che* (1997) (Mexico City: Planeta, 1998).

6 Ernesto Guevara, *La guerra de guerrillas*, in Guevara, *Escritos*, 1: 25–190.

7 See, for example, Che's following works: *Apuntes filosóficos*, ed. María del Carmen Ariet García (Mexico City: Centro de Estudios Che Guevara and Ocean Sur, 2012); "El socialismo y el hombre en Cuba," in Guevara, *Escritos*, 8: 253–72; "Notas para el estudio de la ideología de la Revolución Cubana," ibid., 4: 201–11, and *Marx y Engels: Una síntesis biográfica* (Bogotá: Centro de Estudios Che Guevara and Ocean Sur, 2007).

8 See Jorge Domínguez, "Cuba since 1959," in Leslie Bethell, ed., *Cuba: A Short History* (New York: Cambridge University Press, 1993), 96ff.; Tulio Halperín Dongui, *Historia contemporánea de América Latina*, 13th ed. (Madrid: Alianza, 1996), 515–17; Morris H. Morley, *Imperial State and*

Revolution: The United States and Cuba, 1952–1986 (London and New York: Cambridge University Press, 1987), 40–71; and Marifeli Pérez-Stable, *The Cuban Revolution: Origins, Course and Legacy*, 2nd ed. (New York and Oxford: Oxford University Press, 1999), 80ff.

9 Gérard Pierre-Charles, *Génesis de la Revolución Cubana*, 6th ed. (Mexico City: Siglo XXI Editores, 1985), 111–19 and 152–71. The PSP was among the political organizations that merged in 1961 into the Organizaciones Revolucionarias Integradas (ORI, Integrated Revolutionary Organizations), which was the forerunner of the current Partido Comunista de Cuba (PCP, Communist Party of Cuba).

10 Ernesto Guevara, "Carta a la madre," in Ernesto Guevara, *Otra vez: Diario inédito del segundo viaje por Latinoamérica* (Barcelona: Ediciones B, 2001), 169–70.

11 See Ernesto Guevara, *Gran debate: Sobre la economía en Cuba 1963–1964*, ed. David Deutschmann and Javier Salado (Melbourne: Ocean Press, 2003); Orlando Borrego, *Che: El camino de fuego* (Havana: Imagen Contemporánea, 2011), 1–153; and Helen Yaffe, *Che Guevara: The Economics of Revolution* (London: Palgrave, 2009).

12 Ernesto Guevara, "Mensaje a los pueblos del mundo a través de la Tricontinental," in Guevara, *Escritos*, 9: 371.

13 See Ernesto Guevara, *El diario del Che en Bolivia* (1968) (Mexico City: Siglo XXI Editores, 1988); and Régis Debray, *La guerilla du Che* (1974) (Paris: Éditions du Seuil, 1996).

14 Aviva Chomsky, *A History of the Cuban Revolution*, 2nd ed. (Chichester, West Sussex: Wiley & Sons, 2015), 30.

15 See Alain Badiou, *L'hypothèse communiste* (Clamecy: Lignes, 2009), 7–12 and 181–205; Badiou, "The Idea of Communism," in Costas Douzinas and Slavoj Žižek, eds, *The Idea of Communism* (London and New York: Verso, 2010), 1–14; and Slavoj Žižek, *First as Tragedy, Then as Farce* (London and New York: Verso, 2009), 86–157.

16 Álvaro Vargas Llosa, *The Che Guevara Myth and the Future of Liberty* (Swan Way, Oakland, CA: The Independent Institute, 2006), 7.

17 Korda adopted this name after the film director Alexander Korda. See David Kunzle, *Che Guevara: Icon, Myth, and Message* (Los Angeles: UCLA Fowler Museum of Cultural History in collaboration with the Center for the Study of Political Graphics, 1997), 58.

18 Michael Casey, *Che's Afterlife: The Legacy of an Image* (New York: Vintage, 2009), 5.

19 Luis López and Trisha Ziff, *Chevolution* (Mexico: Red Envelope Entretainment, 2008), DVD.

20 Castañeda, *La vida en rojo*, 26.
21 Ibid., 27.
22 Michel Guillemot, ed., *Dictionnaire mondial de la photographie: Des origines à nos jours* (Paris: Larousse, 1996), 170–1.
23 Hannah Charlton, "Introduction," in Trisha Ziff, ed., *Che Guevara: Revolutionary and Icon* (New York: Abrams Image, 2006), 7.
24 Karl Marx and Friedrich Engels, *Manifest der Kommunistischen Partei* (1848) (Vienna: Sozialistische LinksPartei, 2000), 12.
25 Francis Fukuyama, "The End of History?" *The National Interest*, Summer 1989, 3.
26 Ibid., 8.
27 See, for example, among the works that have been published in the last six years, Badiou, *L'hypothèse communiste*; Bruno Bosteels, *The Actuality of Communism* (London and New York: Verso, 2011); Jodi Dean, *The Communist Horizon* (London and New York: Verso, 2012); Douzinas and Žižek, *The Idea of Communism*; Filip Spagnoli, *The Neo-Communist Manifesto* (New York: Algora, 2010); Tiqqun, *Tout a failli, Vive le Communisme!* (Paris: La Fabrique Éditions, 2009); Slavoj Žižek, ed., *The Idea of Communism 2: The New York Conference* (London and New York: Verso, 2013); and Žižek, *First as Tragedy, Then as Farce*. See also a classic work on the continued relevance of Marxism that was published in the previous decade: Jacques Derrida, *Spectres de Marx: L'état de la dette, le travail du deuil et la Nuovelle Internationale* (Paris: Galilée, 1994).
28 Eric Hobsbawm, *How to Change the World: Tales of Marx and Marxism* (London: Abacus, 2011), 398.
29 Norberto Bobbio, "L'utopia capovolta," *La Stampa*, 9 June 1989, 1.
30 Ibid.
31 David Kunzle, "Chesucristo: Fusions, Myths and Realities," *Latin American Perspectives* 35, no. 2 (2008): 99.
32 I am aware that I am using here the term "reading" to designate the deciphering, comprehension, and interpretation of images that do not fall within the category of written matter. I must therefore clarify that I understand "reading" in the broadest sense of the word, that is, as the action of perusing printed matter.
33 Barthes, "Le Message Photographique," *Communications* 1 (1961): 137.
34 Peter Goodrich, *Law in the Courts of Love: Literature and Other Minor Jurisprudences* (New York and London: Routledge, 1996), 96.
35 Guillaume Bourgeois, "L'heraldique de la faucille et du marteau dans l'univers communiste," in Denise Turrel, Martin Aurell, Christine Manigand, Laurent Hablot, and Catalina Girbea, eds, *Signes et couleurs des*

identites politiques du Moyen Age à nos jours (Rennes: Presses Universitaires de Rennes, 2008), 115–51.

36 See Philippe Button, "L'iconographie revolutionnaire en mutation," *Cultures & Conflits* 91/92 (2013): 31–2.

37 See Anca M. Pusca, *Post-Communist Aesthetics: Revolutions, Capitalism, Violence* (New York: Routledge, 2015), 84ff.

38 Ralf Dahrendorf, *Reflections on the Revolution in Europe: In a Letter Intended to Have Been Sent to a Gentleman in Warsaw* (London: Chatto and Windus, 1990), 103.

39 Vargas Llosa, *The Che Guevara Myth*, 8.

40 Both the terms "*indignados*" (Spanish) and *αγανακτισμένοι* (Greek) can be translated into English as "outraged."

41 Jeff A. Larson and Omar Lizardo, "Generations, Identities and the Collective Memory of Che Guevara," *Sociological Forum* 22, no. 4 (2008): 426.

42 Ibid., 447.

43 Maria-Carolina Cambre, *The Semiotics of Che Guevara: Affective Getaways* (London and New York: Bloomsbury, 2015) 27ff. See also, Cambre, "Stealing or Steeling the Image? The Failed Branding of the 'Guerrillero Heroico' Image of Che Guevara," *Imaginations: Journal of Cross-Cultural Image Studies / Revue d'Études Interculturelles de l'Image* 3, no. 1 (2012): 78ff.

44 Susan Sontag, *On Photography* (1977) (London: Penguin, 2008), 112.

45 See note 32 above.

46 Ariel Dorfman, "The Guerrilla: Che Guevara," *Time Magazine*, 14 June 1999, 212.

47 See Anderson, *Che Guevara*, 442; Casey, *Che's Afterlife*, 25; and Thomas, *Cuba*, 860.

48 See Casey, *Che's Afterlife*, 25–6; Kunzle, *Che Guevara*, 58; Thomas, *Cuba*, 921; Trisha Ziff, "Guerrillero Heroico," in Ziff, ed., *Che Guevara*, 15.

49 Cited in Kunzle, *Che Guevara*, 58; and Ziff, ed., *Che Guevara*, 15.

50 Ibid., 16.

51 Thomas, *Cuba*, 922ff.

52 Ziff, "Guerrillero Heroico," 15–16. See also Brian Wallis, "Che Lives!" in Ziff, ed., *Che Guevara*, 25.

53 Casey, *Che's Afterlife*, 17.

54 See note 13 above.

55 Casey, *Che's Afterlife*, 113–17.

56 A copy of the original poster is reproduced in Ziff, ed., *Che Guevara*, 40. See also Carlo Feltrinelli, *Senior Service* (Milan: Feltrinelli, 1999), 316.

57 Wallis, "Che Lives!" 26.

58 David Kunzle coined the neologism "posterization" to refer to the embodiment, reproduction, and dissemination of Che's political ideals and hopes through political posters. See Kunzle, *Che Guevara*, 25–6.
59 Ziff, "Guerrillero Heroico," 20.
60 Matilde Sánchez, Fernando Diego García, Oscar Sola, and Frank Sozzani, *Che: Sueño rebelde* (Mexico: Diana, 1997), 209. The terms *nonsense* and *look* are actually written in English in the Spanish original version of the text.
61 Fidel Castro, "Una introducción necesaria," in Guevara, *El diario del Che en Bolivia*, 12.
62 See Cambre, *The Semiotics of Che Guevara*, 9; and Ziff, ed., *Che Guevara*, 22.
63 Alison Young, *Judging the Image: Art, Value, Law* (London and New York: Routledge), 13.
64 Kunzle, *Che Guevara*, 26.
65 See Ariana Hernández-Reguant, "Copyrighting Che: Art and Authorship under Cuban Late Socialism," *Public Culture* 16, no. 1 (2004): 15.
66 Ley no. 14, del Derecho de Autor, *Gaceta Oficial de la República de Cuba*, 30 December 1977 (modified by the Decreto-Ley 156, 2 September 1994), art. 1 and 3.
67 Ibid., art. 4.
68 Casey, *Che's Afterlife*, 15.
69 Ibid., 25ff. Copyright does not arguably entail an obstacle for the derivative use of *Guerrillero Heroico* even after 1997. In Cuba, photographs retain copyright protection for twenty-five years from the date the work is first used. Ley no. 14, art. 43. If we consider, just for the sake of granting *Guerrillero Heroico* the most extensive copyright protection, that this work was first published along with Che's *Diario en Bolivia* in 1967 – and not in the advertisements for the conferences on economy that were announced by *Revolución* several years before, in 1961 – it seems that in Cuba the copyright protection of Korda's portrait has already expired. For a detailed comparative analysis of copyright issues around *Guerrillero Heroico* in Cuban, American, and international jurisdictions, see Sarah Levy, "A Copyright Revolution: Protecting the Famous Photograph of Che Guevara," *Law and Business Review of the Americas* 13, no. 3 (2007): 687ff.
70 See Louis Marin, *Le portrait du roi* (Paris: Éditions de Minuit, 1981), 7–22.
71 Ibid., 13. See also Shearer West, *Portraiture* (Oxford: Oxford University Press, 2004), 71ff.
72 Eric Hobsbawm, *The Age of Extremes: A History of the World, 1914–1991* (1994) (New York: Vintage, 1996), 439.
73 *Che Guevara*, 22.

74 Katerina Clark, *The Soviet Novel: History as Ritual* (Chicago and London: University of Chicago Press, 1981), 27ff.
75 Katerina Clark, "Socialist Realism *with* Shores: The Conventions for the Positive Hero," in Thomas Lahusen and Evgeny Dobrenko, eds, *Socialist Realism without Shores* (Durham and London: Duke University Press, 1997), 27.
76 Ibid., 29.
77 Ibid., 28.
78 Kunzle, *Che Guevara*, 22.
79 Chomsky, *History of the Cuban Revolution*, 34.
80 Kunzle, *Che Guevara*, 23.
81 Wikimedia Commons, "File:SculptureCheGuevaraCuba.jpg," https://commons.wikimedia.org/wiki/File:SculptureCheGuevaraCuba.jpg.
82 Marin, *Le portrait du roi*, 12–13.
83 Roland Barthes, *La chambre claire: Note sur la photographie* (1980), in Roland Barthes, *Oeuvres complètes* (Paris: Éditions du Seuil, 2002), 5: 799.
84 Ibid., 851.
85 Ibid., 800.
86 Ibid., 795.
87 Ibid.
88 See Roland Barthes, "La mort de l'auteur," in Barthes, *Oeuvres complètes*, 3: 40–5.
89 *La chambre claire*, 810.
90 Ibid., 822–7.
91 See Cambre, *The Semiotics of Che Guevara*, 39.
92 *La chambre claire*, 810.
93 John Storey, *Cultural Theory and Popular Culture: An Introduction*, 5th ed. (Harlow: Pearson, 2009), 65.
94 See Cambre, *The Semiotics of Che Guevara*, 42.
95 Ibid.
96 Peter McLaren, *Che Guevara, Paulo Freire, and the Pedagogy of Revolution* (Lanham, MD: Rowman and Littlefield, 2000), xix.
97 Ibid.
98 See note 67 above.
99 See Ziff, ed., *Che Guevara*, 104.
100 Casey, *Che's Afterlife*, 29; Ziff, ed., *Che Guevara*, 113.
101 Ziff, ed., *Che Guevara*, 11 and 121. See also Hernández-Reguant, "Copyrighting Che," 4.
102 Casey, *Che's Afterlife*, 313.
103 Hernández-Reguant, "Copyrighting Che," 4–5.

104 Charlton, "Introduction," 11.
105 Stuart Jeffries and Vanessa Thorpe, "The Man Who Gave Che to the World," *The Guardian Online*, 27 May 2001, http://www.theguardian.com/world/2001/may/27/cuba.stuartjeffries.
106 *Che's Afterlife*, 313.
107 *Ch€: Revolución y Mercado* (Barcelona: Ajuntament de Barcelona and Turner, 2007).
108 Richard Rorty, *Contingency, Irony, and Solidarity* (Cambridge: Cambridge University Press, 1989), 74.
109 *On Photography*, 106–8.
110 *Das Kunstwerk im Zeitalter seiner technischen Reproduzierbarkeit* (1936), in Walter Benjamin, *Gesammelte Schriften* (Frankfurt: Suhrkamp, 2013), 1–2: 485.
111 See Desmond Manderson, *Kangaroo Courts and the Rule of Law: The Legacy of Modernism* (New York: Routledge, 2012), 17.
112 "Force of Law: The 'Mystical Foundation of Authority,'" *Cardozo Law Review* 11, nos. 5–6 (1990): 943.
113 *Contingency, Irony, and Solidarity*, 97
114 Cited in Kunzle, *Che Guevara*, 106.
115 On photography as a medium aimed at structuring a temporal bridge between the photograph and the spectator, see David Tomas, "A Mechanism for Meaning: A Ritual and the Photographic Process," *Semiotica* 46, no. 1 (1983): 36–7.
116 Charlton, "Introduction," 12.
117 Badiou, *L'hypothèse communiste*, 193–5.
118 Ibid., 198.
119 Ibid.
120 Ibid., 196–7.
121 Ibid., 199.
122 José Carlos Mariátegui, "Aniversario y Balance," in José Carlos Mariátegui, *Ideología y Política*, 2nd ed. (Lima: Amauta, 1971), 249.
123 Guevara, "El Socialismo y el Hombre en Cuba," 259.
124 See Michael Löwy, *La pensée de Che Guevara* (Maspero, 1970), 27ff.
125 Guevara, "El Socialismo y el Hombre en Cuba," 269–70.
126 Löwy, *La pensée de Che Guevara*, 28.
127 Ernesto Guevara, "Discurso en el Segundo Seminario Económico de Solidaridad Afroasiática," in Guevara, *Escritos*, 9: 343.
128 Karl Marx, "Thesen über Feuerbach," in Friedrich Engels, *Ludwig Feuerbach und der Ausgang der klassischen deutschen Philosophie: Mit Anhang, Karl Marx über Feuerbach vom Jahre 1845* (Berlin: JHW Dietz, 1888), 72.

129 Löwy, *La pensée de Che Guevara*, 29.
130 Guevara, "Discurso," 344.
131 Borrego, *El camino del fuego*, 112ff. Antonio del Conde – also known as "*El Cuate*" (The Friend) – who worked with Che when he was the Cuban minister of industry, summarizes Che's attempt at reforming the economy through a simultaneous reform of the human soul in two key facets: "*disciplina y muchos huevos*" (discipline and big balls). Interview with Antonio del Conde, Mexico City, 9 January 2015.
132 *Che Guevara*, 724.
133 See note 125 above.
134 Guevara, "Mensaje a los pueblos del mundo," 369.
135 Ibid.
136 See Enrique Krauze, "Che Guevara: El Santo Enfurecido," in Enrique Krauze, *Redentores: Ideas y Poder en América Latina* (Mexico City: DeBolsillo, 2011), 328–31.
137 *Che Guevara*, 270.
138 Che does not consider communism as a "utopian system based on man's goodness as a man," but rather – in his own words – as a *historical* possibility which could be objectively glimpsed through the material experience of the Cuban revolution. Thus, he is not utopian because it is impossible to implement the communist idea, but rather because he had a strong vision of a good society that he constantly contrasted with the capitalist mode of production he strived to defeat. See Ernesto Guevara, "Discurso en la Asamblea General de Trabajadores de la Textilera Ariguanabo," in *Escritos*, 7: 39, 47–8. It must be noted that the term "utopia" can be translated either as *no place* (εὐ-τόπος) or as *good place* (εὐ-τόπος). Utopia can therefore be defined as *the good place that is not yet here*. The praise of Utopia supposedly written by the laureate poet Anemolius made for the first time explicit both ways of understanding this concept. See Thomas More, *Utopia*, ed. George M. Logan and Robert M. Adams (1516/18) (Cambridge: Cambridge University Press, 1996), 115–21.
139 *The Che Guevara Myth*, 3.
140 Ernesto Guevara, "Discurso en la Asamblea General de Naciones Unidas: 11 de diciembre de 1964," in Guevara, *Escritos*, 9: 305.
141 See Hilda Gadea, *Che Guevara: Los Años Decisivos* (Mexico City: Aguilar Editor, 1972).
142 See Anderson, *Che Guevara*, 175–6; Taibo, *Ernesto Guevara*, 104–5.
143 "Vieja María, vas a morir / Quiero hablarte en serio: / Tu vida fue un rosario de agonías completo. / No hubo un hombre amado, ni salud,

ni dinero, / apenas el hambre para ser compartida ... Tu vida fue horriblemente vestida de hambre, / acaba vestida de asma. / Pero quiero anunciarte / en voz baja y viril de las esperanzas, / la más roja y viril de las esperanzas, / quiero jurarlo por la exacta / dimensión de mis ideales. / Toma esta mano que parece de niño / entre las tuyas pulidas por el jabón amarillo, / refriega los callos duros y los nudillos puros / en la suave vergüenza de mis manos de médico. / Descansa en paz, Vieja María, / descansa en paz, / Vieja luchadora, / tus nietos todos vivirán la aurora. / LO JURO." Ernesto Guevara, "Vieja María, Vas a Morir," in Mario Benedetti, ed., *Poesía trunca* (Havana: Casa de las Américas, 1977), 13–14.

144 *La chambre claire*, 869.

145 Ibid., 875–8.

12 The Art of Bureaucracy: Redacted Ready-mades

KATHERINE BIBER

It was a monotonous job ... To break the monotony [Yossarian] invented games. Death to all modifiers, he declared one day, and out of every letter that passed through his hands went every adverb and every adjective. The next day he made war on articles. He reached a much higher plane of creativity the following day when he blacked out everything in the letters but a, an, and the. That erected more dynamic intralinear tensions, he felt, and in just about every case left a message far more universal.

Joseph Heller, *Catch-22*[1]

In the final days of its regime, agents of the Ministerium für Staatssicherheit, or Stasi, destroyed documents on a mass scale. Most were pulverized using a *feuchtschredder*, or wet shredder. Agricultural composters were retooled to destroy papers, microfilm, and audio tapes, producing enormous lumps. Some of these were buried, some were discharged into the Leipzig municipal sewer system, which several days later became clogged before spewing watery pulp into the streets. Today these grey rocks, dimensions variable, are exhibited by the artist Daniel Knorr in his series *The State of Mind* (2007). The original documents within these "file-stones" can be vaguely perceived but cannot be read. They testify not only to the secrecy of the regime from which they originated, but also to the malign artistry of its officials.

This chapter investigates official secrecy as bureaucratic creativity. Visual techniques of official secret keeping display the art of administration, driven by the need to create new methods of destruction, obfuscation, and concealment. That these techniques might be imagined *as art* becomes possible through the intervention of contemporary artists whose work is made from the tangible remainders of official secrets. This chapter examines several art projects which draw on redacted or otherwise wilfully damaged official records. Whilst most critics and commentators in this area are interested in exploring what these records might reveal about the secrets that have been removed from them, artworks made from redacted records can also teach us about the creativity and artistry involved in bureaucracy itself. These artworks, whilst attributed to a named artist, are in fact originally made by officials of the state. Usually these officials are unknown, sometimes they work in collaboration with others, mostly we have no idea of how they operate. All we can see is physical evidence of their endeavours, made manifest because they have visibly, tangibly, creatively intervened to hide a secret. The first section, "Redacting Secrets," describes some of the practices and techniques used in contemporary official information management. Section 2, "Making Art from Redacted Records," examines some of the instances in which redaction and official secrecy are appropriated by artists whose work engages with bureaucratic or archival secrets; this part focuses upon some of the art practice of Jenny Holzer and William E. Jones. The third section, "Bureaucratic Arts," traces the long history of bureaucratic creativity and innovation, and engages with the scholarly work of Cornelia Vismann. In section 4, "Bureaucratic Seductions," the chapter shows how some contemporary practitioners engage in collaborations with bureaucrats in order to produce their work. This more collaborative approach, exemplified in work by Jill Magid and Timothy Garton Ash, relies upon a tenacious and intimate dialogue between the official record keeper and the artist.

Collectively, the artworks in this chapter represent those contemporary artists whose practice explicitly invites and provokes engagement with political and legal institutions. Situated within the twenty-first-century sphere of art as critique, this is work *about* the political climate in which it is produced. In each instance, we can see an artist who is self-consciously working with political ideas about government transparency, freedom of information, surveillance, and secrecy. What is distinctive and surprising about all these works, however, is their strict aesthetic formalism. That is, they rely heavily upon the formal properties of composition, structure, line, shape, and colour consistent with the objectives of twentieth-century abstraction. These works are characterized by their reliance upon formalism in order to engage with the political sphere. Significantly, they take their formal properties directly from government records which, following the processes of classification and redaction, come to bear some of the lines, shapes, surfaces, and colours associated with abstract art. Initiating an ironic dialogue between formalism and social critique, these works draw attention to the aesthetic techniques used by bureaucrats charged with maintaining official secrets. In so doing, they draw attention to the fact that bureaucracy can be deliberately aesthetic, and that its practitioners are engaged in a creative – as well as an administrative – enterprise. In the interplay between visible and invisible, present and absent, these artworks use the abstract aesthetics of redaction – sharp lines, black boxes, non-representational shapes – to amplify their critiques of secrecy and surveillance. It is this surprising transaction between formalism and political engagement that produces new tools for charting a legal and political terrain characterized by obfuscation and concealment.

Redacting Secrets

In administrative and legal documents, the concealment of data in the official record is called "redaction." To "redact" is a neologism meaning "to conceal from unauthorized view," "to censor but not to destroy,"[2] or to render "unreadable."[3] The term most often refers to the concealment of specific information within government records prior to their declassification and release. Redaction is one of secrecy's instruments.[4] Some writers have observed that redaction is itself an art form, betraying the "striking individualism" of the classifier; they may use a black marker, opaque tape, sharp razors, or photocopiers.[5] George W. Bush's favourite item of stationery was said to be his black Sharpie, which he referred to by name, and which was included in the gift packs given to all White House aides.[6]

Scholars of official secrets recognize redaction's paradox: in a regime of transparency, redaction enables us to glean the existence of the secret, but not its contents.[7] Open government, open justice, freedom of information, and their analogues all arise from the belief that public processes and data should be available, should be disclosed, and should be seen. The administrative ideals and practices that enable citizens to see the information held by the state have evolved over time, so that transparency in the era of Wikileaks and Edward Snowden looks very different from the visions of transparency imagined by Kant, Rousseau, and Bentham. Contemporary transparency relies upon visibility, but where transparency reaches its limit, that limit also needs to be visible.

The limit of transparency might be the official secret, the trade secret, the privileged or confidential disclosure, or the private, personal, or sensitive information which, for reasons set out in legislative instruments, must not be publicly revealed. In a 1974 amendment to the United States Freedom of Information Act, redaction enabled officers to remove secret portions of official records and release them, rather than use the secret portions to justify withholding entire documents.[8] Now widely practised internationally, redaction might be regarded as a tool of transparency; it is the visible attempt to reconcile secrecy with disclosure.[9]

In the contemporary turn towards transparency, the official secret *itself*, activated by the act of redaction, becomes the object of illumination and transmission. The secret, that which has been removed or hidden from the document, becomes the mesmerizing black hole that lures us towards it. Artworks illuminate not only the fact that a secret has been removed, but the agent who removed it. They make visible the creativity demanded by official document creation, management, and destruction. As the legal anthropologist Annelise Riles urged, the aesthetic qualities of documents are proper subjects for legal inquiry, and when we critique bureaucracy, we must be careful not to miss "the very means by which bureaucratic processes compel … creativity in the first place."[10] Whereas, Riles conceded, most ethnography relies upon documents in order to produce knowledge about "social contexts and institutional purposes," it is also possible and sometimes necessary for users to produce "empathetic accounts" of the aesthetic properties of official records.[11] Importantly, the artworks examined in this chapter derive part, or even all, of their impact because of the creative labour of state officials. The frameworks, policies, and guidelines for official information management provide the preconditions for the aesthetic impact of these artworks. These artworks don't merely *resemble* government records; they are actually made from them. These administrative origins provide the basis for the works' aesthetic and market value.

Making Art from Redacted Records

Jenny Holzer, "Redaction Paintings"

In 2005, the artist Jenny Holzer commenced a multimedia project titled "Redaction Paintings," drawn from United States government records declassified after September 11, 2001. Holzer's "Redaction Paintings" were made from documents that were requested under freedom-of-information legislation by the American Civil Liberties Union. The works were drawn from heavily redacted declassified documents about the war in Iraq, extraordinary rendition from Afghanistan, torture at Abu Ghraib, and interrogation techniques at Camp X-Ray. Her work drew attention to the official origins of these documents as well as their pre-release redaction, and was described as simultaneously abstract and political.[12] In the work's mutual reliance upon aesthetic formalism and *Realpolitik*, Holzer sustained an ironic dialogue between the techniques for achieving secrecy and the horrors that are being hidden.

For some critics, her canvases portraying documents almost entirely obscured by blocks of black were aesthetic citations of Cold War paintings by Mark Rothko or Robert Motherwell,[13] prompting a reassessment of those earlier paintings, with their paint-soaked blocks, blotches, and stains, as foundational artworks about secrecy and paranoia.[14] That Holzer's work has these forebears points to the longer narrative in which formalism appears in political art. But it also draws attention to the brazenness of contemporary bureaucracy, which deploys such traditional abstract devices as cubes, lines, and blocks of colour in the

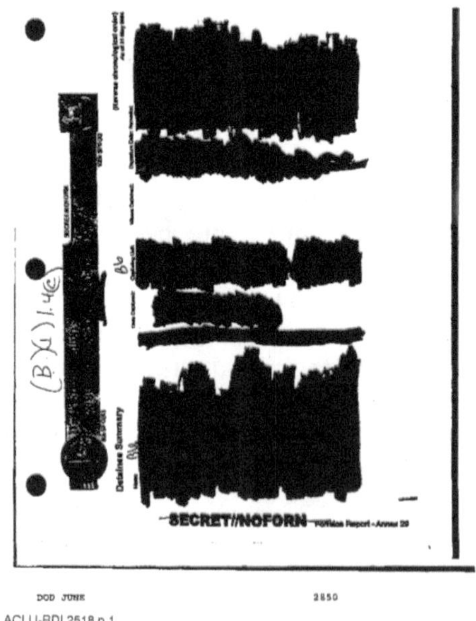
(B)(1)1.4(c)
Detainee Summary
SECRET//NOFORN
DOD JUNE
2850
ACLU-RDI 2518 p.1
DOD056686

Figure 12.1 Formica Report Annex 29 [page 1]: List of Detainee Summaries.[15]

concealment of such materially real and embodied practices of state-sanctioned deprivation and violence.

Joseph Slaughter described the experience of walking through the Whitney Museum in Spring 2009 to see Holzer's exhibition "Protect Protect," which included around two dozen of her "redaction" works. The exhibition featured what he called some of the "infamous masterpieces" of the Bush administration's circumvention of the Constitution and international treaties, alongside what he called "lesser known works of criminal activity, intent and investigation."[16] Here Slaughter was gesturing at the immense creativity that enables state criminality to be effaced by the smooth impassivity of bureaucracy, where the artistic meets the artful. For Conley and Saas, redaction was but one of the Bush administration's systemic practices of "mystification," in which the culture of suppression functioned on a spectrum, with document sanitation (redaction) at one end, and enhanced interrogation techniques (torture) at the other.[17] Holzer's work compresses that spectrum, presenting redacted records about torture. It was reciting the deliberative formalities of redaction, inviting us to recognize, in their use of well-known modes of abstract composition, the careful artistry of bureaucracy. The Bush administration was not a machine, nor was it bound by the strict application of rules. Instead, it comprised creative individuals, endlessly reimagining and reinterpreting, and taking pleasure in their mastery of abstract formalism, with its respect for structure, balance, and harmony, all in the service of concealing official state practices which bore none of these attributes.

For Slaughter, Holzer's work makes invisibility visible.[18] These are secrets that are hiding in plain sight; they are open secrets. Open secrets capture the tension between knowledge and discretion, operating in a zone between what is public and what is private, known yet hidden.[19] Seeing something that was not intended to be seen delivers a voyeuristic thrill to the viewer,[20] so that artworks made from redacted records require official redaction in order to succeed visually and discursively; they achieve aesthetic affect *because* they are open secrets. Alison Young used the related concept of the "public secret," drawn from the work of Michael Taussig.[21] Young and Taussig both recognized the double power of public secrets: first, that they *are* secrets and will not be disclosed, but second, that their existence is *publicly* acknowledged as a secret. These are secrets we can see.

For Slaughter, the redaction marks on Holzer's canvases represented the death of narrative, which he called "un-narration" or "un-telling."[22]

These were stories that refused to be told. By presenting these dead stories, killed by a nameless bureaucrat, Holzer might have been inviting viewers to do several things. Either we were to mourn their loss, or to take action to demand their resurrection, or we might be tempted to try to piece them together from the fragments left behind. Attempts to "peer behind the black bars"[23] present real ethical and legal challenges for scholars, transparency activists, and information managers, as they enable patient and knowledgeable people (including "trained hostile analysts"[24] and "determined researchers"[25]) to reconstitute secrets. Un-redaction is practised by historians and computer scientists using a combination of manual and digital methods;[26] techniques for "mosaic analysis" are cited in the jurisprudence of redaction, litigated by government agencies defending their refusal to grant freedom-of-information requests.[27]

Much of the critical commentary about Holzer's work saw art critics trying to tell, or retell, the "stories" behind the documents.[28] Despite their collective title – "Redaction Paintings" – the works were largely received by viewers and art critics as being "about" the words, facts, or content that have been left behind by the censors. They wanted to tell stories about torture and illegality from documents that had been purged of these narratives. Whilst these works succeeded aesthetically because they perform the brutal, black comedy of redaction, in the end they assumed a kind of political role, informing viewers about secret government operations, and the crafty techniques of government secrecy.[29] These were disclosures about non-disclosures, and in Holzer's works we saw both at the same time.

But there was another crucial withholding in Holzer's paintings. Whereas in the original government records there was *something* behind the black, in Holzer's paintings there were no secrets behind the paint: just canvas.[30] Whilst viewers of redacted records might be engaged in the exercise of trying to see behind the black bar, in Holzer's work we needed to acknowledge that there was actually nothing there. The bureaucrats who redacted these documents were visibly concealing secrets, in full knowledge of those secrets and the laws and policies relating to information management. Holzer's artistry appropriates and mimics the bureaucratic techniques of effacement, but without undertaking – or even acknowledging – the various bureaucratic acts of judgment, decision making, and policy interpretation and application that necessarily preceded them.

William E. Jones, "Killed"

Whereas Jenny Holzer went to a lot of trouble to make artworks that looked exactly like redacted records, William E. Jones is an artist interested in testing the idea that he might "forego the effort" of making an artwork, and instead "give new thought" to existing archival materials, simply by relocating them in an art space.[31] This accords with Hal Foster's assertion that archival art "is as much preproduction as it is postproduction."[32] These are artworks pre-produced by bureaucrats, and the artist's role is to retrieve them.[33] Much of Jones's art practice has involved re-presenting materials drawn from archival sources, usually with the intention of retrieving a hidden queer past from records that might have accidentally captured traces of it.[34]

During the Great Depression, the United States Farm Security Administration (FSA) was charged with alleviating rural poverty among sharecroppers, tenant farmers, and the poorest landowners. The unit's Information Division was led by the economist Roy Stryker, whose enthusiasm for photography saw him establish what would later become one of the most recognizable and significant photojournalism projects. Stryker hired photographers including Walker Evans, Dorothea Lange, Ben Shahn, Gordon Parks, and others. Together they produced over 250,000 images between 1935 and 1943. Jones and others described the Information Division as a propaganda machine; today we would call it a media unit. Stryker alone determined which images might be suitable for publication, rejecting 68,000 images; at least 157 unsuitable images were "killed" by punching holes in the negatives. Apparently it was Stryker who deployed the term "kill," and he himself wielded the hole-punch.[35] Stryker's authority looms over the FSA images, simultaneously claiming and disavowing his own creative influence over the project. He once wrote, "I never took a picture, and yet I felt a part of every picture taken. I sat in my office in Washington and yet I went into every home in America."[36] The FSA was disbanded in 1943, and replaced with the Office of War Information. Stryker left, but before he did so he ensured that the entire photographic collection, including the killed negatives, was preserved by the Library of Congress. When the collection was made available online it included many of these killed images, which have since formed the basis for several artistic projects.[37] Jones's films "Killed" (2009) and "Punctured" (2010) consist of looped montages of the killed images which he found on the Library of Congress online catalogue.

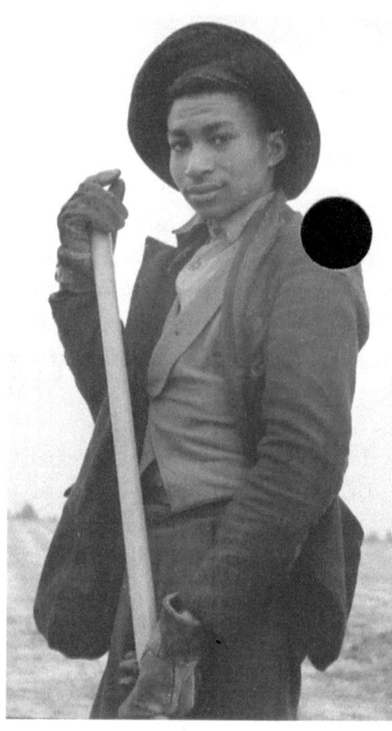

Figure 12.2 Untitled, created between 1935 and 1942, photographer unknown. Photograph from Farm Security Administration/Office of War Information black-and-white negatives, Library of Congress, online catalogue. No rights restrictions. LC-USF33-T01–000498-M4 (b&w film dup. neg.), LC-DIG-fsa-8a01406 (digital file from original neg.).

Jones told an audience: "Roy Stryker himself offered no recorded explanation as to his rationale [for killing negatives]. He was not a photographer. He was a social scientist … He had the good sense to hire photographers like Walker Evans and Dorothea Lange and Ben Shahn for his project. He was not immune to aesthetic discernment. But he had a very different idea of what the project was for."[38] Jones hypothesized about Stryker's motivations for "killing" the negatives, suggesting that it was an act of control, that it had a political dimension given the public criticism of the FSA, and that it warned photographers to be less wasteful with film.[39] "Censorship" is sort of an official word, and I'm not sure it's exactly the right word for what happened [to the killed negatives]."[40] For Jones, Stryker, as a bureaucrat, was self-consciously not interested in art. Jones said, "Because he didn't see this work as art he felt licensed to destroy certain negatives."[41] However, Jones's art practice relied upon Stryker's creative intervention; his hole-punch, and the ragged circle it left behind, provided the aesthetic lure that led Jones and his audience towards the killed works. Had Stryker thrown unwanted negatives into the garbage, Jones's work could not have been made. Instead, he killed them and kept them, transforming the images into open secrets. Jones and others could later see what had been hidden, and make visible the technique of hiding: in this case, the puncture mark, Stryker's unique creative signature.

Jones's videos made from killed negatives are about the hole, and it is the punched hole which activates these works. The animation moves too quickly for us to examine or read the images; we just see the punched hole. Jones said that, by making his films about the hole itself, it gave the works an "extreme and concentrated visual impact, almost like an abstract painting."[42] For Audrey Mandelbaum, the puncture mark in the images was a "mesmerizing graphic element."[43] The hole, she wrote, can be seen as "beautiful," "menacing," "funny," and "hypnotic"; also "darkly erotic."[44] These documents become activated *because* something is missing. The puncture mark is surprising; as viewers we are drawn into the hole. The hole frames the secret at the centre of this work; the hole contains the secret answer to the question of why Stryker killed these images. But the hole is a reminder of Stryker's creative oversight, haunting the contemporary artwork with his own spectral presence.

Bureaucratic Arts

Twentieth-century art inaugurated a range of related terms: "readymade," "found object," "appropriation," and "image transfer." These terms are not synonymous, they are coextensive, and they refer to the process by which an everyday object is transformed by aesthetic alchemy and conceptual deliberation. Readymades are most closely associated with Marcel Duchamp (the artist behind the pseudonym "R. Mutt"), who aimed to conflate art and commerce, and whose work preceded that of Marcel Broodthaers and Hans Haacke, whose practices at times recast these artists as bureaucrats, engaging with institutional and archival documentation within their work. Duchamp's readymades were industrial products relocated into art spaces, although in later work he engaged with papers, files, cheques, and documentation. The relocation or recontextualization itself wrought a transformation: by putting these objects in a museum, Duchamp asserted that he had transformed them into artworks. Art scholars including Thierry de Duve and Margaret Iversen argued that readymades transformed art practice, but they also transformed what we demanded from art.

Readymades didn't need to be beautiful, or masterful, or pleasing to the king. Whereas art usually invited reflection upon the encounter between the artwork and its viewer, the readymade was probative of the encounter between the artist and the object. That object, de Duve reminded us, had been chosen by the artist; readymades, he argued, rather than being called "found objects," were more accurately described as "chosen objects."[45] In the case of contemporary art practice derived from archival sources, de Duve's description might be replaced with the term "chosen documents" or "retrieved documents" or, most precisely, "downloaded documents," since many of these works were derived from archives found on the Internet.

Whilst Jones invoked abstraction as one of his aesthetic aspirations, it is fair to say that his work was more substantially committed to documentation and historical traces, and his creation of these video works was part of his quest to find new ways of presenting archival materials in order to achieve his sociopolitical goals.[46] In this respect, Jones inherits a legacy from earlier artists such as Broodthaers and Haacke. Haacke, in particular, relied upon official documentation to draw attention to how systems worked, particularly the nexus between financial markets, sociopolitical contexts, and the art world. Jones himself invoked the "readymade," reminding us that a century has passed since R. Mutt's "Fountain" (1914) appeared at the Armory Show.[47] Jones worried that, despite the documentary turn, or the archival turn, readymade artworks sourced from official documents were not necessarily politically transformative. He said, "In practice, there is a lot of 'kidding the product,' making the spectator feel smart while truly disturbing or provoking no one."[48]

Marcel Duchamp described a readymade as "something one doesn't even look at."[49] It is unseen because it is banal, or lacks presence. The art theorist Daniel Soutif used the term *présentification* to describe the process by which found objects become art.[50] "Presentification" explains how an "entity belonging to the invisible world is made present ... The invisible *presentified* has a power, a force, a capacity to act."[51] To presentify is *not* to represent; readymades do not resemble or simulate; *they are*.[52] For Soutif, in the early twentieth century, the invisible world being presentified was the market, and the presentification of the market occurred in the museum.[53] The redacted readymade is different. It presentifies the invisible world of official records, bureaucracy, and legal process. And it also presentifies the officers of the state, the invisible makers, keepers, and destroyers of official records, and encourages us to see, perhaps for the first time, the creativity of their endeavours. These contemporary works might achieve a reversal of Duchamp's mission of bringing commercial items into the art world; here we see the labour of public servants commercialized in the art market. Jenny Holzer accessed redacted records online for free.[54] Current redaction artworks by Holzer are priced above US$200,000.[55]

Cornelia Vismann's extraordinary book *Files* traced the immense innovation practised by record makers and record keepers within the long history of administration and paperwork. Contemporary redaction practices have their origins in the early techniques of cancellation and effacement which Vismann wrote about. Traced back to the thirteenth-century court of chancery, cancellation was the drawing of latticed lines or bars on a document, indicating that it was no longer the "original" draft and was not to be copied again.[56] "Canceling endows a writ with authority and force of law. The chancery, the site of this particular activity, derives its name from this act. Crossing out, it seems, is more elementary than the more productive act of writing down. Deleting rather than writing establishes the symbolic order of the law."[57] For Robert Chapman, cancellation was a destruction, an act of violence,[58] but it was a violence that left evidence of the conduct of its agents; where a cancelled leaf survived, it did so because it had not been destroyed. Vismann reminded us that, in Kafka's *The Trial*, there was a scene in which Joseph K. discovered a storeroom containing the tools of cancellation: "Bundles of useless old papers and empty earthenware ink bottles lay in a tumbled heap behind the threshold."[59] Decades before Jenny Holzer did so, Kafka drew the link between redaction and state violence; it was in the same storeroom that Joseph K. witnessed an act of executive torture.

For Vismann, the management of multiple drafts of documents gave rise to the possibility of "slips," "traces," "irregularities, displacements, mistakes" left behind.[60] She recognized the "pleasure" in discovering an "unprotected moment" in which "the law had been caught red-handed" in its manufacture of secrets.[61] By 1500, drafts were no longer cancelled but filed, in a transformation that Max Weber identified as the origin of modern bureaucracy.[62] Vismann only touched lightly upon contemporary official record management, but she offered an important insight into the management of secrets. In light of what she called the "dogma of transparency," secrets are censored *before* they are put on the record;[63] real secrets remain "off the record."[64] Everything put on the file remains a threat to the file maker. A prudent file maker knows never to record real secrets. In light of Vismann's insight, we might see contemporary redacted records assuming a more terrifying spectral tenacity. Knowing that the documents used by Holzer and others recorded the terrible secret facts of torture and atrocity, we now might wonder about how much worse are the secret-secrets, too dreadful to record. The mendacious bureaucratic artistry that enables secrets to go unrecorded demands forms of creative endeavour that might never be known, retrieved, nor visualized – nor monetized in the commercial art world.

Importantly, the bureaucratic creativity relied upon by Holzer, Jones, Knorr, and others shows us how records *used to be* redacted or deliberately damaged. These artworks are anachronisms, and part of their effect is derived from their retro aesthetic. They are haunting and powerful because redacted records don't look like this anymore. As Vismann realized, "In cultural memory … these technologies of effacement have themselves been effaced."[65] Contemporary government records are digital. Declassifying digital documents is done using computer software. The US National Security Agency regularly updates its guide, called "Redacting with Confidence."[66] The guide itself replaces the term "redaction" with "sanitization"; other organizations use an even more invisible term, "data loss prevention." The production of new forms of abstraction – in which language no longer conveys meaning – points to the ongoing creativity of institutions. The logic of "data loss prevention" is that information is "lost" when it is disclosed. The data itself is not lost, it is shared; what is lost is institutional control of the data: where it goes, how it is used, and how it is understood. Data control is preserved by keeping information secret, and so loss prevention demands concealment and effacement. The challenges posed by digital data storage are seized upon by information managers as new creative opportunities. The black boxes are digitally drawn, but the guidelines prefer that the boxes be grey, or that they not be boxes at all; sensitive text should be replaced with innocuous text and the replacements should be of uniform size so that we cannot speculate upon the amount of text that was there before. The hidden data in digital documents needs to remain hidden, and the replacements are encrypted, so that different users with different access rights might be able to see more or less data. Whereas redaction draws attention to a document's sensitivity by visually indicating those portions of it that are missing, a sanitized document hides sensitive content in a way that conceals its own hiding.[67] Whilst the contemporary transparency movement has revealed to us how labyrinthine and creative official secrecy really is, it places new demands upon artists to find ways of making it visible.

Bureaucratic Seductions

Jill Magid

Jill Magid is an example of an artist who has responded to this challenge. Her work relies heavily upon the creativity of bureaucratic and legal processes. She told an audience, "Law has been my most consistent collaborator."[68] Much of her work seeks to document her encounters with state officials, recast as love stories, romances, and seductions. In 2005, Magid was commissioned to make an artwork for the new headquarters of the Netherlands secret service, or Algemene Inlichtingen – en Veiligheidsdienst (AIVD). Magid responded to the brief to "find the human face of the organization" by undertaking a series of authorized meetings with its agents. Prevented from photographing or recording them, from disclosing anything that might identify them, or from accessing the premises in which they worked, Magid endeavoured to mimic the covert nature of their work by arranging to meet agents in nondescript public places, later scrawling notes about her encounters. (Some of these notes were later illuminated in large neon sculptures in the artist's handwriting saying "secretary," or "loud squeaky voice," or "dark puffy bob" in the series "I Can Burn Your Face," 2008. That exhibition was vetted by AIVD agents prior to its opening.)

Prevented from disclosing factual information about its agents and their work, Magid wrote a novel entitled "Becoming Tarden" about her findings, seeking to hide any official secrets beneath a cloak of fiction.[69] She sent the manuscript to the AIVD, which resulted in a protracted legal dispute in which she was threatened with criminal prosecution. She was forbidden from publishing the book, and when the manuscript was returned, 40 per cent of its contents had been removed by the AIVD.[70] Magid later said, "The Dutch redact by removal in white, which is brilliant because you don't know what you don't know."[71] She then came to an agreement in which her unpublishable novel and its redacted manuscript could both be exhibited in the 2009–10 Tate Modern exhibition "Authority to Remove" – displayed in sealed glass vitrines.[72] Within the vitrines, viewers could see only the redacted title page and one page of the novel's epilogue. At the exhibition's conclusion, AIVD agents attended the gallery and seized the novel, retaining it permanently. For the art theorist Pamela M. Lee, Magid's work exposed secrecy as an "ideological contrivance," in which the act of withholding, the power to withhold, is at least as significant as the withheld data itself.[73] In addition, her project highlighted the elaborately performative nature of bureaucratic labour, endlessly improvising and surprising, and its responsiveness to the artist's persistent pressure.

Much of Magid's work has relied upon the collaboration and cooperation of state officials, whose capacity for inventive and creative thinking her work has tested and provoked. In "Evidence Locker" (2004) she collaborated with Merseyside Police and Liverpool City Council. Magid walked daily, sometimes with closed eyes, and always wearing a distinctive red coat through the crowded streets of Liverpool, which were heavily monitored by a CCTV network. When she closed her eyes, she used a mobile telephone to speak to a CCTV operator, asking him to guide her (which he did, with considerable compassion, humour, and patience). In some instances, CCTV operators knew to monitor her movements by training a camera on her; at other times, they did so independently, unaware they were collaborating in her artwork. She later used municipal application forms to seek access to the footage, although she completed the forms in the genre of love letters to the unknown person who was watching her. The video footage was made into several video works including "Trust" (2004). The love-letters/forms were published as *One Cycle of Memory in the City of L* (2004).

Timothy Garton Ash, "The File"

Scholars have suspected for some time that the office and the archive are *themselves* significant sources of inspiration. This has sometimes been referred to as the "archival turn," "archival impulse," "archival shudder," or "archive fever."[74] Much of this work makes passing mention of the workers within these institutions, but doesn't draw attention to their creativity, endlessly making, arranging, discarding, and destroying records. This imaginative labour, much of which is in service to suppressive agencies or secret government operations, is rarely cited as the basis for most of the artistic work that flows from it. Artists have been mining official repositories so that their works, in the words of curator Okwui Enwezor, acquire the aura of "anthropological artefacts" and the authority of a "social instrument."[75] What this artwork often misses is the fact that this "aura" and "authority" are in fact the tangible products of bureaucratic labour. Only occasionally, as in the work of Jill Magid, are we able to see not only the creative outputs of official information workers, but the seductive dialogue that lures them out of the shadows and into the artwork.

Timothy Garton Ash wrote a book largely about the hitherto-unknown state officials who produced his Stasi file. *The File* also drew our attention to the public officers who continued to care for, manage, redact, and release it. As a student, Garton Ash lived in both East and West Berlin, later returning regularly as a reporter for the English press. The Stasi kept a file on him. Following the collapse of the Berlin wall in 1989, and the establishment of the Stasi-Unterlagen-Behörde, or Stasi Records Agency, Garton Ash applied to see his file. When it was released to him, fifteen years after it was created, he was suddenly tumbled back into that earlier world, only somehow askew, as reports in his file bore only a spectral or imagined relationship with his own memories. He described the file as "325 pages of poisoned madeleine,"[76] and set out to write a memoir of that time as recounted by his file, also attempting to track down and interview all those who informed upon him and all the Stasi operatives who kept him under surveillance. Tracking down his file makers demanded, alternately, tenacity and seduction. Eventually, all but one of those people agreed to speak to him, and the result is a strange, moving, and occasionally nerve-wracking account. What is striking is the heterogeneity of the people who created his file, their motivations, their methods, and their subsequent reflection on their past role as Stasi agents and informers. Whilst Garton Ash did not attribute to them any creativity or artistry, at times he compared their file notes with those in his own personal diary from that time, remarking on powerful differences in detail, perspective, interpretation, and contextualization. *The File* is largely about the forgotten or invisible people who made Stasi files, and it is also about how Garton Ash lured them into disclosing *their* secrets.

The File is also a tribute to the officials who continued to keep his file, and all those other surviving files in the custody of the Stasi Records Agency. In 1996, at the time that Garton Ash was researching his book, the agency employed 3000 full-time staff – drawn from both the East and the West – and had a budget of DM 234,272 million ($US164 million).[77] Requested files were pre-read by an archivist and redacted prior to their release. Of this process, Garton Ash wrote, "Frau Schulz [the archivist responsible for his request] has read my file before I did because, in scrupulous bureaucratic implementation of that law, she is supposed to photocopy the pages on which the names of Stasi victims or innocent third parties appear, to black out those names on the copies and then to copy the pages again, just to make quite sure the name cannot be deciphered using a strong light. She is also meant to cover up any passage containing personal information about other people that is not directly related to the inquiry."[78]

Although his remarks about the "scrupulous bureaucracy" suggest rigid and repetitious procedures, Garton Ash found unexpected meaning and memory in the redactions, pointing to the ways that official secrecy is generative of creativity and imagination: "Yet even the partly blacked-out names, the addresses and telephone numbers, unlock memory's doors, and send me back to my diary."[79] Whilst he was hesitant about attributing to his archivists any capacity for departing from stringent guidelines, he was attentive to the fact that their decision making relied upon their compendious knowledge and their ability to draw connections across files and to foresee consequences that might arise from disclosure. He wrote affectionately, if somewhat condescendingly, about "my file ladies," and said: "Everyone who works directly with the files has extraordinary knowledge. However sober-minded and responsible the people, the procedures and the whole atmosphere may be, there is still a voyeuristic thrill to knowing such intimate details of other people's lives."[80]

Garton Ash's book, along with all those artworks made from redacted or destroyed official records, are important reminders of the human agency that underlies legal and government secrecy. Official secrecy, which has been described as the "obsessive hoarding" of the executive branch of government, has been regarded by some critics of transparency as the trigger that actually provokes leaks.[81] Whilst, to date, most attention has been given to the individuals who leak secret data, these artworks return our attention to those who hoard the secrets, and also to those who modify, redact, or damage secret records before releasing them to the public. That all these artworks are, to differing degrees, *made* by bureaucrats points to the fact that official secrecy is *not a system*. It is the result of individual ideas and actions by public servants. These are works that highlight the creative practices inherent in contemporary official information management. Where bureaucrats use recognizable techniques of abstraction – non-representational shapes, black squares, circles, and lines – they achieve the effect of making redacted documents starkly visible to transparency activists, and also aesthetically appealing to those artists who make work from them. These formalist aesthetic interventions have the effect of drawing attention to sensitive data within insurmountable piles of paper. These bureaucratic markings have enabled artists to shed new light upon state secrecy, and bring awareness of it to new audiences. The critical celebration of this work, however, enables us to lose sight of everything else that remains hidden in official records, the sheer volume of which has the effect of making it invisible. Voluminous records can only be examined and understood given considerable time, resources, skill, and tenacity. Lacking the aesthetically pleasing marks of redaction, they – and the important information they might contain – risk being ignored.

Laws and policies about open government and freedom of information rely on the false assumption that the effects of disclosure are predictable and calculable.[82] In fact, information flows in uncontrollable ways, and at inconsistent speeds.[83] These consequences have the effect of demanding endless improvisation by the bureaucrats charged with caring for official secrets. To every disclosure is attached a decision maker, an information manager, a human agent. Record keeping, official disclosure, and record destruction are activities that shape the legal consciousness and legal discourse of the twenty-first century. They are achieved through countless instances of policy application, guideline interpretation, discretion, imagination, and creation. These artworks, made from the records released by public agencies, force us to acknowledge the artists of transparency and secrecy who are their makers.

NOTES

1 Joseph Heller, *Catch-22* (1962) (London: Vintage, 2004), 8.

2 William Safire, "Redact This," *New York Times*, 9 September 2007, accessed online.

3 Eric Bier, Richard Chow, Philippe Golle, Tracy Holloway King, and Jessica Staddon, "The Rules of Redaction: Identify, Protect, Review (and Repeat)," *IEEE Security and Privacy Magazine*, no. 11 (November 2009): 46.

4 Michael G. Powell, "Shadow Elite: WikiLeaks, FOIA and the Cultural Life of Government Secrecy," *Huffington Post*, 2 December 2010, accessed online.

5 Michael G. Powell, "Blacked Out: Our Cultural Romance with Redacted Documents," *The Believer*, June 2010, accessed online.

6 Ibid.

7 Mark Fenster, "The Opacity of Transparency," *Iowa Law Review* 91 (2006): 885–949.

8 See note 4 above.

9 Mark Fenster, "The Implausibility of Secrecy," *Hastings Law Journal* 65 (2014): 346. A group of art-world activists, Liberate Tate, draw attention to arts sponsorship by oil companies. When the Tate Modern attempted to hide details of their relationship with BP by redacting documents, the activists conducted an action described at https://liberatetate.wordpress.com/performances/hidden-figures-september-2014.

10 Annelise Riles, "Introduction: In Response," in Annelise Riles, ed., *Documents: Artifacts of Modern Knowledge* (Ann Arbor: University of Michigan Press, 2006), 20–1.

11 Ibid., 20.

12 Cathy Lebowitz, "Protect Us from What We Don't Know," *Art in America*, October 2006: 163; David Joselit, "Public Image Ltd.," *Artforum*, September 2006: 113.

13 Joselit, "Public Image Ltd.," 113; Joseph R. Slaughter, "Vanishing Points: When Narrative Is Not Simply There," *Journal of Human Rights* 9 (2010): 207–23; Robert Bailey, "Unknown Knowns: Jenny Holzer's Redaction Paintings and the History of the War on Terror," October 142 (Fall 2012): 144–61.

14 Slaughter, "Vanishing Points," 208.

15 Formica Report Annex 29: List of Detainee Summaries. Release date: 30 June 2006. Source: ACLU FOIA Request (7 October 2003). Image in the public domain; accessed online at https://www.thetorturedatabase.org/files/foia_subsite/pdfs/DOD056666.pdf. Holzer claims copyright in her works; when Joseph Slaughter was prevented from reproducing her works in an academic journal, he chose to replace them with photographs of the real redacted documents, which are taken from official sources and are public records. They so closely resemble Holzer's paintings that they can stand in their place. I have done the same, albeit with a different image.

16 Slaughter, "Vanishing Points," 207.

17 Donovan Conley and William Saas, "Occultatio: The Bush Administration's Rhetorical War," *Western Journal of Communication* 74, no. 4 (2010): 341.

18 Slaughter, "Vanishing Points," 211.

19 Katherine Biber and Derek Dalton, "Making Art from Evidence: Secret Sex and Police Surveillance in the Tearoom," *Crime, Media, Culture* 5, no. 3 (2009): 243–67; Katherine Biber, "In Crime's Archive: The Cultural Afterlife of Criminal Evidence," *British Journal of Criminology* 53, no. 6 (2013): 1033–49.

20 Katherine Biber, "Peeping: Open Justice and Law's Voyeurs," in Cassandra Sharp and Marett Leiboff, eds, *Cultural Legal Studies: Law's Popular Cultures and the Metamorphosis of Law* (Abingdon: Routledge, 2016).

21 Alison Young, "The Art of Public Secrecy," *Australian Feminist Law Journal* 35 (2011): 57–74; Michael Taussig, *Defacement: Public Secrecy and the Labor of the Negative* (Stanford: Stanford University Press, 1999).

22 Slaughter, "Vanishing Points," 209, 220. For an analysis of blank spaces in Reformation portraiture, see Peter Goodrich, "The Iconography of Nothing: Blank Spaces and the Representation of Law in Edward VI and the Pope," in Costas Douzinas and Lynda Nead, eds, *Law and the Image: The Authority of Art and the Aesthetics of Law* (Chicago: University of Chicago Press, 1999): "It is precisely the law of law that the empty space both reveals and conceals in its display of nothing" (113).

23 William Brennan, "The Declassification Engine: Reading between the Black Bars," *The New Yorker* online, 16 October 2013. For more about "black" as a code word for clandestine military or government operations, see Kirsten Johnson, "All Eyes," in Meg McLagan and Yates McKee, eds, *Sensible Politics: The Visual Culture of Nongovernmental Activism* (New York: Zone Books, 2012).

24 *National Security Archive v. Federal Bureau of Investigation*, 759 F Supp 872 (DC) 1991 at 877.

25 *Laurie Aarons v. Australian Archives*, [1992] AATA 261 at [9].

26 See note 24 above.

27 See esp. *CIA v. Sims*, 471 US 159 (1985). In one Canadian case, Dawson J actually engaged in mosaic analysis himself, enabling him to deduce the identity of a confidential source. His deduction was verified ex parte by the Crown. He then conceded the difficulty of writing a judgment that wouldn't itself constitute an innocuous piece of a mosaic which could, read together with other pieces, enable others to deduce the identity of protected sources. However, recognizing the need for an appellate court to be able to review his reasons, guided by the Secret Index and ex parte charts provided to the court, he also provided supplementary "private reasons" to the appellate court, which were to be kept under seal. The official judgment was given to the Crown for review and clearance prior to publication: *R. v. Ahmad*, 2009 Carswell Ont 9296.

28 Joselit, "Public Image Ltd."; Bailey, "Unknown Knowns"; Slaughter, "Vanishing Points."

29 Slaughter, "Vanishing Points," 209.

30 Ibid., 212.

31 William E. Jones, cited in Felicia Feaster, "William E. Jones: The Secret History," *Creativeloafing.com*, 20 February 2008.

32 Hal Foster, "An Archival Impulse," in Charles Merewether, ed., *The Archive: Documents of Contemporary Art Series* (Cambridge, MA: MIT Press, 2006), 144.
33 See for example Sven Spieker, *Art from Bureaucracy* (Cambridge, MA: MIT Press, 2008); Okwei Enwezor, *Archive Fever: Uses of the Document in Contemporary Art* (New York: International Center of Photography & Steidl, 2008); Katherine Biber, "Evidence from the Archive," *Sydney Law Review* 33, no. 3 (2011): 575–98.
34 See http://www.williamejones.com. See also Biber and Dalton, "Making Art from Evidence"; Biber, "Peeping." Biber, "Evidence from the Archive."
35 Audrey Mandelbaum, "An Invocation of Ghosts: William E. Jones's 'Killed,'" *X-tra: Contemporary Art Quarterly* 12, no. 2 (Winter 2009). Accessed online.
36 Cited in Eric Banks, "William E. Jones: Punctured," *Paris Review Daily*, 4 October 2010, accessed online.
37 See for example Étienne Chambaud, *Personne* (2008) and Lisa Oppenheim, *Killed Negatives: After Walker Evans* (2007), both of which are discussed in the blog *Carefully Aimed Darts*, 20 February 2009, https://carefullyaimeddarts.wordpress.com/2009/02/.
38 William E. Jones in conversation with Andrew Roth, "An Artist Dialogue – 'Killed,'" New York Public Library, 8 September 2010. Accessed online.
39 Ibid.
40 Rosalind Early, "Artist William E. Jones on His Saint Louis Art Museum Exhibit 'Killed,'" *St. Louis Magazine*, 17 April 2013. Accessed online.
41 Conversation with Andrew Roth.
42 Aram Moshayedi, "500 Words: William E Jones," *Artforum.com*, 26 January, 2011.
43 Mandelbaum, "An Invocation of Ghosts."
44 Ibid. Mandelbaum draws the link between the eroticism of the black hole and Jones's earlier work about illicit gay sex, including *Tearoom* (1962/2007), for more about which see Biber and Dalton, *supra* note 20.
45 Thierry de Duve, "Echoes of the Readymade: Critique of Pure Modernism" (trans. Rosalind Krauss), *October* 70 (Autumn 1994): 72.
46 Jones's works based upon the killed images are part of his ongoing project to find and present evidence of a "historical queer presence" that may be visible in archival sources either unconsciously or accidentally. Proposing that the FSA images were killed because of their queer content, Jones pretty much admits, is a highbrow folly. He said, "I'm not making an argument ... I'm presenting possibilities ... One of the responsibilities we

have [as artists] is to imagine new ways of using these images": "An Artist Dialogue."

47 Matthew Carson, "William E. Jones interview," *Monsters & Madonnas: The International Center of Photography Library Blog*, 20 December 2010. Accessed online.

48 Ibid.

49 See note 45 above.

50 Daniel Soutif, "Found and Lost: On the Object in Art," *Artforum*, October 1989: 158. He derives this from the work of philosopher Lucien Stéphan.

51 Ibid.

52 Ibid.

53 Ibid.

54 Interview with Jenny Holzer, "Jenny Holzer: 'For 7 World Trade' and 'Redaction Paintings,'" *Art21.org*, 4 November 2007. Accessed online.

55 Jenny Holzer's "Dust Paintings" were exhibited at Cheim & Read, New York City, 11 September–25 October 2014.

56 Cornelia Vismann, *Files: Law and Media Technology*, trans. G. Winthrop-Young (Stanford: Stanford University Press, 2008), 26.

57 Ibid., 26.

58 Ibid., 28.

59 Ibid., 28.

60 Ibid., 27.

61 Ibid., 28.

62 Ibid., 91.

63 Ibid., 146.

64 Ibid. For a detailed analysis of visibility and torture, see Hedi Viterbo, "Seeing Torture Anew: A Transnational Reconceptualization of State Torture and Visual Evidence," *Stanford Journal of International Law* 50, no. 2 (2014): 281–317.

65 Vismann, *Files*, 26.

66 National Security Agency, Information Assurance Directorate, *Redacting with Confidence: How to Safely Publish Sanitized Reports Converted from Word 2007 to PDF*, 18 March 2008. Accessed online.

67 Bier et al., "The Rules of Redaction," 52.

68 Jill Magid in conversation with Carey Young, Tate Britain, 7 February 2015, who was in attendance.

69 The title "Becoming Tarden" refers to one character, a former intelligence agent, in the novel *Cockpit* by Jerzy Kosinski. See Pamela M. Lee, "Open Secret," *Artforum*, May 2011: 226.

70 Mark Fenster writes about the publication of Valerie Plame Wilson's memoir, which, following her publisher's failed legal appeals, was printed with the redactions intact. The absurdity, Fenster points out, was that most of the parts of Wilson's story which were redacted are nevertheless recounted in the book's long afterword, written by Laura Rozen from publicly available sources, and which were beyond the jurisdiction of the CIA: *supra* note 9, at 40. In another example he gives, a memoir by Anthony Shaffer about his work in the Defense Intelligence Agency (DIA) was printed with approval of the Army but, prior to release, publication was opposed by the DIA. The Pentagon purchased and destroyed the printed copies, and a new, redacted issue was published. However, several advance copies of the first edition had already been released to reviewers; not only did they have access to the full manuscript, but could also use the second edition to establish the sensitive information that the DIA had redacted: "The Implausibility of Secrecy," 41.

71 See note 68 above.

72 See Lee, "Open Secret."

73 Ibid.

74 Ann Laura Stoler, "Colonial Archives and the Arts of Governance," *Archival Science* 2 (2002), 95; Hal Foster, "An Archival Impulse," *October* 110 (2004): 3–22; Arlette Farge, *The Allure of the Archives*, trans. T. Scott-Railton (New Haven and London: Yale University Press, 2013); Jacques Derrida, *Archive Fever: A Freudian Impression*, trans. E. Prenowitz (Chicago: University of Chicago Press, 1995).

75 Enwezor, *Archive Fever*, 13.

76 Timothy Garton Ash, "The Stasi on Our Minds," *New York Review of Books*, 31 May 2007, accessed online.

77 Timothy Garton Ash, *The File* (New York: Vintage, 1998), 220. Those numbers are likely significantly lower today.

78 Ibid., 21. Garton Ash asks himself this question: "But what is not relevant to understanding a secret police that worked precisely by collecting and exploiting the most intimate details of private life?" (21). Later, he explains (126) that whilst "affected and third parties" are to have their names blacked, "persons of contemporary history" are to be left visible; "protection-worthy interests" are also to be concealed. "Protection-worthy interests" are "sensitive details from the person's private life" and which are not important to understanding the operations of the Stasi. Nevertheless, under the Gauck Authority it is the person accessing the file who assumes legal responsibility for anything that might be done with the information disclosed to them.

79 Ibid., 33.

80 Ibid., 221.

81 See note 9 above.

82 Mark Fenster, "Disclosure's Effects: WikiLeaks and Transparency," *Iowa Law Review* 97 (2012): 753–807.

83 Fenster, "The Implausibility of Secrecy," 329.

13 Illicit Interventions in Public Non-Spaces: Unlicensed Images

ALISON YOUNG

Much of my recent research engages with art that takes place on and in the street, and in what is conventionally called "public space." In this essay, I will examine some instances in which illicit images are created at a very particular part of public space – the public transport stop. By this, I mean the areas on and in which we stand, when waiting for a train, a tram, or a bus. These may take the form of station platforms, or the smaller slices of space set aside on pavements or demarcated within a roadway for passengers awaiting buses and trams. Such locations are paradigmatic examples of what Marc Augé calls "non-space,"[1] a term he gave to airport departure lounges, the space alongside train lines, and similar urban areas. Such spaces seem to lack functions other than suspension and transition: individuals move through these spaces in order to travel from one place to another; they have no desire to spend time within the area of transition itself, which exists merely as territory to be crossed. When not moving through such spaces, individuals are also held in suspension within them, waiting until they are able to traverse or exit them. Public transport stops exhibit many of the features of one of Augé's non-spaces: the stop exists to enable passengers to gather in one place before boarding.

Such spaces are utterly commonplace within contemporary cities. They are both mundane and ubiquitous, their architecture and imagery rarely prompting a second glance from commuters, consumers, and tourists. Occasionally, however, the individual waiting at a bus stop becomes something other than an indifferent user of the space. In this chapter, I will investigate the transformations occurring when the public transport stop becomes a space that can be altered by artists and activists, when the surfaces of the stop are treated as sites to be monetized, when the space is patrolled and policed, and when the commuter, waiting for a train, becomes a spectator. As such, my essay locates itself within broader questions about the co-implicative relationship between the image and law. The image is both desired and regulated by law, whose processes depend upon an iconography, in which word and image together communicate legal rules and prohibitions and imagery, at the same time as the law promulgates a hierarchy of permissible and impermissible imagery and does not hesitate to intervene when an image, such as an artwork, contravenes its regulatory protocols.[2] My essay investigates the relation between law and image at the particular location provided by the public transport stop. It is an unconventional site at which to think about the co-implication of law and the image, but it enables consideration both of ways in which citizens may take for granted the law's underwriting of property and propriety and ways in which the law's responses to unauthorized image making at such sites reveals much about the law's interest in the aesthetics of urban space.

Public Transport, Private Space

Can "public space" be found at a public transport stop? It is an easy contemporary colloquialism to speak of public space within urban centres, but the size, scope, and variety of such spaces have dwindled. There is now little substantive content to the term, at least in the sense that a space is publicly owned. Instead, cities are crammed with what are known as "POPS": privately owned public spaces.[3] Such locations resemble archetypal public spaces – parks, gardens, plazas – but the extent to which they can provide citizens with spaces in which to rest, take refreshment, eat, assemble, relax, play music, or meet people is constrained by the fact that they are owned by entities such as companies or housing developments. Although use of public space has always been subject to various historical limitations (e.g., by laws relating to breaches of the peace, disorderly conduct, and public drunkenness), private ownership usually results in a far-reaching curtailment of the activities open to users of the space, backed up with an enforcement apparatus entirely separate from the police force, such as private security officers whose function is to monitor the space and identify individuals whose conduct might challenge the norms of permitted use.

While a public transport stop is not typically associated with activities such as refreshment, relaxation, and meeting people, its design nonetheless recognizes an obligation to service the public in various ways, for example by the provision of seats, shelter from wind, rain, or strong sun, and information about transport services. Members of the public make use of the space for a range of activities related to their transit from one location to another. And as a way station in the network of transit services, a public transport stop might well appear to be quintessential public space, assisting citizens as they travel around the city. However, transport stops are themselves examples of POPSs: their public location says nothing about ownership. Transport companies own transit stops, and ownership awards them extensive powers as to the designation of activities that are allowed within the space and the policing of the sites themselves.

As both a privately owned public space and a non-space, in Augé's sense, the public transport stop is exemplary of the difficulties in working out what we mean when we talk about "public space." Urban geographers have tended to concentrate on public space as something that is available to some but not all; arguing that it should be accessible to the homeless, poor, disabled, young, and non-white subject as well as to the idealized docile and governable subjects that comprise middle-class consumers. For Mitchell, the "right to the city" took place in urban spaces outside the private home and named a physical space in which people could gather, protest, meet, or conduct any of myriad other activities that are becoming progressively restricted in modern urban environments. While his later work recognized the somewhat mythological nature of this conception of public space, Mitchell has continued to argue that a right of access to public space is an important claim to make. As he puts it, social groups need to be able to exist in spaces we think of as public, "for it is here that desires and needs … can be *seen*."[4] Public space makes possible an envisioning of the affective lives of others, and acknowledges that others have a place.

The notion of public space as an envisioning also inflects its conceptualization in political theory. As Hannah Arendt notably expressed it, "the public" is comprised of "spaces of appearance … where I appear to others as others appear to me."[5] But Arendt's conceptualization is premised on an assumption that we each appear equally to others, whereas the subaltern members of marginalized groups, such as the homeless or the non-white, experience an uncomfortable and contradictory combination of discounted status and excessive visibility as an object of governance.

As Kurt Iveson points out, approaches such as these demarcate two tendencies in thinking about public space, categorizable as either "topographical" or "procedural" models of the public.[6] In addition to these ways of thinking, "public space" can be understood to mean the space of a city's publics. Since Michael Warner set out his account of a plurality of groups and cultures and called them "publics" and "counterpublics," it has become commonplace to think of a shifting realm of social groupings whose discursive efforts constitute themselves as part of a public (or a counterpublic), with the related effect of the exclusion of others.[7] But a sense of incompleteness permeates these paradigms, and scholars have sought to address aspects of public space that do not seem to be accounted for in the conventional modes of its theorization. Concepts such as "public intimacy" elaborate a conceptualization of the paradoxes of, or what it means to live in, public privacy.[8] Critical geographers such as Iveson examine the paradoxes of membership of a privatized public, noting that there has been little attempt to trace publics as they map on and in public space.[9] There has been still less of any attempt to follow the ways in which "publics" and "public spaces" produce a sense of the law and a sense of the image in law. In the remainder of this essay, my analysis will engage with the image and with the laws of the image that might be found in the non-space of a public transport stop, as one of many examples of the paradox that is privately owned public space. Together, these create monetized spaces which operate according to differential norms of access, and according to variable social norms, for different social groups. The effect is such that "public space" cannot be conceived of as a uniform terrain, which all have the potential to enter. Instead of a city in which public space is an ideal or aspirational space, the city is composed of public spaces, privately owned public spaces, private spaces, and non-spaces, whose use is permitted to a greater or lesser extent to different social groups according to class, income levels, age, gender, and mobilities. The city is "fragmenting" or "splintering."[10]

Authority and the Image in Urban Spaces

Irrespective of whether a location in the public sphere is privately owned or a public asset, the images produced for and within them are extensively regulated. Cities are sites of cultural and aesthetic production, engaged in a continual process through which they develop and refine their self-image. A range of aesthetic practices – architectural innovation, statuary, signage and advertising, maintenance of the social environment through street cleaning and public art – make this possible.

This continual cultural production is underpinned by a network of planning regulations, local and municipal laws, and public order law. The space of a public transport stop is no different from any other part of the urban environment in being an aesthetic product as well as a physical location. Train station platforms tend to be long and narrow, with backdrops provided by walls or fences; they may be underground or open to the air, sometimes at ground level and sometimes elevated above the street. Bus stops are usually located on a pavement, and may involve as perfunctory a physical space as that resulting from a metal pole with a sign that designates the bus's stopping area, or the space may be expanded to include an area of shelter, with or without seating. Such structures often include panels made from glass or heavy-duty Perspex or other transparent plastic, inserted into the grey metal frame of the shelter. The appearance is one of unexceptional, bland, municipal function, with little attempt at variation, or brightening of a uniformly dull aesthetic. At station platforms and bus stops alike, the rear walls provide a surface that is used for advertising, forming part of what Iveson has called the "outdoor media landscape," a terrain of surfaces in which "urban outdoor spaces are used as media spaces by those who place text and images on urban surfaces and infrastructure to address strangers who pass through those spaces."[11] Small billboards can be affixed to the wall of train platforms; the Perspex panels of bus stops are hollow, designed to frame and conserve posters featuring a variety of goods and products. The bland aesthetic of the transport stop becomes a backdrop against which an advertisement may be more noticeable (and more memorable).[12]

Images, like conduct, are the object of legal governance. The privatized public places of urban environments require images to conform to an imagined genre of aesthetics for that space. An encounter with an image in which aesthetics and space do not match, for whatever reason, prompts anxiety and uncertainty. Images whose presence seems to lack any authority give rise not only to aesthetic dissonance within the space but also to a challenge to social and legal norms about property and propriety.

The illicit image in public space is commonly referred to as graffiti or street art. Graffiti and street art both tend to involve the application of paint to urban surfaces, but beyond this they are quite different cultural practices. Graffiti is often compared to calligraphy and, like calligraphy, involves writing letters in various unified styles.[13] The graffiti writer usually chooses to write his or her graffiti name, or "tag," which can be done with marker pens, aerosol cans, paint rollers, and even with fire-extinguishers. A tag can easily become what is called a "throw-up" (rapidly written "bubble" letters drawn quickly on a wall) or a "piece" (larger, mural-like designs utilizing multiple colours and complex techniques). A more recent innovation is the use of a high-pressure hose to remove dirt, paint, or other layers from a surface to create a "reverse" tag. Lasers have also been used to project tags onto buildings. Some have even written their tag in three dimensions, carving letters into metal or concrete, which can then be bolted onto a wall.

While graffiti writers remain largely focused on letters and words, street art has no such limit as to content.[14] Street artists use paint, paper, or sculptural objects, and manipulate the built environment; they might incorporate live performance, video, and sound into their artworks. Images may be hand drawn, painted, stencilled, printed, or glued onto walls. Some street artists reference graffiti culture in their work, some openly acknowledge that they started out as a tagger (notably Banksy), but on the whole the relationship between the two communities is contested and uncomfortable.

Street art shares some features in common with graffiti writing: both tend to be unauthorized, in that the graffiti writer and the street artist usually place work on private property without the permission of the property owner, and both are impelled by a desire to alter the environment. Many street artists began as graffiti writers, and subsequently developed an interest in expanding their skills beyond those required for graffiti, thus altering their artistic practices; and many street artists report being inspired by graffiti, or by films and books about it, to try their hand at tagging before they developed other skills such as stencilling or sculpture. However, street art is no simple offshoot of graffiti; many of its practitioners drew inspiration from punk rock, skateboarding, or protest movements (all of which emphasize a DIY, handmade quality in their activities) instead of or as well as from hip hop graffiti.

Other, rather more ambiguous examples of uncommissioned images can be found in public space, and particularly around the non-space of the public transport stop. These illicit images are created when individuals alter, replace, or erase advertising images. Such illicit image making has a substantial history.[15] The activists of the Billboard Liberation Front, formed in San Francisco in 1977, describe their alteration of adverts through the addition or erasure of letters and images as "improvements"; and in Australia the Billboard Utilising Graffitists

Against Unhealthy Promotions (BUGA UP) were active from the late 1970s in altering the messages of billboards that attempted to sell tobacco and soft drinks to consumers, an activity they called "refacing" (as opposed to defacing) the billboard.[16]

Billboard alteration became a recognized technique of "subvertising," in which the texts and images of advertisements are exploited in order to create a message for consumers diametrically opposed to the product originally being sold. In addition to guiding the billboard-altering tactics of activist groups, the Situationist ideas of *détournement* have also inspired artists to take over billboard sites for the purposes of art: Robert Montgomery, for example, pasted over billboards in London with poetry, written in white capital letters against a black backdrop.[17] After an intervention by Montgomery, a billboard at a busy traffic intersection in Shoreditch no longer showed an image intended to sell a product but read as follows:

> THERE ARE WOODEN HOUSES ON LAND IN FAR-AWAY PLACES THAT DON'T COST MUCH MONEY, AND STRINGS OF LIGHTS THAT MAKE PATHS TO THEM GENTLY, AND DO NOT TURN OFF THE STARS. AND 100 BLACK FLAGS OF ANARCHIST SHELD UP AT NIGHT 100 MILES APART / 10,000 MILES OF FLAGS AND A ROW OF TENTS IN FRONT OF THE CATHEDRAL GUARD OUR FUTURE. THERE WILL BE A QUICK SICKNESS, THE KIND THAT KILLS THE BODY BEFORE THE MIND KNOWS THEN THERE WILL BE A SLOW RISING[18]

Montgomery writes "elegant words" in a "sparse presentation" to "vandalis[e] advertising with poetry."[19] Other artists have similarly "vandalised advertising" by replacing it with words or images. The French artist Zevs has "liquidated" numerous adverts in bus shelter panels, adding wounds that drip blood to the foreheads of models advertising clothing companies, or deadening the eyes of models selling cosmetics.[20] Australian artist Kid Zoom in 2012 removed from tram shelter panels adverts for fast food, banks, and business magazines, painted skulls over most of their surfaces, and returned them to the panels. As part of a project called "Unveiling Beauty," the Berlin-based artist Vermibus travelled around cities hosting a "Fashion Week" and replaced advertisements for clothing, perfume, and cosmetics with his own hand-painted images. In New York, a collective of artists known as "Poster Boy" removes, cuts up, rearranges, and then replaces advertising posters on subway platforms.

Also in New York, artist Jordan Seiler decided to replace the advertisements in subway stations by covering them with his own artwork. He photographed the blue siding of houses, printed thirty-two copies of the image, to the dimensions of the subway advertisements, and spent a night "wheatpasting" them in the subway. His aim was "to create a very calm, graphic picture, to go over all these really noisy advertisements ... and to really calm the place down. It was an aesthetic decision that I wanted to alter the feeling of that space."[21]

After his initial "aesthetic" intervention, Seiler decided that he no longer wanted "to bring aesthetics into it ... Because everyone's got their opinion on what constitutes something that's worthy of looking at in public space." Instead, his interest focused upon the ways in which public spaces, particularly those used for transit, are commercially exploited: "We have this large environment that we all travel through ... and one of my issues is questioning commercial use of that space. We should question whether or not we want that kind of imagery to continue to exist in that space."

To further his aim of questioning the presence of advertisements in transit spaces, Seiler became involved in the Public Ad Campaign, coordinating large groups of volunteers who would, in concert, replace advertisements displayed in the Perspex panels of bus stop shelters with artworks, photographs, and other forms of non-commercial imagery.[22] A parallel campaign has formed in Britain: Brandalism is "following on from the guerilla art traditions of the 20th Century and taking inspiration from the Dadaists, Situationists and Street Art movements ... We are tired of being shouted at by adverts on every street corner so we decided to get together with some friends from around the world and start to take them back, one billboard at a time."[23]

In 2012, twenty-six artists collaborated on the "subvertising" of thirty-five billboards in London, Leeds, Glasgow, and other cities. The artists, wearing the high-visibility vests of municipal workers, used special keys to unlock the Perspex panels of bus shelters, sliding out the official advertisement and inserting in its place a print of an artwork created by one of the participants (and perhaps addressing, in Warner's sense, a counterpublic to that with whom the advertisement might seek to engage). Some of the artworks that replaced the advertisements seemed to counterpose the idea of art with the commercial imperatives of advertising. Most took a more overtly politicized approach: "Turn off your television," advises the figure in the poster by Ghostpatrol, while the poster installed by artist Bill Posters in Birmingham, one of the cities affected by rioting in August 2011, showed a man whose triumphant brandishing of shopping bags is revealed by three words to be the result of unauthorized consumerism: "JUST LOOT IT." In November 2015, Brandalism coordinated the subvertising of display panels at bus stops in Paris in the days before the UN 21st Conference of Parties talks on climate change. Brandalism worked with a team of locals to install posters at sites owned by JC Decaux, "one of the world's largest outdoor advertising firms and an official sponsor to the COP21 climate talks." Six hundred posters, by sixty artists from nineteen countries, were installed overnight at sites across Paris, aiming "to highlight the links between advertising, consumerism, fossil fuel dependency and climate change."[24]

Most subvertisers who seek to alter the advertisements displayed at public transport stops make use of a specialist key that opens the Perspex panels in the structure that provides passengers with shelter. (The inexpensive key is sold by hardware stores and online; it was also being given away as a prize in some of the fairground attractions in the "anarchism" section of Banksy's five-week "Dismaland" theme park.) The use of a key allows the activist-artist swiftly to unlock the panel, slide out the advert and slide in the replacement artwork.

The act of alteration can in this way be accomplished within minutes, and is less likely to be detected by the police or transit authorities. Nonetheless, it should be noted that subvertising often results in an encounter with the police. Jordan Seiler has been arrested numerous times; Zevs was arrested altering advertisements for luxury brands in Hong Kong. One of the members of Poster Boy, Henry Matyjewicz, was charged with the felony offence of damaging property and was sentenced to eleven months' imprisonment (although this was later reduced on appeal).[25]

However, within the community of subvertisers working in the non-spaces of public transport sites, the Melbourne-based activities of Kyle Magee are distinctive in several ways.[26] He has evolved a means of altering the advertisements located within these panels that does not rely upon a key or other means of accessing the displayed advert, and which does not aim for speed or to avoid arrest. Magee has engaged in a series of interventions that cover advertisements. His actions take place within a struggle over the image, a struggle that involves his rejection of "corporate/capitalist advertising" and his demand for "a total, world-wide ban on corporate/capitalist/for-profit advertising in public media/space."[27]

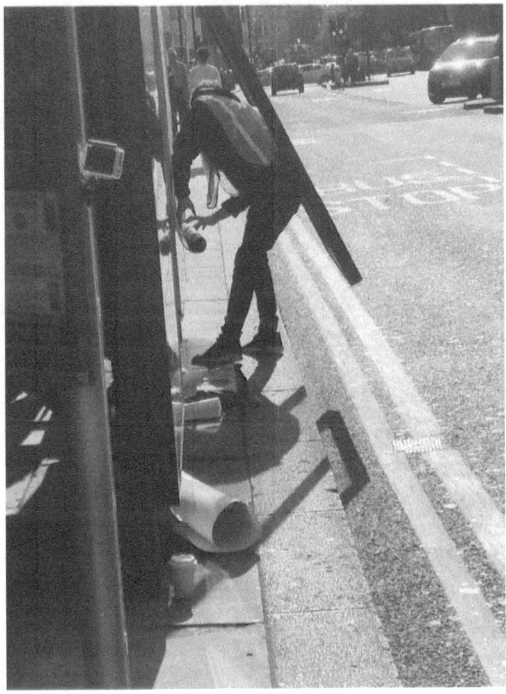

Figure 13.1 Vermibus, replacing a bus shelter advertisement, London, 2016. Photograph by Alison Young.

Magee began his actions around 2005, by painting over billboards. He repeatedly painted over the same three or four billboards: "I would paint them all and then keep an eye on them and then paint them again when the ads were replaced."[28] After quite some months, Magee was arrested by police. When he resumed, he maintained the strategy of painting out advertisements but shifted the location of his interventions to tram stop shelters. Magee's reasons for the shift related to the charges he had faced: painting over the surface of a billboard resulted in larger amounts of damage claimed by the company who owned the billboards: "one of the companies said I caused $30,000 worth of damage." A lawyer also suggested to Magee that he could argue that his actions were a form of political expression and thus protected under the Victorian Charter of Human Rights; Magee reasoned that reducing the "damage" might strengthen that argument in court.[29]

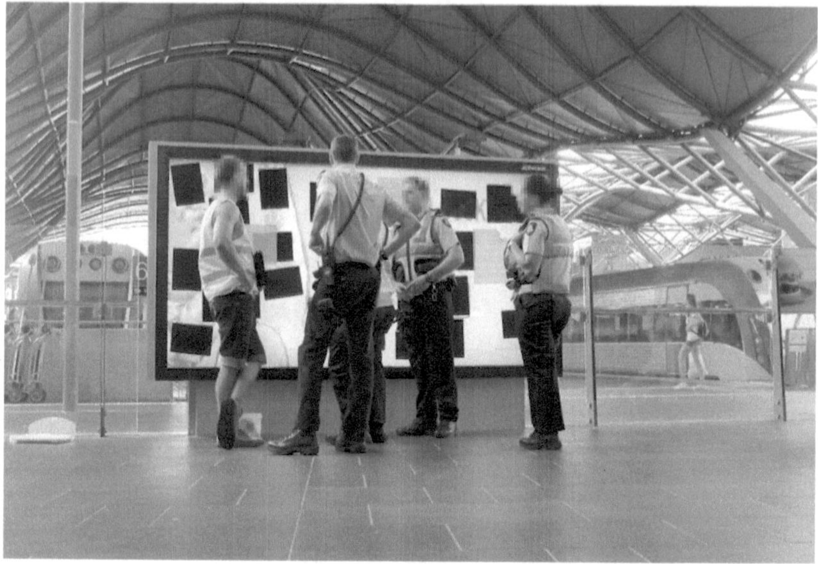

Figure 13.2 Kyle Magee, conversing with police officers prior to being arrested, Melbourne, 2014. Photographer unknown.

Magee decided to concentrate on painting over the glass panels in tram shelters: "I was still making the same point. But if I painted over a glass panel at a tram shelter, they'd just wash it off and that's $40.00, which I think is an exaggeration, cleaning these panels is part of their normal cleaning costs and it probably just doesn't cost them *anything*." Magee painted over panels over a lengthy period, and then switched his mode of intervention, once again attempting to minimize the damage that his acts of subvertisement might cause: over the last two years he has been wheatpasting pieces of paper over the panels in tram shelters around the city centre and has faced several sets of criminal charges related to those activities.

One of the sites he favours is a tram shelter adjacent to the County Court building:

> i'm back covering the same advertisements housed in the tram shelter on the corner of william and lonsdale, out the front of the magistrates, county and supreme courts (i guess because it'll be clear who is responsible as i've been there before, and i am challenging a law that allows

and protects corporate advertisements, so it is a somewhat appropriate place).[30]

Unlike many other subvertising campaigns such as the Public Ad Campaign in New York or Brandalism in the United Kingdom, which coordinates large numbers of individuals acting in concert within a short period of time, and which relies on swift replacement of images by individuals who then leave the scene, Magee acts alone, and makes no effort to flee or to disguise his identity. In fact, he provides his website address and a smart phone identification code on the paper in order to assist the authorities in identifying him. He writes: "i'll just keep going and see what happens, i can't imagine that the ad company won't want me charged or that the police won't want to charge me." In his recent posts, and in the magistrates court hearing for charges of "posting a document on a structure without consent," he reiterates that he is not ashamed of "his expression" and that he chooses busy times of day in busy and heavily surveilled locations as a result.[31]

Magee's aesthetic approach is very different from that of other subvertisers. When his technique of intervention revolved around paint, it was not to alter the wording of an advert or to undermine the content of its imagery: rather, he added paint over the panel until the image beneath was blocked out by a white rectangle. When Magee began using paper and paste, unlike the technique used by the activists of Brandalism and the Public Ad Campaign in replacing adverts with printed artworks or politicized posters critiquing consumerism, Magee simply sticks A4 sheets of plain paper over the panel. He does not glue them in a way that accumulates into a rectangle, as his brushstrokes did, but merely in such a way that they obscure the image.

In his interview with the police after being arrested for one of his attempts to paint over an advertising panel outside the county court, Magee stated that he "just sort of scribbled all over [the advertisement …], tak[ing] away all messages and images."[32] He thus characterizes the result of his paint strokes as *not-an-image*, rather than as an alternative image countering the advertisement. The not-an-image that he has created disputes the presence of an image (the advertisement). He does not create artworks designed as aesthetically pleasing alternatives to an advert or write culture-jamming slogans. Such interventions substitute for what was there; they add something else to the space or edit the image in such a way as to augment or alter its meaning. Magee's paint strokes and pieces of paper add nothing but themselves as paint strokes and paper. Their purpose is to draw attention to the fact that they cover an advertisement. By negating the advertisement they constitute something else.

If we read a glass panel of a tram shelter, after Magee has visited it, as an "encountered sign," this assists in understanding what Magee's actions transmit *as image* to the spectator at the tram stop. The commuter at the tram stop confronts a shape, whether a painted rectangle or patches of glued papers, that are ordinarily not present. Tram shelter glass panels do not normally have anything on their outer surface; any such objects (stickers, chewing gum, paint) are out of place, applied there for a variety of reasons. White rectangles of paint on glass and sheets of A4 paper are not normally part of the bus shelter aesthetic; the composition of the image that now occupies the panel announces itself to the spectator as something whose advent is unusual. The conventional and predictable surfaces of the bus shelter have been disrupted by the appearance of an ambiguous image.

The spectator does not even have to generate an accurate interpretation of what the image might be ("vandalism," "damage," "art," "culture jamming," "subvertising," "political communication"); rather, the image is encountered as something that has already changed the space and thus demands a spectator's engagement in its interpretation. Before any particular intellectual or emotional response is engendered, the image elicits the spectator's engagement as an affective intensity.[33]

If one reads the painted-over or papered glass panel as an affectively charged surface, Magee's additions to the panel must be conceptualized as an active semiotic event whose meaning is generated through the spectator's encounter with them. While a culture-jammed billboard offers the spectator a counterposition to the original advertisement, the results of Magee's interventions offer no comfortable semiotic certainty. When a spectator looks at the sheets of blank paper glued by Magee in no discernible pattern over a tram shelter display panel, what the spectator sees cannot easily be categorized, whether the category is that of political statement, "adbusting," or damage to property. It is not simply that the aesthetic meaning of the sheets of paper is difficult to determine, but more that any visual analysis of the result must ask whether Magee's actions with paint and paper transmit any sense of *image*.

As Adams makes clear in her account of the affective responses to the use of paint by Francis Bacon, paint strokes are never simply a matter of technique or a mechanistic component of an image: "Perception [of the paint] is not just an issue of vision but an issue of desire."[34]

The movement of paint across canvas and the application of paper to a surface can be read as both the evidence of an image and as a form of anti-image in itself. While Magee saw himself as removing an image (the advert) and replacing it with a kind of nothingness ("taking away all messages and images"), his action, as a replacement, means that there is still something there to be engaged with by the spectator.

Engagement with the ambiguous non-images created by Magee occurs in the ambiguous non-spaces of the public transport stop. How are we to understand the spectator's encounter with such an image, in such a place? As discussed at the outset of this paper, the public transport stop is a privately owned location that must offer services to the public: waiting areas in which to assemble, shelter from the weather, and surfaces that can be monetized through commercial use by advertising companies. All of these activities are *licensed* within the space of the train platform or tram stop.

Magee's unlicensed image making both disrupts and confirms the conjunction of criminal law, property law, and administrative law in constructing public space as privately owned and controlled, and behaviour in public space as subject to *licence*. The limits of this licence were considered in *Masterson and another v. Holden*.[35] Two men, at a bus stop on Oxford Street in London, at almost 2 a.m., kissed and fondled each other. Two heterosexual couples were passing by; the girls were shocked when they saw the men; one raised her hand to her mouth. Their male companions addressed Masterson and Cooper: "How dare you in front of our girls?" An act with a spectator, in a bus stop, on a street that is normally busy but which, at two in the morning, might not have been: an act in public that also makes a public – four heterosexuals, the magistrate, the justices of the Queen's Bench, and all the passers-by that might walk down Oxford Street, or wait for a bus. For the law, the kissing men are out in public and *out of place*; their intertwined embrace is an image that offends; their conduct confusing, as Goodrich puts it, the "omnibus and the erogenous."[36] The men make an exhibition of themselves (and their desires) in a space where only certain behaviours can be exhibited; they (and their desire) become an image that exceeds the limits to the images such a space can contain.

Non-Images in Non-Spaces and the Laws of Licence

The image in public space is not just an object to be interpreted by the spectator but exists in an active semiotic relation to the observer.

Meaning emerges through the spectator's affective relation with the image. The notion of "encounter" denotes a dynamic process through which aspects of the image are affectively registered by the spectator (such as shape or setting or colouration), or its artist (his age, gender, motivations, mode of conduct) or its challenge to particular values (such as taking over a space designated for advertisements), or its lawfulness (and, conversely, perhaps its unauthorized and illicit nature). Thinking of our spectatorship of an image as an encounter in which "affects coalesce as social emotions"[37] enables us to attend to relative variations in individualistic responses, to the striations in the judgment of an image that arise from social hierarchy, and to trace how affective spectatorship can lead to dramatic consequences in the lives of those image makers whose images are judged to be unlicensed and unauthorized.

Lorimer notes the far-reaching semiotic consequences of the condensation of affect and image in these everyday encounters, when we see an advertisement in a panel at a bus stop, or when we encounter the counter-image left there by a culture jammer:

> Life takes shapes and gains expression in shared experiences, everyday routines, fleeting encounters, embodied movements, precognitive triggers, practical skills, affective intensities, enduring urges, unexceptional interactions and sensuous dispositions ... In short, so much ordinary action gives no advance notice of what it will become. Yet it still makes critical difference to our experiences of space and place.[38]

When the spectator looks at one of Kyle Magee's painted rectangles or Zevs's bleeding models in a display panel, in which *public* do they position themselves? Each of these images carries an affective charge; but it is the spectator who legislates what is to be made of that charge. The image might engender pleasure or humour, it might inspire a desire to emulate, it might invoke a sense of loss or anger. We are all familiar with Althusser's account of the individual who, upon hearing the shouted words, "Hey you!" turns around, interpellated as a subject of law. But what of the individual who calls (on) law? In every wry smile or surge of outrage at the sight of these images, there also exists the demand for the law. This can take explicit form, as when passers-by call the police when they see Kyle Magee sticking sheets of paper over advertisements, but it would be naive to think that law is not otherwise present. In the encounter, the spectator takes up the subject position of the "juridical individual."[39] Every contravention knows itself by reference to the rule; there is nothing outside of the (law's) text.

Perhaps the ambiguities around Magee's images arise out of a situation that relies on *licence*. The notion of licence is a mainstay of administrative law and of intellectual property. What it performs is law's approval, and also law's self-restraint: in effect it is also a promise, a promise *not to sue* the one who acts in its name. Licensing meets the needs of our appetites, and gives them a proper place and time: the publican licensed to serve alcohol, the brothel licensed to sell sex, the club licensed to host live music, the individual allowed to listen to music on a CD but not to reproduce it. It relies on legal but also on social discretion. To detour briefly back to the bus stop on Oxford Street, what so dismayed the young woman on the street, and later the magistrates and the justices of the Queen's Bench, in encountering one man fondling another? Their dismay derives from their certainty that such a sight is *out of place*. The spectacle of such desire has no place in public; it is licentious. The licentious is libertine and lascivious, lacking self-restraint and lawfulness. So, too, when a man pastes paper over a panel instead of waiting in suspension for the tram, his image-making transcends the boundaries of licence. "The icon separates licit and illicit modes of representation; it establishes a regime of similarity, of repetitions, of the permitted forms of figuration of an absent God, and so also of a law in abeyance, an immemorial tradition."[40] With their origins in actions that contravene the rules of licensed behaviour in public space, Magee's images are configured by the law as non-images, lacking the fealty to law found in an authentic or legitimate image.

The non-images produced by the refusal to conform to the terms governing the licensed subject can be removed or washed off; their makers can be removed from the space, and fined, or confined. But the demands of spectatorship remain; still more images crowd into public space, demanding transmission. To end, then, let us consider again the tram stop visited by Kyle Magee, displaying the non-image that results from an unlicensed conduct failing to show fealty to the terms and territories allocated to the public subject. Such conduct lacks all love of and for the law; and in lacking love for the law, its images must be illicit. Thus, is the boundary of the law in public space re-marked, and the spectator re-constituted as a juridical subject in the city.

NOTES

1 See Marc Augé, *Non-Places: Introduction to an Anthropology of Supermodernity* (London: Verso Books, 1995).
2 On the co-implication of law and the image, see further Alison Young, *Judging the Image: Art, Value, Law* (London: Routledge, 2005).
3 On POPS and their implication, see Bradley Garrett, "The Privatisation of Cities' Public Spaces Is Escalating. It Is Time to Take a Stand," *The Guardian*, 4 August 2015, online at http://www.theguardian.com/cities/2015/aug/04/pops-privately-owned-public-space-cities-direct-action.
4 On the right to the city, see Don Mitchell, *The Right to the City: Social Justice and the Fight for Public Space* (New York: Guilford Press, 2003), 33, emphasis in original. Mitchell later moderated some of his investment in the notion of public space as an ideal: see Don Mitchell, "The S.U.V. Model of Citizenship: Floating Bubbles, Buffer Zones, and the Rise of the 'Purely Atomic' Individual," *Political Geography* 24 (2005): 77–100. See also Kafui A. Attoh, "What Kind of a Right Is the Right to the City?" *Progress in Human Geography* 35 (2011): 669–85. See also Henri Lefebvre, *The Right to the City* (Oxford: Blackwell, 1996). On Lefebvre's version of the right to the city, see Chris Butler, *Henri Lefebvre: Spatial Politics, Everyday Life and the Right to the City* (London: Routledge, 2012). Paul Carter also notes the "mythopoetic" aspects of the idea of public space: see Paul Carter, "Public Space: Its Mythopoetic Foundations and the Limits of the Law," *Griffith Law Review* 16 (2007): 430.
5 See Hannah Arendt, *The Human Condition* (1958) (Chicago: University of Chicago Press, 1998).
6 Kurt Iveson, "Cities for Angry Young People? From Inclusion and Exclusion to Engagement in Urban Policy," in Brendan Gleeson and Nigel Sipe, eds, *Creating Child Friendly Cities* (London: Routledge, 2006), 3.
7 Michael Warner, "Publics and Counterpublics," *Public Culture* 14, no. 1 (2002): 49–90.
8 See esp. Lauren Berlant, ed., *Intimacy* (Chicago: University of Chicago Press, 2000).
9 Iveson's own work constitutes an exception to this: see Kurt Iveson, *Publics and the City* (Oxford: Blackwell, 2007).
10 On the "fragmenting" city see Andrew Kirby, "The Production of Private Space and Its Implications for Urban Social Relations," *Political Geography* 27, no. 1 (2008): 74; and on the argument that urban societies are "splintering," see Steve Graham and Simon Marvin, *Splintering Urbanism* (London and New York: Routledge, 2001).

11 See Kurt Iveson, "Branded Cities: Outdoor Advertising, Media Governance and the Outdoor Media Landscape," *Antipode: A Radical Journal of Geography* 44, no.1 (2012): 160.

12 On the monetizing of public transport surfaces see also Naomi Klein, *No Logo* (London: Flamingo, 2001).

13 On graffiti generally see Joe Austin, *Taking the Train: How Graffiti Art Became an Urban Crisis in New York City* (New York: Columbia University Press, 2001); Craig Castleman, *Getting Up: Subway Graffiti in New York* (Boston: MIT Press, 1984); Martha Cooper and Henry Chalfant, *Subway Art* (New York: Holt Paperbacks, 1988); Jeff Ferrell, *Crimes of Style: Urban Graffiti and the Politics of Criminality* (Boston: Northeastern University Press, 1996); Roger Gastman and Caleb Neelon, *The History of American Graffiti* (New York: Harper Design, 2010); Mark Halsey and Alison Young, "'Our Desires Are Ungovernable': Writing Graffiti in Urban Space," *Theoretical Criminology* 10, no. 3 (2006): 275–306; Lachlan MacDowall, "In Praise of 70k: Cultural Heritage and Graffiti Style," *Continuum: Journal of Media & Cultural Studies* 20, no. 4 (2006): 471–84; Gregory Snyder, *Graffiti Lives: Beyond the Tag in New York's Urban Underground* (New York: New York University Press, 2009).

14 On street art generally and variously see Magda Danysz and Mary-Noelle Dana, *From Style Writing to Street Art: A Street Art Anthology* (Paris: Drago, 2010); Cedar Lewisohn, *Street Art: The Graffiti Revolution* (London: Tate, 2009); Nicholas Alden Riggle, "Street Art: The Transfiguration of the Commonplaces," *Journal of Aesthetics & Art Criticism* 68, no. 3 (2010): 243–57; Anna Waclawek, *Graffiti and Street Art* (New York: Thames & Hudson, 2011); Alison Young, *Street Art, Public City: Law, Crime and the Urban Imagination* (London: Routledge GlassHouse, 2014).

15 On unauthorized spatial interventions see Isis Brook, "Aesthetic Aspects of Unauthorised Environmental Interventions," *Ethics, Place and Environment* 10, no. 3 (2007): 307–18.

16 Simon Chapman, one of the members of BUGA UP, gives an account of the founding of the group and its activities in Chapman, "Civil Disobedience and Tobacco Control: The Case of BUGA UP," in *Tobacco Control* 5 (1996): 179–85. See further on BUGA Up: Kurt Iveson, "Cities within the City: Do-It-Yourself Urbanism and the Right to the City," *International Journal of Urban and Regional Research* 37, no. 3 (2013): 941–56.

17 See Matilda Battersby, "The Artist Vandalising Advertising with Poetry," *The Independent*, 3 February 2012. On situationism and *détournement* in street art, see Janet McGaw, "Complex Relationships between *Détournement* and *Récupération* in Melbourne's Street (Graffiti and Stencil) Art Scene," *Architectural Theory Review* 13, no. 2 (2008): 222–39.

18 This poem was one of three used by Montgomery, printed in white capital lettering against a black backdrop, printed on paper that was then stuck over billboards in London in February 2012. One line of it was subsequently used on a banner by Occupy London, as recounted by Montgomery in an interview, "The Poetics of Robert Montgomery," by Rachel Small for *Interview Magazine* (no date), online at http://www.interviewmagazine.com/art/robert-montgomery-c24-gallery/#_.

19 As described by Matilda Battersby in *The Independent*.

20 See Hugo Vitrani, "Zevs, tueur d'images," *Médiapart*, 18 October 2014. Online at http://www.mediapart.fr/portfolios/zevs-tueur-dimages.

21 In an interview with me, 2010.

22 Seiler has also collaborated on an app for smart phones called NO AD, launched in 2014.The app allows users to hold their phone in front of billboards on subway platforms in New York, so that instead of seeing an advertisement, they can look, through their smart phone screen, at an artwork. See details at http://noad-app.com.

23 See Brandalism's website at http://www.brandalism.org.uk.

24 Full details and press releases can be seen at http://www.brandalism.org.uk/brandalism-cop21.

25 The sentencing of artists and writers who place illicit images in urban spaces is discussed at greater length in Mark Halsey and Alison Young, "'Our Desires Are Ungovernable.'"

26 On other aspects of Kyle Magee's activities, see Susan Bird and David Vakalis, "Kyle Magee: Ad-Busting, Exclusion and the Urban Environment," *Southern Cross University Law Review* 14 (2011): 163–83; and Alison Young "From Object to Encounter: Aesthetic Politics and Visual Criminology," *Theoretical Criminology* 18, no. 2 (2014): 159–75.

27 See Magee's website: http://globalliberalmediaplease.net.

28 In interview with me, 2013.

29 When sentencing someone charged with criminal damage, judges take into account the total amount of damage done by the defendant.

30 A detailed discussion is found on Magee's website at http://globalliberalmediaplease.net/2012/10/back-at-it-again/.

31 See http://globalliberalmediaplease.net/2013/11/first-posting-bills-conviction-magistrate-capell-decides-and-sentences. Magee can be seen sticking paper over the panels in the images on his website: http://globalliberalmediaplease.net/2013/05/date-with-magistrates-court.

32 Quoted in *Magee v. Delaney* [2012] VSC 407 at 410.

33 It should be noted that some of spectators to Magee's interventions have been court protective officers at the county court, security officers

employed by transit companies, and police officers. When encounters involve these spectators, Magee has been arrested and charged with a range of criminal offences, including criminal damage and posting bills. In addition to such criminal charges, Magee has been pursued by the Office of Public Prosecution for the costs ($32,000) of one of his appeals against conviction to the Supreme Court of Victoria; and Adshel, the company manufacturing the tram shelter panels, is also pursuing him for $43,000, which they say is the cost of removing his papers from over 100 panels during a three-month period.

34 Parveen Adams, *The Emptiness of the Image* (London and New York: Routledge, 1996), 111.

35 [1986] 3 All ER 39.

36 Peter Goodrich, *Languages of Law* (London: Weidenfeld and Nicholson, 1990), 236.

37 See Jill Bennett, *Practical Aesthetics* (London: I.B. Tauris, 2012), 188.

38 See Hayden Lorimer, "Cultural Geography: The Busyness of Being 'More-than-representational,'" *Progress in Human Geography* 29, no. 1 (2005): 84.

39 Don Mitchell, *The Right to the City: Social Justice and the Fight for Public Space* (New York: Guilford Press, 2004), 77.

40 Goodrich, *Languages of Law*, 248

14 What Authorizes the Image? The Visual Economy of Post-Secular Jurisprudence

RICHARD K. SHERWIN

What appears in the image field is not subordinate to existing reality, it constitutes that reality.

Katharina Grosse[1]

The soul actualizes truth through the experience of sublimity.

Werner Herzog[2]

On the Nature of "Visual Economy"

Picture a canvas by Mark Rothko: let's say, "Four Darks in Red" (1958) (figure 14.1): Across an expanse nearly ten feet wide, four bands of colour are laid out one after another – brown, the thinnest; black, the most expansive; then maroon and red. The black has the most weight; it is portentous in its depth. All four bands seem to drift in an encompassing sea of roseate light, which suffuses around the cloud-like edges of the slightly darker, lower band. That band has been made to contract further away from the edges of the painting than the other three, as if the light behind it could not be contained. Absent figures or representations of any kind, there are no stories to tell. Words fall away, as will happen when one is immersed in music. All that remains is the slow dance of these shimmering colour forms, and your own gaze feeling its way across, around, and within the canvas. It is a strange visual dance, as if accompanied by an otherworldly score, watching subtle hues (black within black, red within red) separate out and move among themselves within each separate band, as each band oscillates against the unsettled borders of its neighbour, and the ensemble oscillates together as a unified whole within the larger luminous field of incandescent red. Without words, affect surges. An uncanny joy pierces the heart, a deathly despair, an insistent hope – as of daybreak …

Where are we? How did we get here? What does it mean? And what could this possibly have to do with law?

In order to gain our bearings we first need to grapple with the word "economy," and in particular with the notion of a *visual* economy. It is not the exchange of capital, commodities, and labour that I have in mind here, but rather an earlier meaning for "economy" – one that derives from the Greek *oikonomia*: *oikos*, meaning "dwelling place," and *nomia* meaning management or organization, especially of worldly

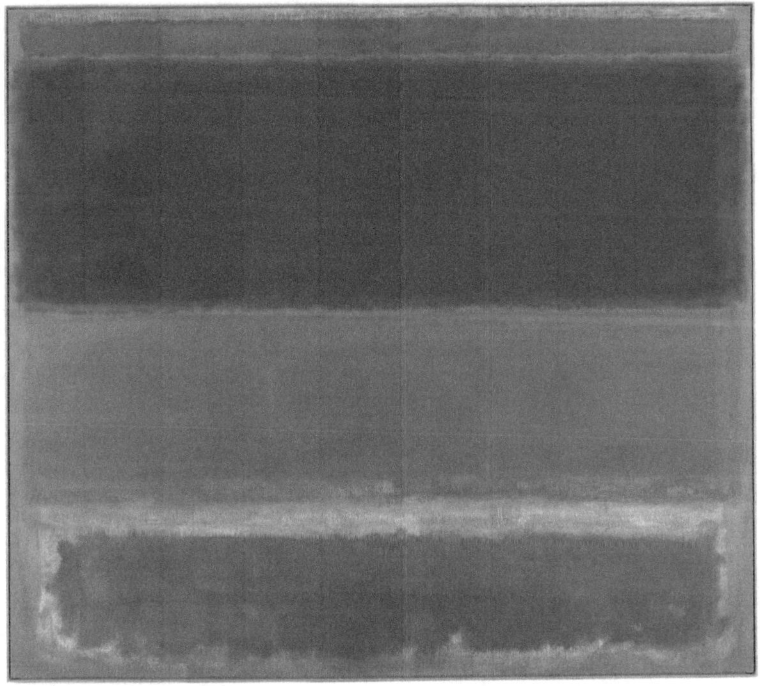

Figure 14.1 Mark Rothko (1903–70). "Four Darks in Red" (1958). Oil on canvas, 10113/16 × 1163/8in. (258.6 × 295.6 cm). Whitney Museum of American Art, New York; purchase, with funds from the Friends of the Whitney Museum of American Art, Mr. and Mrs. Eugene M. Schwartz, Mrs. Samuel A. Seaver and Charles Simon. Photography by Sheldan C. Collins.

affairs. Economy in this sense is the place where things of this world are properly administered.[3] Reflecting on the way we manage the world (or worlds) we live in invites us to consider anew the different moral values and aesthetic registers through which reality takes shape for us. How do things and others in the world appear?

In order to take shape first there must be a space to take place in, an *oikos*. So we ask, what is the nature of the space in which things appear and circulate around us?[4] How are the various elements of what appears organized in that space? What is their *nomia*? As soon as we speak of appearances, we confront time as well as space: a before and after. Out of what did it appear? How do we understand the relation between the appearance and its source? Its authorship, if you will. What is it that authorizes such a presence? "In the image of" what does it appear? What is its mode of emergence, transmission, encounter? How is to be understood? What does it demand of us? These are the sorts of questions a visual economy is meant to account for.

Human institutions, including law, reflect and implement a dominant visual economy. In different eras, different cultures have enjoyed vastly different visual economies. For instance, in Homeric Greece one encounters the economy of display where physical and social worth is constructed by the other's gaze. "Look at me!" Achilles says in the *Iliad*. "Do you not see how beautiful, noble and great I am?"[5] Yet, by the fifth century BCE, in the democratic Athenian polis, the economy of public display has transformed into an economy of public speech. The citizen's gaze now produces (and is a product of) the field of public performance constituted as participatory spectator and political contestant.[6]

Or consider Byzantium, in the eleventh century, the time of Constantine. For Orthodox iconophilic Christians like Nikephoros, the gaze was constituted by the economy of the Incarnation. It is the Incarnation that lets the world be seen. An invisible God must sacrifice an intimate part of himself, his only Son, in order to create a visible space for God's infinite presence in the world. The Incarnation – the way the infinite occupies material space – must be sacrificial, broken, *kenotic*, for the infinite will not appear. It always recedes from view. The icon unified the administration of worldly affairs (including law, belief, and material goods) in the image of God's sacrifice of His only Son. The economic imaginary of the icon modelled that sacrifice. When God became flesh (as word/image/body) the world became visible.[7]

As these examples may suggest, different visual economies establish the world we live in by constituting how the eye sees.[8] How do we know reality? What constitutes its truth? Does it touch the tactile image (in the presence of a pious painter like Giotto)? Does it break with form in the quest for unseen reality (before the uncanny coloured splotches of Fra Angelica, say, or Vermeer)?[9] Closer to our own time, we may ask whether reality is present in the ecstatic, despairing colour fields of Rothko and the numinous, post-secular spaces of Barnett Newman? Or does it appear to us more like a jumble of fragmented remains, disparate feelings, or non-signifying affects, as we dance on the surface of visual forms in ornamental delight, as when we watch a Hollywood blockbuster, momentarily casting our lot with the life of another for a cry or a laugh before the screen goes dark? A matter, we might say, of image as Hollywood idol.

If the visual economy constitutes the reality in which we live, including the network of beliefs, laws, and institutions that make up our worldly existence, who is (or will be) master of the image?[10] What authorizes the image? What is the source of law's legitimacy in the "visiocracy" we call home?[11]

From Iconology to Semiotics (and Back Again)

On the heels of the ruinous, seemingly endless religious and civil wars of the seventeenth century, early modern Europeans began to turn their gaze away from sectarian sources for legal authority. Foremost among them in this regard was Thomas Hobbes. It was Hobbes who gave us the political triad of sovereignty (the "artificial Soul"), positive law ("artificial Reason"), and the state (that artificial Leviathan, also known as the Commonwealth), bound together by contract: ceding power to the one, or the many, who represents the people.[12] In short, it was Hobbes who first blazed the trail for secular positivist legal thinking. The state and its laws were now viewed as manifestly human constructs, authorized not by God but by collective consent. Law ruled semiotically: defining the terms of representation and exchange. Over the years, as transcendental references continued to weaken, the premodern visual economy of living symbols entered a prolonged state of collapse. This development pushed semiotics to the limits of its legitimating power, and perhaps beyond.

What would it be like to reimagine law not simply in terms of semiotics or abstract concepts, but also as a visual economy, a matter of embodied seeing? What would it mean to picture a corpus less akin to Hobbes's legal machinery than to a network of interlinked, living symbols, where rational categories yield at least equal respect to embodied states and embodied knowledge (affects, feelings, emotions),[13] and in which legal institutions that establish and maintain basic concepts (such as due process, equal protection, and liberty for all) also help to express and perform a preferential range of shared emotions? Imagine a state in which everyone recognizes that structures of feelings help to create both individual identity and social reality, and in which legal institutions help us to avoid "bad civic passions" (such as fear, envy, and shame) while promoting the good (compassion, respect, perhaps even love).[14]

What if law were viewed less as a metric system than a musical composition, a public performance, a work of art: not simply a passive archive of written rules, policies, and principles, but also, and perhaps even more importantly, a theatre in which we perform a shared reality, clearing a space – an *oikos* – for reality to appear? What could make that happen?

When semiotics began to displace living symbols, science took over from theology and the humanities, displacing rhetoric in particular as the leading source of authorized knowledge.[15] In the disembodied epistemology of science, non-sensual truth becomes, as Heidegger put it, a matter of discerning the adequation between image and some underlying model. What is "adequate" in this context is a function of some form of imitation or measurement, whether it is based on a Platonic ideal form or an alternative metrical system. In this kind of visual economy – let us call it the economy of "mimesis as imitation" – good images are accurate copies.

Now while science may excel in establishing conditions of accurate measurement based on formal conditions of validity, it is sorely lacking in providing a basis for structures of feeling, or a preferred network of embodied knowledge. Science is not cut out to express what binds us to a particular model or belief. Discerning the source of an uncanny or sublime presence, what Heidegger calls "the ecstatic play of the world," is beyond its ken. The economy of the sublime, of *mimesis* as appearance or event,[16] insists upon a very different ground of truth than accurate imitation. Symbolic or iconic truth coincides with what the image reveals in our encounter with it. This kind of phenomenological exchange in the face of the iconic image is more akin to performance. Something happens. The image brings something (perhaps some form of being) into a clearing, created within the space of the image, for the gaze to encounter.[17]

Experiencing law's validity as a matter of its compliance with the right set of rules or principles without any sense of its felt significance, which is to say, without an adequate account of what binds us to law's authority in the first place,[18] leads us to Kafka's law: a law that is valid, but lacks significance.[19] For Gersholm Scholem, this encounter with the dead spirit of the law describes the nothingness of revelation, the zero point of law and politics, the state of exception. Valid legal forms may proliferate in baroque and neo-baroque spectacle, but that profusion cannot distract us forever from sensing the emptiness at the core.[20] To counter that lack requires an event – the advent of meaning.

Scientific objectivity can tell us nothing about the advent of law's significance. For that we need living symbols in the visual economy of presence. We can see this is so when we consider the genealogy of law's legitimation over time. For example, it was the visual economy of the Incarnation – that phantasmal presence in the imperial coin (the emperor in the image of Christ),[21] the Orthodox icon,[22] the king's two bodies,[23] and the legal emblem[24] – that once authorized law's worldly power, "making power visible,"[25] giving proof to its invisible spiritual source.[26]

In the pre- and early modern visual economy of the living icon the image precedes the word.[27] As Goodrich points out, the tripartite structure of the legal emblem recapitulates the threefold unity of the Incarnation, the image made flesh.[28] But over time, what began as a transcendental, symbolic visual economy devolved into something far different: a secular legal positivism, the modern semiotic economy of signs and definitions.

And yet, there remained a ghost in the secular machinery of positive law: the enigmatic aura, the unrepresentable, inconceivable (but perhaps not insensible) "Other" of law. In the material semiotic age of science and technology, the economy of signs appeared to have displaced the auratic symbol. But like Banquo's ghost, it "will not down."[29] What could be the source today of such a phantasmal legitimating presence? From what visual economy could it arise?

Post-secular Jurisprudence: The New Visual Economy of Presence

Eric Santner locates a crucial shift in the visual economy of the early modern legal emblem from the "King's two bodies" (secular and divine) to the "People's two bodies." The sovereign that the people create by contracting their rights to their representative contains a surplus, an irreducible excess that Santner calls "the flesh" ("a sublime somatic materiality").[30] This uncanny surplus describes what remains of transcendence.[31] It is what passes from the divine sovereignty of the King to the popular sovereignty of the People.

Imagine the Hobbesian contract of civil representation not simply as words in a document, but also as something iconic in its overdetermination. What if, in order to fit on the page, the social contract could not contract enough the foundational source of power it was meant to carry? What if we viewed that constitutive contract as a living symbol, an icon, which is to say, irreducible to words alone?[32]

What spirit hovers behind the visible signs of civil commitment, as if scintillating within a sea of roseate light on a canvas painted by Rothko? If we were to try to imagine such a possibility, how would we describe its visual economy?

In our psychological times, we might well begin with interior space, the domain of libido. That is Santner's point of departure: the flesh imagined as an invisible residue of uncontainable, uncircumscribable transcendence, for libido (unconscious *Eros*) always exceeds the material body. In Freudian terms, when we "cathect" libido – transferring *Eros* from our body to something beyond it, including expressive forms – we enter into relation with those forms, including others and the world around us. We might say that the body politic acts similarly. We collectively invest libidinal energy in, and thus bind with various objects, others, stories, and ideals. These in turn become charged with libidinal excess. If the object in question is a document, a contract or foundational constitution, say, that excess is the felt presence that binds us. In this sense, the social bond is an excess of meaning. It charges and sustains (so long as it lasts) a shared belief in a cultural construct, an *oikonomia*, if you will, that legitimates the power of the state.

This is how we might talk about a contract that rules with uncanny vitality, as an emotional construct, or a symbolic form of life. This is the enigmatic flesh of the law imagined in terms of a sublime materiality.[33] An economy ("*oikonomia*") imagined as that space in which we manage the material world (of goods and institutions) in the image of something uncontainable, something sublime.

Santner calls this uncanny phenomenon "the royal remains." It is, he says, how the king's transcendent body appears in modernity: how the enigmatic presence of the royal remains was reconstituted in the body politic of popular sovereignty.[34] But it doesn't just happen, like a transaction in which goods, or goods and currency, are exchanged in a sale that's final. It persists. Or it doesn't. Its viability depends on a currency that doesn't appear at all, namely, libidinal cathexis. Without that animus, that uncanny surplus, the laws may be valid but lack significance. Under such conditions, legitimacy is but a rumour.

That is the revolutionary ramification of spiritual and libidinal capital: absent its enigmatic presence the social contract fails. If the basis for a particular cultural form of life disappears, if the currency – what Santner calls "biocratic investiture"[35] – that makes a legal regime function, becomes too weak to support the state's demands, the constitutive structure of belief collapses. If libidinal investment sustains the state, libidinal dis-investment (collective de-cathexis) augurs its fall, its deadly spiral into the state of exception, the zero point of law and politics, a state of perpetual terror. That is what happens when we withdraw our love for objects and others in the world around us. The external world crumbles, mirroring an internal catastrophe.[36]

Let's see if there is a visual economy in which we can visualize the flesh of the law in a similarly corporeal representation.

Reimagining the Visual Economy of Post-secular Jurisprudence

In art, the unspoken, unfigurable source of beauty calls to us. It demands a response from the spectator's gaze. The relationship we enter in the poetic space of beauty's presence is described in the phenomenology of *aesthetics*.[37] In law, justice likewise comes to us as an infinite, uncontainable force. We stand before the Other, whose suffering demands a response. In the visual economy of law justice hovers beyond the field of our vision, like an uncanny, enigmatic presence. It haunts us. Always unrealized, always beyond our grasp – and yet, it is justice that animates law, lending it significance. We feel this, particularly in certain forms and performances of law, even if we cannot always name it. That feeling binds us to law. Our cathected relationship to others and objects (including texts and ideals) is a relationship of significance. We may describe this as the phenomenology of the *ethical*.[38]

What Eric Santner calls "the royal remains" coincides with the phantasmal presence that invisibly bestows legitimacy upon law. In the immediate aftermath of the French revolution, Santner senses that presence in Jacques-Louis David's famous painting, "Death of Marat." Santner credits art historian T.J. Clark with the critical insight at work here. Quoting Clark: "In the cult of Marat [David saw] the first forms of a liturgy and ritual in which the truths of the revolution itself would be made flesh – People, Nation, Virtue, Reason, Liberty."[39] But how would such a "liturgy" find an appropriate form of expression? Santner discerns an aesthetic revolution at work in David's painting. It emerges as a new kind of abstraction. The painter "seems to make Marat much the same substance – the same abstract material – as the empty space above him."[40] Equating that enigmatic space with the King's sublime body ("the flesh"), this abstraction of sovereignty, its sudden vacancy, symbolizes "the impossible representation of the People."[41]

Revolutionary, indeed. No less is at stake than the dissolution of the iconic representation of the Incarnation of Christ, established for centuries, as the underlying model for the King's transcendental body. What we are witnessing is a profound shift in the visual economy of law and politics. According to Santner, the inability to represent the royal remains in the transcendental body of the People (an *aporia* he refers to as "representational deadlock")[42] describes the status of popular sovereignty in the post-Revolutionary age of modernity. The masses who once comprised the Hobbesian Leviathan (pictured in the famous frontispiece of Hobbes' mid-seventeenth-century political handbook) have now dissolved into an absence. This charged absence is the abstract animated field we all carry within ourselves: the uncontainable excess of *Eros*. In this new visual economy, popular sovereignty is animated by a libidinal excess, or somatic surplus of immanence that every citizen carries within his or her own body.

With Rothko, and the mid-twentieth-century emergence of abstract expressionism in general, the visual economy of the image that we first witnessed in David's enigmatic abstraction has developed even further. Now all representational form has been evacuated. Only a shimmering coloured field remains. The mysterious legitimating source of somatic excess, the royal remains that have been transferred to popular sovereignty, has become an entirely abstract expression. But this may hardly come as a source of political comfort. After all, how many people see (much less seek out) in the work of Rothko a source of iconic mastery – making a space for the mystery of the infinite to materialize in the world? A source of legitimacy that has grown this esoteric, so far removed from more familiar rites and liturgies of popular investiture, is an unlikely basis for a sustainable visual economy of law.

Yet, without understating the gravity of an incipient legitimation crisis that has dogged the liberal state throughout late modernity,[43] access to a source of legitimation may lie closer to hand. Perhaps as close as the nearest screen.

If we begin with the ontology of the image, before long – amidst the various registers of being, from sublime presence to sensorial delight, that different kinds of images allow (or preclude) – we come across what visual ethnographer David MacDougal calls "the corporeal image."[44] MacDougal's notion of seeing with the whole body may be read against the current cultural backdrop of the "affective turn," including renewed interest in embodied or "synaesthetic" knowledge.[45] Of particular interest here is what the corporeal image cannot configure, which is to say, our encounter with its excess, the sublime shimmer that accompanies its mysterious overdetermination.[46] That excess is what makes us shudder when we gaze upon the charged abstract colour fields of a work by Rothko, or the sudden, inexplicable vacancy in David's "Marat." The surplus of immanence that we encounter in the ontological field of corporeal images is irreducible to what we see there.

Film, television, and video images, on screens large and small, serve as immensely accessible "popular" sites where corporeal (among many other kinds of) images are in continuous play. The vast circulation of images made possible by new visual technologies keeps alive the prospect that the mysterious source of popular sovereignty in the visual economy of law remains before us. At the same time, however, the very profusion of visual images today also keeps alive the prospect of continued obscurity, burying the corporeal image in the neo-baroque clamour and clutter of undifferentiated visual spectacle.[47]

This defines the visual challenge of our time. Before law's legitimation may be stabilized within a still emergent visual economy, enough contemporary artists, cultural critics, and jurists need be amassed to assimilate and clarify its aesthetic and ethical demands and registers. Only then can that vision be broadly and effectively distributed and shared within the body politic. This process of clarification may well be the most profound task of culture, namely: to sustain the legal and political groundwork necessary for both law's and culture's production, maintenance, and vitality.

To illustrate in greater particularity the claim that the "corporeal image" is closer than the example of abstract expressionism may suggest, one could choose from an extensive archive of films which, to a greater or lesser degree, shimmer with a kind of uncanny corporeal excess. The dictates of limited space allow only a brief example here, drawing on two closely interconnected films by the contemporary filmmaker Joshua Oppenheimer.

The Visual Economy of an Ethically Inflected Aesthetic

Oppenheimer's "The Act of Killing" (2012) and "The Look of Silence" (2014) not only recapitulate in their subject matter the genealogy of law's legitimation, but also aesthetically model the way presence in corporeal images – as well as a deadly vacancy in dizzingly baroque forms – work on the screen. In short, the films perform an integrated visual economy for law and politics in which discrete ethical and aesthetic registers dialectically play out.

A group of high-level army officers has staged a coup. To legitimate their action they characterize it as a necessary response to a ferocious "enemy within" that is threatening to violently seize the state. In the aftermath of the coup, they unleash a killing operation in which enemies of the state (alleged "Communists") are rounded up and slaughtered. No exact estimate exists, but more than five hundred thousand people were killed in this way. Violence on such a massive scale exceeded the capacity of the army without assistance. Accordingly, the state enlisted a civilian cadre of willing killers within a widely distributed network of local militias. This happened in Indonesia in 1965–6. The leaders of the coup remained in power for over four decades thereafter. As co-agents of that political and military triumph, the civilian killers were subsequently praised as heroes of the state. And for all these years, the survivors of mass violence, along with the families and friends of the victims, were subjected to continued oppression (from crude shakedowns in the marketplace to the utter silencing of political dissent) by the thugs, gangsters, and neo-fascist militias that continued to serve the state's needs.

Enter Joshua Oppenheimer, who asks: What is it like to live with the knowledge that you have murdered in cold blood scores, perhaps even hundreds, of innocent people? And what is it like for the victims to live within a regime of such repressive silence? "The Act of Killing" poses the first question. "The Look of Silence" poses the second.

Oppenheimer found that the aging killers, when approached, were only too happy to recount the brutal torture and mass murder that they had committed in their youth. And so the filmmaker enters a strange state of play, providing the killers both the opportunity and the technical means to make a film of their violent and sadistic exploits. Anwar Congo, white-haired now, rail thin, charismatic, and tortured by his past, despite the apparent comfort of his social status, is the chief protagonist in this creative venture. As he moves from scene to scene, we are thrust into his visual world. Culturally immersed in the westerns and crime noirs of Hollywood, Congo's visual vocabulary is rich and astute. He uses his film knowledge to play out fantasies of denial together with recollections of violence and death that incessantly fill his mind, some images more persistently, more hauntingly, than others. As it turns out, nightmares disturb Congo's sleep. He can't stop seeing the open eyes of the decapitated head of a random victim that he left like litter on the killing ground. As if to purge his demons, Congo stages his worst deeds, one after another. Brutal scenes of sadistic torture and killing by strangulation with a wire, in which Congo sometimes is the killer, sometimes the victim, are interspersed with majestic waterfalls, beautiful dancing girls, and carnivalesque cross dressing (for Congo, the would-be film director, is well aware that an audience also must have beauty and humour or they will turn their attention elsewhere).

Bizarre, surreal, perverse: the film moves from one scene to the next, accelerating into the terrible fever dream that we come to recognize as Congo's anguished internal state. As if the impossible cognitive dissonance in which he lives, oscillating between "state hero" and "murderous beast," cannot hold. The visual economy of Congo's existence is one of terror and violence. One image follows another, dizzying in their mad profusion. Nothing adds up. Congo's baroque world of proliferating spectacles of extreme violence and sensual delight remains unstable at its core. Perhaps that is what animates the profusion in the first place. The nothingness at the centre of vision must be avoided at all costs, for fear of total collapse.[48]

The folly of Congo's visual staging is soon evident. The cumulative details of self-deceptive denial and self-lacerating violence (as in the scene where a crazed perpetrator forces Congo's decapitated head to swallow his own liver) know no resolution. They can only quicken. And as they quicken, the fever dream intensifies, until it finally reaches a culmination – and the house of cards that is Anwar Congo's mental world falls apart. That collapse appears in the final scene in "The Act of Killing." We see Congo standing on the same rooftop where he killed so many of his victims in cold blood decades ago. He is silent, seemingly reflective. And then he begins to heave, again and again convulsive retching overtakes his frail, wracked body. It is the body's unconscious knowledge enacting what Congo's tortured mind lacks the power to utter. Not just an isolated killer, but a whole society, a political regime based squarely upon a massive outburst of killing, has been revealed in a vertiginous, baroque image world well suited to feverish horror. The root of that horror and the futility of its denial are laid bare: the rottenness at the state's core. As Freud wrote of Daniel Paul Schreber: "His subjective world has come to an end since his withdrawal of his love from it."[49] An internal catastrophe that mirrors the external catastrophe in which Congo all too willingly participated has finally come to dominate the world in which he lives.

Here is a living image of law in the flesh, suited to a failed political state under neo-baroque conditions: a world of incessant tableaux and transmuting personas, one supplanting the other in quick succession, one after another passing away in a wild proliferation of transmogrifying images, bound in the end to run their final catastrophic course: the heaving, mute, destitute body. Congo is trapped in a perpetual state of emergency. No matter how many representational forms or visual images may be placed at his disposal, the result remains the same. *Endgame*. Psychological catastrophe within, legal and political catastrophe without. And here, allegorically speaking, is where Indonesian society might remain, unable to acknowledge its violent past, continuing its acts of denial and oppression. Here at the zero point of politics, a state of terror within collectively mirrors a state of terror without.

In his second film, Oppenheimer shifts from the perpetrator's mindset to that of the victim. Along the way, we witness a corresponding shift in visual economy. Adi is now the main protagonist. His brother, Ramli, was brutally tortured, mutilated, and killed during the Indonesian genocide, a year before Adi was born. Working now as an optometrist, living amidst his brother's killers, Adi's life mission is to speak truth to power. But it is not vengeance that motivates him. Rather, it is the need to pierce the veil of oppressive silence, to confront the killers with their feckless denials, their empty fantasies, their perverse bravado. Do you not see it was wrong? Have you no remorse, no regret? Such is Adi's refrain as (in no idle metaphor) he calmly fits lenses on the eyes of the killers around him, or sits across from them, including those in positions of significant political power.

Forced to hide his identity, resisting threats of renewed violence if he continues to speak the unspeakable about the past, Adi persists in his questioning.

If only the killers could acknowledge the wrongness of their actions, if only they could take responsibility, and apologize, face to face with the survivors of so many innocent victims, perhaps reconciliation might become possible. Perhaps politics may begin anew, based not on violence, but rather on a deep commitment to empathy (even with the

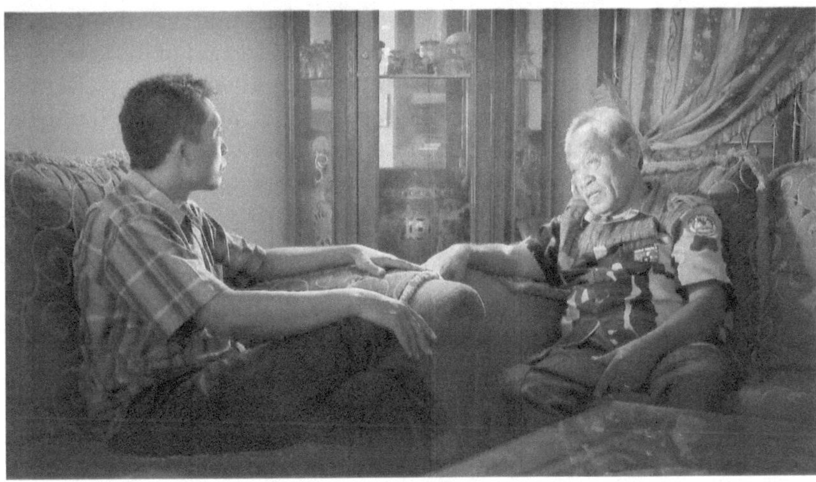

Figure 14.2 Adi questions Commander Amir Siahaan, one of the death squad leaders responsible for his brother's death during the Indonesian genocide, in Joshua Oppenheimer's documentary "The Look of Silence." Courtesy of Drafthouse Films and Participant Media.

perpetrators) combined with a profound moral conviction regarding the necessity of taking responsibility and seeking forgiveness. That is the moral thrust of truth and reconciliation in Adi's steady gaze.

The aesthetic register of Adi's gaze contrasts sharply with that of Anwar Congo. The vertiginous, unstable images of Congo's fever dream have now given way to something calm and steady. Adi's gaze holds us; it is stable, securely rooted. The silence of the dead, and the dignity of the living who survive them, pervades every scene in "The Look of Silence." In these scenes the corporeal image is suffused with the incalculable demands of human suffering, and perhaps, too, the infinite majesty of human nobility. Adi's morally stable universe is sustained by the human capacity for relationship, radical empathy, and the redemptive possibility of forgiveness – perhaps even love. In scene after scene of everyday life, "The Look of Silence" models for us Adi's capacity for love: love of his elderly, long-suffering parents, for whom he must now care, love of his lost brother, who so many years ago set in motion the ethical demand of Adi's life mission, and love for his children who will inherit a legacy of suffering and injustice. We see this in simple scenes of everyday life: Adi washing his blind and nearly deaf and demented father – unable now to escape the prison of his grief; Adi speaking in close intimacy with his careworn mother as she cracks nuts on a stone; Adi playing with his young daughter, jumping delightedly on her bed as she humorously mimics her father's sales pitch for new glasses, and Adi walking with his older son, solemnly explaining the lies his teachers are telling him at school.

These scenes of the survivor's everyday life are suffused with moral fortitude and love. But above all it is the silence of countless victims that animates Adi's gaze in the face of the killers around him, intensifying Adi's morally robust silence against the crude pitch of the perpetrators' threats and deceptions. The filmmaker's love for Adi, and for Adi's parents and children, instantiates and models the moral force that pervades the visual economy of "The Look of Silence," holding out hope for political renewal through redemptive justice.

Two films, two different interventions in the history of mass murder. One, a fever dream of incessantly shifting personas, disguises, oscillating wildly from self-deceit to self-conviction, showing us what it is like to look in the mirror of a perpetrator's life – a life lived in the homeless terror of unacknowledged guilt and shame. The second, almost an idyll – but for the background of violence and death, and the exquisite, almost unbearable suffering left in their wake. Yet, for all that, Adi's calm gaze prevails. We see what it is like to look in the mirror of a victim condemned to live behind a veil of oppressive silence, but who refuses to succumb – not with violence or cries for retribution, but with dignity and moral conviction vouchsafed by the silent authority of the dead. Adi's gaze aims for forgiveness and reconciliation once the killers themselves, along with those whose power can be directly traced to that horrific origin, acknowledge the truth, and take responsibility for the wrongs they have committed.

Two different gazes, two different image worlds – together constituting the visual economy of contemporary Indonesia. But this is not simply an allegory of a society internally riven by a history of unspeakable violence and oppressive silence. It is also a symbolic visualization of the way law confronts violence (or fails to), and the way it moves from its own originary violence to the redemptive possibility of renewed love for the world. It places before us, in corporeal images of almost unbearable intensity, the mute knowledge of the body: its fevers, its fantasies, its wretchedness, as well as its dignity, its sweetness, its moral rightness, and its capacity to empathize and to love. Oppenheimer takes us to the heart of human mystery in a visual economy that pulsates with an unrepresentable surplus. From the esoteric challenge of abstract expressionist fields we have travelled to an almost "microscopically" examined representational particularity: a handful of perpetrators, a single family of survivors, among an unfigurable backdrop of so many others, in a world so intimately portrayed as to ask of us, as Oppenheimer wishes to ask, what would it be like to be this family: to "feel you are Adi, or your brother is Adi, and Adi's parents are your parents, your grandparents; Adi's children are your children?"[50] In this visual economy intimacy, empathy, and love pulsate with an uncanny excess. It is this surplus in representational particularity, Oppenheimer tells us, that makes us care.[51] Perhaps it even makes us want to participate in what is being performed on the screen, inviting, enticing, inducing us to enter and invest in this visual economy, to make it our own, even for law's and politics' sake. In this visual economy, the corporeal image provides a basis for stabilizing and legitimating the way we manage and maintain shared beliefs and values in society, the way we make a place (*oikos*) for normative reality (*nomos*).

And so we see the ethical and aesthetic join together in an integrated visual economy that traces law's tragic origin in violence to its possible future in redemptive justice. Two different interventions, two different ruptures: one, the rupture of the veil of denial and lies; the other, the rupture of an oppressive silence with moral responsibility and the hope of reconciliation. Notably, this dialectical integration of the ethical and the aesthetic draws upon all the resources of the body. As Oppenheimer puts it, in a description of the film editing process: "I wonder whether this ability to find that mystery … has to do with the fact these [editorial] decisions … are like decisions of all your senses, your tastes, your feeling, your ears, your stomach, your smell. I'm working in a place that is not about words."[52] Rather, a fundamental, unfigurable mystery, a sublime presence, if you will, unites us through the corporeal image. In that presence the immorality of social and political corruption is manifest.[53] This is Oppenheimer's ethical phenomenology of the empathic gaze. In empathy, even with a mass murderer like Anwar Congo, we may learn to acknowledge and responsibly confront the vast complexity of human nature. For in this view, Anwar Congo is not simply a killer to be dealt with by the punitive force of law, but also a human being haunted by the internal terror that his violent deeds have wrought.

With this realization of the shocking, almost unacceptable complexity of humanity we are in a position to seek something more than retribution. For retribution remains insensible to the moral responsibility and, along with it, the possibility of reconciliation that comes with redemptive justice. Thus, Oppenheimer's radically empathic visual economy of law and politics invites us not to endlessly repeat the mistakes of supplanting one form of violence with another, or one form of false closure with another – whether it is the perpetrator's self-deceit, in fantasy or other forms of denial, or the victim's (and society's ritual performance of) false hope that now, at last, the monsters among us have been purged from the body politic.[54] This visual economy of law cultivates a deeply embodied moral knowledge that makes reconciliation imaginable. It is, as Oppenheimer puts it, "the only way to achieve the widest possible human dignity."[55]

In confronting violence and terror, empathy and love seek to provide a home for the ghost that haunts the Hobbesian legal machine, and all comparable legal systems that remain valid but lack significance. It is not enough to bind the body politic with fear, as Hobbes believed. Fear may prompt obedience, even acquiescence, but it will never inspire empathy or fidelity based on a libidinal cathexis that makes a shared world truly our own. As Giambattista Vico wrote over three centuries ago: "The soul of man must be enticed by corporeal images and impelled to love, for once it loves it is easily taught to believe. Once it believes and loves, the fire of passion must be infused into it so as to break its inertia and force it to will."[56]

Without that investment, that erotic cathexis as we might put it today, legal validity without significance is bound to decay, and fall back into the nothingness of bare life, a fate akin to the collapse of the vertiginous image world of Anwar Congo at the end of "The Act of Killing." It is this catastrophe to which our prolonged crisis of legitimation points. It is the historic burden of justice to avert that fate. These, then, are the stakes when we ask what constitutes sovereignty in our time, which is another way of asking, in what visual economy does law manage shared beliefs, values, and the circulation of power in the material world?

Conclusion

The challenge of authorizing the image in the visual economy of law is twofold: First, we must learn the different ethical and aesthetic registers that operate within the different visual economies of our time. This is a matter of visual literacy. It portends the ascendance of visual rhetoric as a major player in the theory and practice of law. Second, we must embrace the ontological (perhaps metaphysical) challenge that accompanies the exploration of non-conceptual, non-metrical, embodied forms of knowing, as we grapple with the complexity of the uncanny surplus of corporeal images. Different kinds of images circulate in different visual economies – from the iconic incarnation of early modern legal emblems to modernist abstraction (David and Rothko) and sublime representation (Oppenheimer), to images as measured imitation (in the adequation of copy and model) or brute sensorial intensity, in horror and delight (as we find in the crypto-legitimating charade of the digital simulacrum).[57]

In the modern era, the artwork may have "replace[d] the cult of the holy image."[58] But aesthetics alone will not vouchsafe the visual economy of the law. Law's economy also must be linked to our ongoing commitment to justice. That commitment grows out of a renewed encounter with an interior libidinal source – in painting, film, and video images on screens large and small – whose ongoing collective investment binds us to the *nomos* in which we live. In so doing we legitimate the living spirit of law's humanity.[59] In the ethically inflected aesthetic of post-secular jurisprudence, *justice* is to jurisprudence as *beauty* is to art.[60] The authority of law as image arises out of and circulates within an infinite field that we call justice. *Eros* is the name we give to that creative force out of which political worlds are made, from bare life, from the political unconscious known as the flesh of the law. Law's significance finds its uncanny source in that invisible presence. Where the flesh appears as libidinal excess there lies the source of authority, the spirit of the law that binds us. As distant as an abstract expressionist canvas, as close as any neighbour, or indeed any screen on which the neighbour becomes real to us, that is where we simultaneously behold both the subject and source of law's judgment and authority. This is how law persists, iconically, perhaps kenotically, in shimmering corporeal images.

In every era the visual economy of law as image must be learned, perhaps even created anew, so that the uncircumscribable nature of its ethical source will be understood, remembered, and practised in the ways of its time. This realization augurs a renewed integration of law and the humanities,[61] including a renewed reflection upon political theology and the wisdom of the heart in a post-secular age.

For this task to be realized, artist and judge, poet and legislator, need to engage one another in a joint effort to re-authenticate the symbolic basis for our political union. The remains of transcendental excess, incarnate in the immanent wound of the flesh, must be re-encountered anew. Without this, we risk becoming as destitute as Anwar Congo at the end of "The Act of Killing." That is the contemporary lesson of the poetic and ethically resonant film work of Joshua Oppenheimer, work that may betoken a sea change in the visual economy of values and beliefs in which images and laws circulate in society. With radical empathy and the libidinal excess of love that binds us to the world and to others around us, hope for political renewal remains. That is the redemptive promise that we learn from the visual economy of Adi's steady ethical gaze in "The Look of Silence."

Re-authorizing the image of law in our time calls for a reimagined visual economy in which the ethical sublime, the invisible source of law's excess (justice as an expression of love?) remains before us: achingly out of reach, yet beckoning, demanding, entreating. As before a roseate light, rising.

NOTES

1 Katharina Grosse, http://bombmagazine.org/article/4910/katharina-grosse.

2 Werner Herzog, "On the Absolute, the Sublime, and Ecstatic Truth," *Arion* 17, no. 3 (2010): 1–12.

3 *Oikonomia* carries the general sense of "stewardship" or wise and responsible management or administration of something. It also resonates with "equity" in the sense of easing the letter of the law by invoking its spirit. See John Sabu, "The Theology of Oikonomia and Its Implications for Sacramental and Ecumenical Perspectives," doctoral dissertation (Faculteit Theologie en Religiewetenschappen, Leuven, 2007), https://theo.kuleuven.be/apps/doctoraltheses/69.

4 For Rothko the space the eye inhabits is the key to the artist's vision. See Mark Rothko, *The Artist's Reality* (New Haven: Yale University Press, 1998), 59.

5 Simon Goldhill, "Refracting Classical Vision: Changing Cultures of Viewing," in Teresa Brennan and Martin Jay, eds, *Vision in Context* (New York: Routledge, 1996), 17 [*Iliad*, 21.108].

6 Ibid., 19.

7 See Marie-Jose Mondzain, *Image, Icon, Economy: The Byzantine Origins of the Contemporary Imaginary* (Stanford: Stanford University Press, 2005), 5.

8 See Stuart Clark, *Vanities of the Eye: Vision in Early Modern European Culture* (Oxford: Oxford University Press, 2007) and Martin Jay, *Downcast Eyes: The Denigration of Vision in Twentieth-Century French Thought* (Berkeley: University of California Press, 1993). See also Richard K. Sherwin, *Visualizing Law in the Age of the Digital Baroque: Arabesques & Entanglements* (New York and London: Routledge, 2011).

9 See Georges Didi-Huberman, *Confronting Images* (University Park, PA: Penn State University Press, 2005), 11–52, 200–28.

10 Mondzain, *Image, Icon, Economy*, 8.

11 See Peter Goodrich, *Legal Emblems and the Art of Law* (Cambridge: Cambridge University Press, 2014), 16. Mondzain uses the term "iconocracy." See Mondzain, *Image, Icon, Economy*, 152.

12 See Thomas Hobbes, *Leviathan* (London: Penguin, 1968), 227–34.

13 On the differentiation of affect, feeling, and emotion, see Richard K. Sherwin, "Too Late for Thinking," *Journal of Law, Culture, & the Humanities*, doi:1743872115611500 (13 October 2015).

14 See Martha Nussbaum, *Political Emotions: Why Love Matters for Justice* (Cambridge, MA: Harvard University Press, 2013), 3–15.

15 See Richard K. Sherwin, "Sublime Jurisprudence: On the Ethical Education of the Legal Imagination in Our Time," *Chicago-Kent Law Review* 83, no. 3 (2008): 1160. ("Cartesian epistemology shifts attention from images to words, from the objective eye to semiotic interpretation. Signs have no direct correspondence with what caused them. Signs signify. They stand for a word. This is not a matter of sense impression, as with the flow of species. In short, Cartesian modernity subordinates *physis/themis* [nature and natural law] to *nomos* [law posited as a cognitive and cultural interpretation or convention]. The classical and medieval link to the 'natural' order has been broken, and the modern dis-enchantment of nature has begun. Truth has now become the offspring of artificial linguistic conventions. The sign, on this account, is but an arbitrary association to an object or event rather than a natural resemblance.")

16 Ibid., 1175. ("The mimetic experience of being-as – culminating ultimately in the ethical experience of *being-for-an* Other, embodies a sublime epistemology rooted in self-transcendence and the metaphysics of poetic representation. It is this natural mimetic endowment that allows humans to become one with an object [in the act of naming] or with other cultures and their associated mindsets during other times [in the act of discerning linguistic, philological, and mythic patterns throughout history]. Mimesis, the faculty of imitation through *being-as*, is simultaneously the condition

for knowledge and a basis for wonder.") See also Mihai Spariosu, *Mimesis in Contemporary Theory* (Philadelphia: John Benjamins Publishing, 1984), iii.

17 See Paul Ricoeur, "Between Rhetoric and Poetics," in Amelie Oksenberg Rorty, ed., *Essays on Aristotle's Rhetoric* (Berkeley: University of California Press, 1996), 351. ("It is only through a grave misinterpretation that the Aristotelian mimesis can be confused with imitation in the sense of copy. If mimesis involves an initial reference to reality, this reference signifies nothing other than the very rule of nature over all production … *Mimesis* is *poiesis*, and *poeisis* is *mimesis*.") See also Michael Taussig, *Mimesis and Alterity* (New York: Routledge, 1993), xviii, 38, 40 (adopting Walter Benjamin's understanding of the mimetic faculty as the "compulsion to become the Other" and describing sentience as taking us "outside of ourselves" in the "instantaneous" and "mystical" flash which is the "perception of similarity").

18 Even a legal positivist like H.L.A. Hart seemed to sense the need for such a legitimating source of law. His very insistence on the "minimum content of natural law" belies his positivist pretensions. Hart would lay claim to a purely "sociological" sense, but his willing use of the phrase "natural law" imports more than a strictly empirical sociology would seem to require. See H.L.A. Hart, *The Concept of Law* (Oxford: Oxford University Press, 1979), 189–95. See also Richard K. Sherwin, "Opening Hart's Concept of Law," *Valparaiso University Law Review* 20, no. 3 (1986): 398–410 (on the failure of Hart's minimum content of natural law to ground legal obligation).

19 See Gershom Scholem, *The Correspondence of Walter Benjamin and Gershom Scholem, 1932–1940* (Cambridge, MA: Harvard University Press, 1992), 142.

20 Walter Benjamin, *The Origin of German Tragic Drama* (London: Verso, 1998), 3.

21 Hans Belting, *Likeness and Presence* (Chicago: University of Chicago Press, 1994), 164–5.

22 See Mondzain, *Image, Icon, Economy*.

23 See Ernst Kantorowicz, *The King's Two Bodies: A Study in Medieval Political Theology* (Princeton, NJ: Princeton University Press, 1957); Paul Raffield, *Images and Cultures of Law in Early Modern England* (Cambridge: Cambridge University Press, 2004), 114.

24 See Goodrich, *Legal Emblems and the Art of Law*, 218; Raffield, *Images and Cultures of Law*, 46.

25 See Goodrich, *Legal Emblems and the Art of Law*, xvi.

26 Ibid., 35.

27 See Mondzain, *Image, Icon, Economy*; see Goodrich, *Legal Emblems and the Art of Law*, xxii.

28 Goodrich, *Legal Emblems*, 264.

29 Banquo, a character in William Shakespeare's *Macbeth*, was a general in the army of King Duncan. When Macbeth ascended to the throne of Scotland after Duncan's murder Banquo suspected Macbeth of the regicide. After Macbeth arranges Banquo's death, Banquo's ghost appears to Macbeth – first at a banquet (act 3, scene 4) and later in a vision granted by the three witches wherein Macbeth sees a long line of kings descended from Banquo (4.1).

30 Eric Santner, *The Royal Remains* (Chicago: University of Chicago Press, 2011), 4. Historian Edmund Morgan treats the People's two bodies in terms of the felt need to separate the constitutive and self-limiting power of the People (their so-called transcendent or sovereign power), on the one hand, and the less lofty legislative power of practical governance (as subjects), on the other. See Edmund S. Morgan, *Inventing the People* (New York: W.W. Norton & Co., 1988), 78–93. Deprived of the king's sovereign "majesty," as occurred in England with the departure and ultimate death of King Charles I in 1649, "Parliament ceased to exist, as did the commonwealth of which it was a part" (88).

31 Santner, *The Royal Remains*, 22.

32 See, for example, the living symbols of legal performance in Grace Koch, "We have the song, so we have the land: Song and Ceremony as Proof of Ownership in Aboriginal and Torres Strait Islander Land Claims," AIATSIS Research Discussion Paper no. 33 (Canberra: AIATSIS Research Publications, December 2012) (noting that in land-title disputes by Aboriginal people and Torres Strait Islanders in Australia song and ceremony may serve as title "deeds").

33 Santner, *The Royal Remains*, 4.

34 Ibid., 12. See also Carlo Galli, "Hamlet: Representation and the Concrete," in Graham Hammill and Julia Lupton, eds, *Political Theology and Early Modernity* (Chicago: University of Chicago Press, 2012), 70 (tracing the privatization of the state from the historical moment "when the sovereign monarch was substituted by the sovereign citizen").

35 Santner, *The Royal Remains*, 4.

36 We encounter this terrible collapse in Franz Kafka's short, parable-like story "A Country Doctor" – in the image of the raw wound of the flesh. We encounter it as well in the famous case of Daniel Paul Schreber, a legal scholar and judge who succumbed to the pathology of unsublimated *Eros* – the withdrawal of love from the world and others around him. Having mastered its subject, Schreber's abnormally involuted *Eros* burst out in florid forms of psychotic delusion. See Santner, *The Royal Remains*, 63–86.

37 See Mikel Dufrenne, *The Phenomenology of Aesthetic Experience* (Evanston, IL: Northwestern University Press, 1989).

38 I trace the phenomenology of the ethical sublime to Emmanuel Levinas in Richard K. Sherwin, *Visualizing Law in the Age of the Digital Baroque*, 184–6.

39 Santner, *The Royal Remains*, 91.

40 Ibid., 92.

41 Ibid. See also Morgan Thomas, "Law and the Revolutionary Motif after Jacques-Louis David," chapter 4, this volume. According to Thomas, David's "*Marat*" "embodies a movement ... between visual representation and an empty yet ineluctably material state of indeterminacy" (112). Thomas associates the "affective intensity" and "sublime effect" of that "evanescent presence" (113) with "the ethical notion of an irruption of the infinite *in* the finite" (117).

42 Santner, *The Royal Remains*, 95.

43 See Jürgen Habermas, *Legimation Crisis* (New York: Beacon Books, 1973).

44 David MacDougal, *The Corporeal Image* (Princeton: Princeton University Press, 2006).

45 See David Howes, "Scent, Sound and Synaesthesia: Intersensoriality and Material Culture Theory," in Christopher Tilley, Webb Keane, Susanne Küchler, Michael Rowlands, and Patricia Spyer, eds, *Handbook of Material Culture* (New York: Sage, 2006).

46 See Jennifer Deger, *Shimmering Screens* (Minneapolis and London: University of Minnesota, 2006).

47 See Sherwin, *Visualizing Law*; Galli, "Hamlet," 70 (noting that when popular sovereignty substituted for the sovereign king the citizen became "a sovereign spectator, capable only of consuming, in aesthetic enjoyment, a representation that made itself, over time, more and more irresponsible and ineffective").

48 I believe it is fair to say that in the character of Anwar Congo we are close to the unstable mental reality of Daniel Paul Schreber. Like Schreber, Congo, too, is unable to live in this world. For he, too, has de-cathected his libido from it, and consequently suffers the throes of world loss. See Santner, *The Royal Remains*, ix–xvii.

49 Ibid., 22.

50 Richard K. Sherwin and Danielle Celermajer, *A Cultural History of Law in the Modern Age* (London: Bloomsbury, forthcoming) (quoting from interview with Joshua Oppenheimer).

51 Ibid.

52 Ibid.

53 Ibid.

54 As Primo Levi put it: "Monsters exist, but they are too few in number to be truly dangerous. More dangerous are the common men, the functionaries ready to believe and to act without asking questions." Primo Levi, *The Reawakening* (New York: Simon and Schuster, 1995), 228.

55 Sherwin and Celermajer, *A Cultural History of Law*. See also Mondzain, *Image, Icon, Economy*, 78 (on *skhésis* as the core relation of the incarnational sacrifice). See also Nussbaum, *Political Emotions*, 177, 378–97 (on the relation between fraternal interrelatedness, love, and justice) and Goodrich, *Legal Emblems and the Art of Law*, 231 (on the quality of heart that anchors justice).

56 Giambattista Vico, *On the Study Methods of Our Time* (Ithaca, NY: Cornell University Press, 1990), 38.

57 The violent ritual of pseudo-legitimation in the age of the digital spectacle is on display in the immensely popular *Hunger Games* volumes and films. See Suzanne Collins, *The Hunger Games Trilogy* and the *The Hunger Games* (2012, director Gary Ross) followed by director Francis Lawrence's *The Hunger Games: Catching Fire* (2013), *The Hunger Games: Mockingjay – Part 1* (2014), and *The Hunger Games: Mockingjay – Part 2* (2015). I am indebted to Professor Sidia Fiorato of the University of Verona for this insight.

58 See Belting, *Likeness and Presence*, 490.

59 Caroline van Eck, *Classical Rhetoric and the Visual Arts in Early Modern Europe* (Cambridge: Cambridge University Press, 2007), 9.

60 See Sherwin, *Visualizing Law*, 188–9.

61 For hopeful thoughts along these lines by a Nobel laureate in economics, see Edmund Phelps, "What Is Wrong with the West's Economies?" *New York Review of Books*, 13 August 2015, 54. ("Education systems must put students in touch with the humanities in order to fuel the human desire to conceive the new and perchance achieve innovations.")

Contributors

Katherine Biber is a legal scholar, historian, and criminologist at the University of Technology Sydney. She is the author of *Captive Images* (Routledge, 2007) and *In Crime's Archive: The Cultural Afterlife of Evidence* (Routledge, 2017), and co-editor of *The Lindy Chamberlain Case* (ASP, 2009) and *Evidence and the Archive* (Routledge, 2016).

Shane Chalmers is a doctoral scholar in the School of Regulation and Global Governance (RegNet) and affiliate of the Centre for Law, Arts & the Humanities at the Australian National University. His doctoral thesis examines the life of the rule of law in Liberia.

Maria Elander is a lecturer in criminology at La Trobe Law School, La Trobe University. Her research in international criminal justice engages with theories in cultural and feminist legal studies, and examines questions of representation, victimhood, and encounters between the local, national, and international. Her monograph *The Figure of the Victim in International Criminal Justice* is forthcoming in early 2018.

Peter Goodrich is professor of law at Cardozo School of Law and affiliate professor in the School of Social Science at NYU Abu Dhabi.

Stefan Huygebaert is an art historian at the Ghent Legal History Institute (Ghent University). As a Research Foundation – Flanders (FWO) PhD fellow, he scrutinizes the iconology of law in nineteenth-century Belgium. Stefan recently co-edited the catalogue for the exhibition *The Art of Law: Three Centuries of Justice Depicted* (Bruges, Groeningemuseum).

Desmond Manderson is a professor at the Australian National University, where he is jointly appointed in the ANU College of Law and the College of Arts and Social Sciences, and founding director of the Centre for Law, Arts and the Humanities. His *Concepts of Law and Time in the Visual Arts* is scheduled to be published by Cambridge University Press in 2018.

Cristina S. Martinez is an adjunct professor at the Department of Visual Arts, University of Ottawa. She is currently completing a book entitled *Art, Law and Order: The Legal Life of Artists in Eighteenth-Century Britain*, to be published by Manchester University Press.

Sherally Munshi is associate professor of law at Georgetown University Law Center. Her current scholarship focuses on histories of Indian immigration to, and exclusion from, the United States in the early twentieth century.

Connal Parsley is lecturer in law at Kent Law School. His research concerns the intersection of law, politics, and visual culture, focusing on the image as a material technology of legal power, authority, and juridical paradigms of ethics. He is currently working on a visual jurisprudential rereading of Giorgio Agamben.

Luis Gómez Romero joined the School of Law at the University of Wollongong in 2013, where he is a member of the Legal Intersections Research Centre. Prior to this, he was a postdoctoral fellow at the Institute for the Public Life of Arts and Ideas at McGill University.

Richard K. Sherwin is the Wallace Stevens Professor of Law and director of the Visual Persuasion Project at New York Law School. He is the author and editor of numerous books, including *A Cultural History of Law in the Modern Age* (Bloomsbury, 2017) and *Visualizing Law in the Age of the Digital Baroque* (Routledge, 2011).

Morgan Thomas teaches in the art history and film and media studies programs at the University of Cincinnati and has also worked as an editor, translator, curator, and critic. Her research focuses on interrelationships between aesthetics, modernism, and contemporary art.

Honni van Rijswijk is a senior lecturer in the Faculty of Law, University of Technology Sydney.

Alison Young is the Francine V. McNiff Professor of Criminology in the School of Social and Political Sciences at the University of Melbourne. She is the author of *Street Art World* (University of Chicago Press, 2016) and *Street Art, Public City* (Routledge, 2014).

Index

Page numbers in **bold** refer to illustrations.

www.ingramcontent.com/pod-product-compliance
Lightning Source LLC
LaVergne TN
LVHW090148080826
844660LV00013B/712/J

9781442630314